ActiveX™

How to Order:

For information on quantity discounts, contact the publisher: Prima Publishing, P.O. Box 1260BK, Rocklin, CA 95677-1260; (916) 632-4400. On your letterhead include information concerning the intended use of the books and the number of books you wish to purchase. For individual orders, turn to the back of this book for more information.

ActiveX™

Bud Aaron

PRIMA PUBLISHING

Acquisitions Editor:
Ian Sheeler

Development Editor:
Andrew Fritzinger

Project Editor:
Susan Christophersen

Technical Reviewer:
Donald Doherty

Indexer:
Lynn Moncrief

Cover Design:
Vanessa Perez

P ™ is a registered trademark of Prima Publishing, a division of Prima Communications, Inc.

Prima Publishing is a registered trademark of Prima Communications, Inc.

Prima Publishing, Rocklin, California 95677.

Publisher *Don Roche, Jr.*
Associate Publisher *Ray Robinson*
Acquisitions Manager *Alan Harris*
Managing Editor *Tad Ringo*
Product Marketing Specialist *Julie Barton*

ISBN: 0-7615-0801-5

Library of Congress Catalog Card Number: 96-69519

Printed in the United States of America

96 97 98 99 BB 10 9 8 7 6 5 4 3 2 1

Dedication

To Tashie, Shado, Twinky, and ShuShu, who really didn't understand when "daddy" wasn't there to feed them cookies!

Acknowledgments

When I started writing, almost 40 years ago, a book could take a year or more to write. An editor checked my grammar and I received galleys to proof read and return. In these modern times, even though the writer does much of the writing, books are a team effort. The author's name appears on the cover and, without acknowledgments, other team members would go unrecognized. Some members of the excellent team behind this book consist of the following:

Ian Sheeler, Acquisitions Editor (making it all happen); Jill Byus, Acquisitions Coordinator (keeping it going); Andrew Fritzinger, Development Editor (making it a better book); Don Doherty, Technical Editor (keeping me honest); Susan Christophersen, Project Editor (putting it all together); Tom Barich, the CD Man!

And thanks to my family, Dina, Alex, Bill, Erica, Roy, David, and others for understanding the brutal schedules and keeping me fed.

About the Author

Bud Aaron has been actively involved in electronics, computers, and software for more than 50 years in electronic engineering, systems analysis, and teaching. Bud taught military and civilian classes in electronics and programming, and has sold more than 100 magazine articles and books to major publishers. In 1976, Bud helped found BusinessMaster to write accounting software in a family-owned-and-operated business. That led to the founding of CheckMaster in 1992. Working in Microsoft Visual Basic and Visual C++, Bud has been actively involved in writing software and Custom Controls for several years. When Microsoft introduced ActiveX, CheckMaster and CheckMaster developers took a fast track to develop Internet-enhanced and digitally signed check-printing software and other controls for the Internet in close cooperation with the Microsoft Component Builders Team. Bud and CheckMaster are active beta testers for many Microsoft products. Bud is a biographee in Marquis *Who's Who in the West*, *Who's Who in the World*, and *Who's Who in the Media* for his writing contributions.

Contents at a Glance

Table of Contents

Chapter 5 Using the ActiveX Control Pad 111

Introduction

In the Gulf War, President George Bush fielded half a million troops, hundreds of aircraft, and a fleet of ships. His strategy was to build an absolutely overwhelming force of arms to accomplish his intended goals. In a similar manner, businesses need strategies to achieve goals, especially when they start out behind. Like the Gulf War, if enough resources are thrown at a project, it has a good chance of succeeding.

Microsoft started behind the pack in the Internet "war." It needed a strategy to overtake other contenders such as Netscape and Sun Microsystems. Without a doubt, Microsoft could throw massive resources into the effort, but those resources needed a direction. Microsoft's motto became "embrace and extend." The notion was to embrace the existing technology and extend it to cover new venues.

To that end, early in 1996, Microsoft rebranded an entire product line. All OLE Custom Controls became ActiveX Custom Controls—or simply ActiveX Controls. Essentially, Microsoft gave an old, and what some may have considered a stagnant, technology an exciting new name and a new direction by allowing Internet Enhanced components to be built using this technology. To "Internet Enhance" ActiveX Controls, the interface requirements are relaxed. OLE Custom Controls *required* several interfaces. ActiveX Controls are required to implement only the *IUnknown* interface. The IUnknown interface provides three functions: `QueryInterface`, `AddRef`, and `Release`. This relaxation makes porting ActiveX Controls across platforms easier. Thus, ActiveX controls can be made available for the Macintosh and UNIX platforms, among others.

Ultimately, this is all directed to seamlessly integrating the Windows world to the Internet. Until quite recently, the World Wide Web consisted largely of static pages written in HTML. Using CGI, information can be passed to other applications in a limited way. Also, forms that can be filled in for passing data can be implemented. With ActiveX technology, the world will see the WWW more closely integrated to underlying databases and applications. Discerning where your local machine leaves off and the Internet takes over will be difficult.

All of this requires changes across the entire range of clients and servers. This book will not compete with books on building OLE Custom Controls. It will cover the world of ActiveX technology required to activate the Internet on the client side. There is a tendency to think of ActiveX as strictly ActiveX Controls. In fact, the ActiveX SDK (Software Development Kit) was initially called "sweeper." Although I have never seen it stated, it appears that everything that could not be neatly included in an existing API or application category was "swept" into "sweeper." So, in a sense, this book covers sweeper, and to cover sweeper, I must also cover the technology required to bind it all together.

The Internet has been successful over the years largely because standards were developed and maintained. Developing these standards rests with organizations such as the World Wide Web Consortium (W3C) and the Internet Engineering Task Force (IETF).

Microsoft is working closely with these organizations to evolve new standards for HTML, layout, Cascading Style Sheets, objects, and other standards that will allow the Internet to become an extension of the desktop. Some of these technologies may seem out of place in a book called *ActiveX*, but these are the environments in which ActiveX Controls will live.

Who Should Read This Book

This book provides intermediate to advanced information to anyone involved with the Internet or intranets. Some may find the expression trite, but this is Bill Gates' world of "information at your fingertips." This is the world in which future computer users will buy products, hold conferences, make decisions, cooperatively edit documents, run software, do accounting, file legal briefs, hold conversations, and, yes, play games.

It is the world that readers of this book will be building, and I suspect that we have only just scratched the surface of potential applications. For now, I cover the technology available at the time of this writing.

The world to which I refer here is a world of component software using the Component Object Model (COM). Software will be designed as an interface between the desktop and the Internet or a server and the Internet. You wouldn't think of designing an audio amplifier without knowing the interface with which it works. In a similar manner, you would have trouble building ActiveX components without knowing how they will interface to the Internet, Internet browsers, and Internet servers.

Webmasters, Internet Service Providers, Network managers, Web page designers, and everyone involved with designing and implementing the Internet from the client or server side will find useful information in this book.

How This Book Is Organized

Chapter 1, "What is ActiveX?," provides an overview of the ActiveX initiative in general. It shows you how ActiveX Custom Controls fit into the Internet world. It also gives you information about ActiveMovie, Active VRML, and other X technologies. This chapter is recommended reading for everyone to gain a focus on the emerging technologies represented by ActiveX.

Chapter 2, "Installing and Using Internet Explorer," brings you up to speed on the installation and utilization of Microsoft's Internet Explorer. It also shows you how to use the free viewers (OLE servers) that Microsoft makes available for Excel, PowerPoint, and Word.

You will learn how to install and set up Microsoft NetMeeting. NetMeeting provides the user with a white board, voice communication, application sharing, and a chat capability. You will also learn about Microsoft Mail and News. These are currently available Web client tools and most are based on ActiveX Custom Control technology, or can make use of the technology.

Chapter 3, "Using Microsoft FrontPage," gives you a look at Microsoft's FrontPage Web development tool. FrontPage provides a number of tools for building and managing Web sites and the HTML content. The editor is WYSIWYG, but version 1.1 still needs the help of the ActiveX Control pad to implement controls and scripting.

Chapter 4, "Using Other Authoring Tools," teaches you a number of additional Web authoring tools. These are designed to make HTML development easier. They provide you with an easy way to get the lion's share of a Web site designed. After the main authoring is complete, you can use other tools (such as the ActiveX Control Pad, discussed in Chapter 5) to add controls and embellishments. Testing and using ActiveX Custom Controls will be much easier if the designer has a good understanding of the HTML code that makes up most of a Web page. Additionally, well-designed pages allow better use of the functionality exposed by new controls.

Chapter 5, "Using the ActiveX Control Pad," takes you on a tour of a new Microsoft development tool called the ActiveX Control Pad. Underlying this software is the HTML Layout Control (another ActiveX Control), which is incorporated into the Internet Explorer. You will learn how to use the ActiveX Control Pad to develop sensational Web sites using ActiveX Controls and scripting.

Chapter 6, "Understanding Cascading Style Sheets," introduces style sheets, the acknowledged way to provide well-formatted documents and text. An emerging standard from the World Wide Consortium is Cascading Style Sheets, Level 1, or CSS1. This chapter shows you what the style sheets are and how to use them. TrueType fonts on the Web are also covered.

Chapter 7, "Building Web Pages with Scripting," covers the use of VBScript and JScript, Microsoft's implementation of JavaScript. Both these languages make use of components in their implementation, allowing the functionality of ActiveX Custom Controls and other COM objects to be exposed in programming languages very similar to Visual Basic. Oddly, both languages are nearly identical in many respects, even though they were developed by diametrically opposed companies. This similarity speaks very well for the underlying value of the Component Object Model (COM) as a technology.

Chapter 8, "Introducing ActiveX Custom Controls," provides a brief introduction to ActiveX Controls.

Chapter 9, "Building Controls with Visual C++," gives you a small taste of developing ActiveX Controls in C++.

Finally, you'll find three appendixes at the end of the book. Appendix A provides a glossary of terms, and Appendix B is a complete HTML 3.2 reference.

Appendix C explains the CD-ROM included with this book. This CD contains a large number of tools that you would otherwise need to download from Microsoft's Web site. I have also included some of the longer code samples from the book.

Chapter 1

What is ActiveX?

Early in 1996, Microsoft did an unprecedented thing: it rebranded an entire technology. What had been known as OLE and particularly OLE Custom Controls were rebranded to ActiveX Controls. Software vendors were not required to do anything. The .OCX extension still applied; recompiling was not required; the controls simply had a new name. There was another thing. For vendors who wanted to make their controls available on the Internet, controls could now be "Internet Enhanced." To this end, the interface requirements were relaxed and coding was made much simpler.

In mid-1996, Microsoft did yet another unprecedented thing. To make the ActiveX initiative a more generally available technology, Microsoft released it to an independent standards body. The real impact of this decision still remains to be seen, but in principle, this will make ActiveX available to the world of PCs, the Macintosh, UNIX, and, presumably, any operating system manufacturer that cares to implement the technology.

This technological rush is being driven by the Internet. In January, 1993, there were roughly 1.3 million host computers on the Internet. That rose to 2.2 million in January 1994; 4.8 million in January 1995; and 9.4 million in January 1996. Projecting those figures amounts to 144 million hosts by January 2000—an exponential rise. Each of these hosts needs one to hundreds of Web pages written by people with a strong grasp of the latest Web site technology, and these are the skills I intend to help you build throughout this book.

NOTE:
I haven't mentioned the much larger potential market for your Web skills: corporate intranets. TCP/IP and Web technology are being embraced by corporations as a better way to get everyone connected, and these corporations will need people with good Web and Internet skills.

The ActiveX Family

Renaming OLE Custom Controls to ActiveX Controls is only part of the ActiveX story. The underlying principle is to get the world interconnected in such a way that productivity will be raised to new levels. People will be able to work locally, over intranets, or over the Internet as easily as they now work on their local desktop. Microsoft refers to the many faces of this business as ActiveX Technologies. Although it may appear that I stray from the subject of ActiveX Controls (as one of the many faces), the fact is that all the technology is interrelated.

ActiveX Controls

ActiveX Controls are live objects that can be used with Visual Basic, Visual C++, Visual FoxPro, Microsoft Access, or any other container application or development application. Other containers include the Netscape Navigator (via the NCompass ActiveX plug-in) and, of course, Internet Explorer 3.0. Unlike Netscape plug-ins that can be used only with Netscape Navigator, ActiveX Controls can be used in a wide range of applications, and Microsoft is working on making them cross-platform.

ActiveX Controls can also be written using tools such as Visual J++ (Java). J++ applets are compiled to byte code and, for this reason, are platform independent. The possibilities are endless as the technology moves forward. Always think "Internet enabled" when you are considering the development of controls. This will help ensure that any controls you write will have a place in the scheme of things as this technology continues to grow.

> **NOTE:**
> **Microsoft frequently uses the term ActiveX *component* when referring to ActiveX Controls (old OLE Custom Controls). This is related to the fact that these controls are based heavily on the Component Object Model specification, or COM. An ActiveX component is an ActiveX Control.**

ActiveX Document Objects

One of the less publicized items emerging now is the *ActiveX Document* (formerly OLE DocObjects). If you use Microsoft Office 95, you may have had occasion to use the binder. If you have, it may have seemed like just a new-fangled container—and that is exactly what it is. The Microsoft Binder was the one and only ActiveX Document container. Internet Explorer 3.0 is the second ActiveX Document container, and more are on the way. It is a virtual certainty that someone—possibly you—will produce an ActiveX Document container.

What Is an ActiveX Document?

If you have followed the emergence of OLE, you are familiar with its starved beginnings and its growth into a major technology in the form of OLE Custom Controls (now ActiveX Controls) in applications such as Visual Basic, Visual C++, and other development environments. You may also be familiar with the culmination of this technology in the form of in-place activation or visual editing.

Figure 1-1 shows in-place activation (visual editing) of an Excel sheet in a Word 95 window. Notice that menus have been added for Excel, but that this doesn't look exactly like Excel. If you were to examine the Help menu, you would find that it shows Excel Help but no Word Help.

Now I'll have you bypass the Office Binder and look at Internet Explorer 3.0. Figure 1-2 shows a sample Excel document running in Internet Explorer 3.0. Note particularly that full toolbars are available for *both* applications, the menus have been merged, and, particularly, the Help menu includes help for both applications. Once again, this is emerging technology that Microsoft is making available. At present, there are, as mentioned previously, two ActiveX Document

Figure 1-1
In-place activation of an Excel sheet in Word

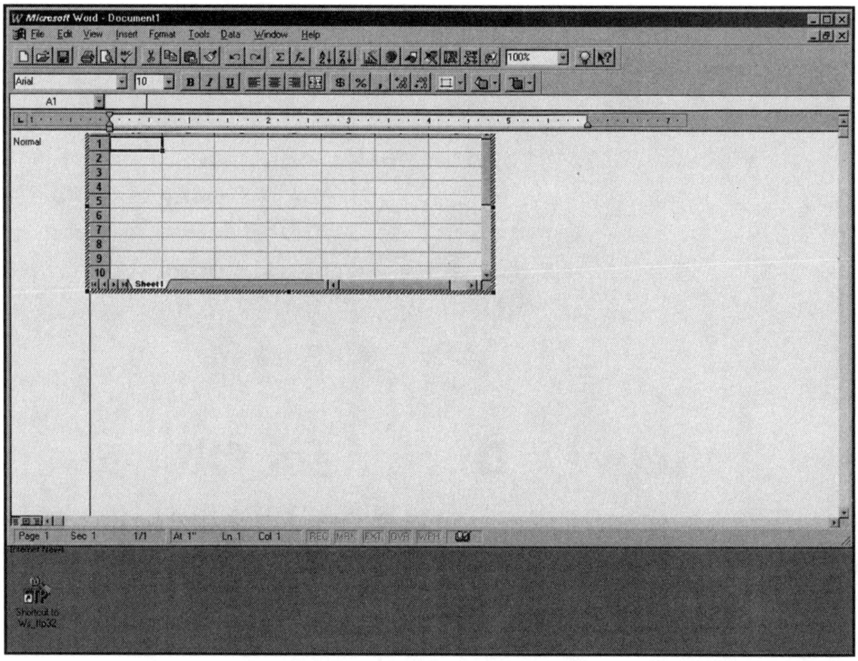

containers. There are also three ActiveX Document Servers; Microsoft Word 95, Microsoft Excel, and Microsoft PowerPoint.

> **NOTE:**
> **Oddly, the Help menu is the key to learning whether you are running a Document container. Help for both applications will appear there. Notice that both Microsoft Excel Help and The Microsoft Network Help are available in the Excel sheet loaded into Internet Explorer, as shown in Figure 1-2.**

ActiveX Server Framework

Although this book will not go deeply into the server side, it is important to keep in mind that the server provides much of the high-level functionality required by current and future applications on the Internet. In the World Wide Web realm, servers traditionally simply send content to the client's browser. Common Gateway Interface (CGI) provides some help by allowing forms to be built and data collected, but this capability will not scale well into the client/server world.

Figure 1-2
In-place activation of an Excel sheet in Internet Explorer

Again, Microsoft has come to the rescue (so to speak) with the Internet Server API (ISAPI). ISAPI—one of the server side pieces of ActiveX technology—allows developers to extend the capabilities of the server to allow more robust functionality. Real applications can be developed to allow, among other things, access to databases on the server side. James Utzschneider, Product Manager of Microsoft Developer Division, characterizes it, as in a title on Microsoft's Web site, "The Internet: Just Another Name for Client/Server Computing." He also discusses multitier architectures that separate client presentation services, business process rules, and data management services in such a way that one can be modified without impacting the others.

Active Scripts

Browser capabilities can be improved and the information that is displayed can be made more functional and attractive using Visual Basic Scripting (VBScript) or Microsoft's implementation of JavaScript called JScript. VBScript is a subset of Microsoft Visual Basic that allows control over ActiveX Controls and provides added functionality to HTML. I show you how it works later. JScript provides similar capabilities. JScript is different from Java applets. JScript allows Java byte codes to be compiled and run as long as the browser being used provides a Java Virtual Machine (Java VM). Both Internet Explorer 3.0 and Netscape's more recent browsers provide a Java VM. Internet Explorer also employs a Just-In-Time (JIT) compiler to speed these operations.

In later chapters, I show you how to write VBScript and JScript, and how to reuse the same code throughout many applications. I also show you how to use the ActiveX Control Pad to manipulate the browser (client) side.

Digitally Signed Code

The Internet is a vast array of interconnected computers. The possibility of downloading code that might do significant damage to your system grows with each new connected host. A virus could be downloaded from any number of sources, and using a virus scanner is not the ideal way to protect your system. Virus-checking software must be used each time that you obtain a new application that might be infected, and the virus scanner must be kept up-to-date with the latest virus information. If you are downloading a component that is going to start immediately in your browser, you would need to stop long enough to scan it, and that would significantly impact your Web surfing.

Microsoft, in conjunction with VeriSign and other code signing authorities, has developed a system now named Authenticode. This system allows software vendors to obtain certificates from a code signing authority (an Internet notary, if you will). Using digital signing technology from Microsoft and RSA Data Security, vendors can give you the equivalent of Internet shrink-wrap.

NOTE:
When you go into a store to buy your software, it comes in a shrink-wrapped package. This package gives you pretty strong assurance that the software came from a particular vendor and is probably safe to install on your computer. In a similar manner, software signed by the vendor using Public Key Encryption Technology, implemented with Authenticode, means that it is just as safe as (and possibly safer than) software purchased in shrink-wrapped packaging from a local store. If you trust the vendor, you can trust the code to be installed and activated immediately, because it's virtually impossible for anyone to have added a virus or otherwise tampered with the software.

Figure 1-3 shows the type of credential that you will see presented more and more as this technology is adopted by software vendors to assure that you get code that has not been modified or tampered with. You can also elect to bypass this display for code delivered using Authenticode. This may prove one of the most useful items available in the ActiveX world.

> **NOTE:**
> **VeriSign charges $20 for a personal certificate and $400 for a corporate certificate at this point. Corporate certificates require that you have a Dun & Bradstreet listing.**

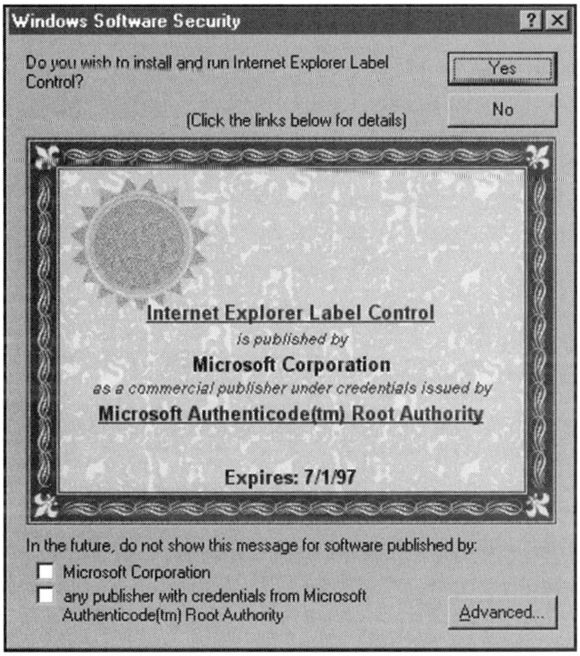

Figure 1-3 A sample Authenticode certificate

Notice that you can make a number of elections regarding whether you want to see certificates. If you trust the certificate holder (Microsoft, for example), you can elect to allow software from that vendor to be downloaded automatically after the system has checked the certificate.

HTML Extensions

HyperText Markup Language, or HTML, is at the center of everything that occurs on the World Wide Web and the vehicle in which client-side ActiveX controls work. Literally everything that happens is determined by how the browser being used interprets the tags delivered to your computer from the Internet site that you happen to be visiting. Attempts to dictate the adoption of new tags instead of leaving that process to the World Wide Web Consortium (W3C) have led to Web pages that are unreadable by some browsers. Both Microsoft and Netscape have been "guilty" of adding tags that are not part of any standard.

Tim Berners-Lee designed the first HTML in the late '80s. The first demo browser, written for a NeXT machine, was tried in early 1990—just six short years ago. The HTML allowed text and images to be delivered with links that allowed moving from document to document.

In the fall of 1993, Marc Andreesen and others at the National Center for Supercomputing Applications (NCSA) developed the Mosaic browser. This browser added new tags, including *fill-in forms*. These forms allowed a degree of interaction with the client in that the client could now send information to the server. Although this capability would later become standard, it created an immediate problem for browsers that were not forms aware.

Marc Andreesen started Mosaic Communications in mid-1994, and in October of that year, Mosaic released the first Netscape browser. That's just two short years ago. The browser added a number of features that enhanced how downloaded Web pages were displayed. It also added some additional tags. The Netscape Version 1.*x* feature set became the basis for HTML version 2.0. Netscape had little real competition through version 2.0 of its browser, which introduced yet another incompatibility, called *frames*. Frames allow the computer screen to be split up, making very attractive displays possible. It also provided a much easier way to navigate a Web site. I go into much more detail on frames later.

Netscape's first real competition came with the release of Microsoft Internet Explorer. Version 2.0 of Internet Explorer did not yet support frames, but frames are now fully supported with Internet Explorer Version 3.0, released August 13th, 1996. That's two highly competitive browsers from Mosaic Communications in just two short years. That, folks, is "Internet Time"! You must be nimble of foot to keep up.

The newest draft HTML standard is HTML 3.2 (notice that 3.0 was abandoned before it could become a standard). Oddly enough, frames are not part of HTML 3.2, but frames are supported by Netscape 2.0/3.0 and Internet Explorer 3.0. Frames are also part of a draft specification now making its way through W3C. HTML 3.2 does include tables, which are composed of a header, body, and footer. Internet Explorer has added some table features that still are not part of the specification. Both Microsoft and Netscape are expressing their intent to follow the standards route with their browsers on the Internet, but each still has features that are not part of any standard.

I cover tables, frames, objects, and scripting in this book. I also include details about the latest working draft information on cascading style sheets, Level 1—or CSS1 as it's more commonly known. One good thing: the two most prevalent browsers will almost certainly work to incorporate any features introduced in a competitive browser. Both browsers are working to make your Web experience more like a desktop publishing scenario. In short, Web sites are becoming ever more attractive as long as you are visiting them with a browser capable of using the latest and greatest tags.

Activating the Internet

Although the Internet is composed of a wide rage of technologies (FTP, SMTP, POP, NNTP, Gopher, and others) the World Wide Web using HyperText Markup Language (HTML) has become the chief technology on the Internet. You will need a number of things now or later to get a good handle on the entire process. The tools you will need in order to utilize the examples in this book are available from a number of sources, and many are included on the CD-ROM to save you hours of download time. You should have a connection to a local Internet Service Provider (ISP), because many of the tools and other material are available only through downloads from Microsoft and other Web sites.

Getting Started

A connection for browsing the Internet and downloading software tools is made through a modem, preferably running at least 28.8 Kbps. An even better choice is an ISDN line, but these can incur expensive ISP charges and are not available in some areas. A valuable start-up tool is the Windows 95 Plus pack, which provides dial-up networking and the ability to easily set up new connections.

Your Internet Service Provider should provide the following information when you sign up for a service:

- A user name
- A password
- A connecting phone number or numbers
- A primary and secondary DNS (IP) number

Many ISPs will provide software and connection instructions, but you may want to set your connections up to best suit your needs. After you have this information, you are ready to configure a connection to your ISP.

NOTE:
In Windows NT 4.0, double-click My Computer, and then double-click Dial-Up Networking and follow the instructions. The help files are very complete and very easy to follow.

From the Dial-Up Networking folder in Explorer, double-click Make New Connection. The connection wizard should start as shown in Figure 1-4. I've left the default as My Connection, but you can make this the name of your choice. Your modem should already be configured from the installation of Windows 95. Now, select Next.

In the dialog box shown in Figure 1-5, enter your ISP's phone number. You may have been given a choice of several numbers. You'll probably want to choose the one nearest you. Leave the area code as it is unless your ISP resides outside your area code.

Select Next, and then, in the dialog box shown in Figure 1-6, select Finish. Your basic connection is complete but you still have a little work to do.

Right-click your new connection in the Dial-Up Networking folder, and select Properties. The dialog box shown in Figure 1-7 should appear. Your ISP's telephone number and other information should already be present. The Configure button allows you to configure your modem. Again, it is probably already set up correctly.

Select Server Type... to bring up the dialog box shown in Figure 1-8.

Figure 1-4
The Make New Connection wizard

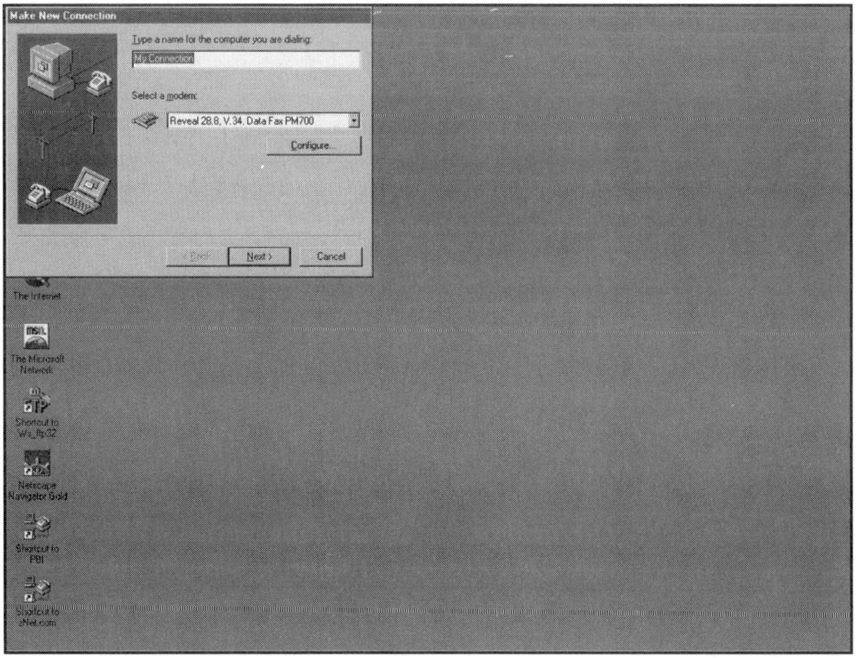

Figure 1-5
Telephone number entry

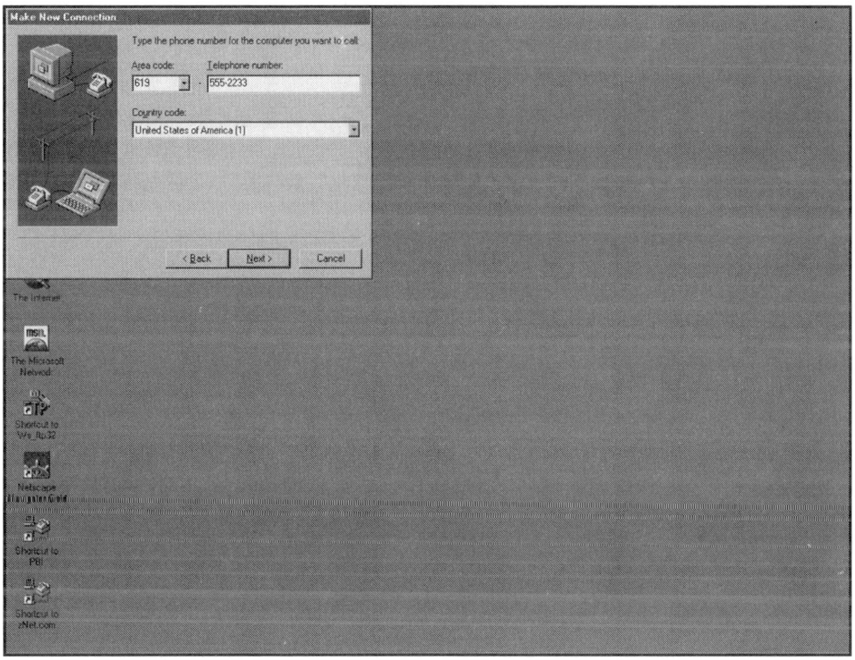

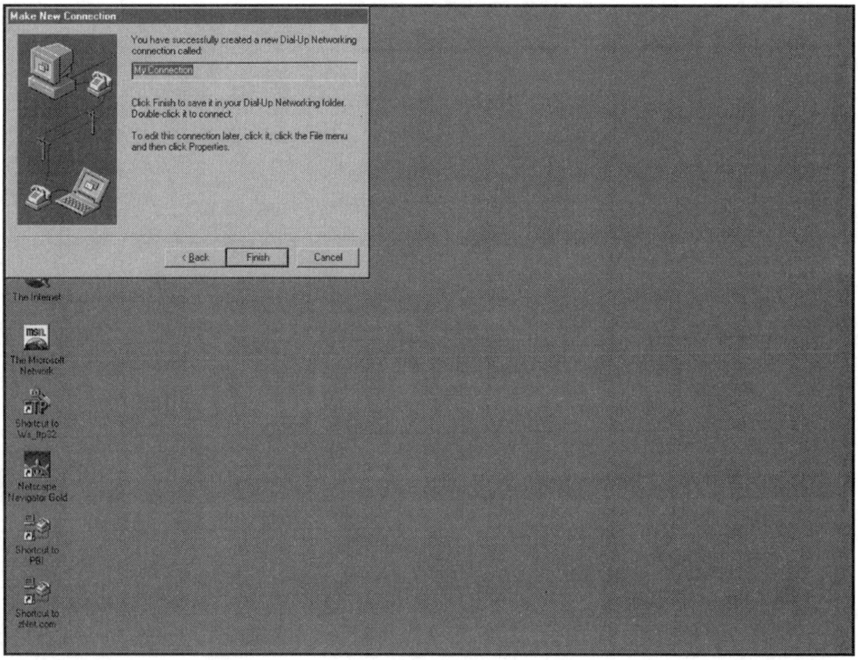

Figure 1-6
Finish dialog box

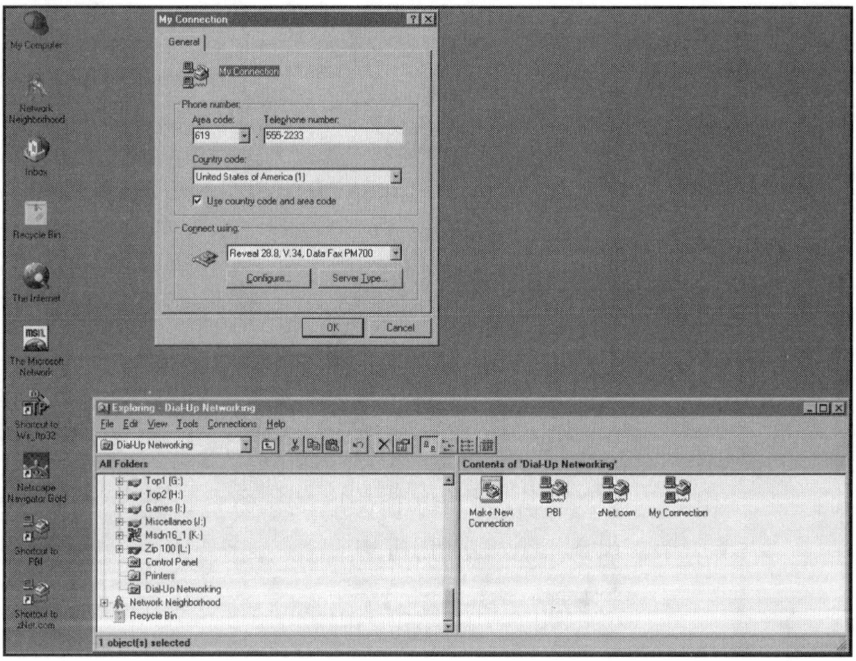

Figure 1-7
Setting up your dial-up service

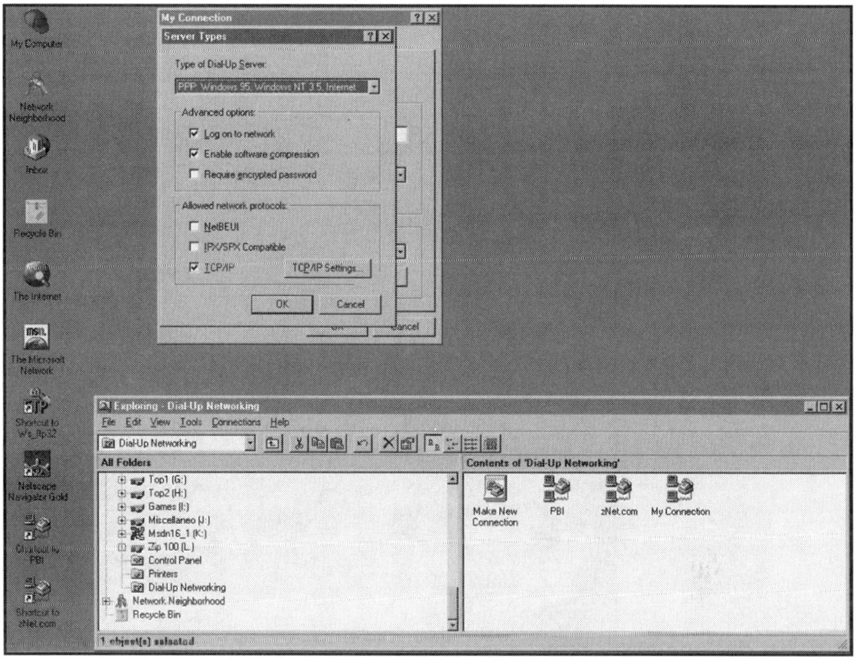

Figure 1-8
Server Type dialog box

Be sure that "PPP: Windows 95, Windows NT 3.5, Internet" appears in the top drop-down box. This assumes that you have a normal PPP connection from your Internet Service Provider, which will usually be the case. Uncheck "Require encrypted password," "NetBEUI," and "IPX/SPX Compatible." TCP/IP should be the only selected item in "Allowed network protocols."

> **NOTE:**
> **Most Internet Service Providers now provide PPP (Point-to-Point Protocol) Internet connections. You should choose a provider that uses PPP. There are other protocols, such as SLIP (Serial Line Internet Protocol), but they are not used extensively. You can use SLIP but you will need to obtain help from your service provider in setting up the Dial-Up Networking.**

Click TCP/IP settings... to bring up the dialog box in Figure 1-9. Unless your ISP has told you to the contrary, set "Server assigned IP address." Most ISPs have a pool of IP addresses that they assign in rotation as users log on. Some ISPs will provide you with a static IP address if you ask. This static address allows other people to log on to your computer.

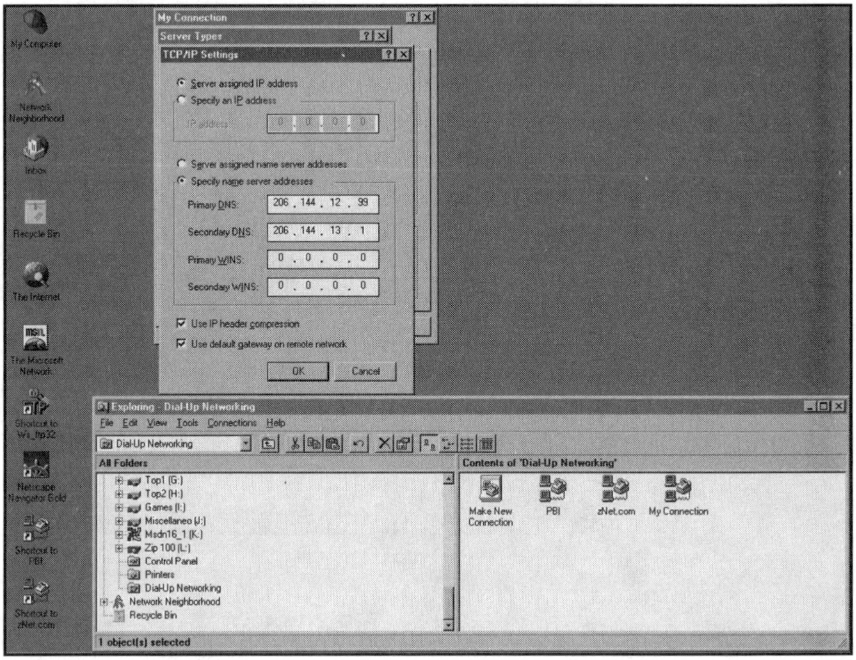

Figure 1-9
Setting your IP addresses

Select "Specify name server addresses" and enter the primary and secondary DNS numbers that your ISP should have provided to you. Leave the two check boxes at the bottom checked as they are by default. Select OK for all the open dialog boxes, and your connection settings should all be ready. You might want to drag a shortcut to the desktop or simply double-click the new connection to start it.

You will be asked for your user name and password when you log on as shown in the sample in Figure 1-10. When you have entered these, they can be saved and reused the next time you connect. The connection can be made at any time without regard to a browser or any other software running to access the connection. You simply have an open line to your ISP that will be used by any Internet-related application that you start at this point.

Next Steps

Although you can work with a browser alone to learn HTML coding as well as many topics covered in this book, you will ultimately need additional things. If you have worked with the design of Web sites, you can probably breeze through what follows. I bypass some initial

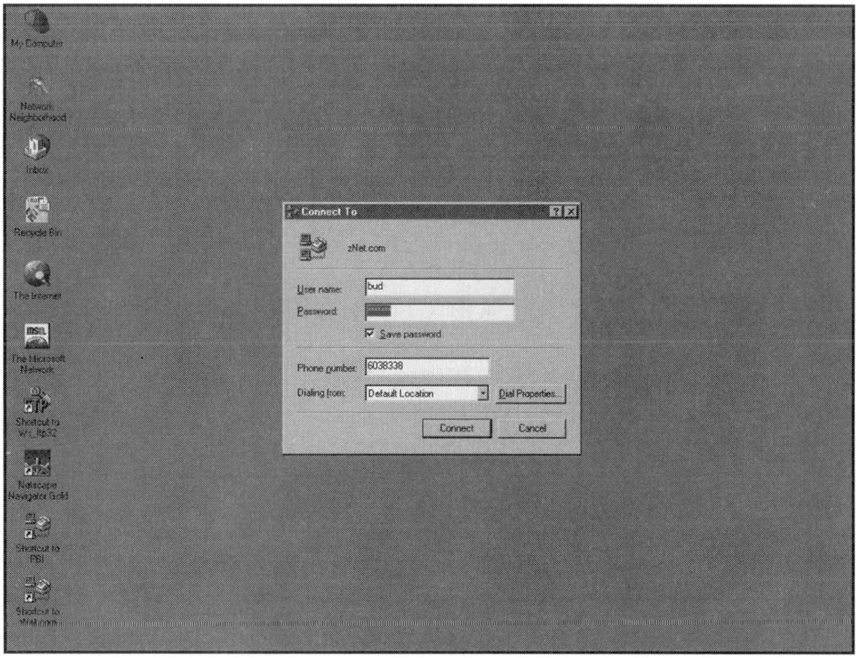

Figure 1-10
The Connect To dialog box

planning stages and explore the general process of setting up a Web site to ensure that you can follow further discussions in this book.

After the planning is complete, the site designer begins writing HTML code. The code can be tested locally using the Web browser of your choice. For your purposes here, the latest version of Microsoft Internet Explorer is the browser that you should probably use for testing. The following code represents a bare-bones version of the HTML code for a Web page:

```
<HTML>
<HEAD>
<TITLE>New Page</TITLE>
</HEAD>
<BODY>
Hello World!
</BODY>
</HTML>
```

This code should be saved with either an .htm or .html extension, depending on the site you intend to run it on. Most Web sites will expect a file called INDEX.HTML for UNIX server sites or

INDEX.HTM for Windows NT server sites. You should check with your host service provider for the default names that you can use. Most servers will provide several different defaults.

The preceding code will print "Hello World!" in your browser window, and the title bar will show "New Page." As you have probably guessed, the preceding code could be entered using Notepad, but better tools are available. I discuss them later.

The code, written on your own computer, can be transferred to your Internet host provider's server via FTP (File Transfer Protocol) as shown in Figure 1-11.

Figure 1-11 An illustration of Internet interaction

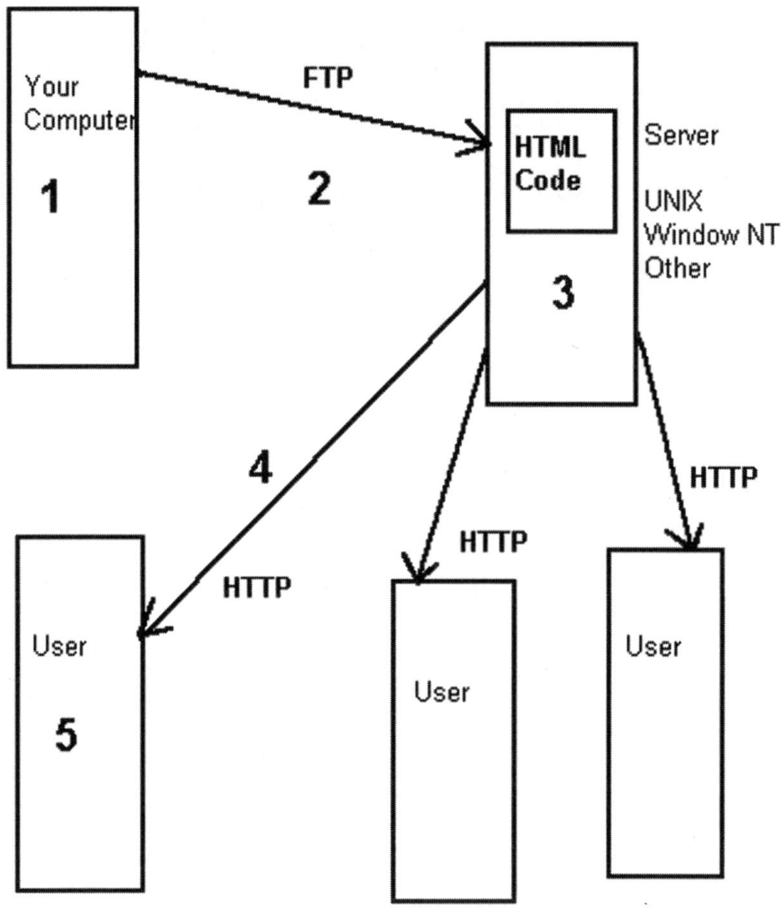

The servers available on the Internet today are mostly UNIX-based computers, and the file and directory structures follow UNIX protocols. This means, for the most part, that the directories are separated with forward slashes on the UNIX side and backslashes on your PC. If you are running Windows 95 or Windows NT, you might want to visit the following site:

```
http://www.ipswitch.com/
```

and obtain a copy of WS_FTPLE. This is an excellent way to transfer files via FTP, and it removes problems associated the file and directory structures of Windows and UNIX.

You build your HTML code (1 in Figure 1-11) and transfer it via FTP (2 in Figure 1-11) to an Internet host. Host service providers can be located anywhere in the world. Visitors to your site will probably never know exactly where your host server is located physically. I actively use three host service providers.

Host Service Provider Number One

zNet provides UNIX hosting services including HTML, FTP, and CGI. These services are located in San Diego, California and my experience with them has been excellent. They will help you with domain name services and can set you up with a "virtual site." This means that your site name will be something like the following:

```
http://www.yourcompanyname.com/
```

> **NOTE:**
> **In a normal host situation, your Internet name will include the name of your host service provider. Virtual hosting makes it appear that you have your own dedicated server. This is important because it makes it easier for Web crawlers and search engines to find you on the Internet.**

ZNet's Web address is as follows:

```
is-http://www.znet.com/zweb/web.html
```

Host Service Provider Number Two

`pair.com` provides UNIX wholesale hosting services. You can buy sites from it and resell them to others or use them yourself. Pair also provide HTML, FTP, and CGI, and provide an excellent level of service. Pair can also provide a secure site and virtual hosting. Pair is located in Pennsylvania.

Pair's Web address is the following:

`http://www.pair.com/`

Host Service Provider Number Three

Joey Foutz runs `biznetc.com` in Farmington, New Mexico. This is a Windows NT site running Internet Information Server. I use this site to test the functionality of a number of things in this book. Joey provides good service and "free roam." Essentially, this means that you can do what you like on your site and Joey will provide you with the tools to do most of what I discuss in this book. It also means that you have a higher level of responsibility to ensure that you don't damage anything on the server.

Biznetc's Web address:

`http://www.biznetc.com/`

This is item 3 of Figure 1-11. You

- Write your HTML code
- Transfer it via FTP to your host computer

If you would like to check out other hosting services, visit the following:

`http://www.search.com/`

Use a search engine such as Alta Vista, Excite, or Lycos and search for "hosting services" (use the quotation marks). You will find thousands of other hosting services listed. You may not find a large number of NT servers at this time.

After your code is in place on the server, users can access it via HTTP (this is item 4 in Figure 1-11). From that point, the code you transferred to your Web site is downloaded to the user's computer and displayed in that user's Web browser. Assuming that you've put only text on the server, this is a completely static Web site. Graphics would improve the appearance. CGI would allow users to fill in forms, but that is about the limit of functionality. In this book, I show you how to make your Web site active in a number of ways—and far more attractive.

You always have the option of running your own hosting service, but doing so can become very complex. My original intent was to do exactly that, but I've found host servers to be far easier to cope with. They get the high-speed connections to the Internet, the CSU/DSUs and routers, and all the other services needed to connect to the Internet backbone. You need only transfer your Web content to the site and users can immediately begin using your new Web site. Just a hint: setup costs for a T1 line are around $5,000 to $7,000, and the T1 line will cost you about $2,000 per month.

Extending Functionality

So far, the Web has been about publishing and moving software or other information from one place to another. It is growing to include commercial and retail sales and similar content. It is hampered by the fact that it is a low-bandwidth, high-latency medium. In other words, it's *slow!* Working on a local area network, these same tasks are quite fast. The advent of ISDN and other technology just beginning to emerge will improve the situation. In the meantime, we all need to deal with this speed deficit by making our sites as small and fast as possible while still delivering content.

ActiveX is about providing greater functionality without negatively affecting the available bandwidth. This greater functionality is obtained in a number of ways. The ActiveX Controls that are being made available now are small bits of code based on the Component Object Model, or COM. The Microsoft ActiveX Controls gallery contains, for example:

- Animated Button
- Chart
- Gradient
- Label
- Marquee
- Menu

- PopUp Menu
- PopUp Window
- Preloader
- Stock Ticker
- Timer
- View Tracker

I cover these in more detail later, but I will say here that these items obviously do not constitute the next "killer apps." They do improve appearance in a number of ways and, at this point, that is about all you can do. On the other hand, at this early stage, these improvements can make a significant difference in how your pages appear to users. They can also make a difference in how people you might work or consult for view your work.

Again, I'm talking about a disparate group of new technologies. When you factor in HTML Version 3.2 with frames, objects, cascading style sheets, TrueType fonts, and scripting, and then add things such as ODBC capabilities and the new dbWeb for database management, things begin to improve still further. All of this revolves around and is based on the Component Object Model. It would be difficult to stress this point too strongly. COM underlies everything on both the server and client side. Virtually everything is based on components and interfaces to components, and these make up the heart of ActiveX.

Microsoft NetMeeting

Consider a scenario for a moment. Margaret, John, Ralph, and Erica are scheduled for a 10 a.m. meeting in the only available conference room. They had difficulty finding the room available and should have had the meeting the previous day.

They intend to discuss and hammer out the details of a new organization and a fairly complex business plan, so each takes copies of the necessary papers. In the conference room are a whiteboard with a bad supply of pens and a damaged eraser, an overhead projector, a table, and chairs. Finally, another group has the room scheduled for 10:45 a.m. Sound familiar?

Needless to say, the meeting may accomplish very little. The attendees will be frustrated, they will be pushing against the clock, and they will likely have forgotten some of the material they needed to bring. At 10:45, they are likely to leave with only a small part of what they needed to finish actually accomplished.

Now try an alternative scenario. The same participants each start a session of NetMeeting (Figure 1-12) *at their own desk*. Each has the information needed on his or her own computer. Each has the time available *at a time they have mutually* selected–not a time dictated by the availability of a conference room.

With no outside distractions, they are ready to get on with the meeting, and unless one of them has other time constraints, they are not being pushed by the clock. Assume that they also are all on the corporate intranet, and thus are not starved for bandwidth, although the same thing can be accomplished on the Internet.

> **NOTE:**
> **Consider these folks located in San Francisco, Los Angeles, New York, and Atlanta. Then, consider the travel costs and associated problems with getting them all together for a productive meeting or meetings.**

Now, when NetMeeting is running, each user goes to the local copy of the User List Service, or ULS, as shown in Figure 1-13. Each finds the other three participants and connects with them. NetMeeting might well be the next "killer app." The users can talk (using a sound card and microphone), use a shared whiteboard, chat using the chat service, and share running applications.

These meeting participants can make modifications to contracts, edit user manuals, change spreadsheet figures, do new charts, and save everything that they do on their own local computer. Now, that should be a low-cost, productive meeting. Best of all, NetMeeting is free! You will find it on the CD with this book or you can download it from Microsoft's Web site.

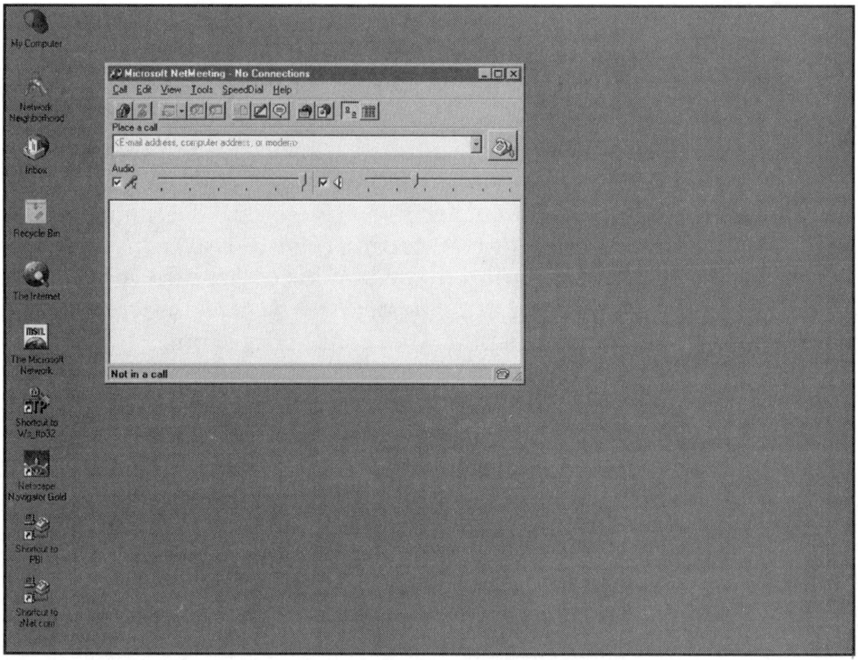

Figure 1-12 The main screen of Microsoft NetMeeting

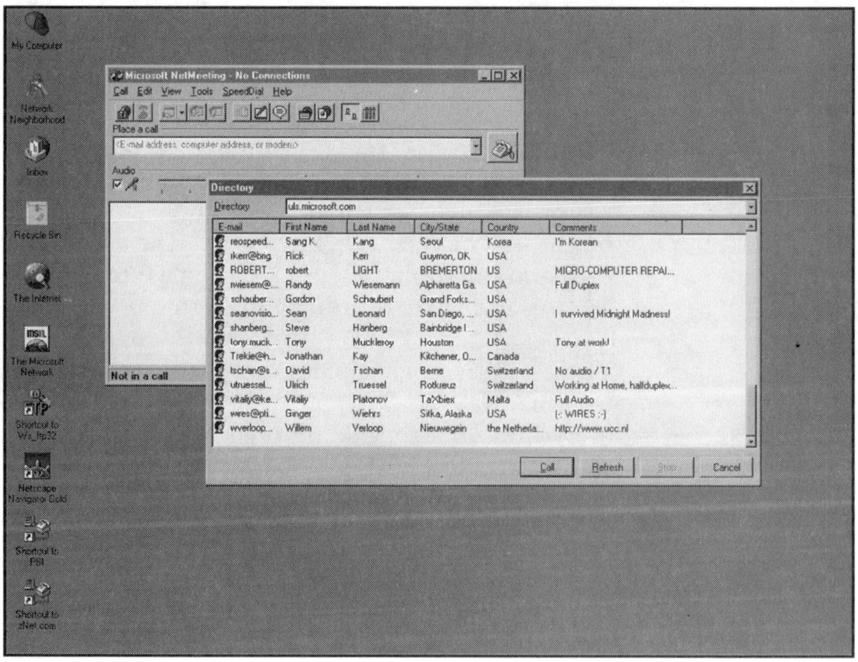

Figure 1-13 Microsoft User List Service (`uls.microsoft.com`)

> **NOTE:**
> **With the necessary bandwidth and a small video camera, that functionality could extend to holding conferences with each attendee at his or her own computer with full video. Not a mandatory requirement, but the final neat touch.**

Remember the lousy selection of pens? Well, with the NetMeeting whiteboard shown in Figure 1-14, you have at least 28 possibilities, each with four different stroke widths.

Figure 1-14
The NetMeeting Whiteboard

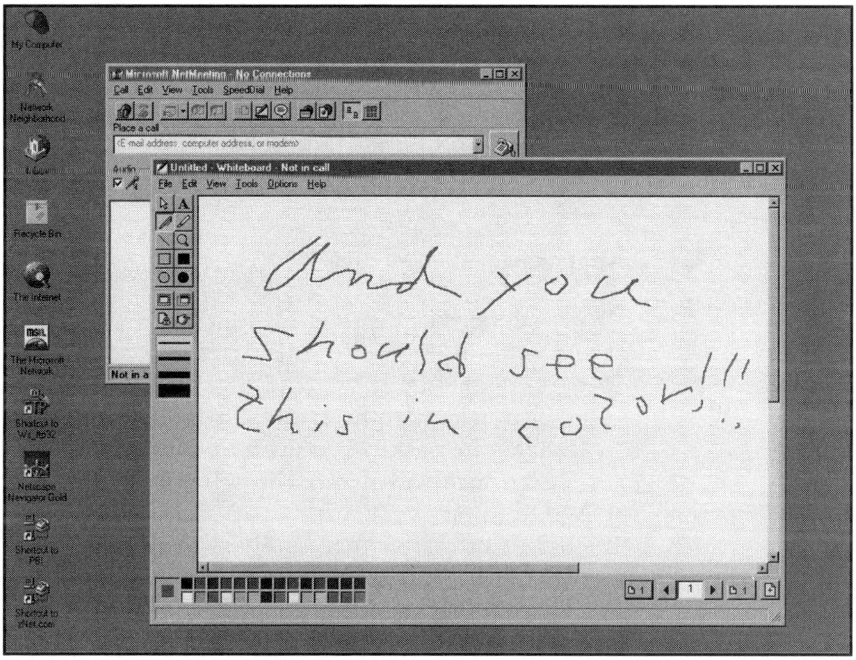

When was the last time you saw a conference room whiteboard with multiple pages and a way to save the contents? Now, add the ability to run a chat session as shown in Figure 1-15 and you have the most...words do fail me. It's one of those Microsoft tricks of bouncing something out there and having someone say, "Holy cow, Batman!"

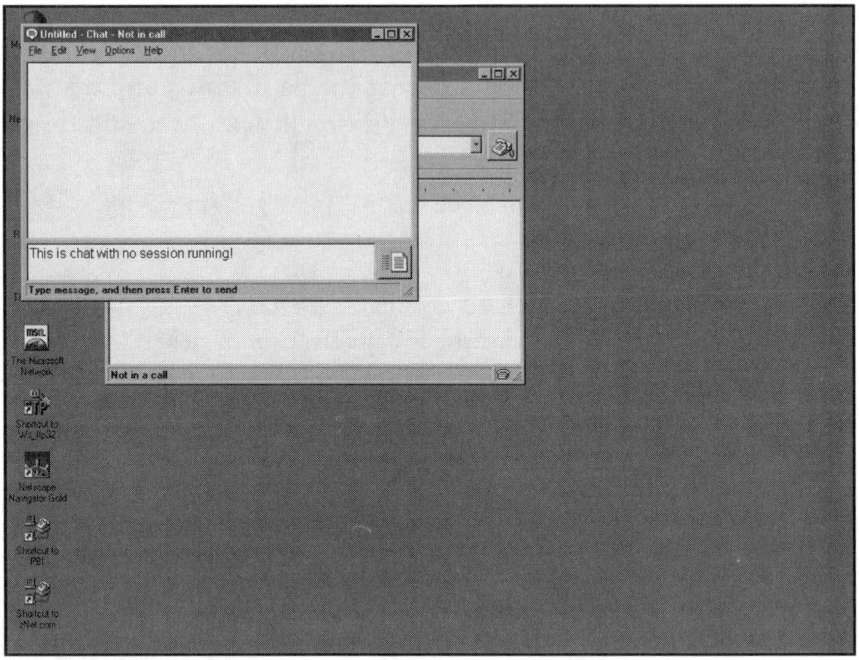

Figure 1-15
The Chat screen

Summary

With Public key cryptography and the various security capabilities built around PKCS, the ability to sign contracts in a secure environment becomes an easy technological step. ActiveMovie, VRML, and a host of other capabilities are all part of the emerging capabilities that will make the desktop your home-based office. Again, the secret is increased bandwidth and, though not directly related, cable companies and others are working to build the bandwidth needed into the Internet's infrastructure and backbone.

Finally, add Visual Basic Scripting Edition (VBScript) and JScript to the mix, and the possibilities extend still further. These are the emerging technologies—some of which are fully functional now—that I explore further in this book to give you the best possible handle on the present and the future of this technology. I've mentioned a few of the more important items already. When you're finished with this book, you should have numerous tools that you can apply to building your career on the future of the Internet.

Chapter 2

Installing and Using Internet Explorer

Microsoft Internet Explorer 3.0 was released to the Internet world on August 13th, 1996 in what Microsoft dubbed "Midnight Madness." For the first time that I know of, `www.microsoft.com` was repeatedly displaying the message "too many users." Thirty-two thousand copies were downloaded from midnight to 6 in the morning. Internet Explorer 3.0 is one of the best values in the world—yours for the cost of download time. Bill Gates has characterized it as being "as important as the release of Windows 95."

NOTE:
It could be said that whereas Windows 95 redefined the PC desktop, Internet Explorer is destined to redefine the enterprise. Like your HiFi cabinet, it is nothing more that an *COM object* container. This container can be ported to other environments, and the COM objects—including ActiveX Controls or components—that make it function can be ported to other environments. If it succeeds in becoming the default browser for the world, it could replace every initiative for windowing in the world of computers.

Internet Explorer is, without question, a milestone in the history of the Internet. The months to come will determine whether Internet Explorer or Netscape Navigator becomes the world's default browser. The browser is the cornerstone of everything that you do on the Internet, an intranet, and in this book. Your thorough understanding of the browser is important in that such an understanding will allow you to make better use of the technology that drives it.

Internet Explorer 3.0 is the culmination of months of work by Microsoft. ActiveX, Java, Plug-in, and broad HTML support are built in to ensure that you have everything the Internet makes available in one place. Internet Explorer provides an advanced development platform for users, corporations, and Web developers.

NOTE:
Internet Explorer is nothing more than ActiveX Controls or components running in a Document Object container. The interfaces to these components are exposed in a number of ways that I discuss later with the scripting object model.

Architecture

The architecture of a browser defines performance, extensibility, and future feature capabilities. Internet Explorer 3.0 is built as a set of ActiveX Controls based on the Component Object Model (COM). In other words, we now have an application that makes full use of what was once known as OLE Custom Controls. This means that pieces can be replaced just as you might replace only the speakers or the preamplifier in an audio system. Replacing one piece does not make the remainder obsolete; thus, functionality can be improved incrementally and in an evolutionary manner.

These pieces can also be written in any number of compatible languages. One piece might use Java, another Visual Basic, and still another Visual C++. More important, new features can be integrated into the system simply by adding components that talk to the system as a whole. You will see the term *interface* used in this book and in other places. The interface represents the connectors that allow the glue (scripting languages) to bind everything together.

Applications can be built that distribute Internet capabilities to the entire desktop. Applications that you write can incorporate Internet functionality by using Internet Explorer as an ActiveX Control. Also, Internet Explorer can use other ActiveX-enabled applications. The result is an infinitely extensible system now and for the future. Additional functionality can be added without having to change the underlying code. When new functionality is developed, a user can simply download the new addition rather than download a huge new application.

Internet Explorer offers full HTML support, including HTML 3.2 and Cascading Style Sheets; broad programming and scripting language support; ActiveMovie support for better multimedia; the security of Authenticode to ensure safe downloads; real collaboration using NetMeeting; and flexible customization.

Feature Set

The feature set ensures that Internet Explorer takes advantage of everything the Web offers, whether it be content, security, communicating and collaborating, or personalizing the browser.

Support for the following HTML features is built into Internet Explorer:

- Standard Frames. Several panes within the browser window or an embedded single frame can be placed along any edge of the page. Frames make navigation of a Web site much easier and more attractive. Various options for the frame borders are also supported.
- Standard Tables. This feature allows greater control over the display of text, graphics, and background colors, making a Web site more interesting and readable.
- Full HTML 2.0 support.
- Full support for HTML 3.2. Specifically:
    - Enhanced Frames. This feature allows frames within frames, floating frames (a frame can be inserted anywhere that a graphic might be), and nonscrolling frames.
    - Enhanced Tables. In addition to background colors, Internet Explorer supports background images, wrapped text, and cell groupings within tables.

    - Enhanced and TrueType Font Support
    - "HTML and STYLE" specification. Covers SPAN, DIV, and STYLE elements, as well as the linking of style sheets to HTML documents; this specification is the glue that binds style sheets to HTML.
    - Full support for Cascading Style Sheets (Level 1). Style sheets bring desktop publishing capabilities to the Web.
    - Embedding style information via the STYLE attribute allows in-line style information.
    - Linked Style Sheets. Style information can be included in a separate file and used with many HTML documents. A site builder can change the look and feel of an entire Web site with changes to a single style sheet. Although not directly related to COM, this is one more example of componentization.
    - Full Font Control. Provides control of font families, weights, and typographic measurement units including centimeters, inches, pixels, percentages, and others.
    - Full Whitespace Control. Margins can be set in typographic units around all edges of elements realizing real desktop publishing-style pages.
    - Full Background Control (nontiled). The Web author can place images behind objects such as in a table cell in a number of ways. Besides the standard full-tile, an image can be tiled vertically or horizontally, or be positioned anywhere on the page.
    - Backgrounds. Background colors and images can be added to tables and paragraphs, or anywhere you like.
    - Typographic Space Control. Now you can include leading spaces between your text lines and other elements.
    - Indenting. Indent a line or paragraph of text on an HTML page.
    - Negative Margins. Allow elements to float over other elements on a page.
- <OBJECT> Tag Support. The heart of scripting.
- Scrolling Marquees. Can be used to convey time-critical information.

I cover the use of most of these features in Chapters 3 and 7. Keep in mind that many of these features could make your Web site readable only with Internet Explorer. Always provide alternatives if you want your site to be read by other browsers.

Broad Support for Added Functionality

HTML is the basis for all Web content, but the World Wide Web Consortium, better known as W3C, is adding new capabilities to the standard in cooperation with Microsoft and others on a steady basis. The result will be more dynamic Web pages and greater Internet interactivity. These extensions to HTML require applications such as ActiveX Controls or Netscape plug-ins to extend beyond the present state of HTML. This added functionality combined with scripting will allow new software in the form of ActiveX Controls and Java applets to provide new and impressive functionality on the Internet.

For the future of corporate intranets (and the Internet), it is extremely important that corporations can make use of their existing knowledge and investments in tools, software, and operating systems. These needs are addressed in the very way Internet Explorer 3.0 (and its upcoming successor, Internet Explorer 4.0) is built—as a group of components using the COM object model.

Internet Explorer supports:

- Java applets, which are software components created using the Java language. Microsoft's new Visual J++ provides the means for developing Java applets and compiles them into Java byte code, making them cross-platform compatible.

- Just-In-Time (JIT) Java Compiler, which is built into Internet Explorer and provides greater performance for interpreting Java byte code. The Microsoft Just-In-Time (JIT) Java Compiler provides the fastest way to run Java applications in a Web page, but Internet Explorer is extensible to use any JIT compiler.

- JScript (Microsoft's implementation of JavaScript) and VBScript, which allow Java applets and ActiveX controls to be used within HTML code.

Java is a great way to build ActiveX controls. Using ActiveX, Java applets can communicate or be scripted with any other ActiveX Controls, regardless of the language in which they were created. Internet Explorer's use of COM architecture allows the same Java applets to be used in either the browser or other COM-based applications.

ActiveX Controls are fast and light-weight software components based on the Component Object Model (COM). ActiveX Controls can be created in a wide variety of languages, including Java, Visual C++, and other languages. By making use of existing technology, ActiveX Controls can be used both on Web pages and in stand-alone applications that are ActiveX component containers (such as Visio, Visual FoxPro, Microsoft Access, Visual Basic, and others). There are currently more than 1,000 ActiveX Controls commercially available and usable in Web pages.

ActiveX Scripting provides great flexibility in tying together software components. Microsoft Internet Explorer 3.0 supports Microsoft's JScript scripting language, as well as VBScript or any other ActiveX scripting language. This provides developers with the ability to choose any scripting language available, including custom languages.

ActiveX Documents allow the common use of the Internet and intranet for disseminating and sharing information. Many systems force users to port existing documents from their original forms into HTML format. Using ActiveX Documents enables the user to open richly formatted documents, such as a Microsoft Excel spreadsheet, a chart, or a Word document, directly in the browser. For those without the native application, viewers are available for free download from Microsoft's Web site. This also means that real Windows documents can be used on Web sites as part of the actual content.

Multimedia on the Internet

Internet multimedia is an opportunity for Web developers and authors to dynamically provide new content on the Internet/intranet. Internet Explorer supports:

- AIFF, AU, MIDI, and WAV audio formats
- AVI video format
- In-line (streamed) sound support
- QuickTime video playback, 3D animation, and VRML
- MPEG audio format
- MPEG video format
- Any ActiveX Controlled in-line (streamed) sound

- In-line (streamed) video
- ActiveMovie Streaming Format (ASF), allowing synchronization of visuals with audio
- ActiveMovie, which supports MPV, MPA, MPE, MPEG, AU, AIF, AIFF, SND, MID, RMI, Wav + AVI, MOV, and QuickTime formats in a single control and is open and extensible for future technologies
- ActiveX scripting support and HTML layout control for more and better multimedia development possibilities

It is worth noting that no other browser supports this broad range of functionality. Microsoft Internet Explorer uses DirectX technologies, which are tightly integrated with the operating system, to ensure that hardware is optimized for various forms of multimedia. Most important, Internet Explorer's COM architecture and ActiveMovie allow multimedia to be integrated with the browser to provide the best multimedia performance on the Internet.

Secure Communication and Interaction

The Microsoft Internet Security Framework provides a comprehensive security solution for the Internet and intranet. It lets Web users communicate and collaborate privately, download code they can trust with Authenticode, and identify themselves to others across the Internet. Web users on the Internet or intranet can conduct transactions and purchase products or do business with privacy and security.

Internet Explorer (and Netscape) supports the following:

- Server and client authentication using a digital ID or certificate to identify yourself to Web servers. Web servers can also identify themselves to the user so that the user knows that he or she is connected to the appropriate server.
- SSL 2.0/3.0. A Netscape-developed protocol intended to provide secure communication over a TCP/IP connection.

Internet Explorer goes further and supports:

- Code signing, with Authenticode providing accountability for software and software components downloaded from the Internet, including Java applets and ActiveX Controls. Internet Explorer 3.0 lets end users identify who published the software before it is downloaded, and verify that it has not been tampered with.

- CryptoAPI 2.0, providing the underlying security services for the Microsoft Internet Security Framework, and specifically for secure channels and code signing. The delivery of CryptoAPI through Internet Explorer 3.0 lets developers easily integrate strong cryptography into their applications.

- PCT 1.0, which is Microsoft's integrated protocol for secure TCP/IP communication.

Microsoft participates in the Internet Engineering Task Force (IETF), World Wide Web Consortium (W3C), and other group's activities to develop Internet security standards. This along with an adherence to existing certificate and cryptography standards will ensure that Microsoft security technologies are interoperable and open.

Communicating and Collaborating on the Web

Features such as Internet telephony, data and video conferencing, mail, news, chat, and application sharing are all parts of a complete communications solution. Internet Mail and News users can create and read mail and news messages in HTML. Any URL automatically becomes a link, with only a double-click required to send the default browser to the site.

Application sharing makes NetMeeting and shared applications a true business feature. This is the most important data/document conferencing capability yet offered for Internet standard software. A user can share any application with other users, and all can see, contribute to, and discuss changes that are made, whether they have the shared application on their machine or not.

Multipoint chat, whiteboard, and application sharing allow the user to hold meetings with three or more people, allowing everyone to receive the transferred files, draw on the whiteboard, and see and control the shared applications. NetMeeting also adheres to T.120 protocols, the International Telecommunications Union standards for data conferencing used by telephone companies, PTTs, bridge manufacturers, video conferencing vendors, software vendors, and service providers worldwide.

Internet Explorer 3.0 is the first step into the future of the Internet, intranet, and the future of computing. History shows that changes in direction are not always clear in the beginning. The Internet has brought about profound differences in the way computing will be done in the future. It is always possible for the direction to change; it is also possible to see the main driving force left rudderless. IBM dominated the computer industry years ago. It is still a major force to consider, but Microsoft holds a similar lead now. As long as Microsoft can maintain its lead, it will likely define the market of the future.

Even if the foregoing sounds like marketing hype, that is not the intention. Internet Explorer 3.0 and the underlying ActiveX technology cover such an incredibly broad spectrum that it is important to attempt to bring it all into perspective. The surface appearance of Internet Explorer is deceptively simple. It would be easy to conclude that "it really doesn't do much—it's just another Web browser." That conclusion would be a huge mistake. You will see how the pieces fit as you continue in this book.

Installing Internet Explorer

The full version of Internet Explorer 3.0 is a file called MSIE30M.EXE and there are different versions for Windows 95 and Windows NT 4.0. An update file is available that works for either installation. To start installation, simply double-click the icon associated with this file. After the EULA (End User License Agreement) presentation, you can click the Yes button to continue with the installation, or the No button to quit. Many people recommend that you first remove beta 3.0 versions, and you can certainly remove old 2.0 versions. Installing over an earlier beta will preserve your favorites folder automatically, and I've yet to see any problems with installing over an earlier beta. Favorites will also be preserved if you uninstall earlier versions.

If you elect to continue installation, the setup will begin extracting the files to be installed. The MSIE30M.EXE version contains Internet Explorer 3.0, Internet Mail, Internet News, NetMeeting, ActiveMovie, and the HTML Layout Control. The HTML Layout control will be used later in this book when you're working with the ActiveX Control Pad, so be sure to install it.

The installation will then ask whether you want to select optional components, as shown in Figure 2-1. Although the installation will install everything by default, you might elect to look at what is actually being installed.

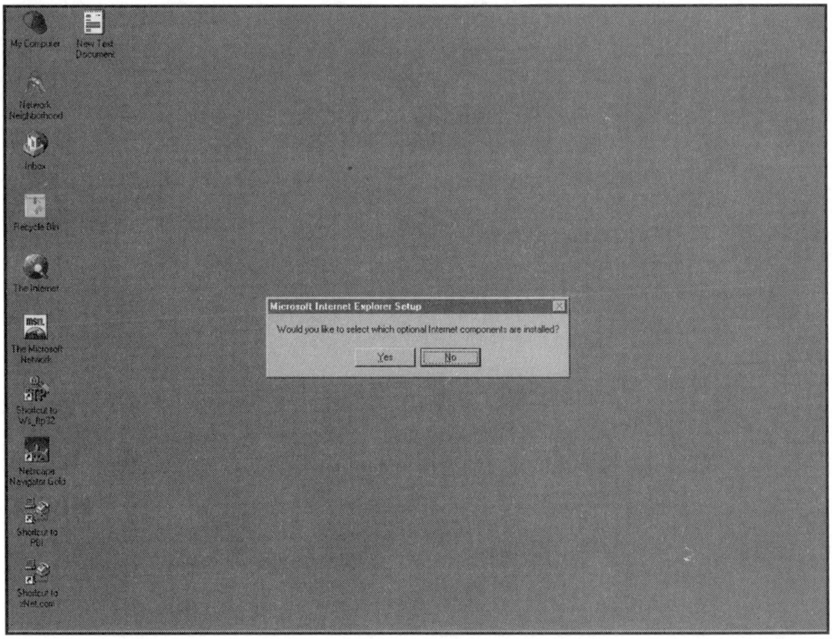

Figure 2-1
The Internet Explorer 3.0 Option dialog box

Figure 2-2 shows the optional items available. If you intend to do the work associated with this book, you should elect to install everything. The total comes to just under 9MB.

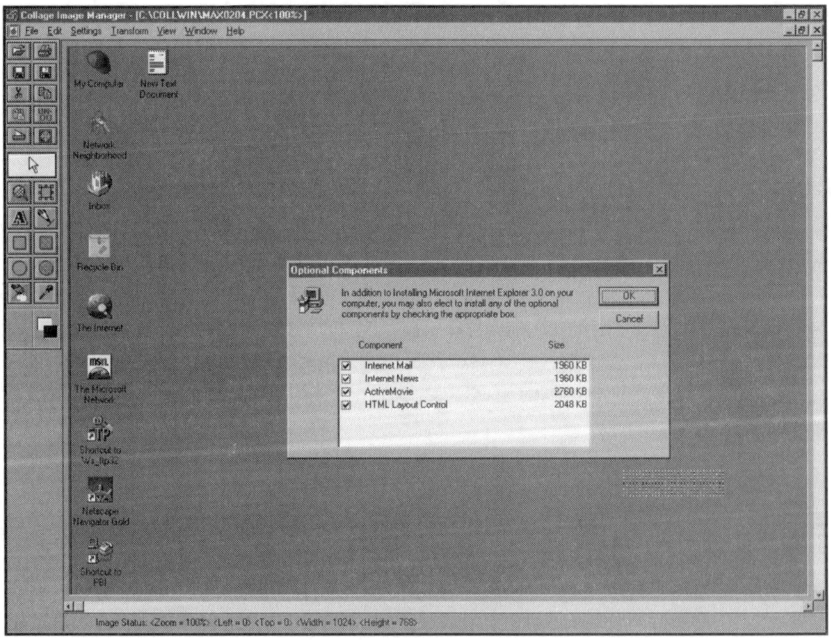

Figure 2-2
The Internet Explorer 3.0 Optional Components dialog box

After you have selected the options that you want to install, click OK to continue with the installation. A dialog box will show which components are selected, and step through the list as each one is completed.

When installation is complete, you will be prompted to restart your computer. Although you can elect not to restart (you may want to close applications or save files) immediately, you must restart to complete the installation. When you restart, the system will update shortcuts and make additions to your Start menu.

Installing NetMeeting

Although not technically a part of Internet Explorer, NetMeeting has such a close tie that you would do well to install it. The full version is included with the latest IE 3.0. I just reinstalled the latest version. Part of the setup involves connecting to the Internet to read the Microsoft User List Service (ULS) at `uls.microsoft.com`. This list has hundreds of people connected every day. While reading this list, an Andrew Rollins from London requested a connection. In the course of voice, chat, and whiteboard goofing, Andrew said, "mention me in your book<g>," so, Andrew, here it is. The point is, this wee application has some incredible potential for collaboration.

The installation is quick and easy and does not require a computer reboot. The first time that you start it, however, you will be stepped through a group of setup dialog boxes. The Welcome screen shown in Figure 2-3 will give you a list of the capabilities.

Clicking Next will take you to the screen shown in Figure 2-4. Here you fill in particulars that you would like made available about you. Please be advised that the information you supply here will be added to the Microsoft ULS when you connect and elect to be added to the ULS. You must supply your first and last name and an e-mail address. The rest is optional.

When you are satisfied with the information that you have entered, click Next to proceed. The dialog box in Figure 2-5 allows you to elect to be listed in a ULS and prompts you for the ULS service that you want to be listed on. The default is `uls.microsoft.com`. You can install a ULS service on your Internet or intranet. Software is available to make this addition. The ULS Server (beta 3) is available for free download at:

`http://www.microsoft.com/intdev/msconf/.`

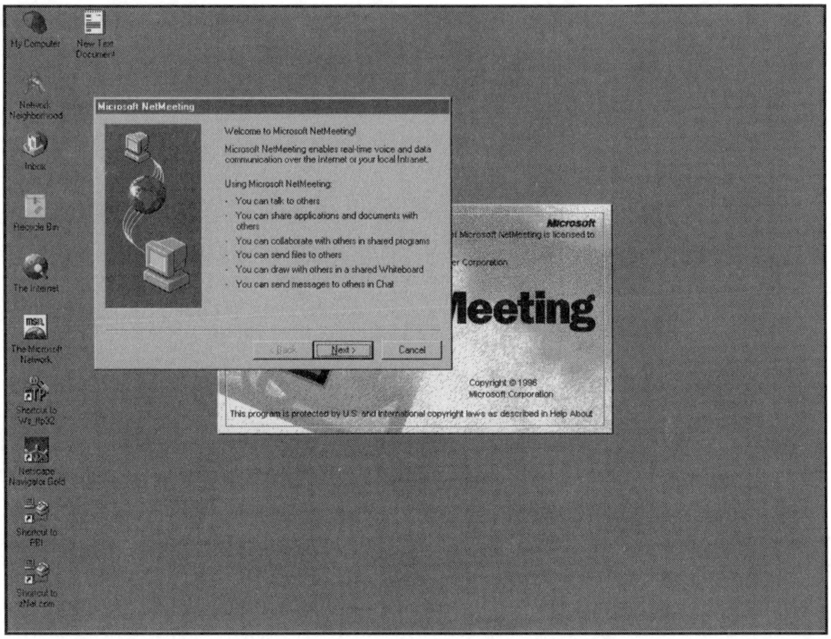

Figure 2-3
The NetMeeting Welcome Wizard

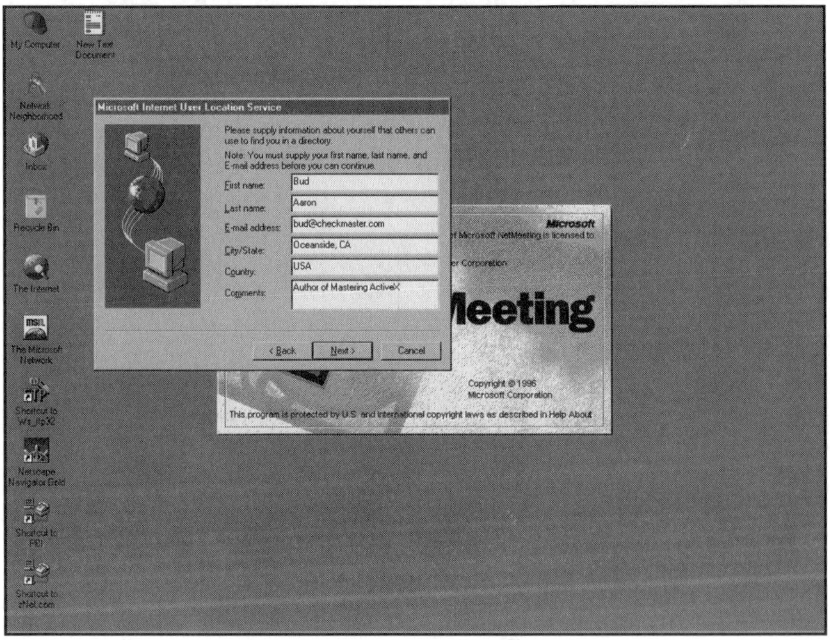

Figure 2-4
The NetMeeting User Profile dialog box

Figure 2-5
The NetMeeting User Profile service selection

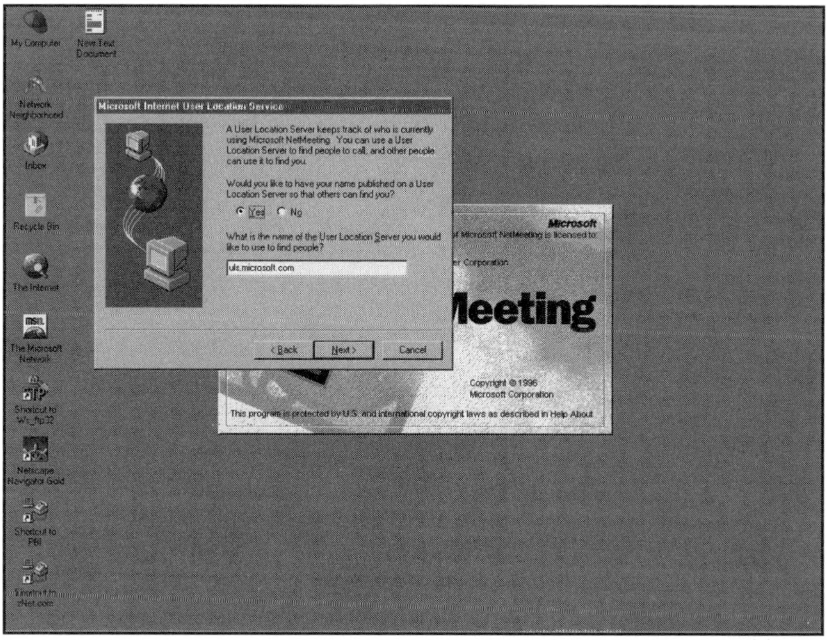

The final steps involve setting the microphone audio levels. This assumes that you have a sound card and a microphone attached. I wouldn't rush out and buy these items right now. A 28.8 connection does *not* provide very good audio capabilities. I did hear Andrew sneeze today and dutifully blessed him, but otherwise, sound was lousy. Until the world is wired with ISDN at a minimum, the ability to talk on the Internet will probably be less than perfect. Anyway, your next screen will be the one shown in Figure 2-6.

As suggested, the next screen shown in Figure 2-7 will tell you whether your audio card is capable of half or full duplex. Half duplex is like a push-to-talk button on a microphone. Only one person can talk at a time. If both talk, nothing gets through. Your telephone is full duplex. Both parties can talk simultaneously and still hear each other. Creative Labs now has full duplex drivers available for their sound cards.

The text implies that you can later change to full duplex. In fact, the full duplex check box will be disabled unless NetMeeting Audio Tuning wizard determines that your sound card is capable of full duplex. The wizard in Figure 2-8 asks you to indicate your connection speed. It will likely default to 14,400 and, with connection speeds running 24,000 (as a rule), this might be a good setting to use. You can always experiment.

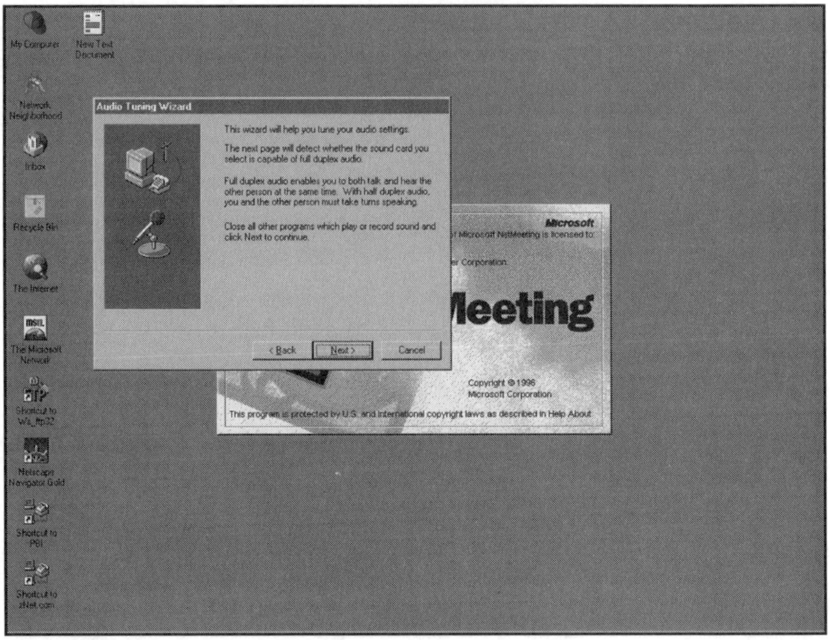

Figure 2-6
The NetMeeting Audio Tuning wizard

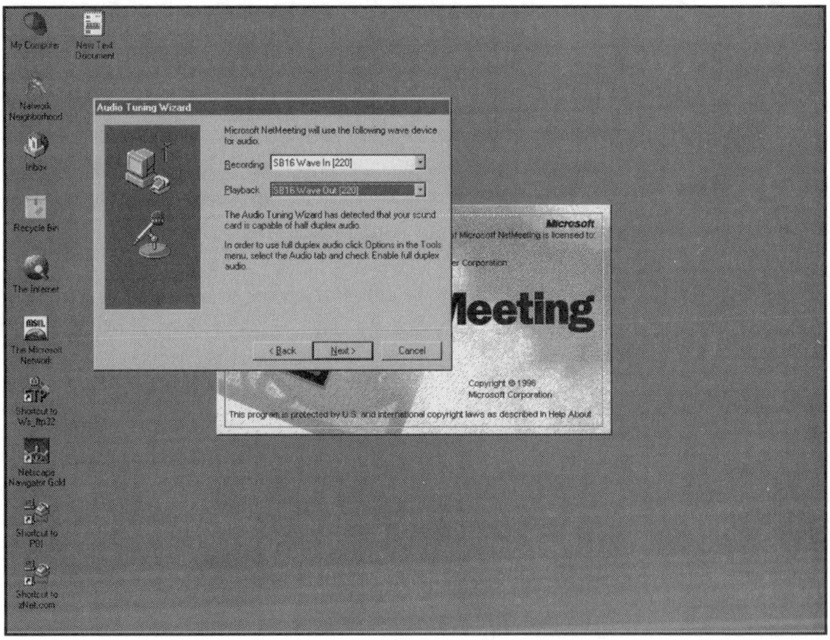

Figure 2-7
The NetMeeting half- or full-duplex indicator

NOTE:
Although you will probably purchase a 28,800 bps (bits per second) modem, the modem will seldom run at rated speed. The speed at which it runs will depend on telephone line noise, the modems being used by your Internet Service Provider, and other factors. My connections are usually at 24,000 and often 21,600. The odd numbers are a function of serial communications, and that subject would comprise another book this size.

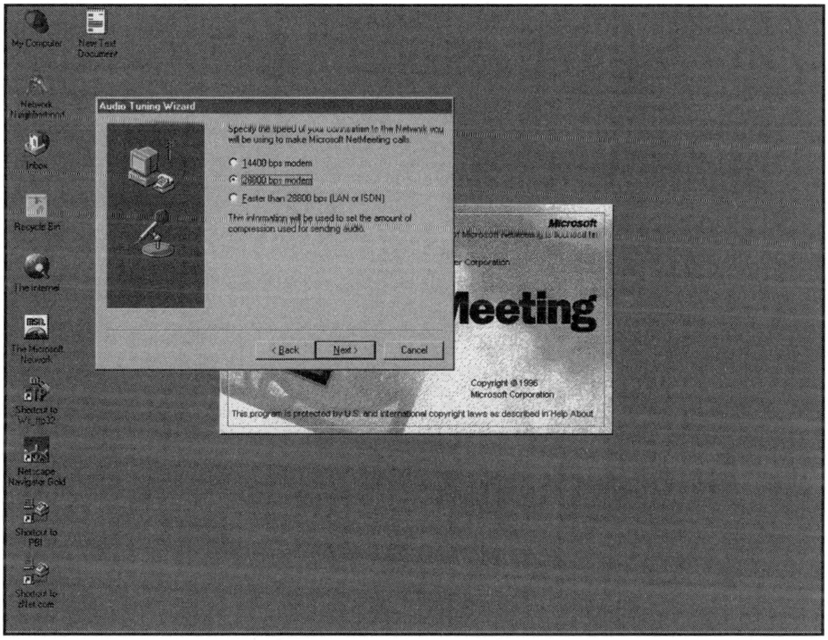

Figure 2-8
The Audio Tuning wizard

In the wizard shown in Figure 2-9, you are asked to click the Start Recording button and then speak for about nine seconds. Just read from the screen in a normal tone of voice at a comfortable distance from the microphone. When the time runs out, the wizard will have determined the optimum setting for your microphone volume, as shown in Figure 2-10.

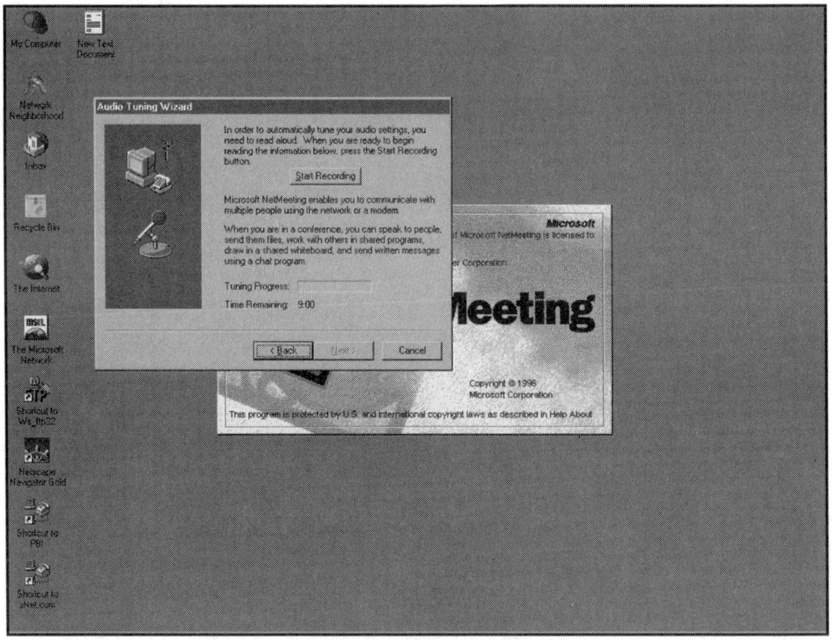

Figure 2-9
The NetMeeting audio recording session

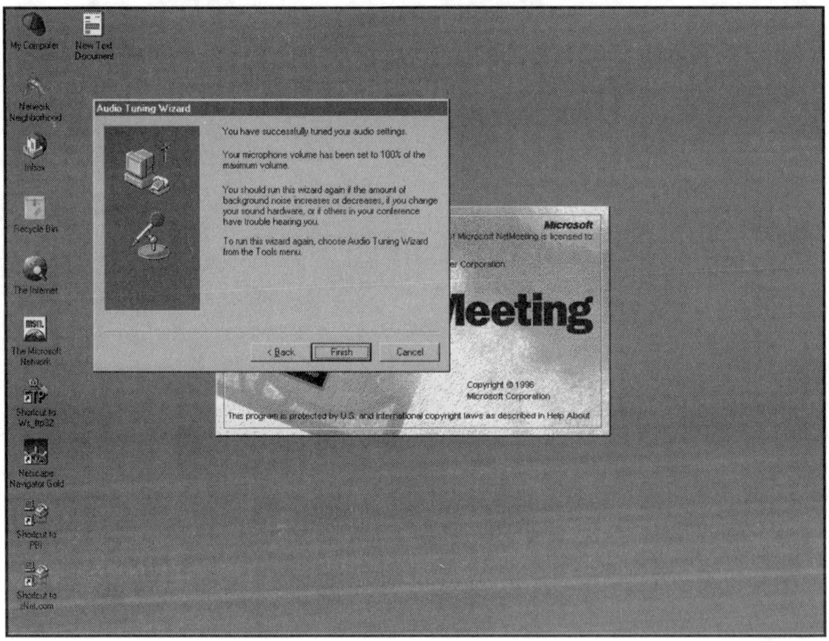

Figure 2-10
The NetMeeting Finished wizard

At this point, NetMeeting will start. It will attempt a connection to your Internet Service Provider and, after it's connected, will go to uls.microsoft.com. It will add your name to the ULS and begin downloading a list of users online. You may be surprised at the numbers, but don't be surprised if someone attempts to establish a connection. You can accept or decline the connection.

If you accept a connection and audio is not good, try a chat session just to get the feel of things. I found myself bouncing from voice, to chat, to whiteboard, and finally settled for a chat session to begin. Don't be bashful, as I tend to be. Almost everyone is somewhat new to this business and is probably new to NetMeeting. If you use it for a few days, you may become the resident expert. So, don't be afraid to experiment. Mistakes here are seldom life threatening, and you may endear yourself to someone else by making a mistake or two.

Using Internet Explorer

If, on starting Internet Explorer 3.0, you hear a "soft rumbling under the hood," don't be surprised. Despite its simple appearance, it is, in fact, a powerhouse application. Surfing the Web with Internet Explorer 3.0 is like driving a Jaguar XJS on city streets. You are not using anything like its full potential. You will find a few newer Web sites that begin to exploit its capabilities, but the browser is built to be comfortable with the next generation of the Internet, where greater bandwidth and more modern sites will begin to use its potential.

Although destined to be cross-platform, Internet Explorer has a small flaw at this point. It assumes that Windows 95 and Windows NT will be the client and server of choice in the years to come. It works well in the existing Web world, but its full potential will not be realized until server-side functionality is improved or until the cross-platform possibilities are fully utilized. With the majority of Internet hosts on the World Wide Web of the UNIX variety, tight integration may be some way away.

Now, grab a chair and pay attention<g>. I'm taking you on one of the last picture book tours in this book. The reason is simple: your understanding of what follows in other chapters depends to a large extent on your intimate understanding of what Internet Explorer 3.0 really is. You also need to tune it to your taste.

Toolbars

The first unconventional thing that you will notice with Internet Explorer is the toolbar. The icons are on a neat background, and as your mouse passes over them, they present themselves as buttons. Future versions will provide the capability to customize the background and probably the buttons. Figure 2-11 shows a full-screen view of Internet Explorer 3.0. In this view, the Address and Links toolbars are positioned off-screen.

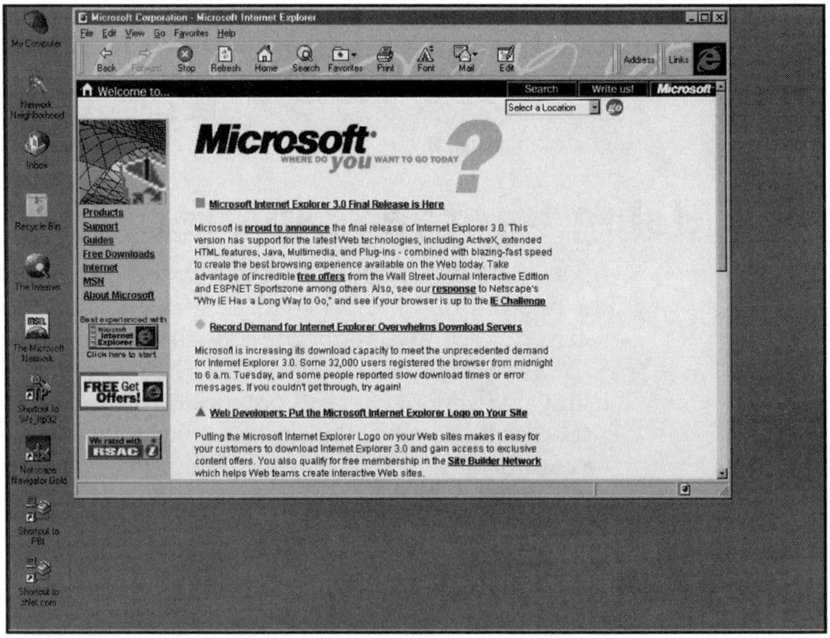

Figure 2-11
Internet Explorer 3.0

In Figure 2-12, the toolbar is expanded by dragging Address and Links to more appropriate positions. That's what is appropriate for me; you, however, can set the toolbar up as you like it.

The usual Back, Forward, Stop, Refresh, and Home buttons are part of the toolbar. The Back and Forward buttons are enabled only when you have pages that you have visited during the current session. The Stop button will stop the downloading and display of a page that you may be trying to load. The Refresh button will cause the browser to download a new page rather than display the page in the cache.

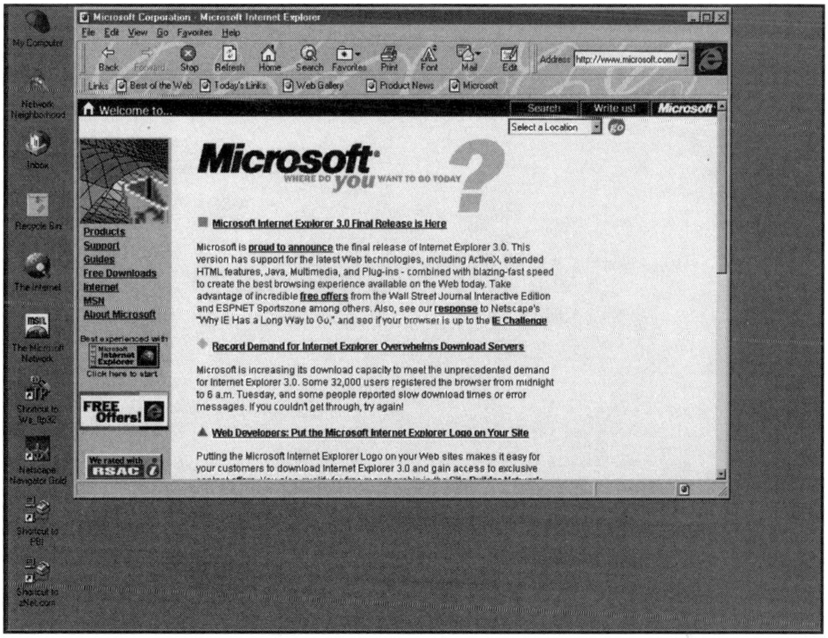

Figure 2-12 New toolbar appearance

The Home button will take you immediately to the page that you have defined as a starting page. The default home page is `www.msn.com` after you install the browser. The Search button will take you to `home.microsoft.com/allinone.asp` and give you a wide range of search options. The Favorites button duplicates the functionality of the Favorites menu selection.

The Print button prints the contents of the displayed page formatted as it appears on the screen. If the page you are on is frame based, simply left-click in the desired pane before printing to ensure that you print what you want to print. The Font button allows you to change the size of the font used for display. This is an excellent tool for ensuring readability for users in an adaptive circumstance. The Mail button brings up a menu that allows you to select various mail operations or read newsgroups.

The Edit button will start your default HTML editing tool. It is one way to examine and save the HTML code associated with a page. It is of limited use, in my view, because it cannot be used to interactively edit Web pages. In any event, it is there for you to use.

Menus

The standard Internet Explorer 3.0 menus hold few surprises, but some items are worth expanding on. The File menu is shown in

Figure 2-13. You can create a New Window, allowing you to leave the contents of one window at a site that you like and navigate in a second window. You can Open... a local HTML file, or enter the name of a URL (Uniform Resource Locator) that you want to load into the browser.

> **NOTE:**
> **Many menu items will not be available unless you have a live HTML document displayed in the browser.**

You can Save or Save As... the page being displayed as an HTML document. You can create a shortcut to a page on your system or on the Internet using Create Shortcut. Close exits Internet Explorer; it does not simply close the displayed document.

Figure 2-13
The File menu

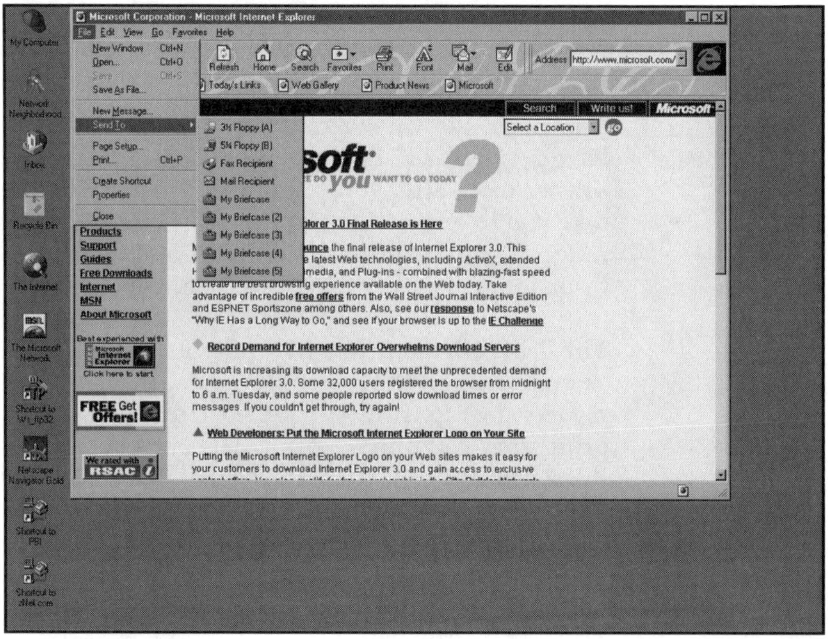

Figure 2-14 shows the Edit menu. This menu consists mostly of standard windows and holds no real surprises. Select All is an excellent way to select the contents of a window for cut-and-paste operations.

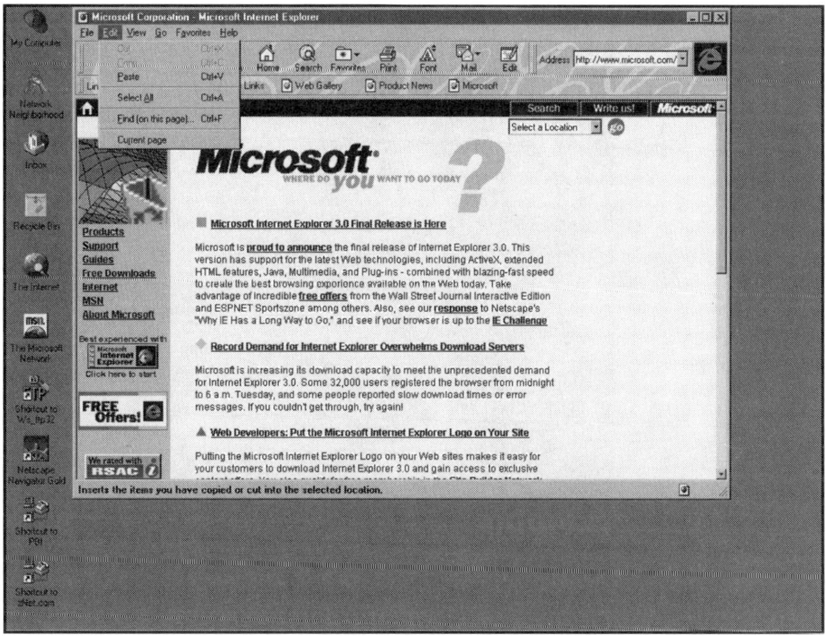

Figure 2-14
The Edit menu

The View menu shown in Figure 2-15 allows you an election for displaying the toolbar and status bar. It also allows you to adjust the displayed font size and to do Stop and Refresh functions as on the toolbar. The Source item brings up a Notepad display of the HTML source code on the page. It is an excellent way to examine what others have done to implement various functionality. I go into more details on the Options... selection a little later in this chapter.

The Go menu (Figure 2-16) duplicates a number of the items on the toolbar. Refer to earlier material for details. The Open History folder allows a more complete view of the sites that you have visited since you started using Internet Explorer. You can set the number of entries allowed in the History folder, which I discuss doing later.

The Favorites menu, shown in Figure 2-17, allows you to keep bookmarks (so to speak) on sites you have visited that you may want to revisit in the future. You can organize this folder in virtually any way you like and at any time. Figure 2-17 shows only one of an infinite number of possibilities. Add To Favorites... allows you to add the site currently being displayed in the browser window to your Favorites folder and in the folder of your choice. Organize Favorites... takes you to a more complete view of your Favorites folder displayed in the browser window.

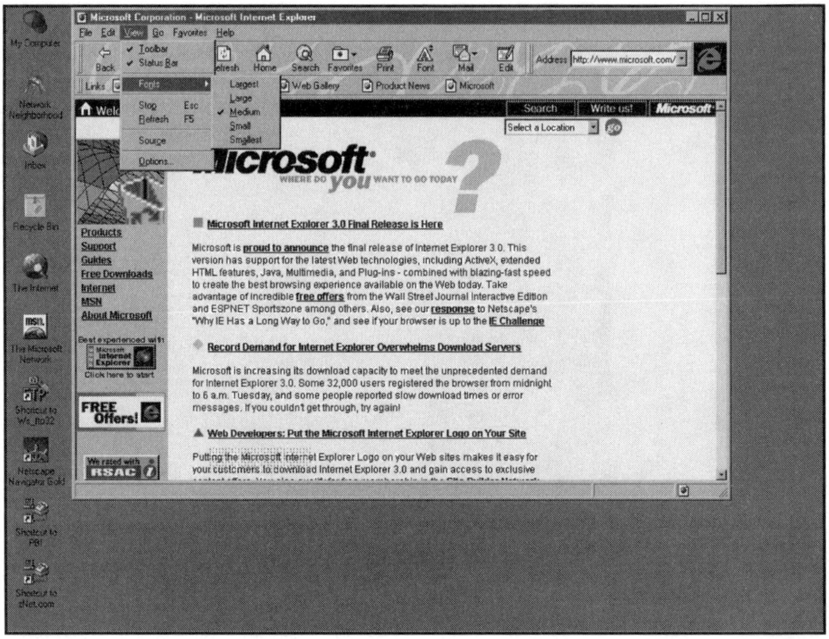

Figure 2-15
The View menu

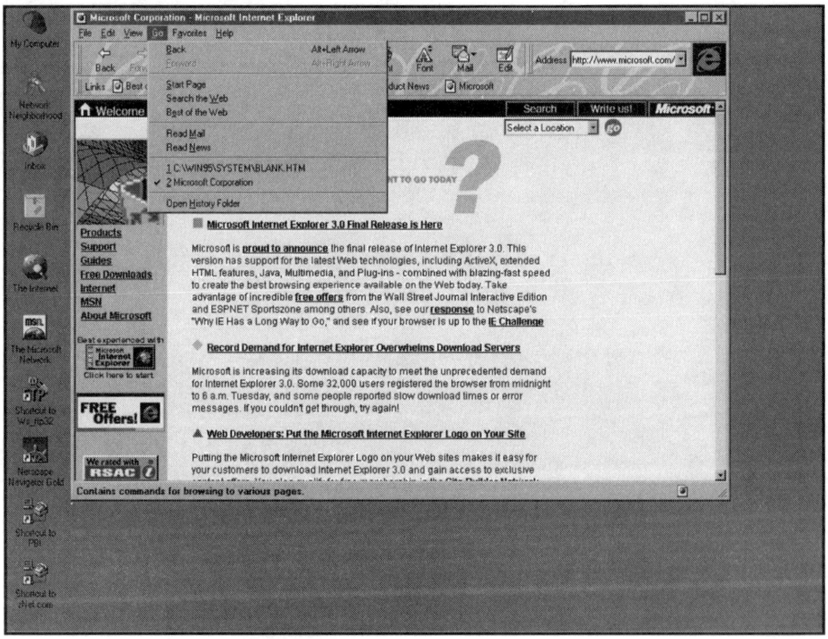

Figure 2-16
The Go menu

Figure 2-17
The Favorites menu

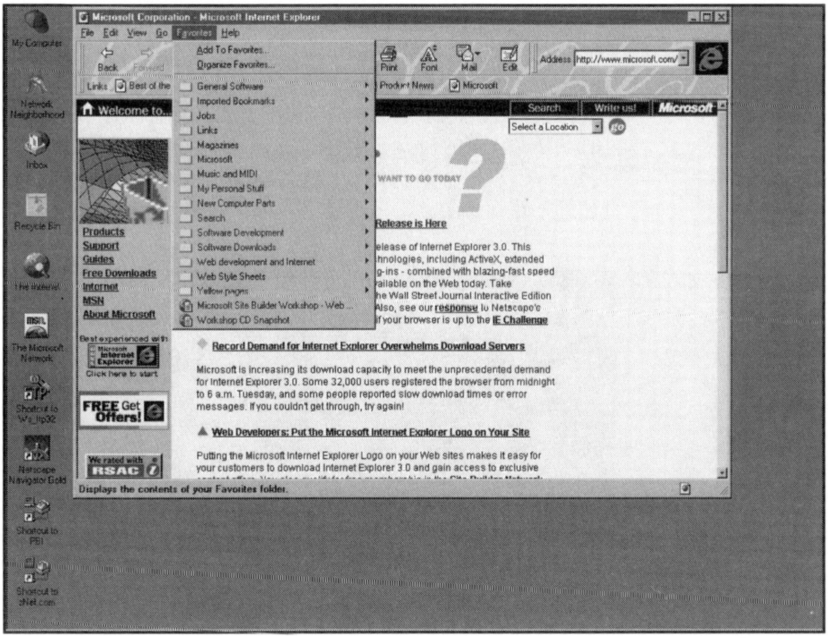

The Help menu is illustrated in Figure 2-18. The only surprise here is that some of the help items take you to locations on the Web as opposed to local help.

Figure 2-18
The Help menu

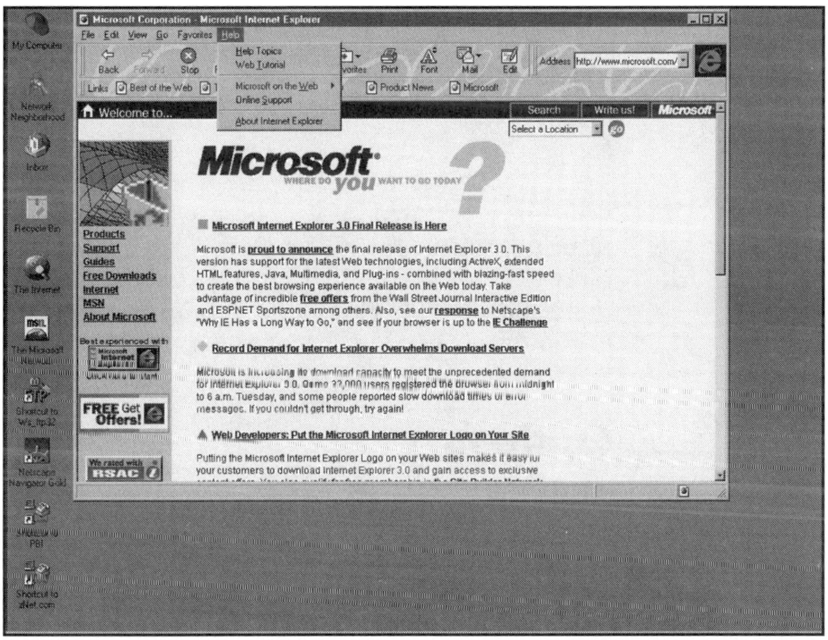

Clicking About Internet Explorer in the Help menu will bring up the dialog shown in Figure 2-19. The first thing to note is the version number. It should read "Version 3.0(4.70.1155)" or higher. The delivered version is build number 1155. If your version is older, please download the latest version in order for this book to be most useful. And, as if you wouldn't expect it, Internet Explorer 4.0 (code named Nashville) will probably be available in beta as you read this book.

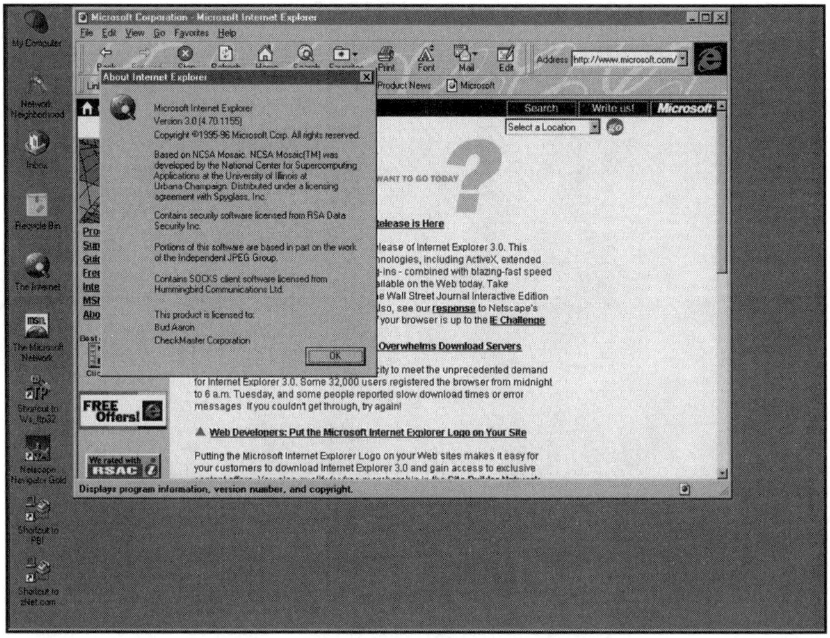

Figure 2-19
The Help About menu

Next, notice the number of people contributing to Internet Explorer 3.0. It is based on NCSA Mosaic—the granddaddy of all browsers, which is distributed under a license from Spyglass, Inc. It contains security software from RSA Data Security Inc., a company I discuss more later in this book. It incorporates functionality from the Independent JPEG Group. It contains SOCKS from Hummingbird Communications Ltd. The point is as follows: *this is component software directly related to ActiveX.*

Options

As with most browsers, there are a number of options that can be set to determine the functionality of your browser. The Options dialog is available (as mentioned earlier) from the View menu. Figure 2-20 shows the Options dialog with a total of six tabs. The General tab provides selections for customizing multimedia, colors, and the toolbar. Most of the selections are self-explanatory, but you might want to experiment with the possibilities. A Font Settings button allows the font names and sizes to be set within a limited range.

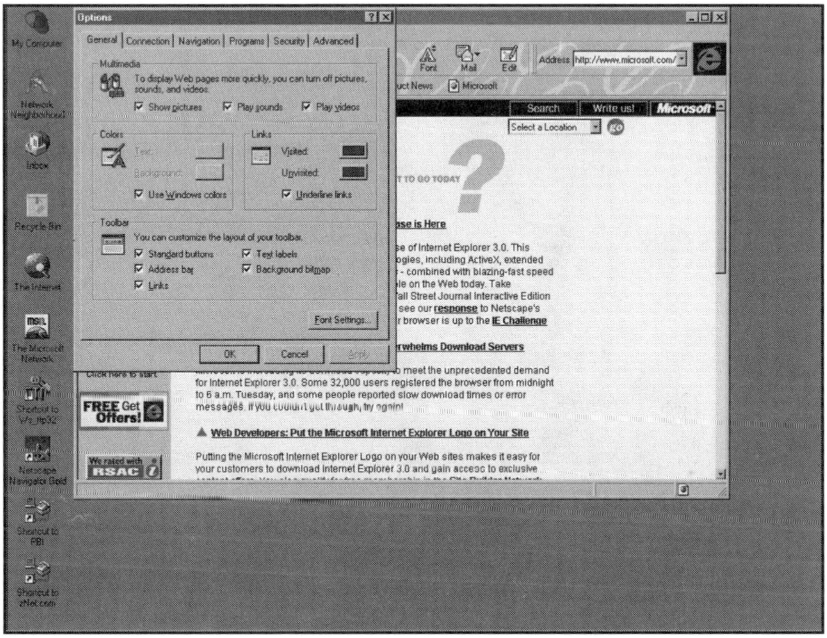

Figure 2-20 The Options General tab

In the Connection tab (Figure 2-21), you can elect to connect to the Internet as needed, set the default dial-up connection (or add additional connections), and set Disconnect for idling time and security options. You can also elect to use a Proxy server. Proxy servers are normally used to buffer a local area network from the Internet—creating a *firewall,* basically.

The Navigation tab shown in Figure 2-22 allows you to tailor a number of things to your preferences. You can set the Start Page, Search Page, and the five Quick Links to point to pages you prefer. The Start page defaults to `www.msn.com`, the Search page to `home.microsoft.com/allinone.asp`, and the Quick links to those sites shown on the toolbar. You can set your history to keep up to 999 days (close to three years) of history of the sites you've visited. The default is 20 days and the amount of disk space used to store the history will depend on how much Web surfing you do. You can also elect to View History... or Clear History.

Figure 2-21
The Options
Connection tab

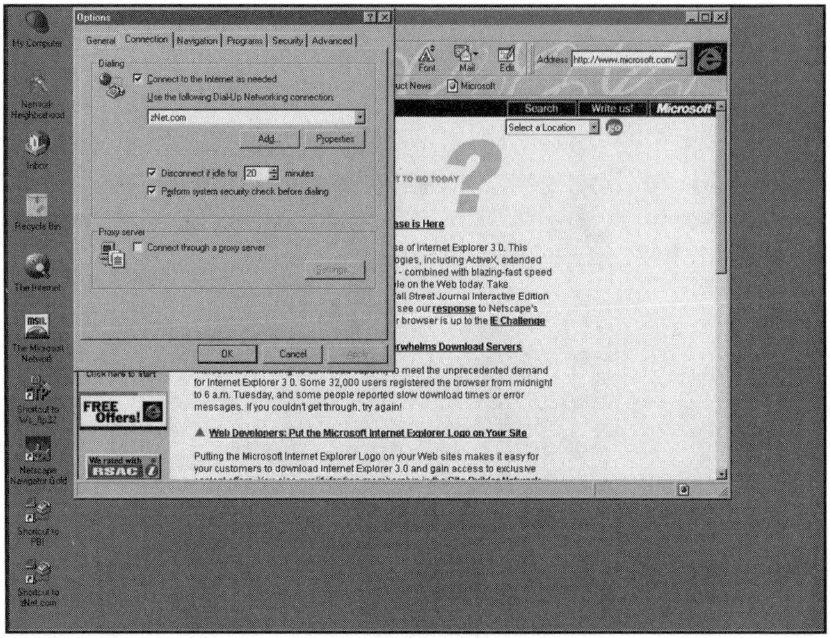

Figure 2-22
The Options
Navigation tab

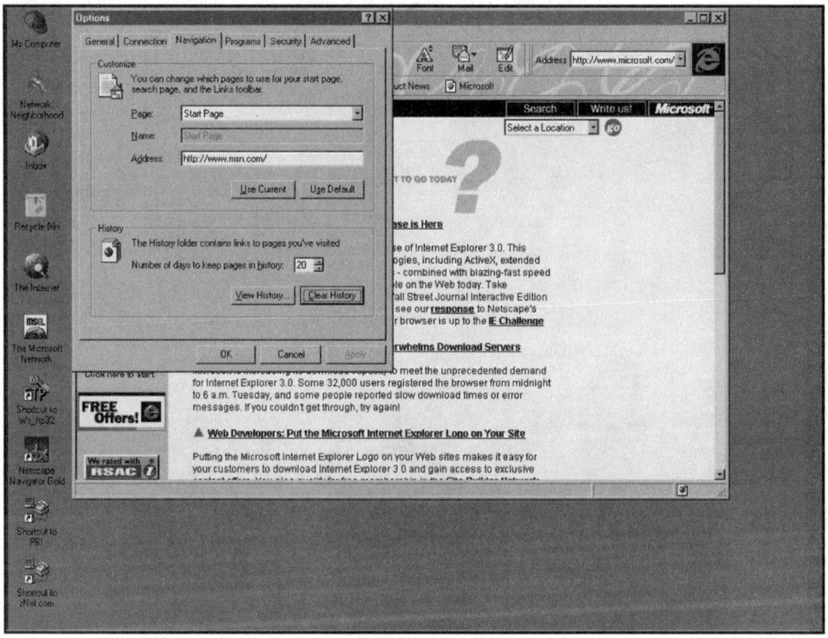

The Programs tab, shown in Figure 2-23, is mostly self-explanatory and will likely need little adjustment. If you are using multiple browsers, you may want to leave the default browser check box selected.

Figure 2-23
The Options Programs tab

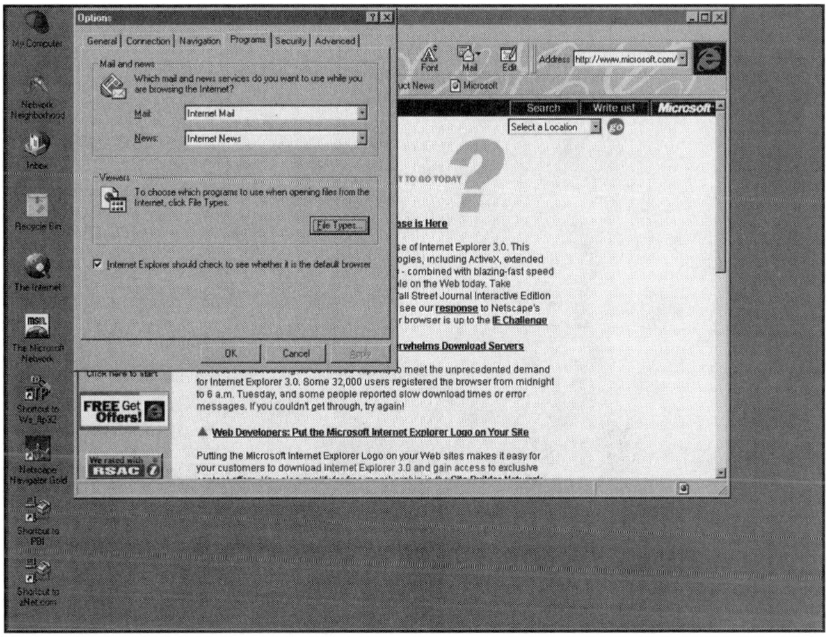

The Security tab provides a number of options. The Content Advisor allows you to implement PICS for protecting your kids, assuming that host sites have implemented the PICS system. It will certainly be useful when the PICS system is adopted on the Internet, but it does not help a lot right now; in any event, it's available for future use.

Certificates deals with the Authenticode checks made by your browser when downloading controls and applications from the Internet.

The Active content section allows you to indicate how ActiveX components and Java should be handled on your system. The Programs tab is shown in Figure 2-24.

You can elect to view and manage Personal..., Sites..., and Publishers... Certificates. Figure 2-25 shows the Site Certificates present on my computer. The issuer is indicated with the option to View the Certificate.

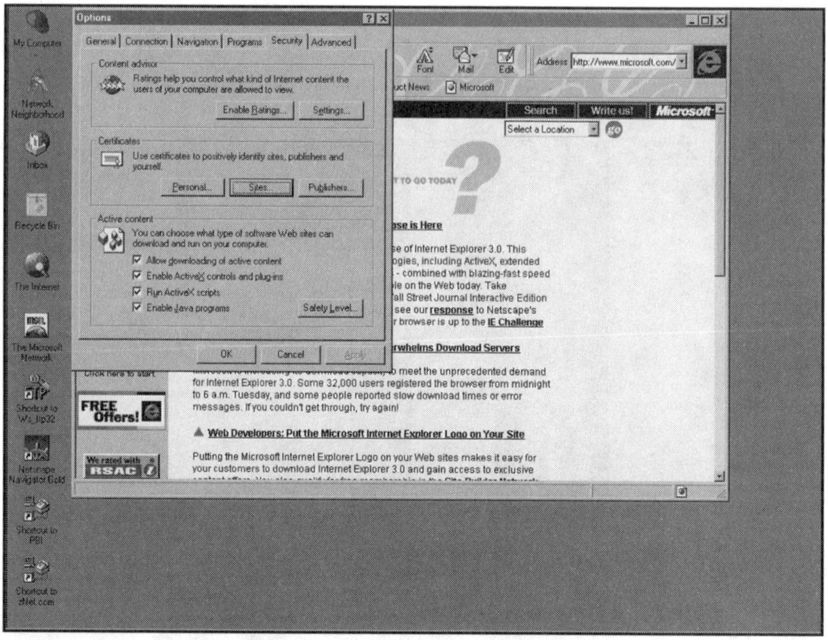

Figure 2-24
The Options Security tab

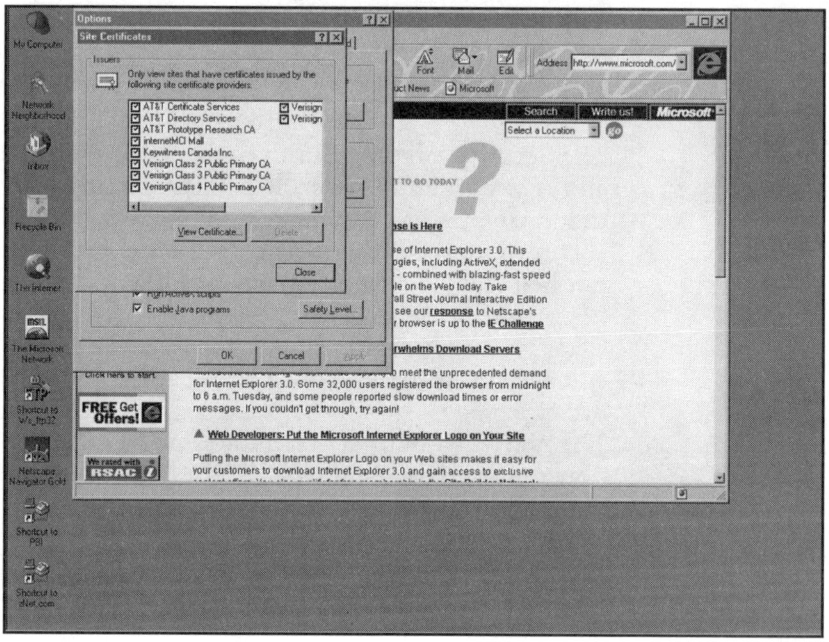

Figure 2-25
The Options Security Site Certificate dialog box

The Publishers Certificate dialog box is shown in Figure 2-26. The elections are self-explanatory for the most part. It should be noted that you can always remove a certificate if you consider it no longer reliable.

Figure 2-26
The Options Security Publishers Certificate Management dialog box

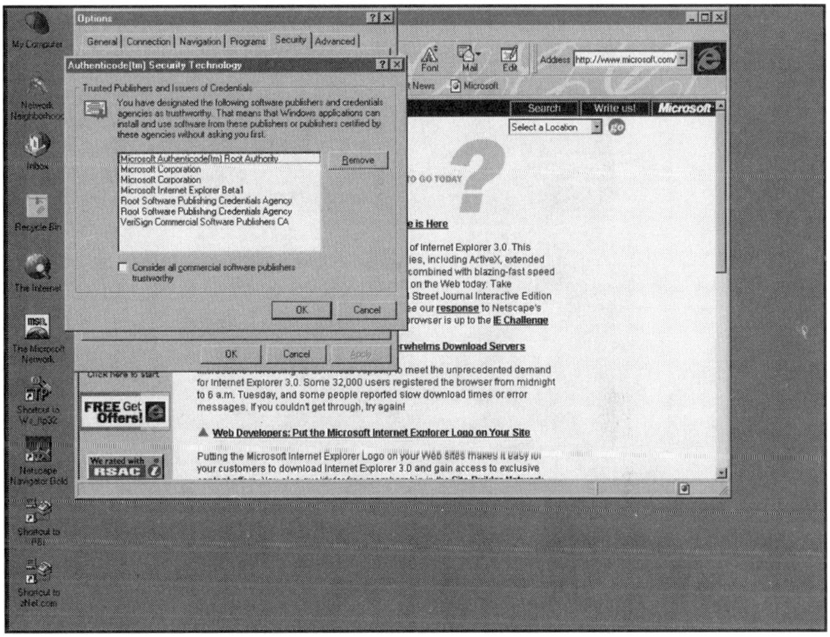

The Safety Level... button brings up the dialog box shown in Figure 2-27. Here you can set the level of protection that you want your browser to apply to material downloaded from the Internet. Medium is the best selection for users working through this book.

The Advanced tab is shown in Figure 2-28. You will need to determine what Warnings you want Internet Explorer to give you. The Temporary Internet files section allows you to manage your Internet Explorer cache. Without some care, the cache can grow out of hand even on very large hard drive partitions. Also, although the cache will speed the loading of some pages, it doesn't always contain the latest information on a Web site.

Show Friendly URLs

This check box lets you display friendly URLs that are significantly shorter than the full path to a resource. You might try it checked and unchecked and decide which you prefer

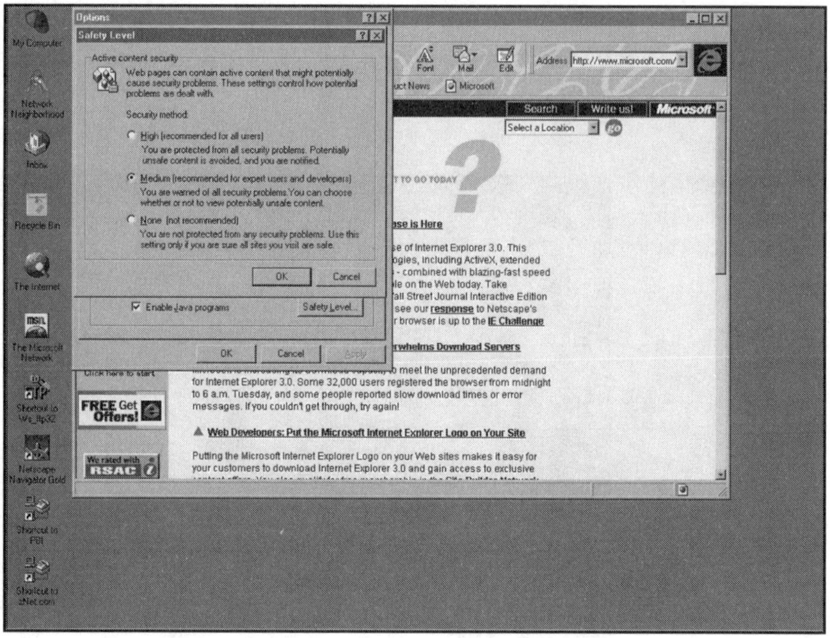

Figure 2-27 The Options Security Safety Level... dialog box

Highlight Links When Clicked

This option puts a box around a link.

Use Smooth Scrolling

When checked, the page scrolls smoothly. When unchecked, the page jumps when scrolling. Again, it's a matter of preference.

Use Style Sheets

This selection determines whether the browser will use style sheets if they are available on the Web sites that you are visiting.

Enable Java JIT Compiler

Internet Explorer provides a JIT (just in time) Java compiler that allows Java to be compiled as read from a Web site.

Enable Java Logging

This option allows you to keep a log of all Java activity.

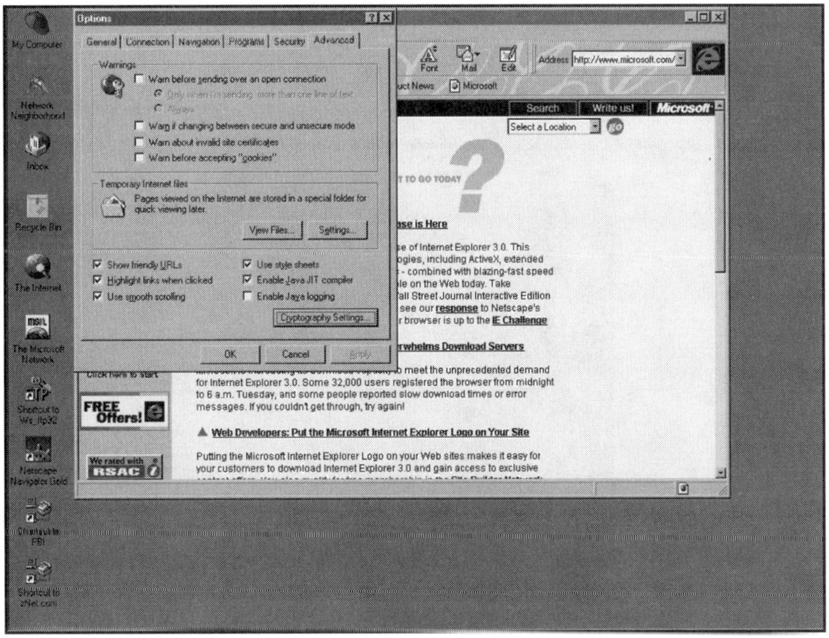

Figure 2-28
The Options Advanced tab

The Settings... button in the Temporary Internet files section will bring up the dialog box in Figure 2-29. Here you can check the frequency with which the caching system checks for new content on the Web sites that you visit. Most important, you can select the percentage of your cache drive (usually drive C) used for the cache files. The election here is three percent of a 1GB C partition. You can also use the bottom buttons to manage your cache files.

Finally, you can view and manage your Security protocols as shown in Figure 2-30. You can elect which protocols to use and whether you want files from secure sites stored on disk or not. The settings depend very heavily on the security requirements at your location. If you are a single user running a dial-up connection, you may want secure site information saved on your hard disk, because there is very little likelihood that anyone but you will have access to the material.

This "picture book" tour should help in lieu of a manual. As indicated previously, Internet Explorer is a very powerful piece of software with many things happening as you run and use it. The interpreting of HTML to present attractive information displays is only a small part of the overall task of a browser.

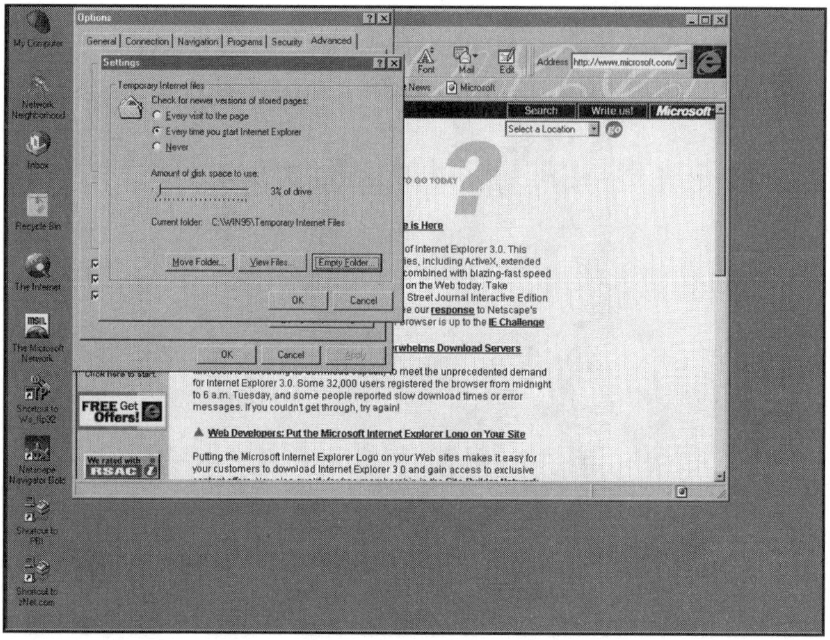

Figure 2-29 Temporary Internet Files dialog box

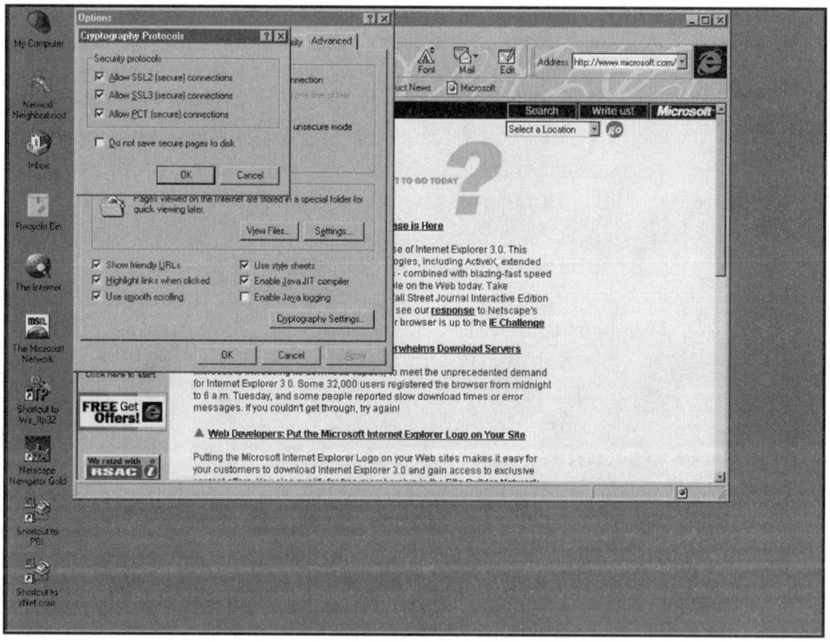

Figure 2-30 Cryptography Protocols dialog box

Although you have a number of issues to consider regarding personalizing the browser for your use in working with this book and on the Internet, I have covered all of the items that have any consequence in your use of Internet Explorer 3.0.

Using Special Viewers

I've discussed ActiveX Documents. What happens if someone sends you a Word 95 document and you do not have Word 95 installed on your computer? You use a viewer. Microsoft has written three applications that are available at its Web site for download that you can also distribute to friends. They are an Excel Viewer, a PowerPoint Viewer, and a Word Viewer. They are exactly what they say they are: viewers. They do not allow editing or otherwise manipulating files, but they are ActiveX Document servers in that they will run inside Internet Explorer 3.0.

The Excel Viewer

The Excel Viewer is shown in Figure 2-31. Notice that you can do a few things from the menu and toolbar. You can open and close files, print files, search, and copy to the clipboard. You might want to download this and other viewers to see the functionality firsthand.

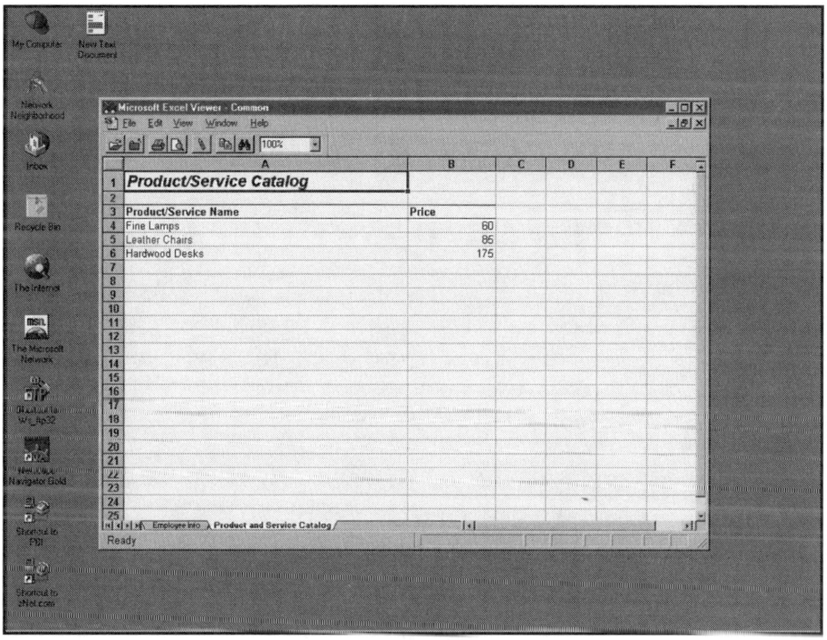

Figure 2-31 The Microsoft Excel Viewer

The PowerPoint viewer

Figure 2-32 shows only the start-up screen for the PowerPoint viewer. If you want to distribute PowerPoint presentations on the Internet, you can always make this application available for download. You might want to look it over first to be able to tell people viewing your presentations how to use the viewer. It is a fairly comprehensive and capable viewer.

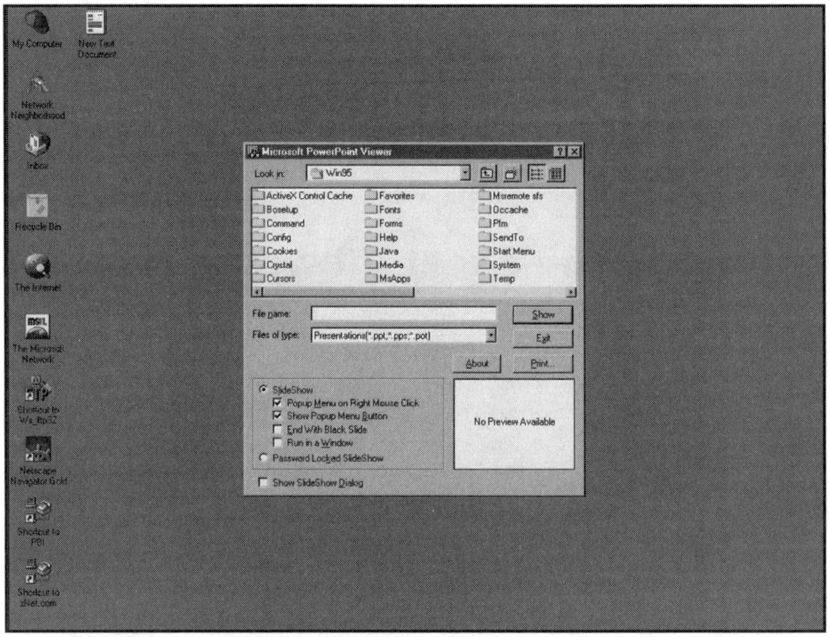

Figure 2-32 The Microsoft PowerPoint viewer

The Microsoft Word Viewer

The Word Viewer shown in Figure 2-33 looks very much like the Excel Viewer. It makes it possible for users without Word installed to open and read Word documents with all formatting in place. In other words, users will see your documents as you intended them to be seen.

> **NOTE:**
> **As ActiveX Document servers, all of these viewers provide a way for users without the parent application to view documents in an ActiveX Document container.**

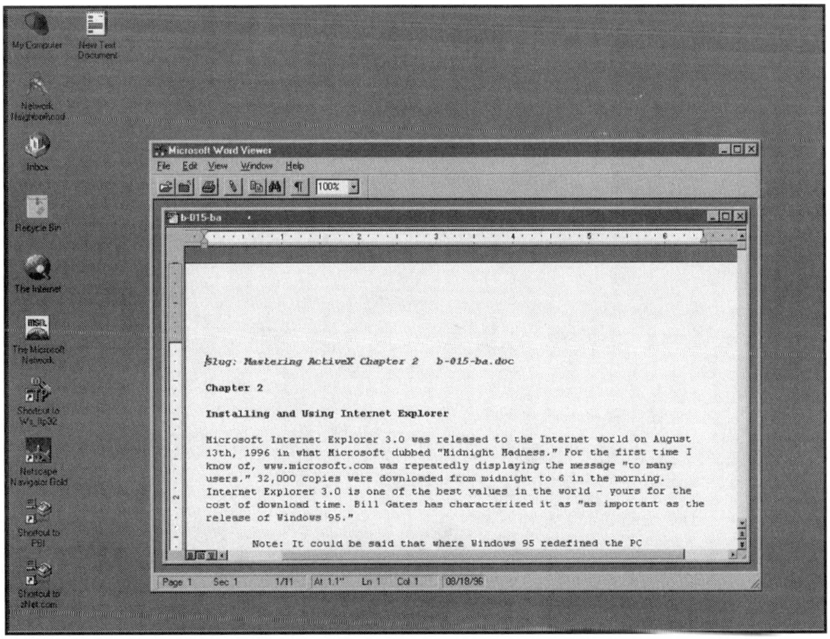

Figure 2-33 The Microsoft Word viewer

Summary

In Chapters 1 and 2, I've introduced you to the tools and technology underlying the ActiveX initiative. In a sense, this all goes beyond just ActiveX, but it's indicative of the very beginnings of new technology. I would tend to view Internet Explorer 3.0 as much like Windows 3.0 (it's certainly not 1.0 or 2.0) in that it is a new beginning. The next months will see Internet Explorer 4.0 (code named Nashville) and other software emerging from Microsoft.

You may never see a Windows 95 or any other number again. You will see new file systems, new display systems, and dozens of new components that will plug into the existing framework. Remember, I'm talking about component software: preamps, speakers, tuners, amplifiers, and the like. The small cabinet is already in place (Internet Explorer 3.0 running in the OS—Windows 95 or Windows NT) and Internet Explorer 4.0 will be the new, grand cabinet!

You are seeing what I believe is the dawn of a new era, and this book will help give you a solid start in understanding the underlying technology. In the next chapter, I examine the "glue" that holds it all together—using HTML 3.2 and additional items such as frames, tables, style sheets, and the rest. You will need a good handle on the newest HTML tags and capabilities contained in Appendix B. They can make Web sites nothing short of spectacular.

Chapter 3

Using Microsoft FrontPage

You would think, with the prevalence of the Web, that lots of tools would be available to make life easier for the Web page developer. With that thought in mind, I went visiting a bunch of Internet sites that once had tools available (some fair, some not so good) and discovered that the tools are not there anymore. My intention was to tell you that you had alternatives to Notepad, but that doesn't seem to be the case.

In fact, you can write:

```
<HTML>
<HEAD>
<TITLE>This will display in the Explorer Title Bar</TITLE>
</HEAD>
<BODY>
<H1>This will display as a large heading</H1>
<P>And this will display as default text.</P>
</BODY>
</HTML>
```

using Notepad or any other text editor. Save the file with an .HTM extension and double-click it to start your browser. You will see a page displayed in Internet Explored like that shown in Figure 3-1.

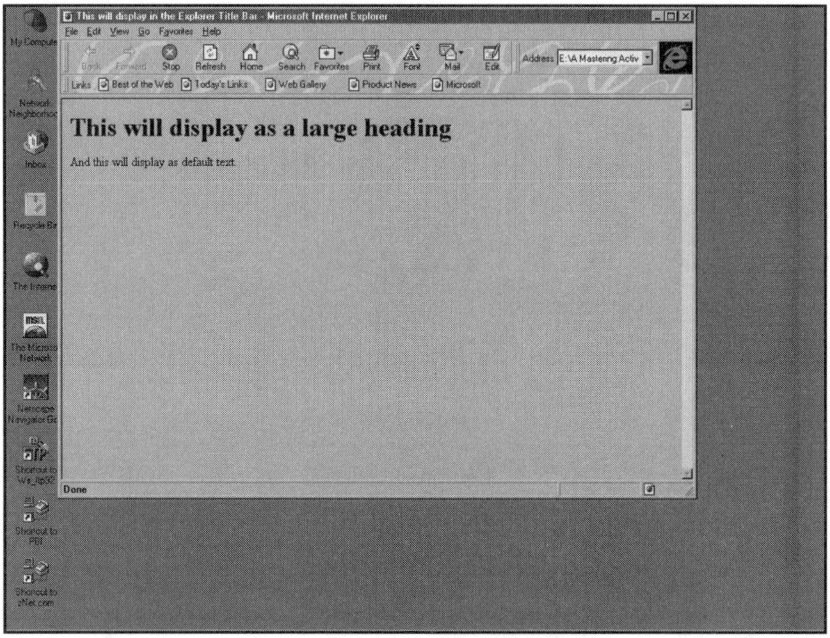

Figure 3-1
A short Web document

Now, I realize that this is not extremely hard to do. It probably takes only a few minutes to type. But what do you do if you have dozens of linked pages with text, graphics, sound, scripts, and other content? The task of building such a Web site using Notepad would be very difficult, to say the least. So, a tool such as FrontPage is almost a necessity for anyone developing real Web content.

You do have a free alternative HTML editor if you are running Word 6 or Word 95: the Microsoft Internet Assistant for Word is available for free download and is included on the CD, but this assumes an investment in Word. There are alternative editors but none of them provides the Web site management provided by FrontPage Explorer. So, at $149, Microsoft FrontPage is a real bargain if you intend to develop Web sites. I discuss alternatives in the next chapter, but for now, I'm giving you some insight into one of the neatest WYSIWYG HTML editors and comprehensive Web site management tools around.

> **NOTE:**
> **Although FrontPage is designed to be run in conjunction with its built-in personal server or in a real server environment, you can use the FrontPage Editor as a stand-alone application. The personal server environment provides far better control over links and other aspects of a multipage Web site.**

Overview of Microsoft FrontPage

Microsoft FrontPage (originally Vermeer) is made up of five applications. The FrontPage Explorer and FrontPage Editor are the two main applications. The third application is A Personal Web Server (administered with the fourth, Server Administrator), which provide and administer a server running on your local machine. The fifth application is FrontPage TCP/IP Test, which is used to test connections to a server, whether local or remote.

Installing FrontPage

FrontPage uses conventional wizard install routines. There are no real surprises but some minor differences. Near the completion of the installation, you will be presented with the dialog box shown in Figure 3-2. The name that you enter may not contain spaces, and you must enter a password. Please make a note of *both*: they will be needed when you're making changes to authoring rights on the Web sites that you build.

You will also be asked whether you want to start FrontPage Explorer. This is a check box selection, as shown in Figure 3-3. Uncheck the box if you do not want to start FrontPage Explore.

FrontPage Server Administrator

Any time you start FrontPage Explorer, the Personal Web Server will start automatically. You can make changes to the server selections using the FrontPage Server Administrator shown in Figure 3-4. The Select Port Number list box shows port 80. This is the normal port for Web servers. The dialog box also lists the Server type as FrontPage Personal Web Server. It also shows the server configuration directory and content directory, and it indicates that Authoring is enabled. Most of the selections here should be left to someone familiar with server setup.

If you click the Security button, the dialog box shown in Figure 3-5 will show you the Web name and administrator name, and will allow you to change the administrator password.

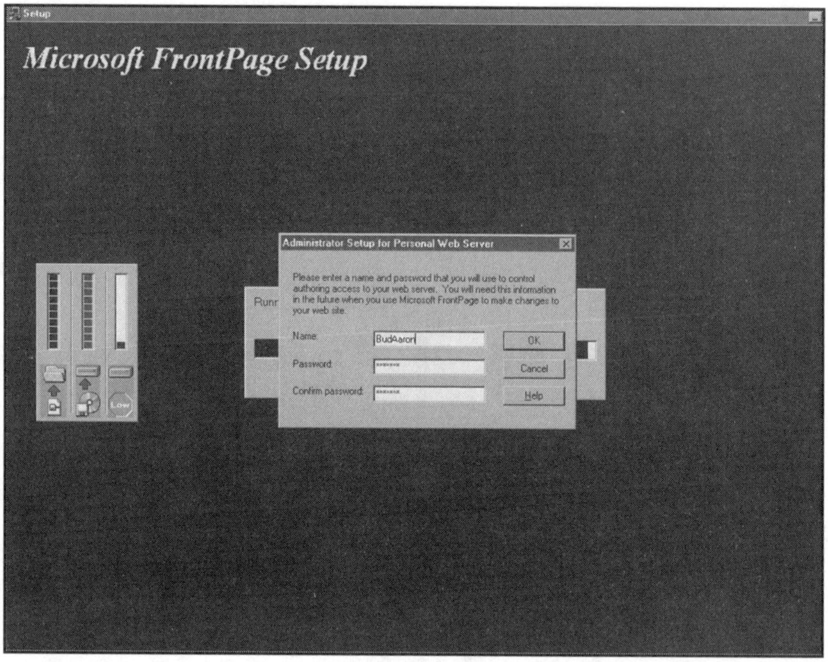

Fig. 3.2
The Administrator setup for Personal Web Server

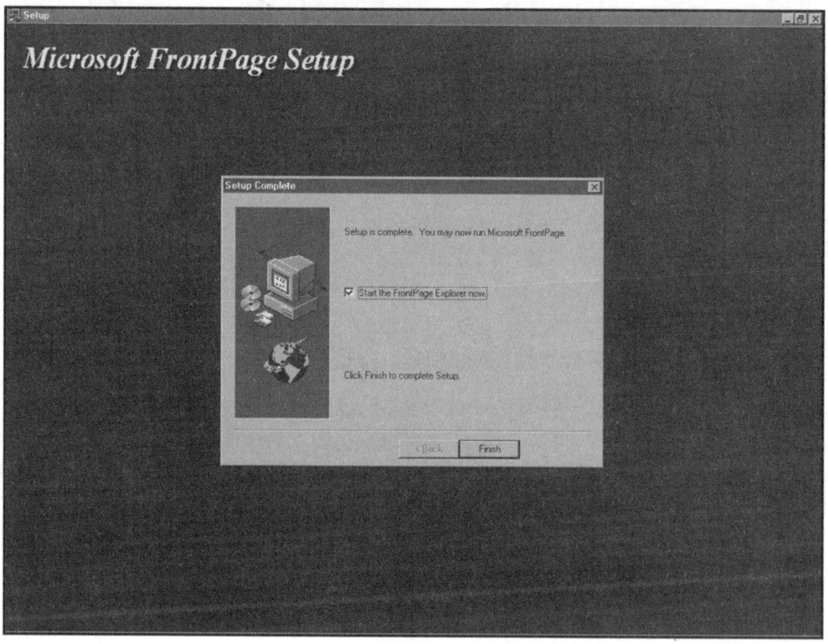

Figure 3-3
The Setup Complete dialog box

You should run the FrontPage TCP/IP Test after installing the Personal Web Server or any other server. The screen shown in Figure 3-6 is displayed. A Start Test and Exit button are available. Run the

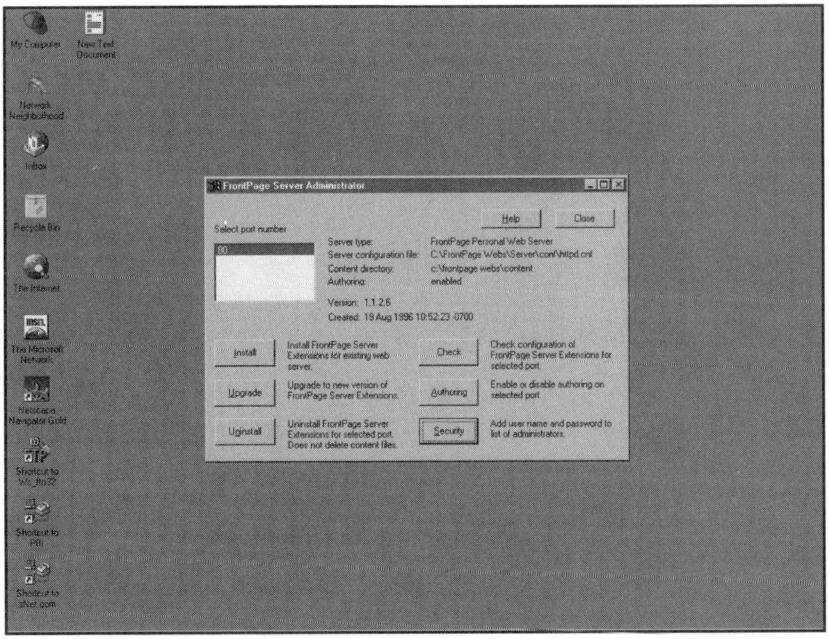

Figure 3-4
The Server Administrator dialog box

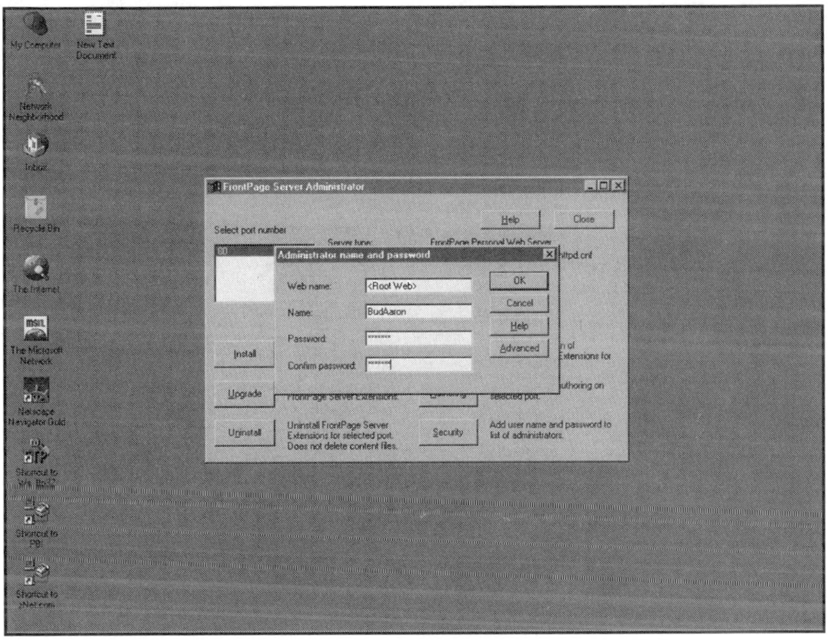

Figure 3-5
The Administrator name and Password dialog box

test by clicking the Start Test button. On completion, the various tests will show results to confirm that everything is working properly, as shown in Figure 3-7. The local host IP should always be 127.0.0.1.

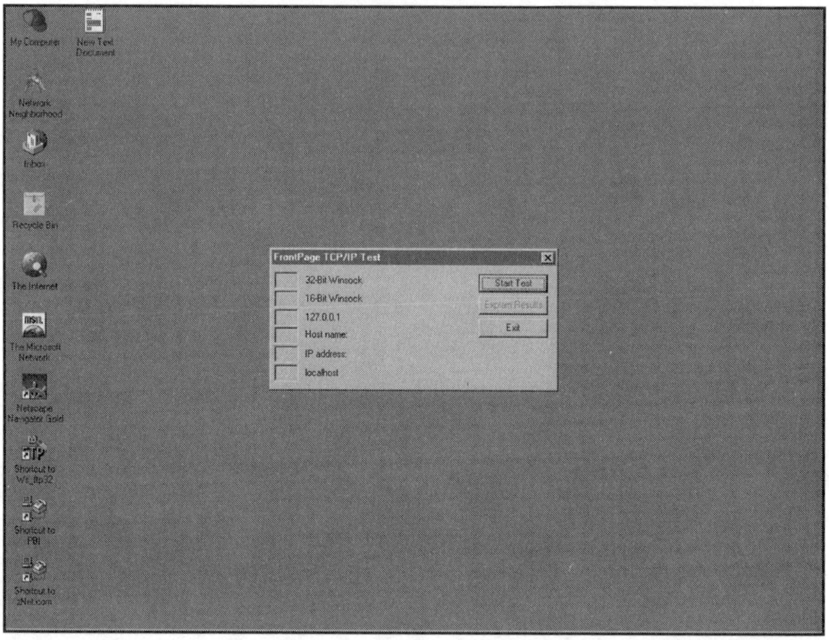

Figure 3-6
The TCP/IP Test dialog box

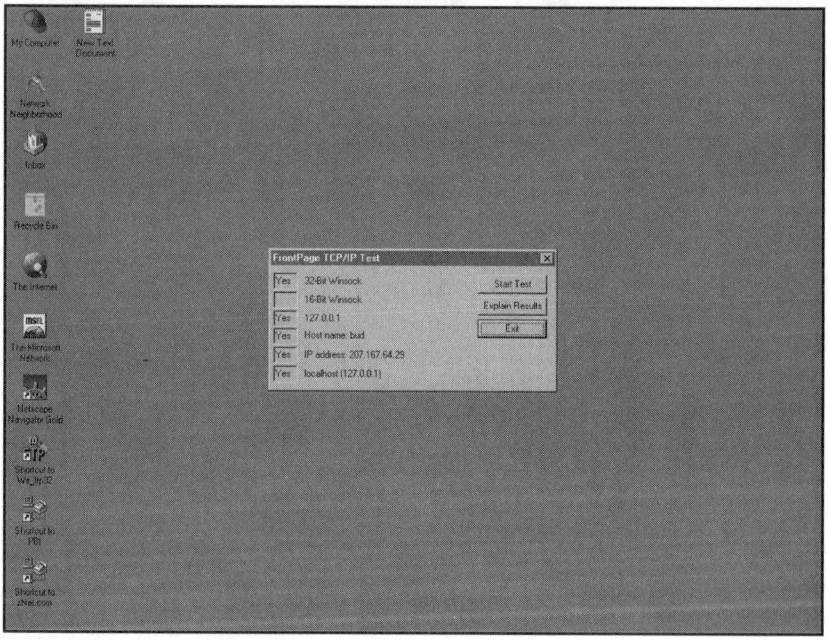

Figure 3-7
The TCP/IP Test dialog box with test complete

Clicking on Explain Results will bring up the Results Explanation dialog box shown in Figure 3-8. The text of the results can be scrolled to show what the test has determined about your setup. If the tests are satisfactory and you have completed the installation, you are ready to start using FrontPage for Web site editing and development.

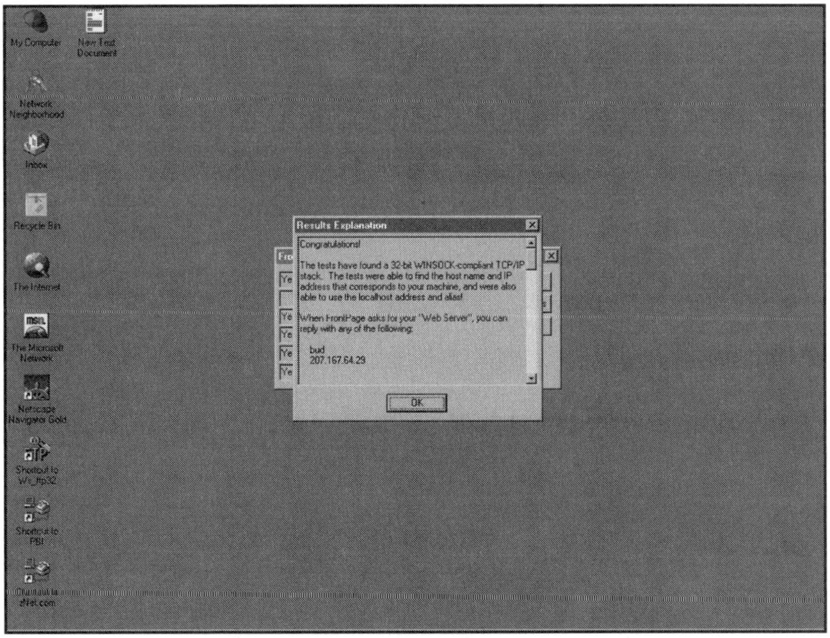

Figure 3-8 The Results Explanation dialog box

The text in the dialog box will be something like the following:

Congratulations!

The tests have found a 32-bit WINSOCK-compliant TCP/IP stack. The tests were able to find the host name and IP address that corresponds to your machine, and were also able to use the localhost address and alias!

When FrontPage asks for your "Web Server", you can reply with any of the following:

bud

207.167.64.29

When you supply a URL (sometimes called a "Location") to your browser, you can reply with any of the following:

http://bud/

http://207.167.64.29/

NOTE: Under certain circumstances your browser may appear to hang for about 90 seconds the first time you access your server by its host name, even though this TCP/IP testing utility says that your host name is OK.

This happens because many browsers always use DNS to resolve host names, even the host name of the local machine. This TCP/IP testing utility does not catch any problems because it (like the FrontPage Explorer) typically does not use DNS to resolve the local host name. Therefore, if your TCP/IP stack uses DNS and your machine is not connected to the network or is experiencing a

continues

continues

network setup or connectivity problem to the DNS server, then the browser hangs for 90 seconds until the connection to the DNS server times-out. For example, this situation commonly occurs when you unplug a laptop computer from its network.

To work around this delay, you have two choices:

1) Fix your DNS configuration/connection or disable DNS. For mobile computers, this often means setting up multiple configurations where the DNS is disabled when the computer is not connected to a network.

2) Use your machine's IP address when you supply a URL/location to your browser:

http://207.167.64.29/

In addition, you will want to set the ServerName directive in your Web Server configuration file so that when the server redirects, it will redirect to your IP address, not your host name.

To do this, use the Window Notepad to open the file c:\FPWebs\Server\conf\httpd.cnf (replace c:\FPWebs with your PWS installation location). Near the bottom are comments regarding ServerName. Add a line (without the # sign in the left column) under those comments that says:

ServerName 207.167.64.29

Save the file and exit Notepad. Then, restart the Personal Web Server. If you fail to follow these instructions exactly, your Personal Web Server may still appear to work, but these things may still cause your browser to hang for 90 seconds:

Browsing a directory URL without the trailing /

Image Maps

SmartHTML pages such as searches, form results, discussions, etc.

Graphic and Other Material for Your Web Site

FrontPage provides a wealth of sample graphics and other material that can be used to embellish your Web site. You need not be a graphic artist to develop Web sites material. You will find bullets, backgrounds, icons, bars, and dozens of other graphic items available for free download. You might start with `www.microsoft.com/workshop/` and `<www.microsoft.com/gallery/>`. You might also visit `www.stars.com` (Figure 3-9) and check out some of its content. Finally, do a Web search to find many good and useful things to use free. Keep in mind that unless you are told that material is free, it is probably someone's intellectual property and you should get permission before using it.

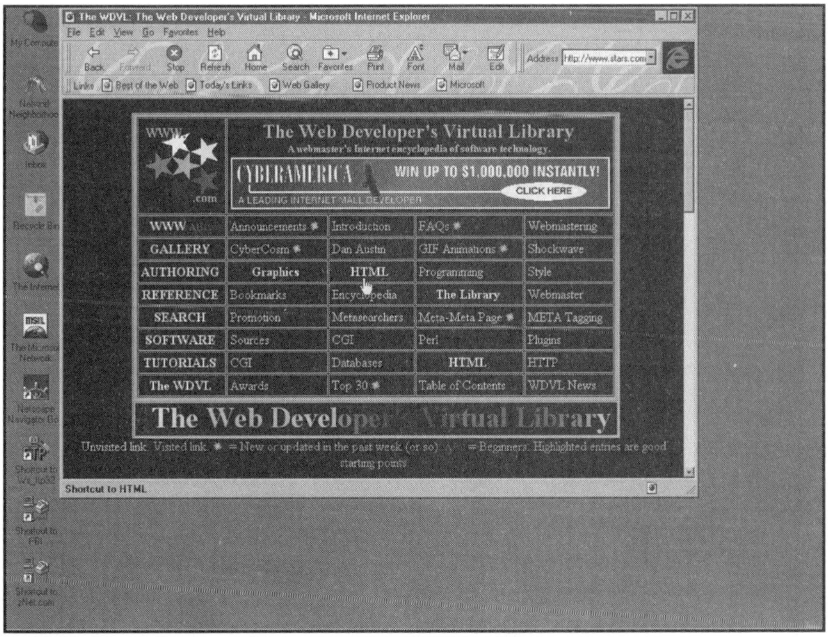

Figure 3-9
The `www.stars.com` home page

DNS, IP, and the World Wide Web

Every Internet host has an IP address in the form *nnn.nnn.nnn.nnn*. You can, for example, reach my showcase site by entering `http://204.134.94.74`. You can consider this number as similar to a telephone number: it is unique to the individual, site, or host using it. When you connect to an ISP, the ISP's server assigns you a temporary IP address (from a pool that the ISP owns) for your connection. At that point, your computer has a unique address through which you can be reached.

When you have telephones installed, the telephone company associates a telephone number with your name. That, in a sense, is how DNS (Domain Name Service) works. Huge databases are maintained on central servers to maintain your domain name and relate it to your IP address. These services are usually rented by ISPs at figures of around $35 a year. Thus, the ISP is not required to manage this huge task.Domain name ownership and assignment is in the hands of AT&T and NetWork Solutions. The site is `http://www.internic.net/`, and you can always point your browser there to look up domain names. My site, `checkmaster.com`, is a domain name, as are `stars.com` and `internic.net`. Each of these names, once assigned, is entered in the DNS databases so that when you type, for example, `www.checkmaster.com` into your browser address window, the name will be *resolved* to its appropriate IP address and you will be linked to that site. It's like having a perpetual White Pages directory at your disposal.

This information should help when using FrontPage Explorer and the associated tools. It should also help you troubleshoot problems with the Personal Web Server. Please keep this in mind: during installation, FrontPage Explorer will attempt to connect to your ISP through your default dial-up connection. If you intend to maintain a site at that location and maintain your Web pages through that connection, let FrontPage Explorer connect. If not, cancel the connection so that FrontPage Explorer sees only your Personal Web Server.

Using FrontPage Explorer

FrontPage Explorer is the "glue" for your Web site regardless of how large it may grow. It provides an Outline View in the left panel to show you pages, graphics, and links. It provides a Link View or Summary View in the right panel and, of course, it bears a resemblance to Explorer. When you first start FrontPage Explorer, you see the view shown in Figure 3-10. You can import existing pages or you can start a new Web site.

Figure 3-10
FrontPage Explorer

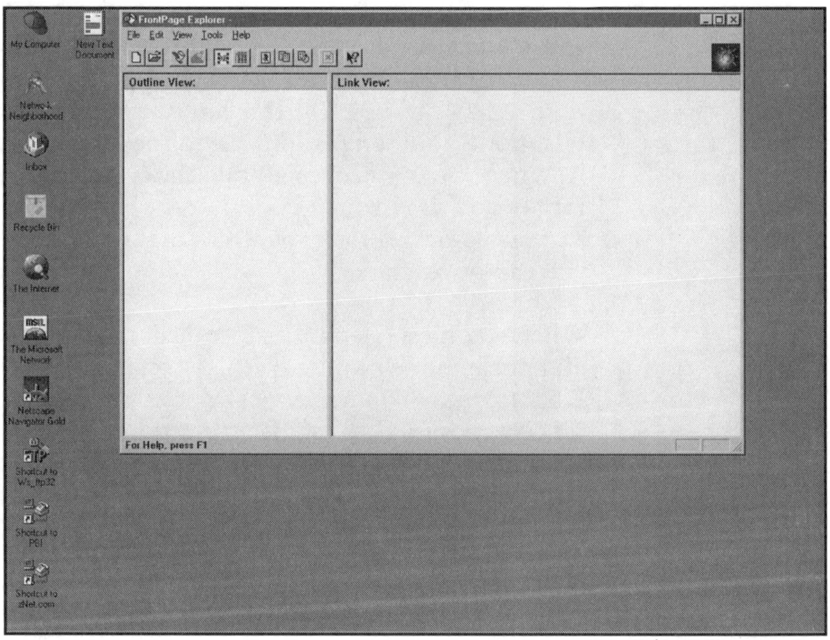

If you choose New Web from the File menu, you will be presented with a selection of templates or wizards as shown in Figure 3-11. The selections are as follows:

- Normal Web
- Corporate Presence wizard
- Customer Support Web
- Discussion Web wizard
- Empty Web
- Learning FrontPage
- Personal Web
- Project Web

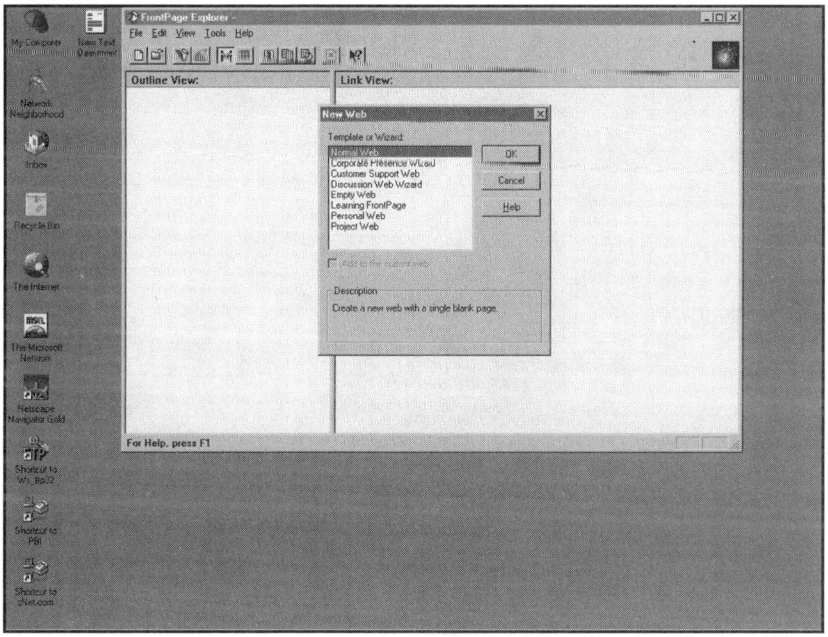

Figure 3-11
FrontPage Explorer New Web dialog box

The wizards will generate very significant Webs with graphics, backgrounds, and attractive content. The templates also generate fairly extensive sites depending on various things. When you select one of these and click OK, you will be asked for a Web server and a Web name, as shown in Figure 3-12. A drop-down box is provided that lists the Web servers available. If you have chosen to use the Personal Server, you will be presented with that name. You can name the Web anything you like.

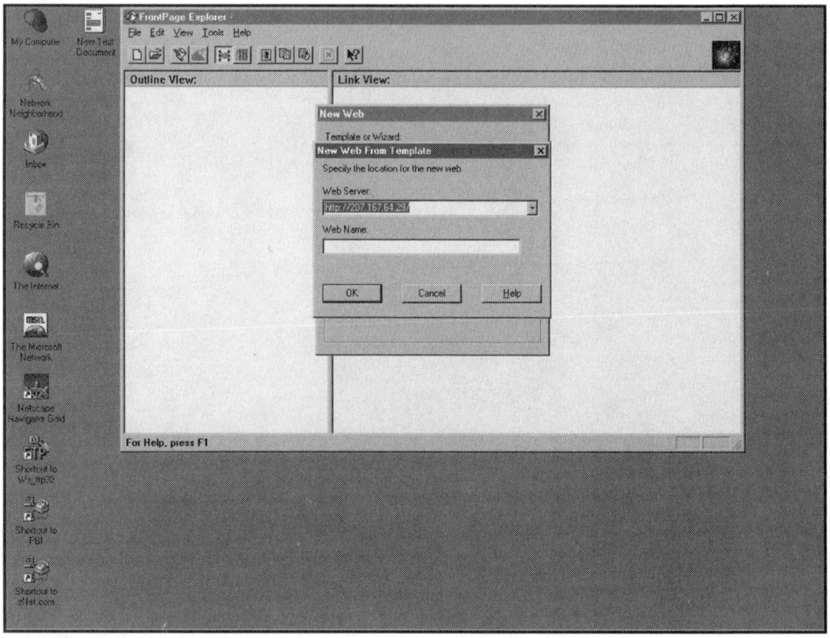

Figure 3-12
New Web from Template dialog box

In Figure 3-13, *bud* and *MasteringAX* are the selections chosen.

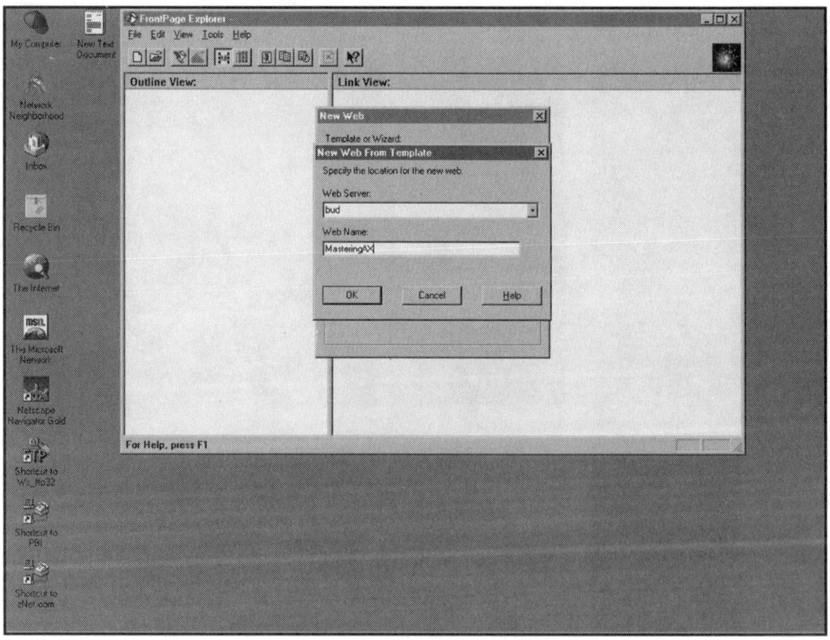

Figure 3-13
New Web from Template dialog box filled in

When you click OK, you will be asked for your name and password (saved from the installation dialog box), as shown in Figure 3-14. Filling these in and clicking OK will generate the Web shown in Figure 3-15.

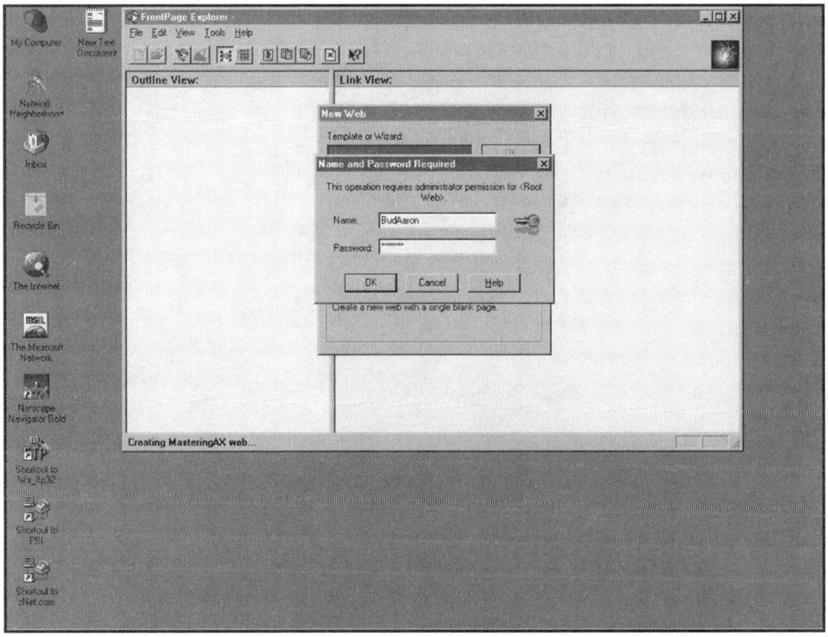

Figure 3-14
Name and Password dialog box

Figure 3-15
The generated Web

A look at Figure 3-16 shows the names and directories generated when a Web is built. Web administrators may understand the use of these directories, but you really don't need to know more than that they are generated by FrontPage Explorer, unless you will be the server administrator on a large site. This would, for example, be the directory structure that an Internet host would build for you on the server.

Figure 3-16
The file and directory structure for the MasteringAX Web

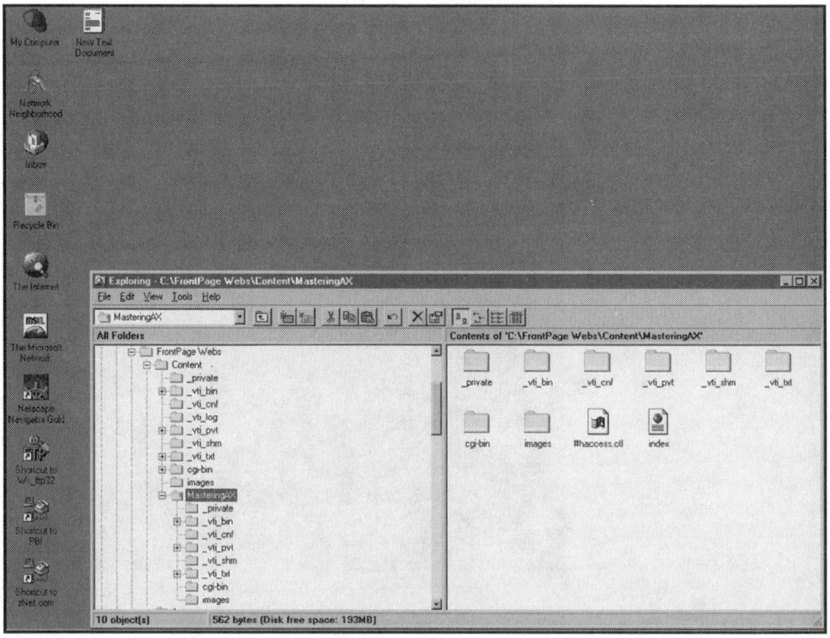

The Summary View of this Web is shown in Figure 3-17. Notice that the default name for the single page is `INDEX.HTM`. Notice also that there is a single link to `IMAGES/UNDERCON.GIF`. You will normally store images in an IMAGES directory on the server.

As shown in Figure 3-18, I've generated a Web using the Learning FrontPage template. This gives a better picture of the Outline and Link Views of Web sites under FrontPage Explorer. I'm trying to get you started here, not teach you all of FrontPage.

Although FrontPage Explorer is not difficult to use, managing Web sites with several to hundreds of linked pages can be a huge task. FrontPage Explorer is one of the only software packages I am aware of that provides this functionality. The best way to understand it is to work with it.

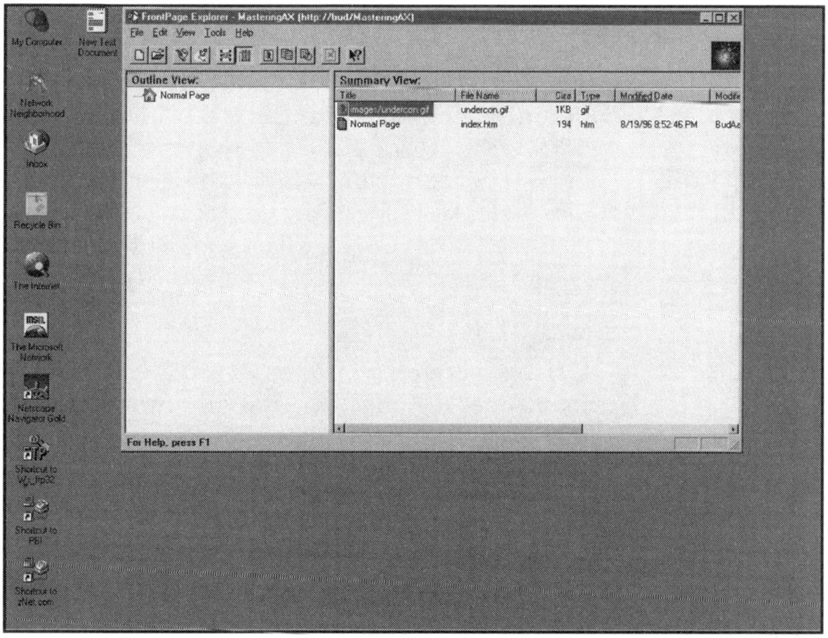

Figure 3-17
The Summary View of MasteringAX

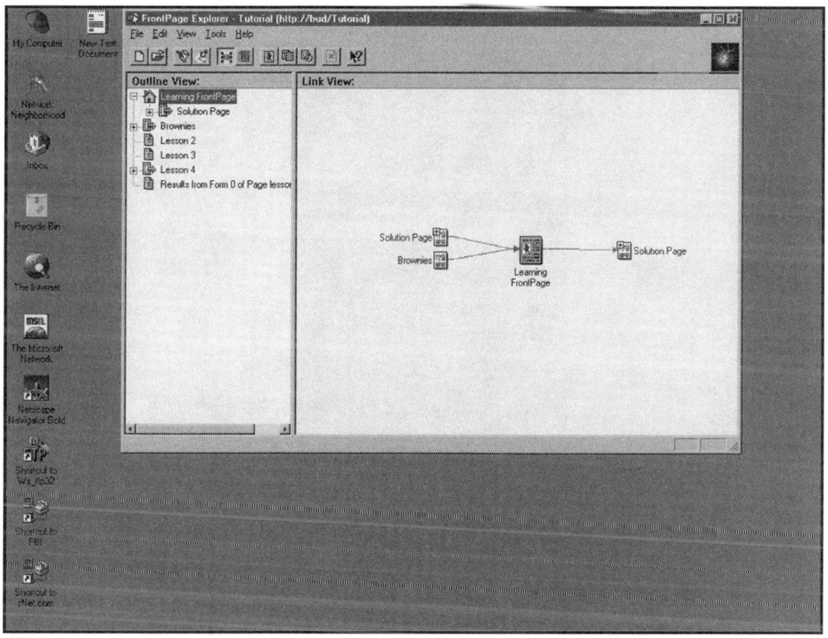

Figure 3-18
A Web called Tutorial, based on the Learning FrontPage template

Using the FrontPage Editor

The FrontPage Editor can be used as a stand-alone HTML Editor or in conjunction with FrontPage Explorer. It stands as one of the best WYSIWYG HTML editors I am aware of. Perhaps more important, it provides support for frames, tables, and forms. These three items fall just under style sheets and scripting with ActiveX objects in terms of degree of complexity. I take a look at frames, tables, and forms shortly, and follow in later chapters with style sheets, scripting, and ActiveX controls.

First, you can crank up the FrontPage Editor and do a trick. Remember the page at the beginning of this chapter? Well, try the following: Start FrontPage Editor. You will be presented with a blank screen. Enter the following:

This will display as a large heading

And this will display as default text.

Your screen should appear as shown in Figure 3-19.

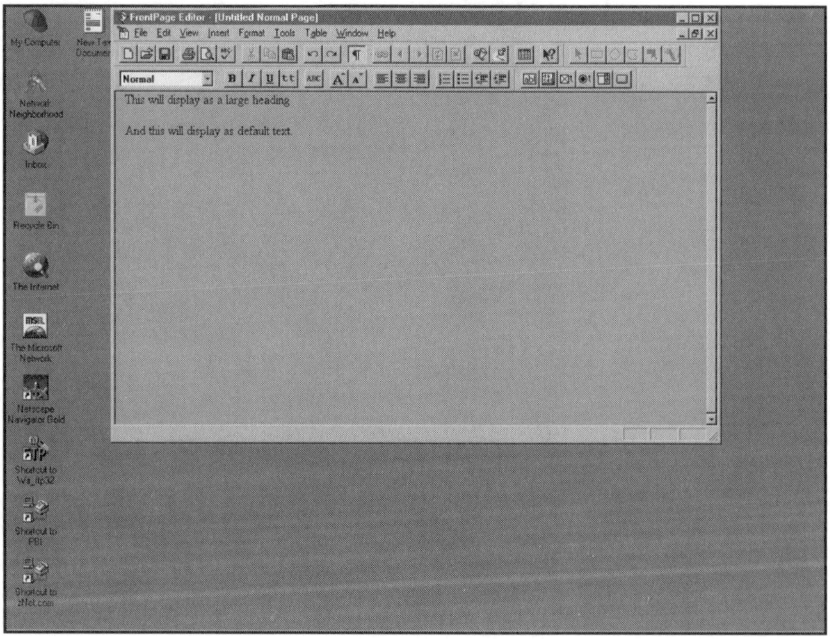

Figure 3-19
The raw text

Now, place your cursor just in front of the first line. You can select Heading 1 from the drop-down list on the toolbar, or select Format and then Paragraph to get the dialog box shown in Figure 3-20.

Select Heading 1 and click OK. The result should be as shown in Figure 3-21.

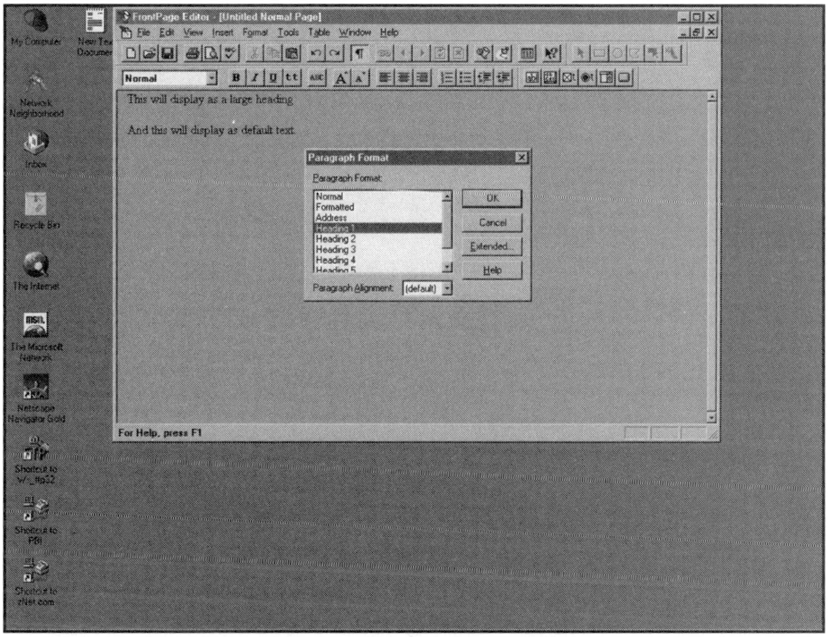

Figure 3-20
Formatting the heading

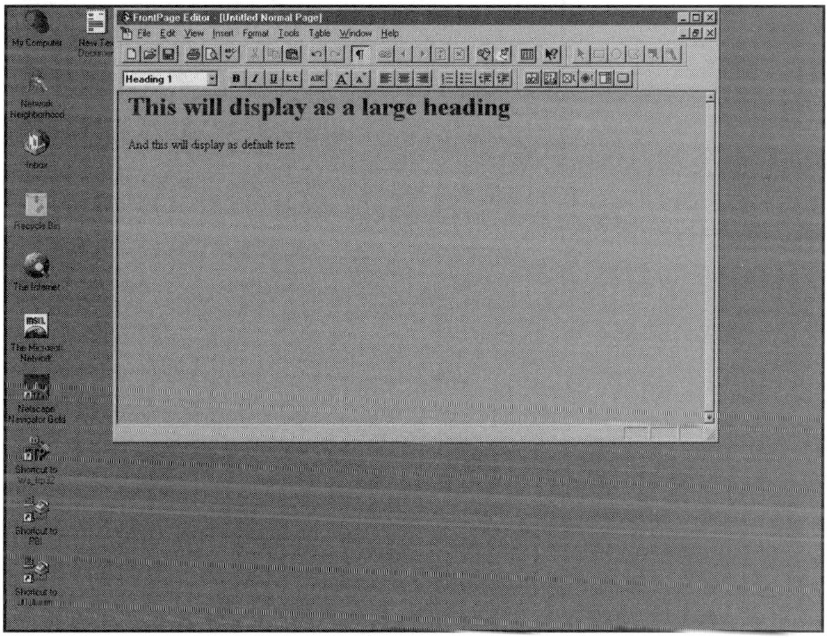

Figure 3-21
The new Heading 1

To finish up, select Page Properties from the File menu to bring up the dialog box shown in Figure 3-22. Enter the following:

This will display in the Explorer Title Bar

and click OK. Select HTML... from the View menu to see that you have just generated HTML code almost identical to the code that you typed at the beginning of this chapter (Figure 3-23). Now, that's gotta be easier than using a text editor! The additional content added by FrontPage is covered in Appendix B.

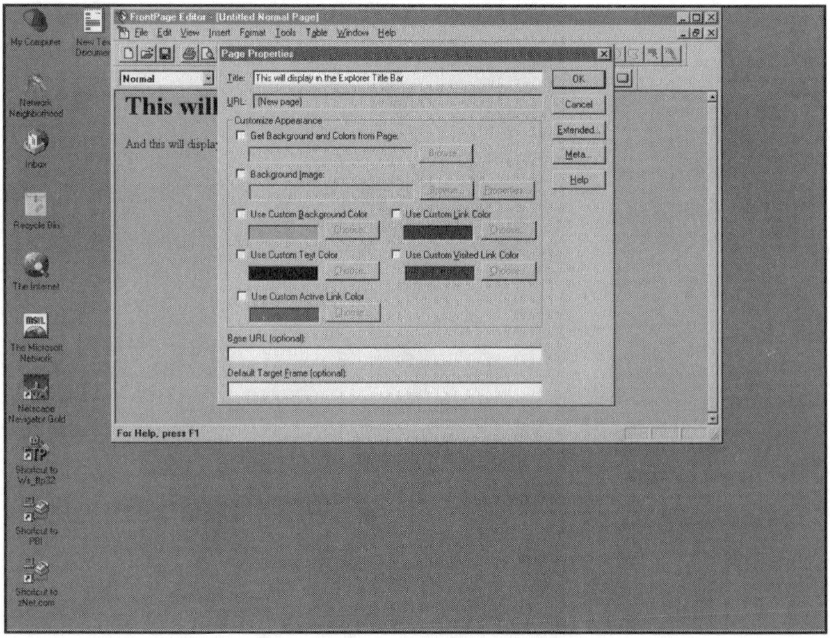

Figure 3-22
Changing the page title

As a final check, save the file to the name of your choice and double-click the result to bring it up in Internet Explorer, as shown in Figure 3-24.

Before continuing, you might want to browse through the menus and toolbar buttons to get a picture of how extensive the FrontPage Editor is. Compare the various capabilities with the HTML code discussed in Appendix B. There are very few of the tags discussed in the Appendix that are not managed in one way or another by this editor.

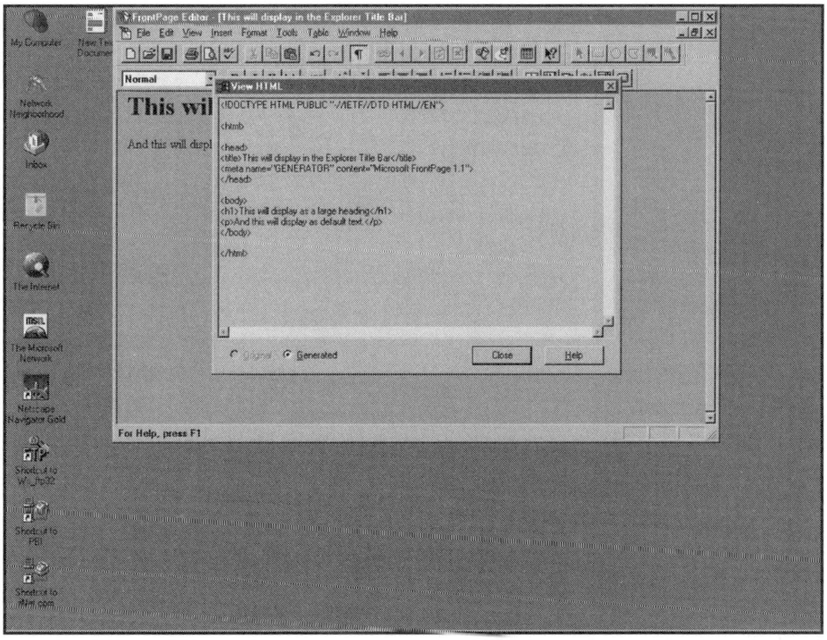

Figure 3-23
The HTML code generated by FrontPage

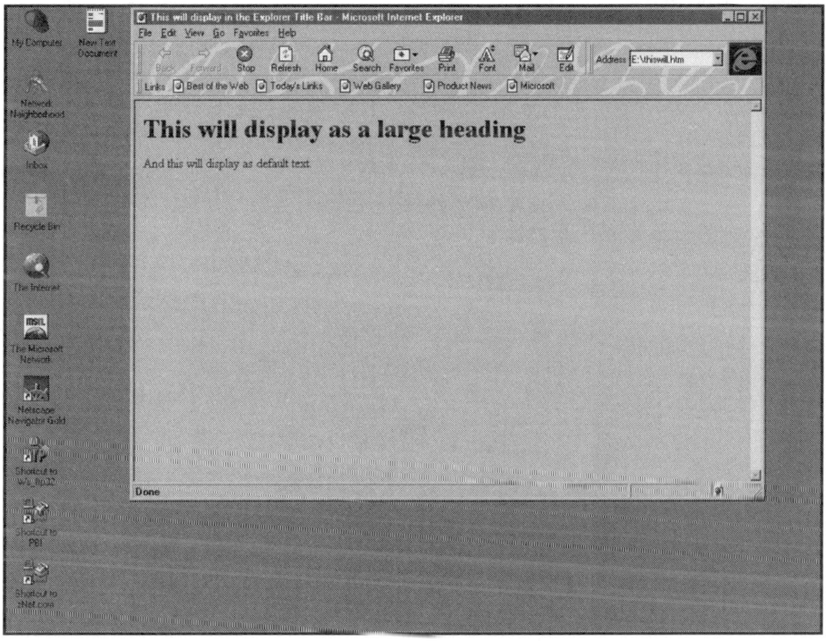

Figure 3-24
The code just generated in Internet Explorer

Forms, Tables, and Frames

In Appendix B, you may notice that most tags required little explanation and are used, by and large, to format text. Forms, tables, and frames required significantly more to describe. The Web has been a means to deliver information in the form of text and graphics as static information for users to read.

Forms were developed to allow some degree of interaction. It would be nice to learn more about people visiting your Web site. It would be even nicer to allow them the ability to order products and make payments. Forms provide a limited amount of information return. The ideal way at present it is through CGI scripts, but this book is not about CGI.

Tables are an ideal way to present some types of information, but throughout the history of publishing, they have been difficult to build. The popularity of spreadsheet software should attest to their desirability. Of course, tables can be built in HTML using a text editor, but I have an easier way.

It would be hard to find a publishing corollary to frames. Web sites usually present text and graphics with appropriate links in a linear fashion. The ideal way would be to maintain a masthead and table of contents as stationary or static elements on the page with a separate area to present the actual content. A banner across the top, a table of contents on the left, and a scrolling window on the right has become rather standard on the Web. These elements may or may not be surrounded by borders.

In the next several pages, I give you some simple examples of these three major elements. In the chapters that follow, I show you how to accomplish even more outrageous things. The aim, after all, is to give you the necessary information to build killer Web sites using every tool possible, including ActiveX Controls, and to make those sites active and attractive.

Building Forms

FrontPage provides a wealth of capability in building forms. You can add elements by hand or use templates or scripts. Here, I'm walking you through the construction of one common type of form. I strongly encourage you to then look at the other available possibilities.

If you select New page... from the File menu, you will see the New Page dialog box shown in Figure 3-25. The available selections are shown in Table 3-1. As you can see, FrontPage has many available templates and wizards. Here, I'm using the Form Page wizard.

Table 3-1
New Page selections

Page	Description
Normal Page	Create a blank Web page.
Bibliography	Create a bibliography page that makes references to printed or electronic works.
Confirmation Form	Create a page to acknowledge receipt of user input from Discussion, FormResult, or Registration forms.
Directory of Press Releases	Create a directory pointing to all of your press, sorted by date.
Employee Directory	Create an alphabetized listing of the employees in your company, with a hot-linked table of contents.
Employment Opportunities	Create a listing of available positions in your company, with a form to request more information.
Feedback Form	Create a page where users can submit comments about your Web site, products, or organization.
Form Page Wizard	Create a form page by selecting the types of information you need to collect.
Frames Wizard	Create a page divided into tiled areas called *frames*. Each frame contains another page or image.
Frequently Asked Questions	Create a FAQ page that answers common questions about some topic.
Glossary of Terms	Create a page defining related terms, divided into alphabetized sections.
Guest Book	Create a page where visitors to your Web can leave their comments in a public guest log.
Hot List	Create a page of links to your favorite sites, divided into categories.
HyperDocument Page	Create a page in a hierarchical document divided into sections.

continues

Table 3-1
Continued

Page	Description
Lecture Abstract	Create a page describing an upcoming lecturer; use this with the Seminar Schedule template.
Meeting Agenda	Create and agenda for a scheduled meeting.
Office Directory	Create a page listing the locations of all your company's offices.
Personal Home Page Wizard	Create a Home Page customized to meet your needs.
Press Release	Create a press release ready for linking into the Press Release Directory template.
Product Description	Create a page describing a product according to features, benefits, and specifications.
Product or Event Registration	Create a page where users can register for product support or an upcoming event.
Search Page	Create a page where users can search for keywords across all the documents in a Web.
Seminar Schedule	Create main page in a hierarchy describing a seminar event. Use the Lecture Abstract template.
Software Data Sheet	Create a data sheet describing features and benefits for a software product.
Survey Form	Create a survey form to collect information from readers and and store it in a file on your Web server.
Table of Contents	Create a page with links to every document in your Web, displayed in an outline format.
User Registration	Create a page where users can self-register for a protected Web. Only useful in a root Web ('/').
What's New	Create a page telling users about changes to your Web site over the last couple of months, sorted by date.

Figure 3-25
The New Page Selection dialog box

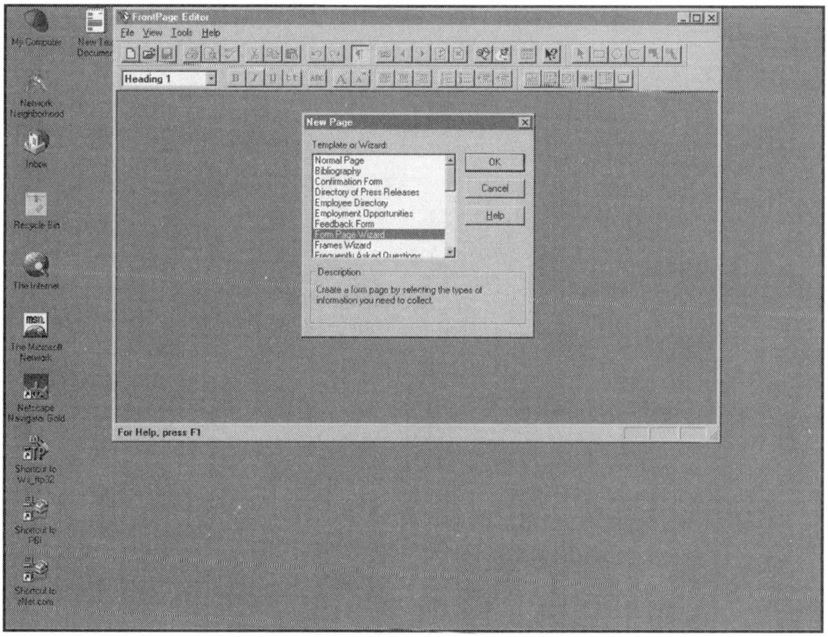

FrontPage Wizard presents the dialog box shown in Figure 3-26 to explain the function of the wizard being run.

Figure 3-26
The Form Page Wizard explanation

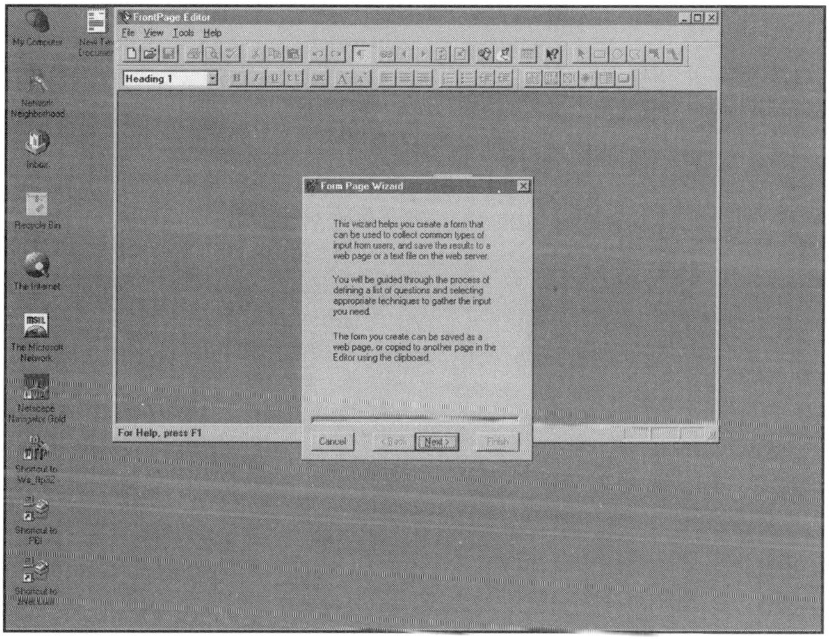

In Figure 3-27, you are prompted to enter a Page URL and Page Title. The Page URL corresponds to a filename and should have a name consistent with the rest of your Web site. The Page Title will be displayed on the Internet Explorer title bar.

Figure 3-27
Naming tour form

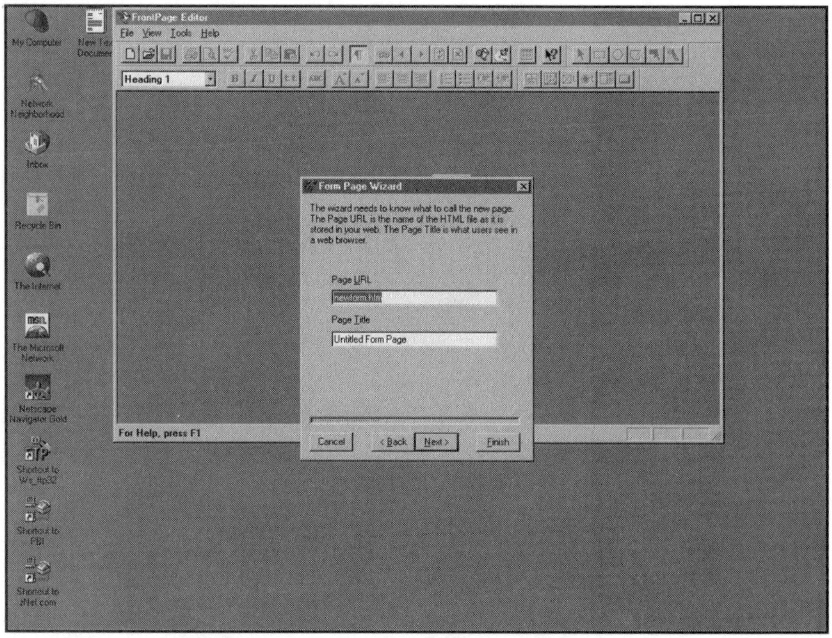

You can build this form to collect contact, account, product, ordering, or personal information, among many possibilities. The dialog box shown in Figure 3-28 allows you to enter a number of questions, as shown in Figure 3-29. It is wise to keep the amount of information requested on any one page small enough that it does not discourage a visitor filling in the form. It is better to break forms up into short, specific forms rather than one long form. In Figure 3-29, you are also allowed to edit the question that will be used on the form. Keep in mind that you can always change things by editing the finished form.

After you have selected contact information, you go to the next step, which gives you a choice of information to be requested in your finished form. The Name check box also gives you format options. You can select as many check boxes as you like. You might also want to change the default Group name to something that suits the site you are building. The dialog box is shown in Figure 3-30.

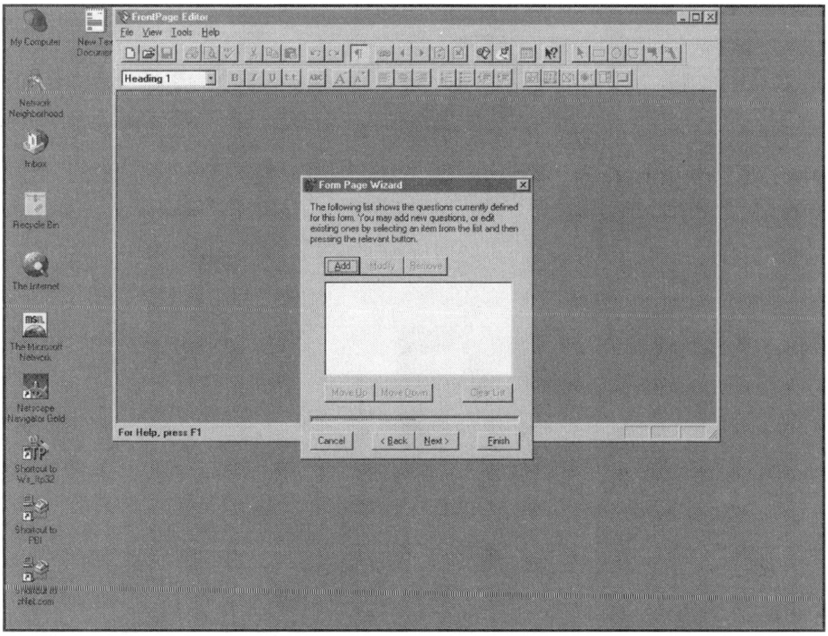

Figure 3-28
The Form wizard Questions dialog box

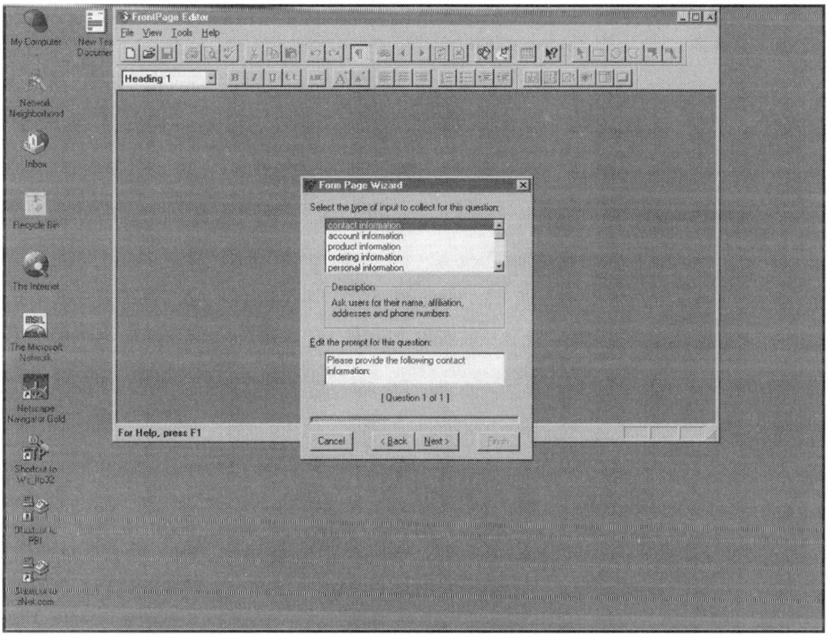

Figure 3-29
The question type and prompt

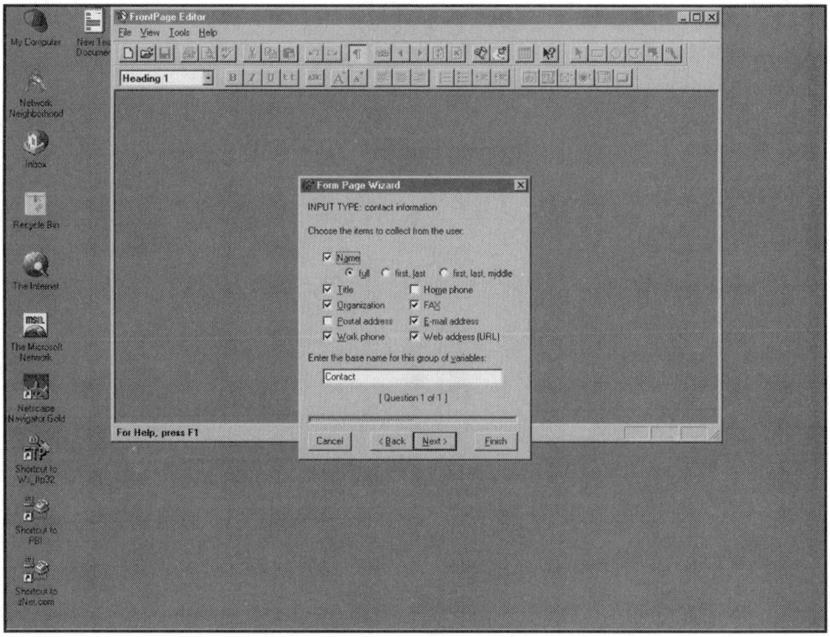

Figure 3-30
Selecting information for this form

The question is posted in the list box, as shown in Figure 3-31. Again, one group at a time is probably better than a lot of questions on a single form. There are exceptions, for which collecting a lot of information is of critical importance to the user—as in a contest application, for example.

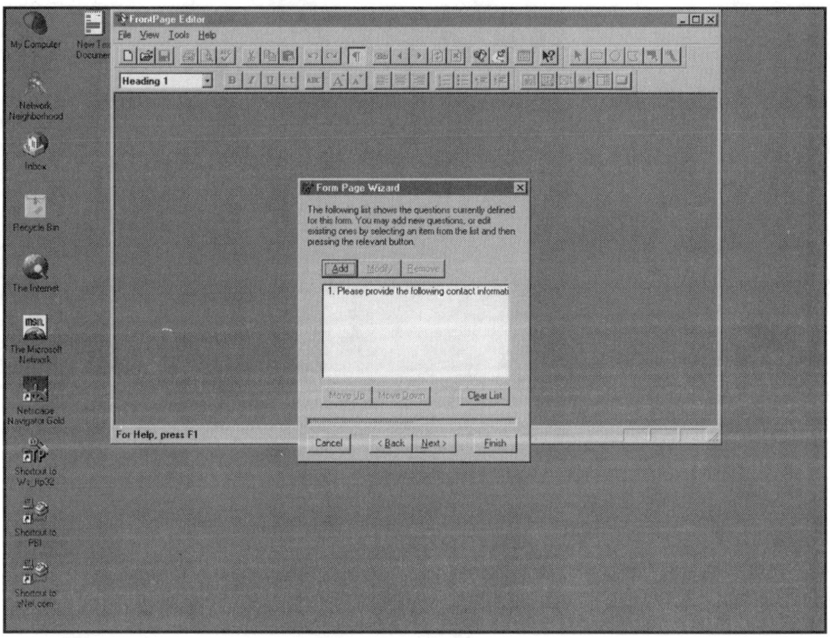

Figure 3-31
The question posted in the dialog box

As shown in Figure 3-32, you are presented with Presentation Options. You can elect to have the material formatted in several ways, and can elect to have a Table of Contents generated for the page. The TOC is desirable if the form is quite large.

Figure 3-32
The Presentation Options dialog box

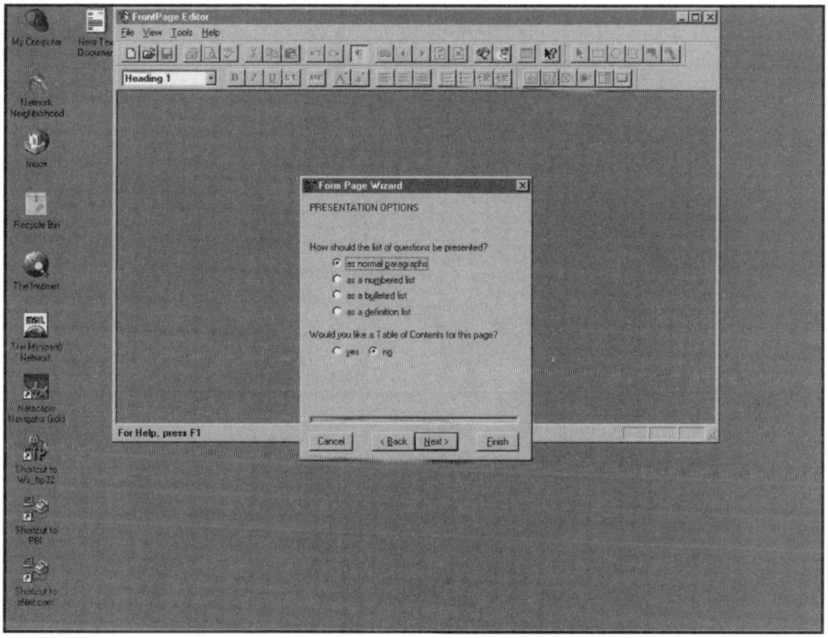

The final dialog box, shown in Figure 3-33, prompts you to indicate how you want the output handled. There are a number of possibilities, including simply saving the result to a file. As I mentioned earlier, the Web started life as a static presentation system, not an interactive system. The need for interactivity has grown. That is one reason for this book, and one reason that forms, in general, are such an important part of the picture.

Figure 3-34 shows the Finish page for this wizard, and part of the result is shown in Figure 3-35. Again, this takes far longer to explain than it takes to actually do. The point is that FrontPage makes building Web pages much easier than using most available systems, such as Notepad.

I've illustrated the basics for building Web forms using FrontPage. I've also shown you that the support for this part of Web design is very extensive in FrontPage. You will find that experimenting with the possibilities can be very rewarding. Always take the trouble to look at the HTML code generated for ideas about fine-tuning your Web sites.

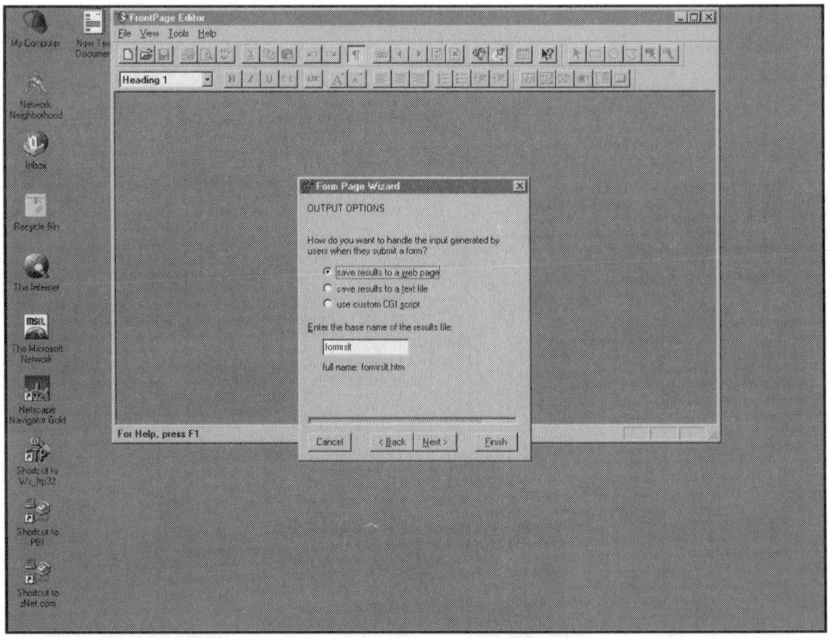

Figure 3-33
The Output Options dialog box

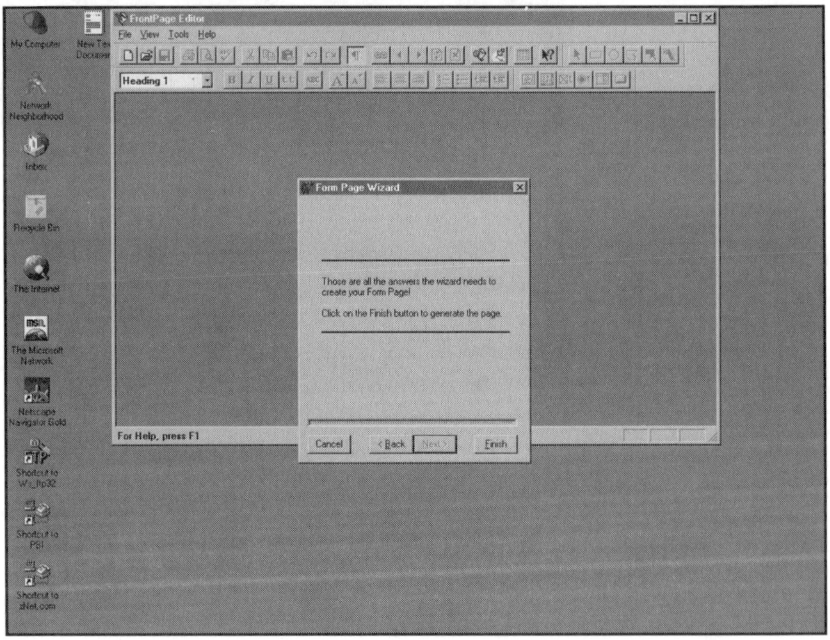

Figure 3-34
The Finish screen for this wizard

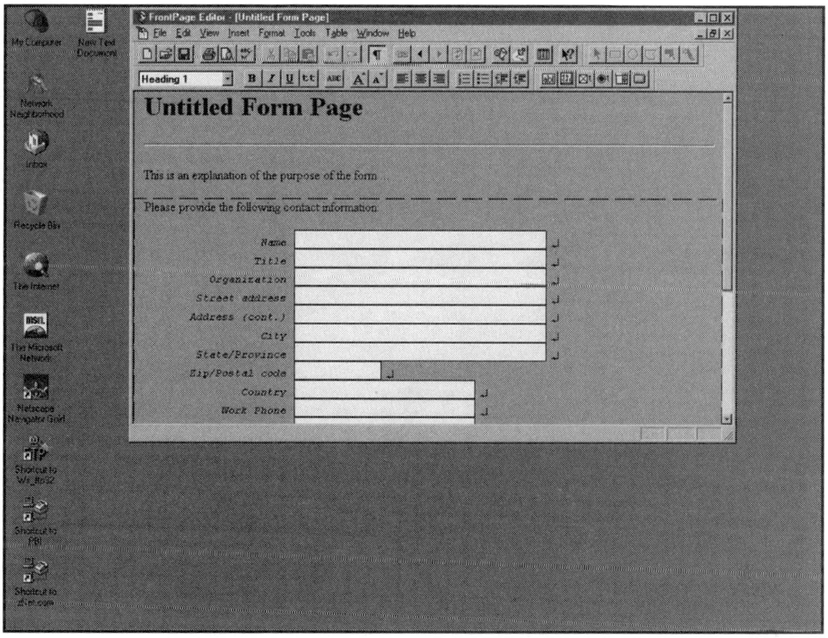

Figure 3-35 The result in FrontPage Editor

Building a Table

Tables, in any publishing venue, are notoriously difficult to assemble and present in an attractive and meaningful manner. That is no less true on Web design. Hand coding tables is very difficult just in terms of placing tags. FrontPage comes to the rescue with its Table editor.

Figure 3-36 shows the Insert Table dialog box. You can specify the size, layout, and width of the table that you would like to build. As shown in Figure 3-37, I've set 10 rows and 4 columns. I've also elected to align the contents to the center of each cell and set a border width of 2. Assembling a table is really that simple, and the result, ready to be filled with data, is shown in Figure 3-38.

After your tables are built, you can always fine-tune them using either FrontPage Table menu commands or by adding tags of your own with a text editor. Practice will always improve your skills in any occupation, and Web design is no exception.

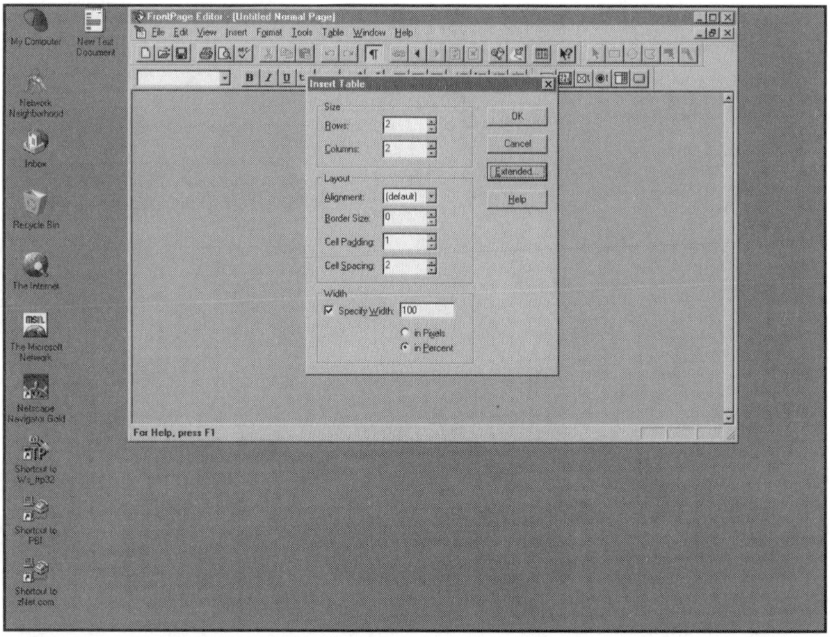

Figure 3-36
The Insert Table dialog box

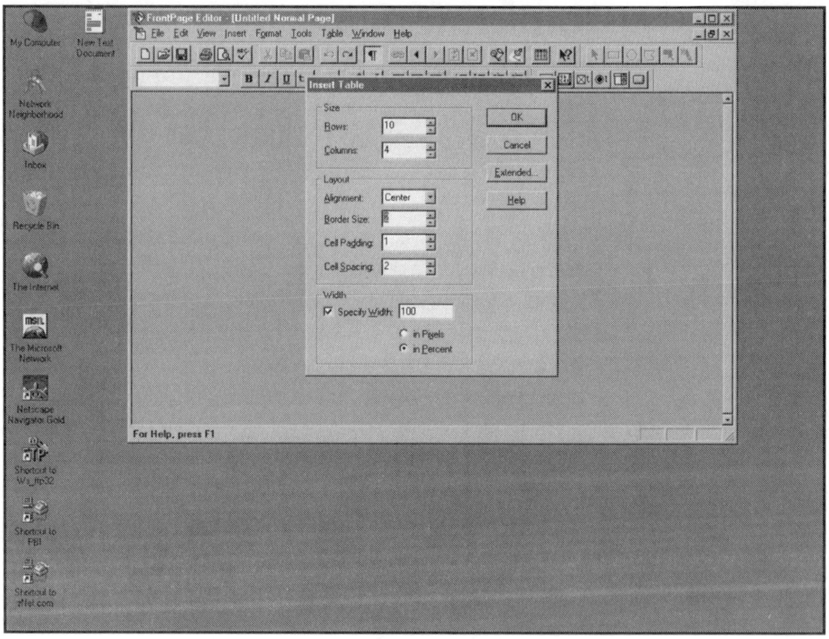

Figure 3-37
New values for the table

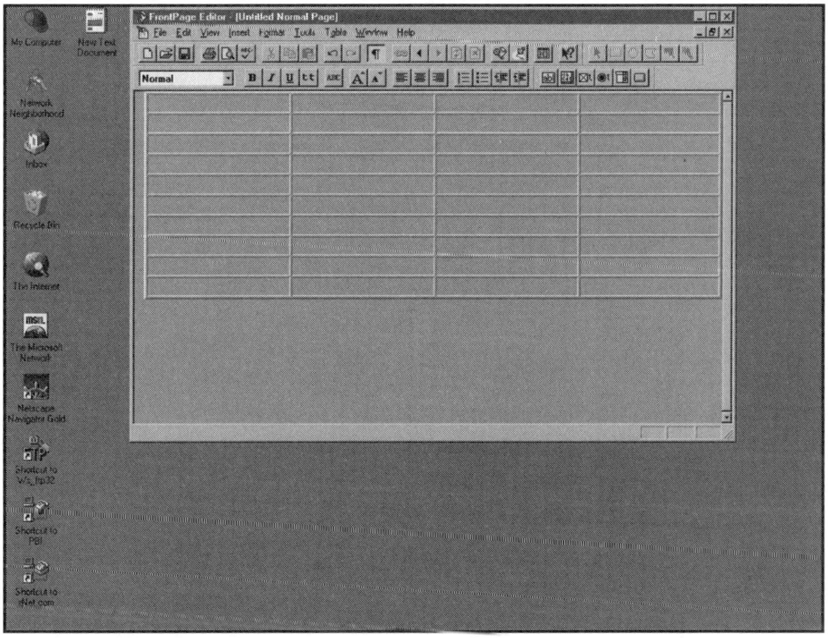

Figure 3-38
The new table in FrontPage Editor

Building a Frameset

Frames are not part of HTML 3.2. They are fully supported by both Netscape Navigator 3.0 and Internet Explorer 3.0. There are a number of other browsers being used that may not support frames. For this reason, you should always provide alternative content for browsers that are not frame enabled.

Frames are not exceptionally difficult to hand code. In fact, you will normally use only one frameset on any Web site, and you'll use that frameset to display all of your Web content. Once again, FrontPage provides a wizard to build framesets.

> **NOTE:**
> **Although FrontPage will build a perfect frameset, it will not display that frameset in FrontPage Editor. It will show you the links and setup in FrontPage Explorer, but double-clicking the representation page will simply start the frameset editor. You can always test the appearance by opening the frameset in Internet Explorer.**

You build a frameset by selecting New Page... from the File menu of FrontPage Editor and selecting the Frames wizard, as shown in Figure 3-39.

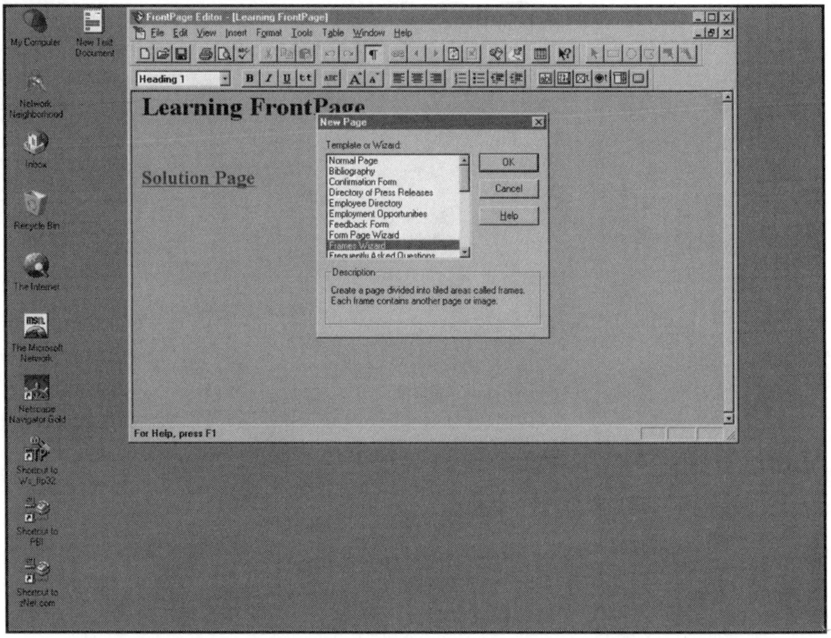

Figure 3-39
The New Page dialog box

Frames wizard's Choose Technique dialog box allows you to go it on your own with the Make a Custom Grid option, or you can use the easy way with the Pick a Template option. In the dialog box shown in Figure 3-40, I've chosen Pick a Template.

A fairly standard template layout is displayed in Figure 3-41. You might want to select the other options just to see the layouts available. Also keep in mind that each can be fine-tuned to suit your needs and the appearance of your Web site. The template shown has a banner to present your company information and logo if you choose. An HTML contents file will fill in the left panel, and the main panel will be the place to which you direct all links. Click Next to go to the next dialog box.

The next dialog (Figure 3-42) allows you to select the URL (HTML file) that will run in browsers that are not frames enabled. You can always come back and fill this in later if you have not yet done an alternate file.

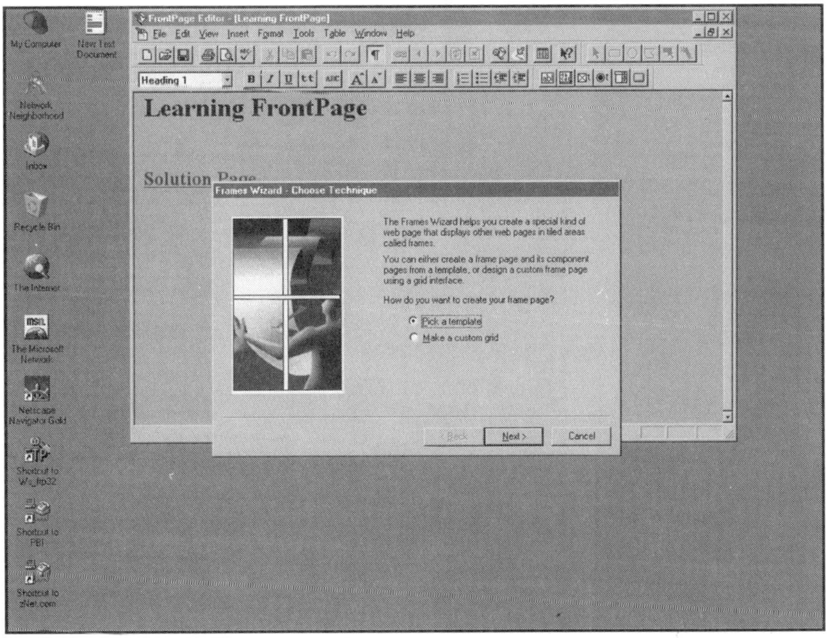

Figure 3-40
The Frames wizard's Choose Technique dialog box

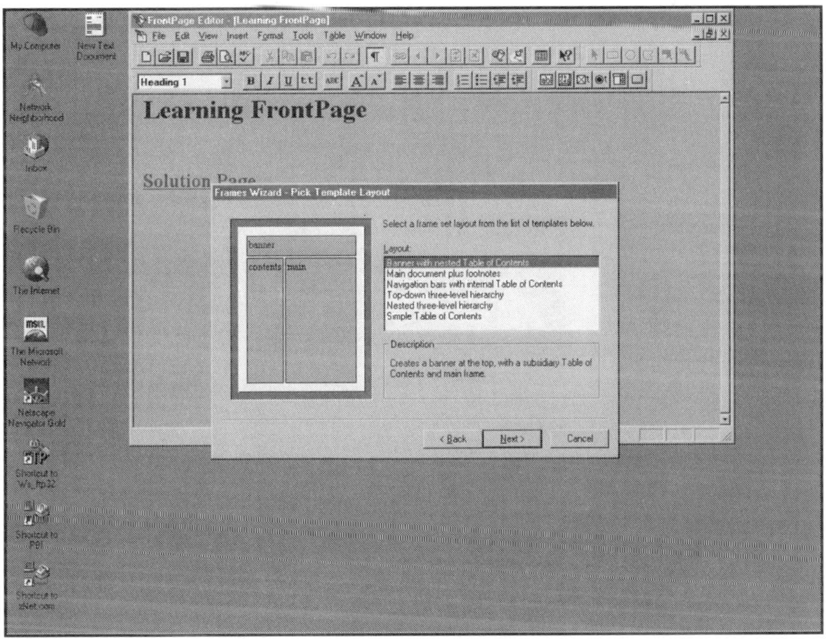

Figure 3-41
Choose the layout to suit your needs

Figure 3-42
Select an alternate URL

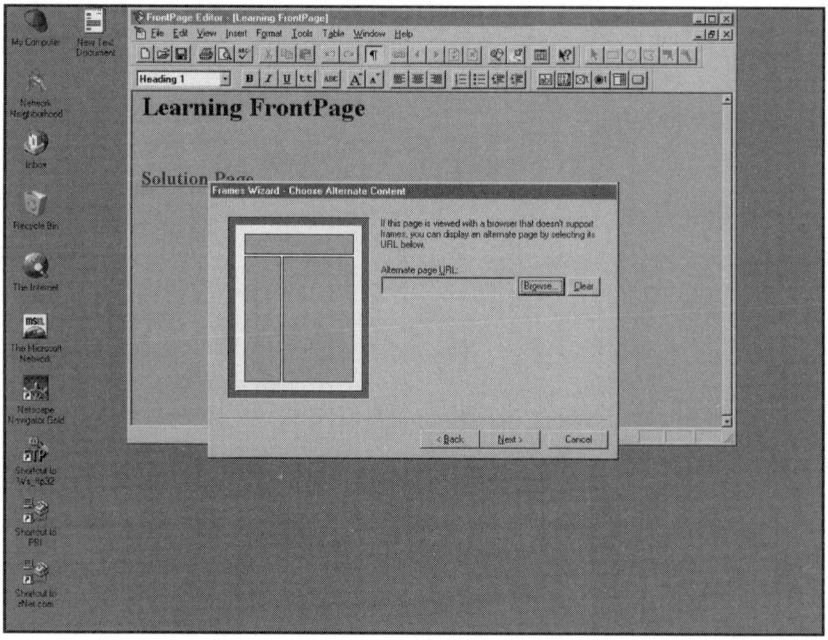

The Save Page dialog box shown in Figure 3-43 allows you to enter a Title for the page and select the URL (HTML file name) under which the frameset will be saved. You can make this the default by naming it INDEX.HTM or INDEX.HTML, depending on the host site using it. Click Finish to complete the frameset.

Figure 3-43
The Finish dialog box

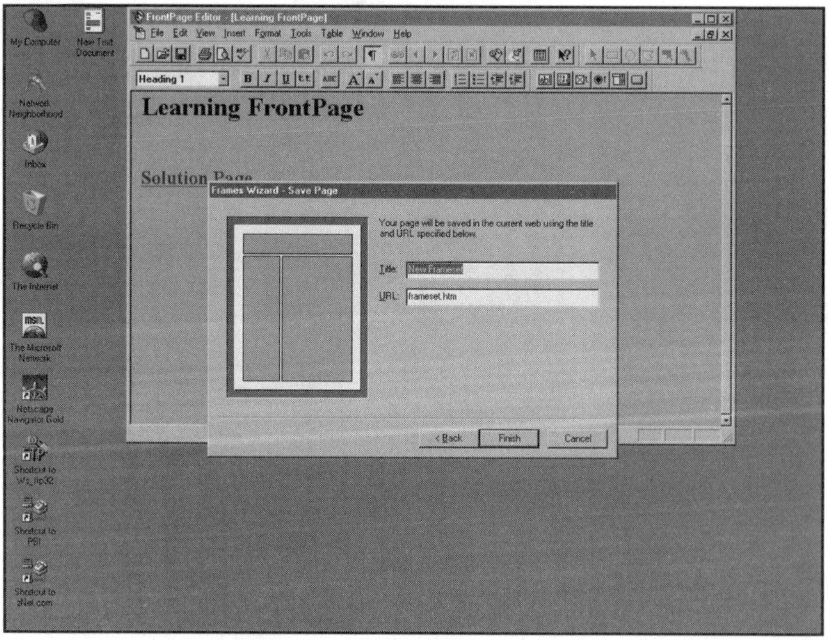

The resulting frameset and links are shown in FrontPage Explorer in Figure 3-44 and displayed in Internet Explorer in Figure 3-45. You can, once again, always fine-tune the results with the various tools in FrontPage or by opening the file in a text editor and coding additional tags or attributes.

Figure 3-44
The Frameset in FrontPage Explorer

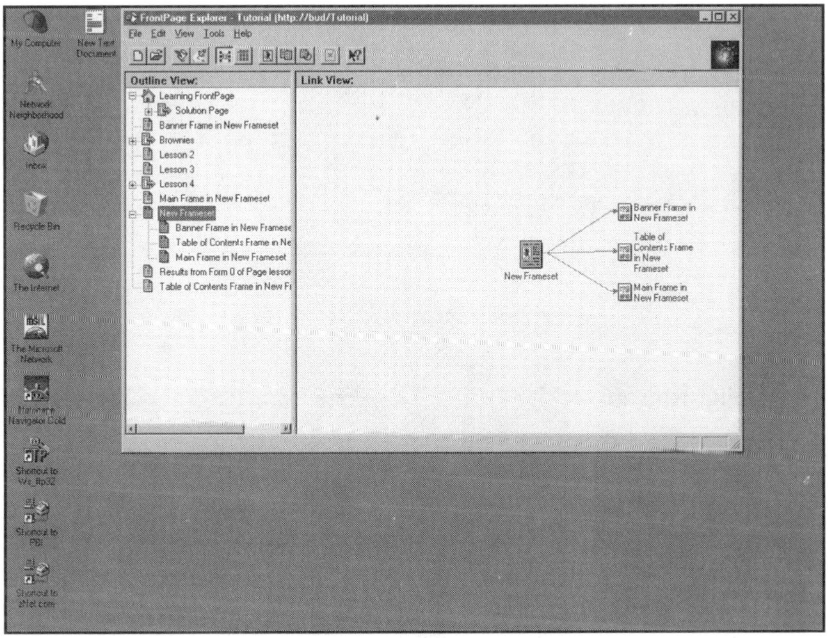

Figure 3-45
The Frameset in Internet Explorer

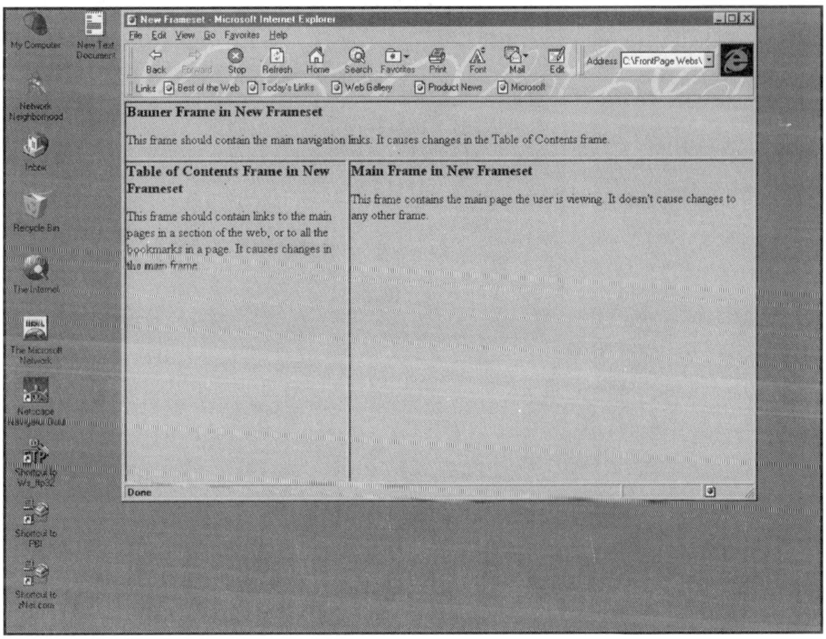

Finally, I present a close approximation of what you may want to do. My showcase site's front door is shown in Figure 3-46. What you do not see is the black marble and gold, or the white clouds on blue that make up the theme of this site. You will not hear the music or see the animated icons in this book, either. The fact is, the World Wide Web is a fantastic place to use content that would be far too expensive to put in a computer book. The URL for this site is

```
http://204.134.94.74/
```

or you can navigate to it from

```
http://www.checkmaster.com/
```

or

```
http://www.instachecks.com
```

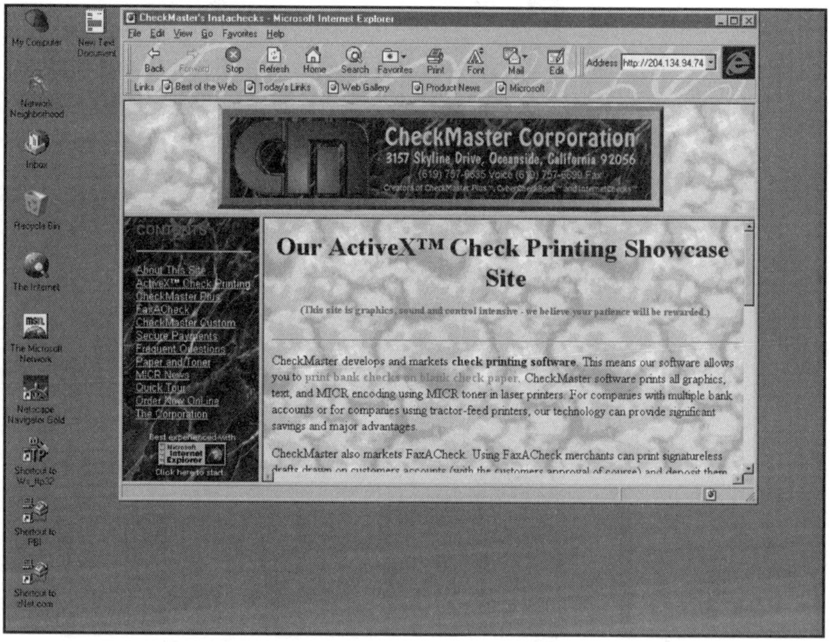

Figure 3-46 The Internetchecks.com Web site

I add some bells and whistles, including various scripts at these sites. You are welcome to examine and use the code. These sites may give you additional help in crafting your own content or scripts.

Summary

In this chapter, I've discussed Microsoft FrontPage. FrontPage represents a very good value for editing Web pages and Web sites. I have also expanded on forms, tables, and frames. You can always improve your knowledge of these areas by using FrontPage to generate code and then examining the code to see what works and how things are being done. There may be times when you can generate HTML here, and then cut and paste it to other applications that you build with tools presented later in this book.

In the next chapter, I briefly go over some alternative tools for editing HTML and show you how you might use them. I follow that with another tool called ActiveX Control Pad, which allows more extended functionality, and then I take a look at style sheets.

Chapter 4

Using Other Authoring Tools

If you change the file extension of an HTML source file to .TXT, and then open the file using Notepad, you will discover that it is nothing more than a standard text file with HTML tags to tell the browser how it should be interpreted. You can also make changes as long as you are quite familiar with HTML coding. Some Web developers still insist that this is the best way to develop Web pages.

So, Notepad or any text editor certainly falls in the category of "other authoring tools." Attempting to use a text editor to maintain a complete Web site will certainly be tortuous, but it is frequently the easiest way to make small, quick changes to existing HTML.

In this chapter, I introduce you to some additional tools to generate HTML code. All these tools except HoTMetaL Pro 3.0 are available on the CD or can be downloaded free from Microsoft or other Web sites. Each tool provides an additional way to prepare HTML code for the Web. This code can either be used as stand-alone pages or incorporated into other pages in some cases. HoTMetaL Pro 3.0 allows the addition of ActiveX Controls and scripting, and therefore is, in a sense, one of the more complete single editors available.

Word Internet Assistant

Word 95 with Internet Assistant installed is a chameleon. Figure 4-1 shows it functioning as a browser at `www.msn.com`. Notice that the toolbar contains Forward and Back buttons. To the right of those buttons are URL, History, Open Favorite, and Add Favorite. The Home, Stop, and Refresh buttons are also included. It is not the most elegant browser in the world, but it does point up the multiple options provided by component-oriented software using ActiveX.

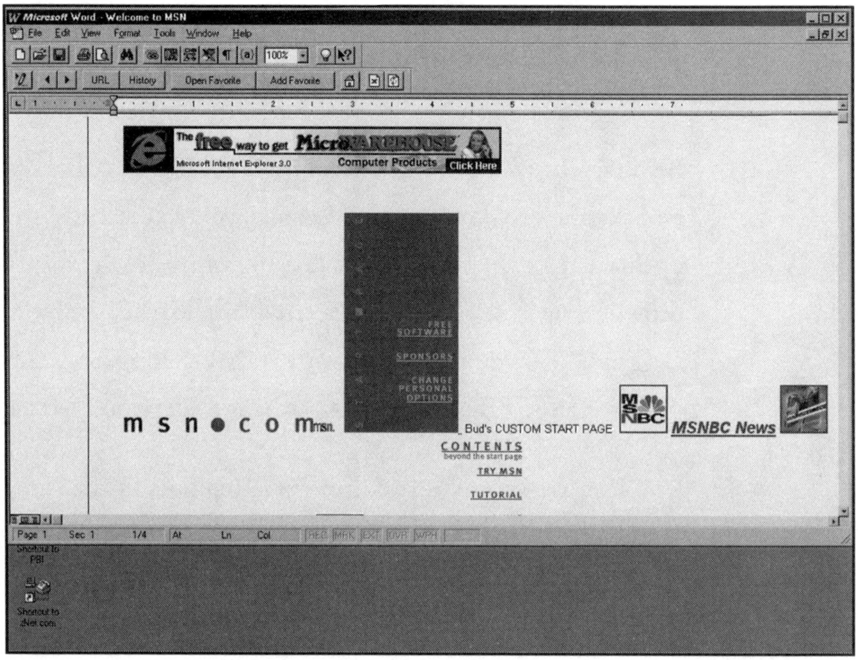

Figure 4-1
Word 95 as an Internet browser

Word 95 provides an HTML template, as shown in Figure 4-2. If you start a new document with this template, it will automatically set up the tools to edit HTML in a WYSIWYG fashion. It does not understand frames and has limited support for forms.

Figure 4-3 shows a document including a table, so Word 95 Internet Assistant does understand tables to a limited extent. This is not an ideal editor for HTML documents, but it provides the functionality needed for a lot of HTML work in the absence of other alternatives. A drop-down styles box is available with HTML formatting alternatives. The ability to insert graphics and links is also provided.

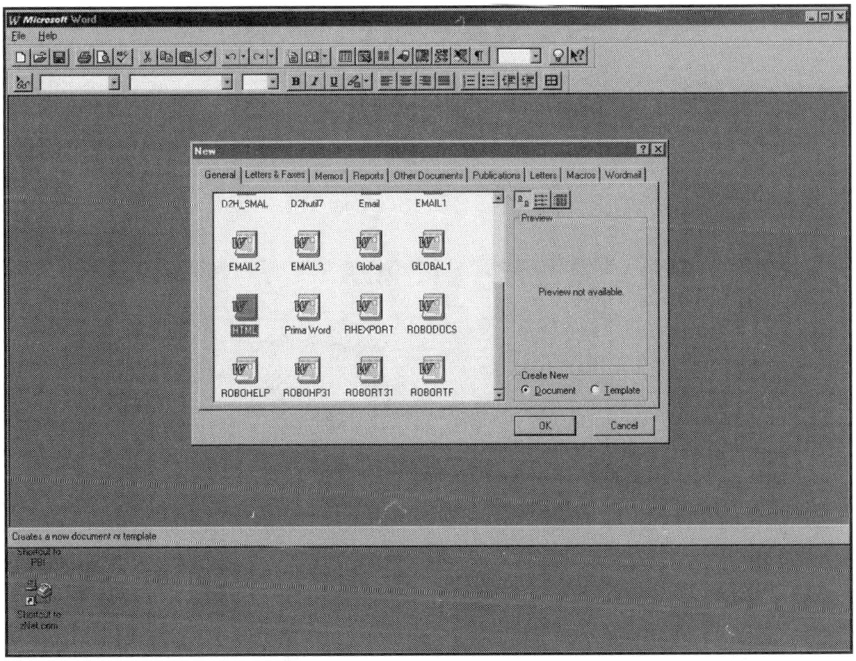

Figure 4-2
A new HTML format document

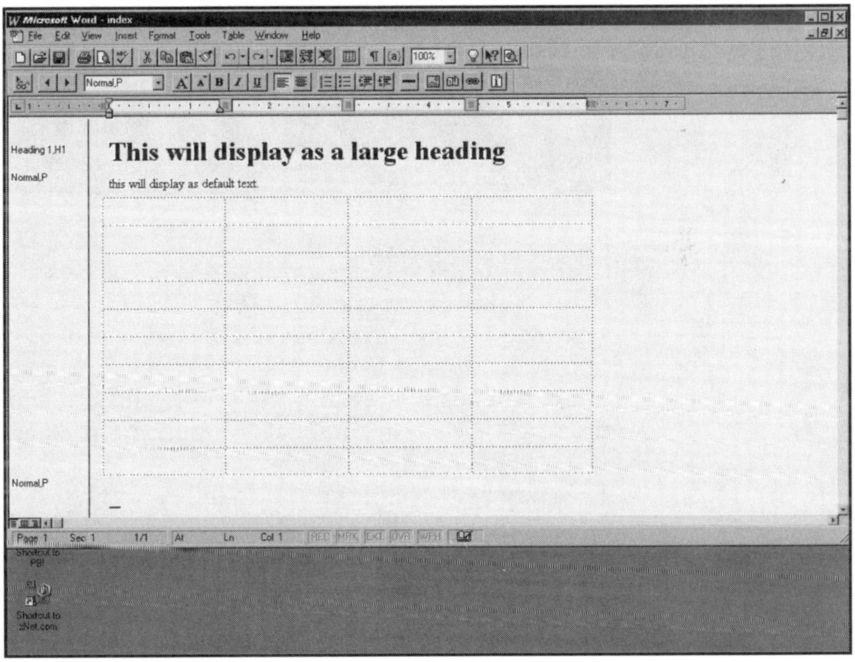

Figure 4-3
A document displayed in Word HTML

Access Internet Assistant

The Microsoft Access Internet Assistant is an add-in wizard. It can be installed from the Add-In selection in the Tools menu. After it's installed, you can start it and the first screen will appear as shown in Figure 4-4.

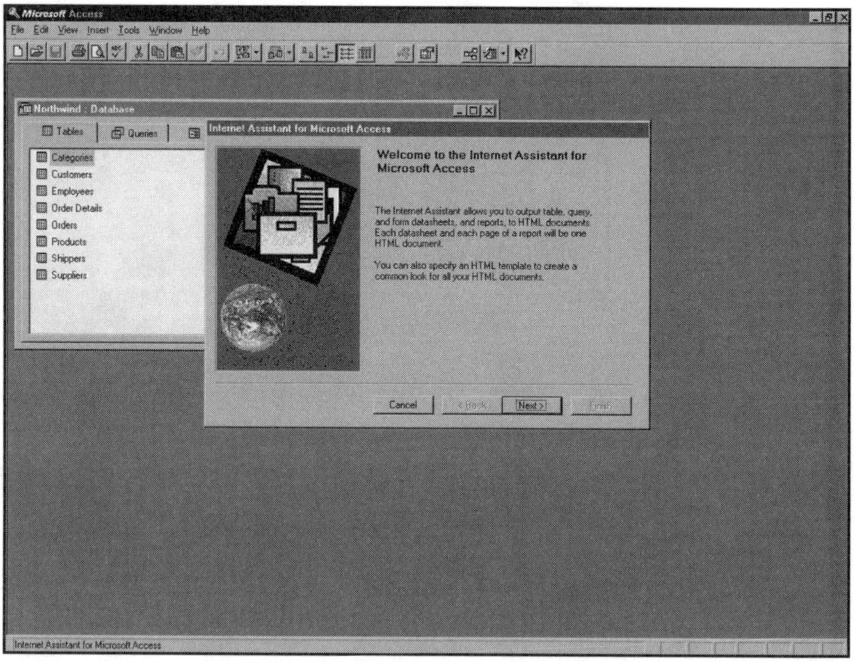

Figure 4-4 Microsoft Access Internet Assistant wizard

Clicking the Next button will take you to the screen shown in Figure 4-5. Here you can select the various types of information that you would like to export to HTML. The idea is to provide a way to make database information available to others on the Internet or intranet. The selections made in this example are arbitrary, and you would probably make different selections in a live situation. This is simply a way to give you a start.

The (very bad looking) result is shown in Figure 4-6. This page would definitely require work but would probably look better if the wizard had been run with more careful attention to details.

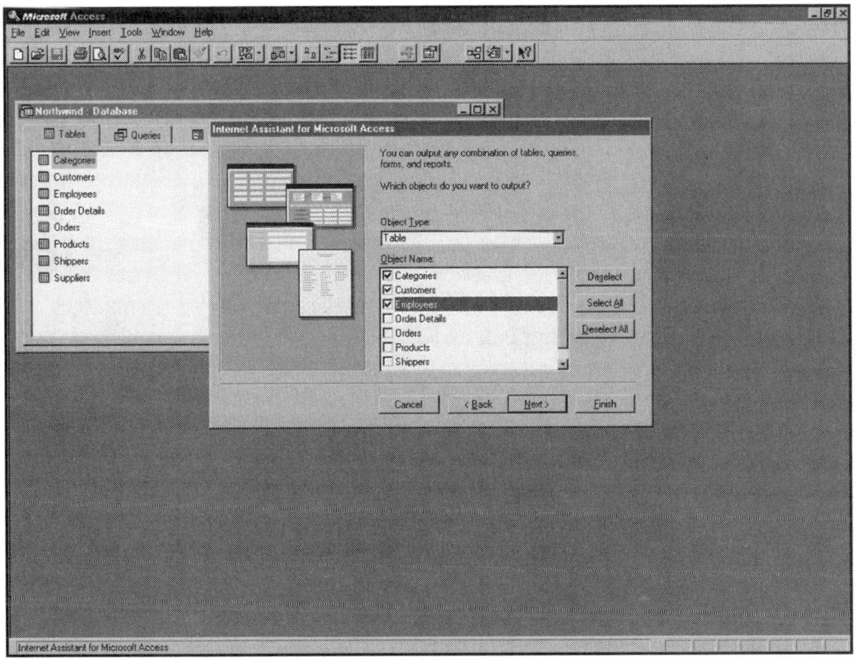

Figure 4-5
The Internet Assistant for Access selections

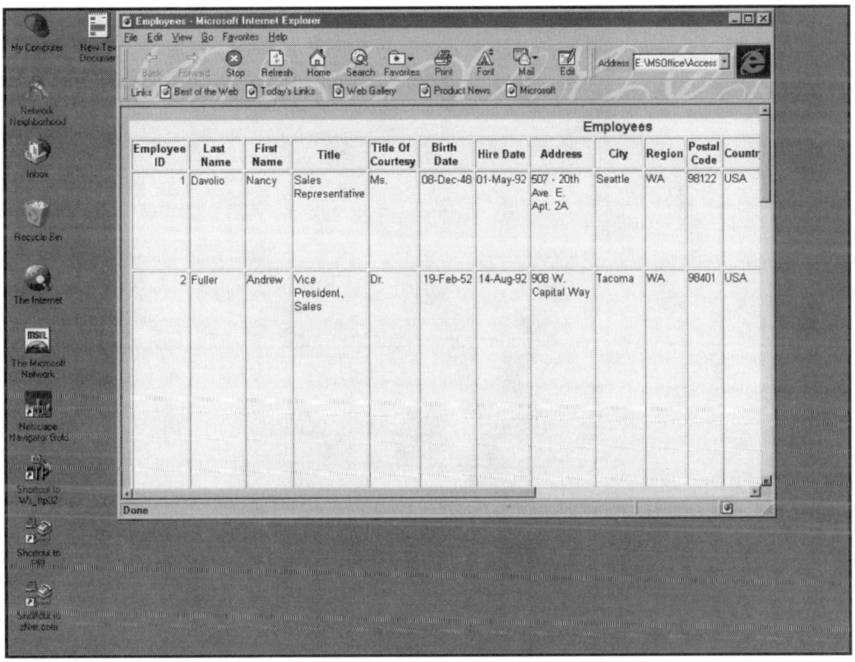

Figure 4-6
The Output from Internet Assistant for Access

Excel Internet Assistant

Internet Assistant for Excel is supplied as HTML.XLA. To begin, move this file to the Excel Libraries directory. Start Excel and, from the Tools menu, select Add-Ins.... In the dialog box, choose Internet Assistant Wizard. This will add the Internet Assistant wizard to your project, and it should now be part of the Tools menu. You can start it at any time to convert your spreadsheet information to HTML. Again, I'm showing only the steps. Figure 4-7 shows the first step of the Excel HTML wizard requiring you to select a range of cells to use. The default is A1.

Figure 4-7
Step 1 in Internet Assistant Wizard for Excel

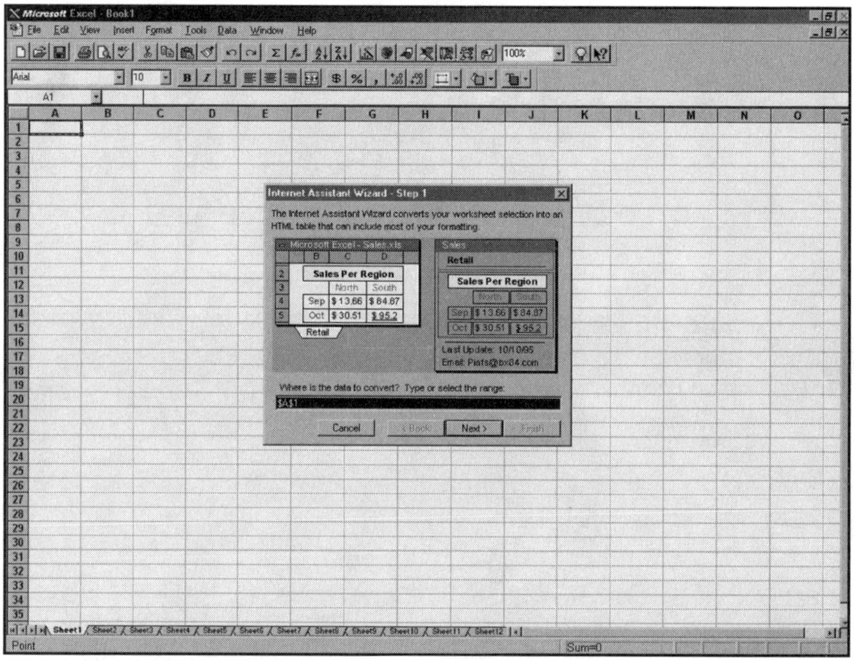

The second step allows you to indicate whether you want a full HTML document or a table that you can insert into an existing document. The Wizard step is shown in Figure 4-8.

Step 3 allows you to specify a title and header with a possible description. It also allows you to apply footer information, as shown in Figure 4-9.

Step 4 (Figure 4-10) and Step 5 (Figure 4-11) let you make decisions about how much formatting to retain and the filename to use.

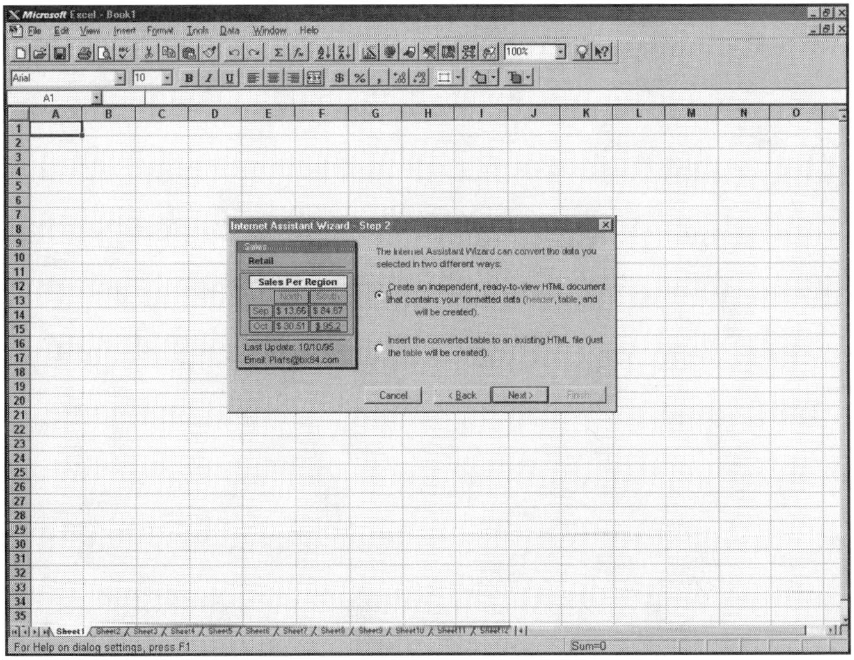

Figure 4-8
Step 2: Selecting the form of output

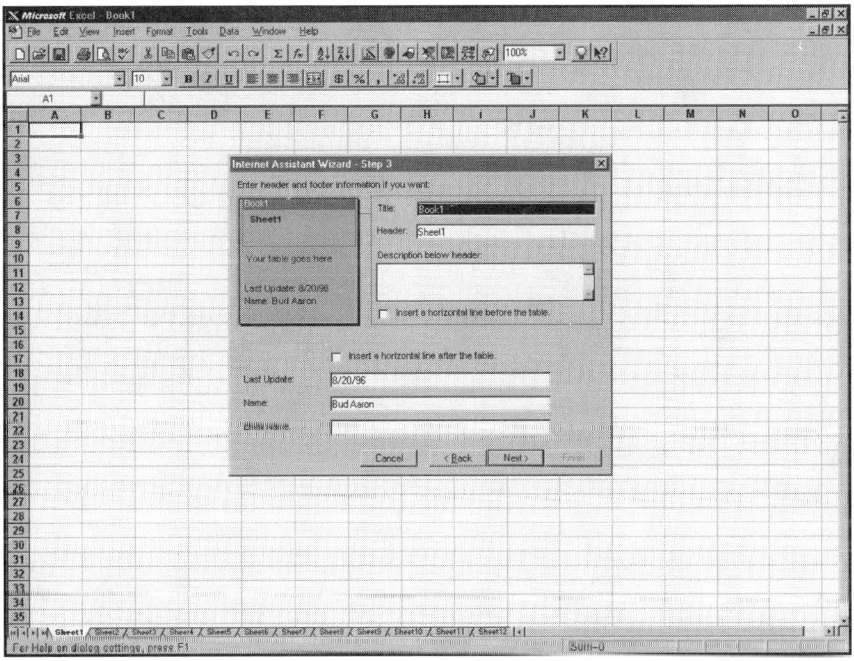

Figure 4-9
Step 3: Specifying the HTML header and footer

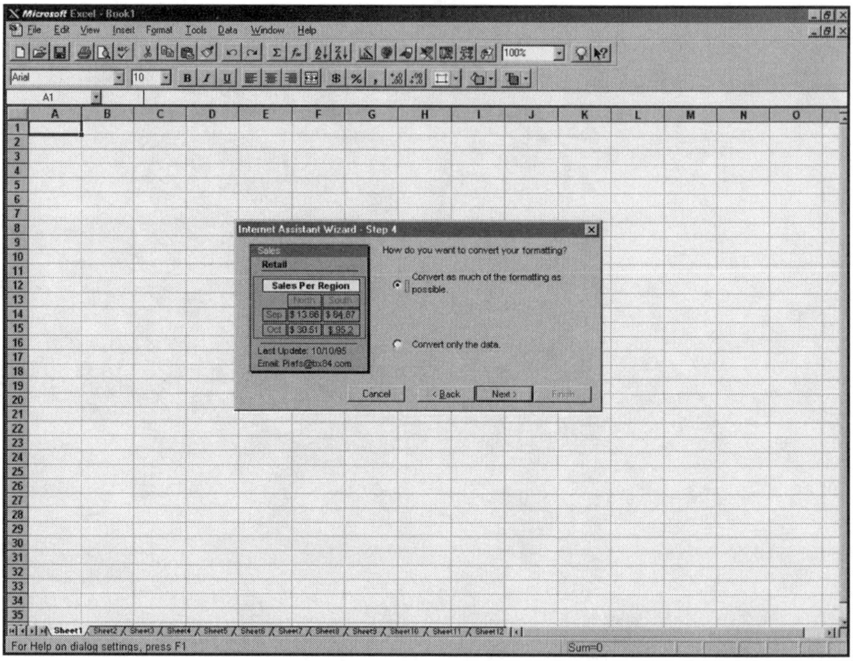

Figure 4-10 Step 4: Setting up formatting

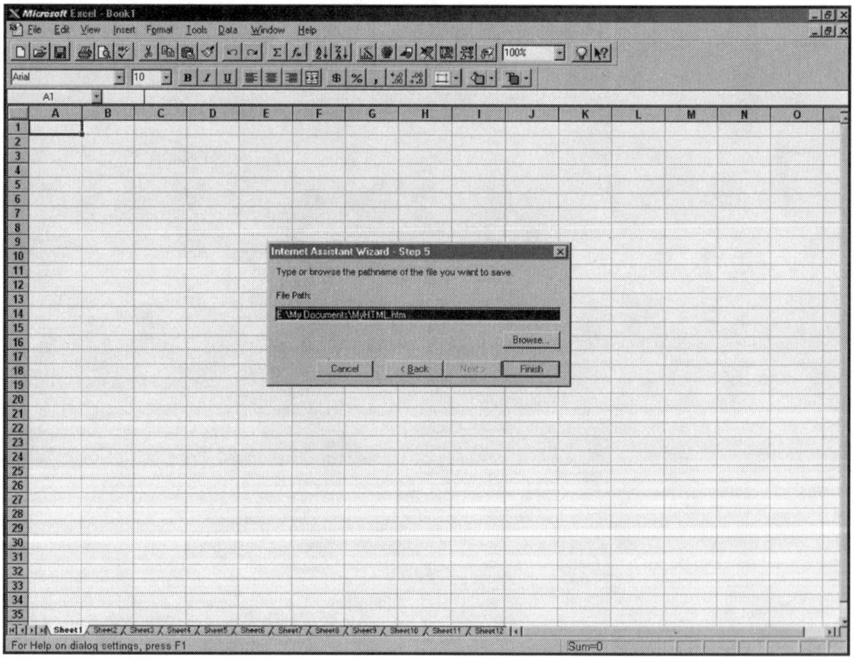

Figure 4-11 Step 5: The finished file name

Again, these are devices to allow information to be converted to HTML for display in Web browsers. They are not editors, just HTML generators. If you find that you have a need to generate this type of information, you will know which tools to use.

PowerPoint Internet Assistant

Microsoft's PowerPoint presentation software is an excellent package to use in creating presentations. When you add Internet Assistant for PowerPoint and know that you can distribute the PowerPoint Animation Player software, you have a powerful tool for generating presentations for the Web. I'm not going into detail here on the use of these tools.

Figure 4-12 shows the the File menu for PowerPoint. Notice that Export for Internet actually allows three possiblities on the submenu. You also have an election to Export as HTML.

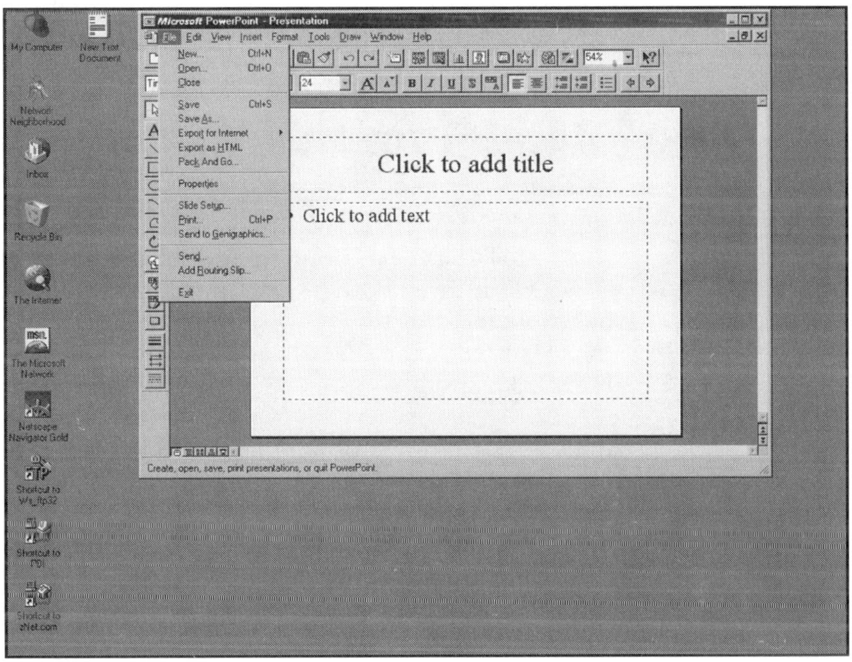

Figure 4-12
PowerPoint Internet Assistant choices

Schedule+ Internet Assistant

The final item in this group is Internet Assistant for Schedule+. The File menu for Schedule+ with Internet Assistant installed is shown in Figure 4-13. You may find a use for it on some of your Internet or intranet sites.

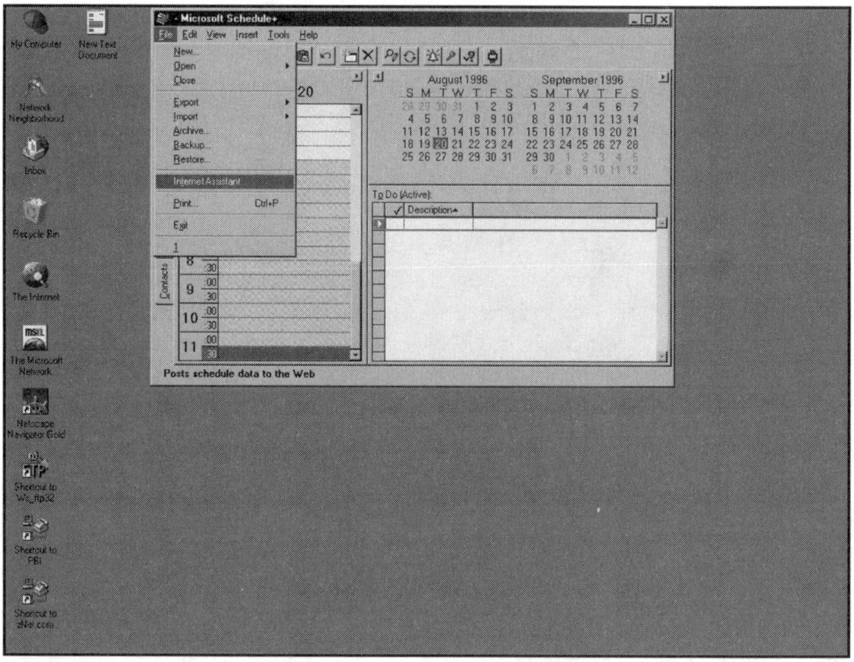

Figure 4-13 Schedule+ File menu with Internet Assistant installed

HoTMetaL Pro 3.0

I feel that SoftQuad's HoTMetaL Pro is worth mentioning here as another WYSIWYG HTML editor. This package is loaded with features. HoTMetaL has been around for a number of years and has steadily improved both its appearance and capability. As an editor, it has more features than FrontPage at this time. It does frames, forms, tables, scripts, style sheets, and virtually everything else contained in HTML 3.2 and beyond.

It also has a number of templates and wizards that you can use. HoTMetaL is shown running in Figure 4-14. Be aware that you can turn off the tag display. Be aware also that HoTMetaL will arrange your HTML to suit its model of the world, and you can use Rules Checking to ensure that the HTML you do is rigorously correct.

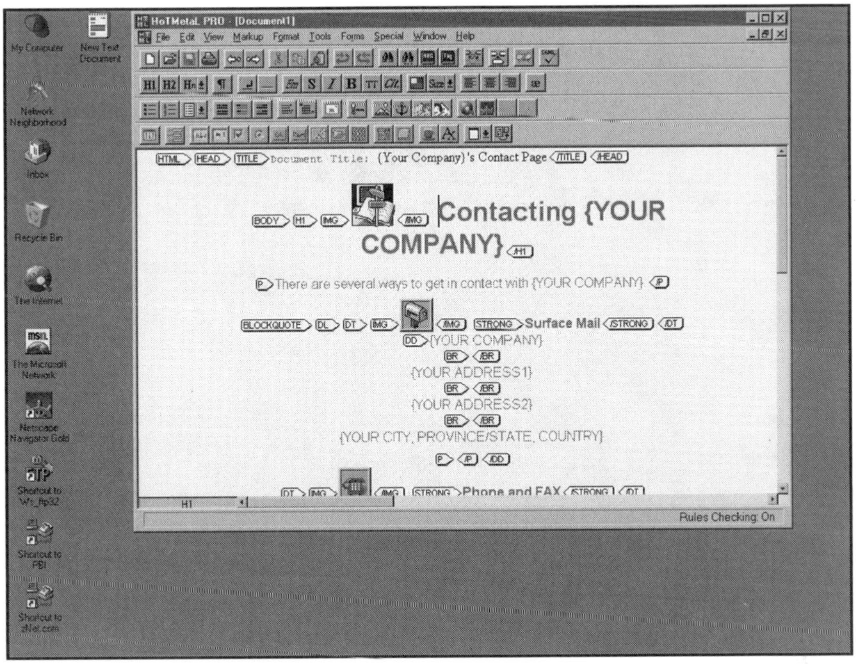

Figure 4-15
SoftQuad's HoTMetaL Pro 3.0

> **NOTE:**
> **HoTMetaL is by SoftQuad, and more information can be found at** `http://www.sq.com/homepro.htm`**. You might also find HomeSite a useful editing tool. HomeSite 1.2 is included on the CD in the back of the book. It is freeware. HomeSite 2.0, a shareware version with additional capabilities, is available from** `http://www.dexter.com/homesite.html`**.**

Summary

In this short chapter, I've touched on a number of alternative HTML editors and HTML generators. All except for HoTMetaL are free for download from Microsoft and are included on the CD in the back of this book. I have done little more than present the tools to let you know that they exist and to let you know how to get them started.

Up to this point, I've given you information that is rather generic to the Internet. In the next chapter, I go into detail on the ActiveX Control Pad and show you how to use the tools included with it. It might even be good to tell you here that the ActiveX Control Pad is heavy on right-click pop-up menus. Anytime you think that something is missing, think right-click. This will begin the real trip into the world of ActiveX technology.

Chapter 5

Using the ActiveX Control Pad

In previous chapters, I covered a lot of territory. The Internet presence that Microsoft is establishing under the ActiveX umbrella is far reaching, and it is sometimes difficult to get a handle on all the disparate pieces. For that reason, and before I jump into more pieces of the puzzle, I'm taking some time to get you better acquainted with the majority of those pieces. I'm also including a couple of tables that will work in conjunction with HTML (see Appendix B for an HTML reference). First, let me give you a Web address where you will find much additional, up-to-date information:

`http://www.microsoft.com/workshop/.`

This is the most likely place to find new information, new software, and upgrades to old software as this technology advances, and it will most certainly advance. If something doesn't work or if things appear to have changed, look to Microsoft's workshop Web site. Practically everything involved with ActiveX can be found from the URL preceding this paragraph. It might be worth taking an hour to visit the site and browse the contents.

The Technologies

First, take a brief look at the technologies that make up the ActiveX initiative.

ActiveX Conferencing

This encompasses the product called NetMeeting and the ActiveX Conferencing SDK that allows other vendors to build products like NetMeeting or products that work with NetMeeting and other Microsoft conferencing products. I discuss NetMeeting in Chapters 1 and 2.

ActiveX Components

ActiveX Components (controls) can come from Microsoft or other vendors. These COM controls are designed to work with many different products and, frequently, on the Internet. It is not mandatory that an ActiveX Control or component be Internet enabled. ActiveX components can be developed using a number of languages. You will find additional material in Chapters 8 and 9.

ActiveX SDK

The ActiveX SDK will ultimately be completely incorporated into the Win32 SDK. At present it is a separate software development kit provided as a free download from Microsoft. It is the kit that allows the development of Internet-enabled ActiveX Controls.

CAB

CAB is Microsoft's high compression "cabinet" technology. Higher levels of compression are provided making this an ideal way to deliver and install components as Internet downloads. It is also an excellent way to deliver software on disk. You will find additional information available at the Microsoft Web site mentioned previously.

Code Signing

Microsoft's code signing (Internet shrink-wrap) using Authenticode is a crypto signing system based on RSA Data Security public key encryption technology. It ensures that the software downloaded to your machine is from a vendor who has been identified and given credentials from VeriSign. It also ensures that the software has not been tampered with and thus does not contain viruses.

Common Internet File System

This is a complex specification working its way through various standards committees. It will provide a common file system for use on all computer platforms. It is especially significant for the Internet, where servers and clients may have a number of different file systems in place.

CryptoAPI

Cryptography is a complex subject both in terms of its mathematical structure and in terms of how it can best be used in a communications environment. It is also hampered by the fact that, since World War II, it has been considered a nonexportable munition! It is today the subject of hot wars and discussions between Congress, the U.S. Administration, and users of the Internet.

Microsoft has simplified things by building a CryptoAPI. This API is designed to talk to the *real* cryptography engine provided by a number of third-party Crypto Service Providers (CSPs). In this way, the strength and treatment of the underlying technology is kept separate from the implementation. Thus, the CryptoAPI can be freely distributed. whereas the CSP part is subject to the International Traffic in Arms (ITAR) regulations of the U.S. government.

Internet Server Application Programming Interface (ISAPI)

Microsoft's Internet Information Server (IIS) is designed to run under Windows NT Server. To allow outside vendors to make use of the functionality provided in that package, Microsoft has made the Internet Server API available to the development community. ISAPI can be used to build extensions to the functionality of IIS.

Microsoft Internet Security Framework

This is the overall security strategy being taken by Microsoft and Microsoft partners. It involves a number of specifications, and includes the following:

- Personal Information Exchange (PFX)
- Private Communications Technology (PCT)
- Point-to-Point Tunneling Protocol (PPTP)

- Secure Electronic Transactions (SET)
- Security Technologies

Further information can be found in the table of contents at Microsoft's workshop Web site mentioned previously.

WebPost API and WinInet API

These are two additional APIs that make the inner functionality of Internet Mail, Internet News, and Internet Explorer available for use by other vendors.

ActiveX Scripting

I cover ActiveX scripting, the scripting object model, and scripting using the ActiveX Control Pad in this chapter.

As you can see, the ActiveX initiative covers a broad range of technology and functionality. I give you additional insight into these pieces as the book progresses.

Products

A number of products are already in place to support the ActiveX initiative. In addition, Internet Explorer 4.0 (Nashville) is to be released in the fairly near future. This product will integrate the Windows 95/Windows NT 4.0 desktop with the Internet. Possibly, a a new *full* release of Windows 95 or Windows NT will never come about. If you consider that virtually the entire system is built of components, you may see only releases of new drives, new DLLs, and new interfaces. Internet Explorer 4.0 will certainly be a new front-end.

Keep the component orientation of the various pieces of this technology in mind as you review the software presently available.

Internet Explorer with VBScript, JScript, and VRML

Internet Explorer 3.0 is the Internet browser presently available from Microsoft. It is also an ActiveX Document container. It incorporates the VBScript engine, the JavaVM, and the Virtual Reality Modeling Language engine. If you install the full system, it also installs Mail, News, and the HTML Layout control discussed later. The amount of functionality incorporated into Internet Explorer will probably increase with time. Internet Explorer (MSIE30M.EXE) is available for free download from `http://www.microsoft.com/ie/` with the functionality mentioned previously.

Microsoft NetMeeting

NetMeeting is the ActiveX Conferencing tool made available as a working application. NetMeeting is available for free download. NetMeeting is discussed in more detail in Chapters 1 and 2.

Microsoft Viewers

Viewers are available for Word, Excel, and PowerPoint. Either Microsoft or another vendor could possibly supply viewers for other document content. In fact, Adobe's Acrobat is such a reader. With the viewers, users can open and read documents without having the underlying application on their machine. Viewers are available for free download.

FrontPage and the Internet Assistants

These products constitute the currently available authoring tools or HTML generators available from Microsoft other than ActiveX Control Pad—the subject of this chapter and of the next item. FrontPage is a commercial product; the Assistants are available for free download from Microsoft's free download area. You can get to the free download area from `http://www.microsoft.com/`. FrontPage is covered in Chapter 3.

ActiveX Control Pad and the HTML Layout Control

This application, which appears deceptively simple, will be developed fully in this chapter. This just seemed a good place to update you on what exists as of today in the ActiveX world. The ActiveX Control Pad is available as a free download from Microsoft's free download area mentioned previously.

Internet Information Server

The Internet Information Server is Microsoft's World Wide Web server software. This software runs `www.microsoft.com` on six quad Pentium computers. Each computer has 512MB of RAM and 10GB of SCSI hard disk storage. Connection to the Net is over three DS3 lines. The site handles 14,000,000 visitors a day. IIS is supplied as part of Windows NT Server and requires Windows NT Server to run.

dbWeb

dbWeb provides the ability (on the server side) to build database functionality into Web sites. It is ODBC compliant. The ability to process user information and provide database connectivity is one of the less-than-perfect parts of the Internet. dbWeb provides part of the answer. It is a free download from Microsoft's free download area.

Visual Basic, Visual C++, and Visual J++

These products are some of the available development environments to author ActiveX controls or Java applets. They are all commercial products available in your local computer store. They are *not* necessary for most of this book, but Visual C++ would help in Chapter 9.

Extra Help

I am including some tables that will give you more help with HTML. Table 5-1 is a list of HTML tags supported by Internet Explore 3.0. The list is in alphabetical order and includes the relevant attributes for each tag with an indication of the supporting specification, if any. You will note that some tags are from Netscape and others are from IE 3.0. Tags that are not HTML may be working their way through standards committees.

Table 5-2 is a list of characters. Each of these characters can be included in HTML code or scripted either as decimal codes (&#192, for example) or using HTML À. Please note that the preceding ampersand and trailing semicolon must be included in your HTML code.

Table 5-1
Tags, attributes, and source specification

Tag	Attribute	Originally Specified
!DOCTYPE		HTML 3.2
A		
A	HREF	HTML 2
A	NAME	HTML 2
A	REL	HTML 3.2
A	REV	HTML 3.2
A	TARGET	Netscape
A	TITLE	HTML 3.2
ADDRESS		HTML 2

Tag	Attribute	Originally Specified
APPLET		HTML 3.2
APPLET	ALIGN	HTML 3.2
APPLET	ALT	HTML 3.2
APPLET	CODE	HTML 3.2
APPLET	CODEBASE	HTML 3.2
APPLET	HEIGHT	HTML 3.2
APPLET	HSPACE	HTML 3.2
APPLET	NAME	HTML 3.2
APPLET	PARAM NAME	HTML 3.2
APPLET	VSPACE	HTML 3.2
APPLET	WIDTH	HTML 3.2
AREA		
AREA	COORDS	IE 3.0
AREA	HREF	IE 3.0
AREA	NOHREF	IE 3.0
AREA	SHAPE	IE 3.0
AREA	TARGET	Netscape
B		HTML 2.0
BASE		
BASE	HREF	HTML 2.0
BASE	TARGET	Netscape
BASEFONT		
BASEFONT	COLOR	Netscape 2.0
BASEFONT	FACE	Netscape 2.0
BASEFONT	SIZE	Netscape
BGSOUND		
BGSOUND	LOOP	IE 3.0
BGSOUND	SRC	IE 3.0
BIG		HTML 3.2
BLOCKQUOTE		HTML 2.0
BODY		HTML 2.0
BODY	ALINK	HTML 2.0

continues

Table 5-1
Continued

Tag	Attribute	Originally Specified
BODY	BACKGROUND	HTML 3.2
BODY	BGCOLOR	Netscape
BODY	BGPROPERTIES	IE 2.0
BODY	LEFTMARGIN	IE 2.0
BODY	LINK	Netscape
BODY	TEXT	Netscape
BODY	TOPMARGIN	IE 2.0
BODY	VLINK	Netscape
BR		
BR	CLEAR	HTML 3.2
CAPTION		
CAPTION	ALIGN	HTML 3.2
CENTER	Netscape	
CITE		HTML 2.0
CODE		HTML 2.0
COL		HTML 3.2
COL	ALIGN	HTML 3.2
COL	SPAN	HTML 3.2
COLGROUP		HTML 3.2
COLGROUP	ALIGN	HTML 3.2
COLGROUP	VALIGN	HTML 3.2
COMMENT		HTML 2.0
DD		HTML 2.0
DFN		HTML 2.0
DIR		HTML 2.0
DIV		HTML 3.2
DL		HTML 2.0
DT		HTML 2.0
EM		HTML 2.0
EMBED		HTML 2.0
EMBED	SRC	HTML 2.0
EMBED	WIDTH	HTML 2.0
EMBED	HEIGHT	HTML 2.0

Tag	Attribute	Originally Specified
EMBED	PALETTE	HTML 2.0
EMBED	NAME	HTML 2.0
EMBED	OPTIONAL PARAM=	HTML 2.0
FONT		
FONT	COLOR	IE 3.0
FONT	FACE	IE 3.0
FONT	SIZE	Netscape
FORM		
FORM	ACTION	HTML 2.0
FORM	METHOD	HTML 2.0
FORM	TARGET	Netscape
FRAME		
FRAME	FRAMEBORDER	IE 3.0
FRAME	MARGINHEIGHT	Netscape
FRAME	MARGINWIDTH	Netscape
FRAME	NAME	Netscape
FRAME	NORESIZE	Netscape
FRAME	SCROLLING	Netscape
FRAME	SRC	Netscape
FRAMESET		
FRAMESET	COLS	Netscape
FRAMESET	FRAMEBORDER	IE 3.0
FRAMESET	FRAMESPACING	IE 3.0
FRAMESET	ROWS	Netscape
Hn		HTML 2
Hn	ALIGN	HTML 3.2
HR		HTML 2
HR	ALIGN	HTML 3.2
HR	COLOR	IE 3.0
HR	NOSHADE	Netscape
HR	SIZE	Netscape
HR	WIDTH	Netscape

continues

Table 5-1
Continued

Tag	Attribute	Originally Specified
HTML		HTML 2.0
I		HTML 2.0
IFRAME		
IFRAME	FRAMEBORDER	IE 3.0
IFRAME	MARGINHEIGHT	Netscape
IFRAME	MARGINWIDTH	Netscape
IFRAME	NAME	Netscape
IFRAME	NORESIZE	Netscape
IFRAME	SCROLLING	Netscape
IFRAME	SRC	Netscape
IMG		
IMG	ALIGN	HTML 3.2
IMG	ALT	HTML 2
IMG	BORDER	HTML 3.2
IMG	CONTROLS	IE 3.0
IMG	DYNSRC	IE 3.0
IMG	HEIGHT	HTML 3.2
IMG	HSPACE	HTML 3.2
IMG	ISMAP	HTML 3.2
IMG	LOOP	IE 3.0
IMG	SRC	HTML 2
IMG	START	IE 3.0
IMG	USEMAP	IE 3.0
IMG	VSPACE	HTML 3.2
IMG	WIDTH	HTML 3.2
INPUT		
INPUT	ALIGN	HTML 2.0
INPUT	CHECKED	HTML 2.0
INPUT	MAXLENGTH	HTML 2.0
INPUT	NAME	HTML 2.0
INPUT	SIZE	HTML 2.0
INPUT	SRC	HTML 2.0
INPUT	TYPE	HTML 2.0

Tag	Attribute	Originally Specified
INPUT	TYPE=CHECKBOX	HTML 2.0
INPUT	TYPE=HIDDEN	HTML 2.0
INPUT	TYPE=IMAGE	HTML 2.0
INPUT	TYPE=PASSWORD	HTML 2.0
INPUT	TYPE=RADIO	HTML 2.0
INPUT	TYPE=RESET	HTML 2.0
INPUT	TYPE=SUBMIT	HTML 2.0
INPUT	TYPE=TEXT	HTML 2.0
INPUT	TYPE=TEXTAREA	HTML 2.0
INPUT	VALUE	HTML 2.0
ISINDEX		HTML 2.0
ISINDEX	ACTION	Netscape
ISINDEX	PROMPT	HTML 3.2
KBD		HTML 2.0
LI		HTML 2.0
LI	TYPE Netscape	
LI	VALUE	Netscape
LINK		IE 3.0
LISTING		HTML 2.0
MAP		
MAP	NAME	IE 3.0
MARQUEE		IE 3.0
MARQUEE	ALIGN	IE 3.0
MARQUEE	BEHAVIOR	IE 3.0
MARQUEE	BGCOLOR	IE 3.0
MARQUEE	DIRECTION	IE 3.0
MARQUEE	HEIGHT	IE 3.0
MARQUEE	HSPACE	IE 3.0
MARQUEE	LOOP	IE 3.0
MARQUEE	SCROLLAMOUNT	IE 3.0
MARQUEE	SCROLLDELAY	IE 3.0
MARQUEE	VSPACE	IE 3.0
MARQUEE	WIDTH	IE 3.0

continues

Table 5-1
Continued

Tag	Attribute	Originally Specified
MENU		HTML 2
META		
META	CONTENT	Netscape
META	HTTP-EQUIV	Netscape
META	NAME	HTML 3.2
NOBR		Netscape
NOFRAMES		Netscape
OL		HTML 2
OL	START	Netscape
OL	TYPE	Netscape
OPTION		HTML 2
OPTION	SELECTED	HTML 2
OPTION	VALUE	HTML 2
P		HTML 2
P	ALIGN	HTML 3.2
PLAINTEXT		HTML 2
PRE		HTML 2
S		HTML 2
SAMP		HTML 2
SCRIPT		HTML 3.2
SCRIPT	LANGUAGE	HTML 3.2
SELECT		HTML 2
SELECT	MULTIPLE	HTML 2
SELECT	NAME	HTML 2
SELECT	SIZE	HTML 2
SMALL		HTML 3.2
SPAN		HTML 3.2
STRIKE		HTML 2
STRONG		HTML 2
SUB		HTML 3.2
SUP		HTML 3.2
TABLE		
TABLE	ALIGN	HTML 3.2

Tag	Attribute	Originally Specified
TABLE	BACKGROUND	IE 3.0
TABLE	BGCOLOR	IE 3.0
TABLE	BORDERCOLOR	IE 3.0
TABLE	BORDERCOLORDARK	IE 3.0
TABLE	BORDERCOLORLIGHT	IE 3.0
TABLE	FRAME	HTML 3.2
TABLE	RULES	HTML 3.2
TBODY		HTML 3.2
TD		
TD	ALIGN	HTML 3.2
TD	BGCOLOR	IE 3.0
TD	BORDERCOLOR	IE 3.0
TD	BORDERCOLORDARK	IE 3.0
TD	BORDERCOLORLIGHT	IE 3.0
TD	VALIGN	IE 3.0
TFOOT		HTML 3.2
TH		
TH	ALIGN	HTML 3
TH	BGCOLOR	IE 3.0
TH	BORDERCOLOR	IE 3.0
TH	BORDERCOLORDARK	IE 3.0
TH	BORDERCOLORLIGHT	IE 3.0
TH	VALIGN	IE 3.0
THEAD		HTML 3
TITLE		HTML 2
TR		
TR	ALIGN	HTML 3
TR	BGCOLOR	IE 3.0
TR	BORDERCOLOR	IE 3.0
TR	BORDERCOLORDARK	IE 3.0
TR	BORDERCOLORLIGHT	IE 3.0
TR	VALIGN	IE 3.0
TT		HTML 2

continues

Table 5-1
Continued

Tag	Attribute	Originally Specified
U		HTML 2
UL		HTML 2
VAR		HTML 2
WBR		Netscape
XMP		HTML 2

Table 5-2
The character set

Character		Decimal Code	HTML Description
À	À	À	Uppercase A, grave accent
à	à	à	Lowercase a, grave accent
Á	Á	Á	Uppercase A, acute accent
á	á	á	Lowercase a, acute accent
Â	Â	Â	Uppercase A, circumflex
â	â	â	Lowercase a, circumflex
Ã	Ã	Ã	Uppercase A, tilde
ã	ã	ã	Lowercase a, tilde
Ä	Ä	Ä	Uppercase A, diæresis / umlaut
ä	ä	ä	Lowercase a, diæresis / umlaut
Å	Å	Å	Uppercase A, ring
å	å	å	Lowercase a, ring
Æ	Æ	Æ	Uppercase AE ligature
æ	æ	æ	Lowercase ae ligature
Ç	Ç	Ç	Uppercase C, cedilla
ç	ç	ç	Lowercase c, cedilla
È	È	È	Uppercase E, grave accent
è	è	è	Lowercase e, grave accent
É	É	É	Uppercase E, acute accent
é	é	é	Lowercase e, acute accent
Ê	Ê	Ê	Uppercase E, circumflex
ê	ê	ê	Lowercase e, circumflex
Ë	Ë	Ë	Uppercase E, diæresis / umlaut
ë	ë	ë	Lowercase e, diæresis / umlaut
Ì	Ì	Ì	Uppercase I, grave accent

Character	Decimal Code	HTML	Description
ì	ì	ì	Lowercase i, grave accent
Í	Í	Í	Uppercase I, acute accent
í	í	í	Lowercase i, acute accent
Î	Î	Î	Uppercase I, circumflex
î	î	î	Lowercase i, circumflex
Ï	Ï	Ï	Uppercase I, diæresis / umlaut
ï	ï	ï	Lowercase i, diæresis / umlaut
Đ	Ð	Ð	Uppercase Eth, Icelandic
∂	ð	ð	Lowercase eth, Icelandic
Ñ	Ñ	Ñ	Uppercase N, tilde
ñ	ñ	ñ	Lowercase n, tilde
Ò	Ò	Ò	Uppercase O, grave accent
ò	ò	ò	Lowercase o, grave accent
Ó	Ó	Ó	Uppercase O, acute accent
ó	ó	ó	Lowercase o, acute accent
Ô	Ô	Ô	Uppercase O, circumflex
ô	ô	ô	Lowercase o, circumflex
Õ	Õ	Õ	Uppercase O, tilde
õ	õ	õ	Lowercase o, tilde
Ö	Ö	Ö	Uppercase O, diæresis / umlaut
ö	ö	ö	Lowercase o, diæresis / umlaut
Ø	Ø	Ø	Uppercase O, slash
ø	ø	ø	Lowercase o, slash
Ù	Ù	Ù	Uppercase U, grave accent
ù	ù	ù	Lowercase u, grave accent
Ú	Ú	Ú	Uppercase U, acute accent
ú	ú	ú	Lowercase u, acute accent
Û	Û	Û	Uppercase U, circumflex
û	û	û	Lowercase u, circumflex
Ü	Ü	Ü	Uppercase U, diæresis / umlaut
ü	ü	ü	Lowercase u, diæresis / umlaut

continues

Table 5-2
Continued

Character		Decimal Code	HTML Description
·	Ý	Ý	Uppercase Y, acute accent
″	ý	ý	Lowercase y, acute accent
°	Þ	Þ	Uppercase Thorn, Icelandic
˛	þ	þ	Lowercase thorn, Icelandic
ß	ß	ß	Lowercase sharp s, German sz
ÿ	ÿ	ÿ	Lowercase y, diæresis / umlaut
	&#00;		Unused
	&#01;		Unused
	&#02;		Unused
	&#03;		Unused
	&#04;		Unused
	&#05;		Unused
	&#06;		Unused
	&#07;		Unused
	&#08;		Unused
			Horizontal tab
	Line feed
	&#11;		Unused
			Unused
	Carriage Return
	&#14;		Unused
	&#15;		Unused
	&#16;		Unused
	&#17;		Unused
	&#18;		Unused
	&#19;		Unused
	&#20;		Unused
	&#21;		Unused
	&#22;		Unused
	&#23;		Unused
	&#24;		Unused
	&#25;		Unused

Character	Decimal Code	HTML	Description
	&#26;		Unused
	&#27;		Unused
	&#28;		Unused
	&#29;		Unused
	&#30;		Unused
	&#31;		Unused
			Space
!	!		Exclamation mark
"	"	"	Quotation mark
#	#		Number sign
$	$		Dollar sign
%	%		Percent sign
&	&	&	Ampersand
'	'		Apostrophe
(	(		Left parenthesis
)	)		Right parenthesis
*	*		Asterisk
+	+		Plus sign
,	,		Comma
-	-		Hyphen
.	.		Period
/	/		Solidus (slash)
0	0		Number 0
1	1		Number 1
2	2		Number 2
3	3		Number 3
4	4		Number 4
5	5		Number 5
6	6		Number 6
7	7		Number 7
8	8		Number 8

continues

Table 5-2
Continued

Character		Decimal Code	HTML Description
9	9		Number 9
:	:		Colon
;	;		Semi-colon
<	<	<	Less than
=	=		Equals sign
>	>	>	Greater than
?	?		Question mark
@	@		Commercial at
A	A		Uppercase A
B	B		Uppercase B
C	C		Uppercase C
D	D		Uppercase D
E	E		Uppercase E
F	F		Uppercase F
G	G		Uppercase G
H	H		Uppercase H
I	I		Uppercase I
J	J		Uppercase J
K	K		Uppercase K
L	L		Uppercase L
M	M		Uppercase M
N	N		Uppercase N
O	O		Uppercase O
P	P		Uppercase P
Q	Q		Uppercase Q
R	R		Uppercase R
S	S		Uppercase S
T	T		Uppercase T
U	U		Uppercase U
V	V		Uppercase V
W	W		Uppercase W
X	X		Uppercase X

Character	Decimal Code	HTML Description
Y	Y	Uppercase Y
Z	Z	Uppercase Z
[	[	Left square bracket
\	\	Reverse solidus (backslash)
]	]	Right square bracket
^	^	Caret
_	_	Horizontal bar (underscore)
`	`	Acute accent
a	a	Lowercase a
b	b	Lowercase b
c	c	Lowercase c
d	d	Lowercase d
e	e	Lowercase e
f	f	Lowercase f
g	g	Lowercase g
h	h	Lowercase h
I	i	Lowercase i
j	j	Lowercase j
k	k	Lowercase k
l	l	Lowercase l
m	m	Lowercase m
n	n	Lowercase n
o	o	Lowercase o
p	p	Lowercase p
q	q	Lowercase q
r	r	Lowercase r
s	s	Lowercase s
t	t	Lowercase t
u	u	Lowercase u
v	v	Lowercase v
w	w	Lowercase w

continues

Table 5-2
Continued

Character	Decimal Code	HTML	Description
x	x		Lowercase x
y	y		Lowercase y
z	z		Lowercase z
{	{		Left curly brace
|				Vertical bar
}	}		Right curly brace
~	~		Tilde
	&#127;		Unused
≠	€		Unused
			Nonbreaking Space
¡	¡		Inverted exclamation
¢	¢		Cent sign
£	£		Pound sterling
¤	¤		General currency sign
¥	¥		Yen sign
¦	¦		Broken vertical bar
§	§		Section sign
¨	¨		Diæresis / Umlaut
©	©		Copyright
ª	ª		Feminine ordinal
«	«		Left angle quote, guillemot left
¬	¬		Not sign
–			Soft hyphen
®	®		Registered trademark
¯	¯		Macron accent
°	°		Degree sign
±	±		Plus or minus
≈	²		Superscript two
Δ	³		Superscript three
´	´		Acute accent
µ	µ		Micro sign
¶	¶		Paragraph sign

Character	Decimal Code	HTML Description
·	·	Middle dot
¸	¸	Cedilla
¹	¹	Superscript one
º	º	Masculine ordinal
»	»	Right angle quote, guillemot right
¼	¼	Fraction one-fourth
½	½	Fraction one-half
¾	¾	Fraction three-fourths
¿	¿	Inverted question mark

The Scripting Object Model

This chapter is about gluing HTML and ActiveX controls together using scripting. You might think that scripting applies only to ActiveX controls. The fact is that you can script virtually any object, HTML tag, or any other element. This chapter concentrates on VBScript because both VBScript and JScript have strong similarities. In Chapter 7, I show you how to use either language to accomplish similar tasks.

To understand scripting, you can take a look at the scripting object model as it is implemented in Internet Explorer 3.0. Doing so will give you good insight into the rest of the material. The Internet Explorer scripting object model is a structure for embedding and controlling Visual Basic Scripting Edition (VBScript) and JScript. The model is designed to provide compatibility with Netscape Navigator for existing pages, while easing the transition to VBScript. The object model is compatible with the object model used in the JScript language. The object model is accessible from any scripting language that is compatible with the ActiveX scripting framework.

> NOTE:
> **All properties and methods that modify HTML content must be called during HTML parse time. The code must reside in a script block that runs inline during the loading of the HTML document. This is called *immediate execution* in the ActiveX scripting model.**

The Object Hierarchy and Scope

There are eleven objects associated with a running instance of Internet Explorer. The objects are as follows:

A Window	The Window is the top level object.
Frames	Frames, as in HTML frames. Frames can be multiple.
History	One History object with one to multiple entries.
Navigator	Just below the window object. Makes code compatible with Netscape Navigator.
Location	The Location object represents the current URL.
Script	As in VBScript of JScript.
Document	The Document object is just below the Window object. It may have an array of links, an array of anchors, and an array of forms.
Link	Resides as an array of links below the Document object.
Anchor	Resides as an array of anchors below the Document object.
Form	Resides as an array of forms below the Document object. Forms can contain arrays of Elements.
Element	Resides below the Document. Elements are intrinsic HTML controls or objects. Controls are placed on a document with the <INPUT> tag, whereas objects are placed on a document with the <OBJECT> tag.

A graphical view of this hierarchy is shown in Figure 5-1.

The top level object is a Window. Every window contains:

Frame	Each frame is a window that has its own properties, including a document.
History	This object is used to Navigate the history list from the browser.
Navigator	The navigator object contains information about the browser application.
Location	Provides information about the location of the window's URL.
Script	Any scripting function defined using the SCRIPT element in the window scope.
Document	The document in the current window.

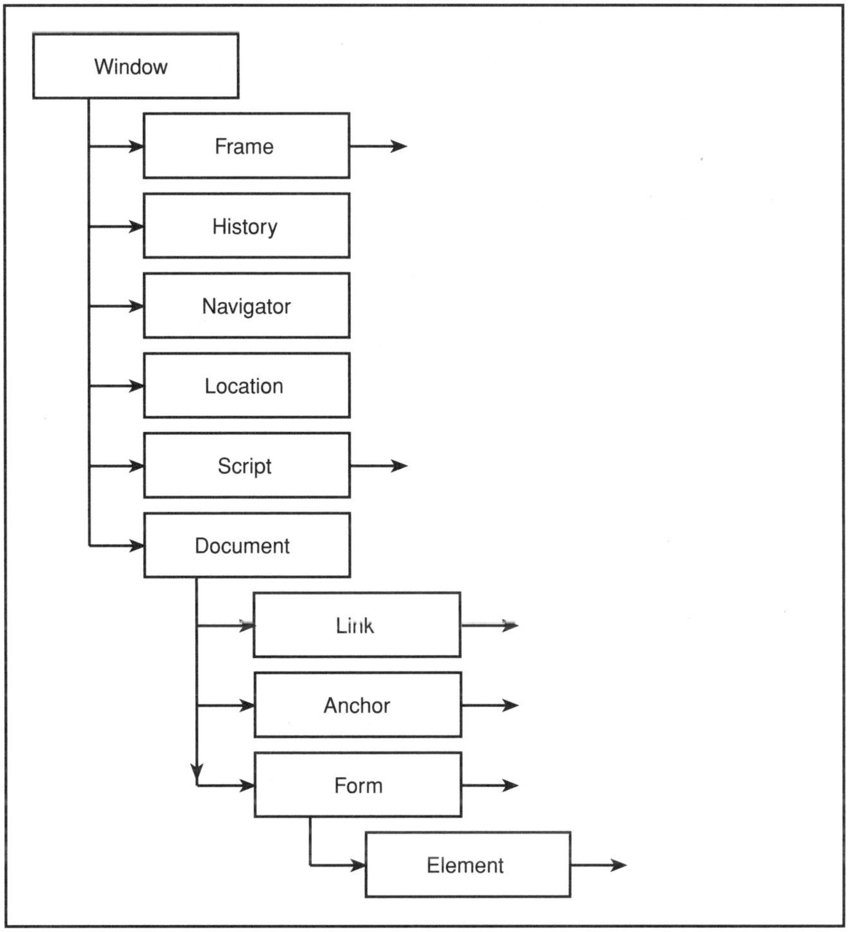

Figure 5-1 The scripting object hierarchy

The Window object properties can be referenced directly by scripts in the Window scope. So, for example, script authors do not need to use:

```
window.name
```

to reference a window name. Just use:

```
name
```

It is also possible to call scripts from one window object to another. To execute the script `myscript` in the topmost window, use:

```
top.myscript()
```

The Document Object

Just below the Window objects is the Document object. It may contain:

Link	**An array of hyperlinks in the document**
Anchor	**An array of forms in the document**
Form	**An array of anchors in the document**

Scripts are in the window object's scope and are accessed with something like Document.property to access document properties. To get the title of the document, use:

```
<script language="VBScript">
'...
string1 = document.title     'Move the title to string1
'...
</script>
```

The Form Object

To access forms in a document, you can either refer by name or through the form array. You might use the following:

```
<form name="Form1">
  <input type="button" name="Button1" value="Click me"
onClick="clicked">
</form>
```

Then, access the object named `Button1` either by name:

```
<script language="VBScript">
sub clicked
  document.Form1.Button1.value="I was clicked"  ' access the form
by name
end sub
</script>
```

or by index:

```
<script language="VBScript">
sub clicked
  document.forms(0).Button1.value=" I was clicked" ' access the
form by index
```

```
end sub
</script>
```

An unusual part of document naming is contained elements that are not form types. Scripts can refer to these elements directly, without using `document`. So, if you create an object called `myObject`, it can be referenced directly in script as follows:

```
<object name="myObject" ... >
</object>
<script language="VBScript">
sub foo
    myObject.color = "green"    ' access the form by index
end sub
</script>
```

The final scope level is a form. The Form object contains:

Element	The array of objects and intrinsic controls contained in the form.

Scripts can reside either in the form object or in the window object. If a script is outside the form, it needs to access the elements in the form, either by name or through the form array. If the script resides inside the form, it can access the elements in the form directly.

```
<form name="Form1">
<input type="button" name="Button1" value="Click me">
<script for="Button1" event="onClick" language="VBScript">
alert "I've been clicked"
document.Form1.Button1.value="Quit it!"  ' usual use the fully
qualified name
Button1.value=" Quit it!"  ' but you might use this.It's in the
scope of form
</script>
</form>
<script language="VBScript">
sub foo
document.Form1.Button1.value="Quit it!"  " here we can only use
the fully qualified name
end sub
</script>
```

Placing Scripts in HTML Code

There are three basic ways to place scripts in HTML: contain them in the <SCRIPT> tag, use attributes of HTML elements, or use a custom URL type.

The SCRIPT Element

The SCRIPT element is used to add scripts to HTML. SCRIPT elements can be added anywhere in the document HEAD or BODY. The SCRIPT element can be used to reference external scripts, using the SRC attribute, and to include script statements within the HTML document. There can be multiple SCRIPT elements in the HEAD or BODY, allowing script statements to be placed near a corresponding FORM element.

The following is a simple VBScript example:

```
<SCRIPT language="VBScript">
'... Additional VBScript statements ...
</SCRIPT>
```

The same example in JScript would read:

```
<SCRIPT language="JScript">
//... Additional JScript statements ...
</SCRIPT>
```

Evaluation of SCRIPT

SCRIPT elements are evaluated as the document is loaded. All code is executed at load time. For functions such as `document.write`, the order of script elements can affect the output of the document. For example, the page:

```
<HTML><HEAD>
<TITLE>New Page</TITLE>
</HEAD><BODY>
<script language="JScript">
document.write ("Hello ActiveX.")
</script>
This is ActiveX Scripting.
</BODY></HTML>
```

results in:

```
Hello ActiveX. This is ActiveX Scripting
```

ss shown in Figure 5-2.

Figure 5-2
Hello ActiveX

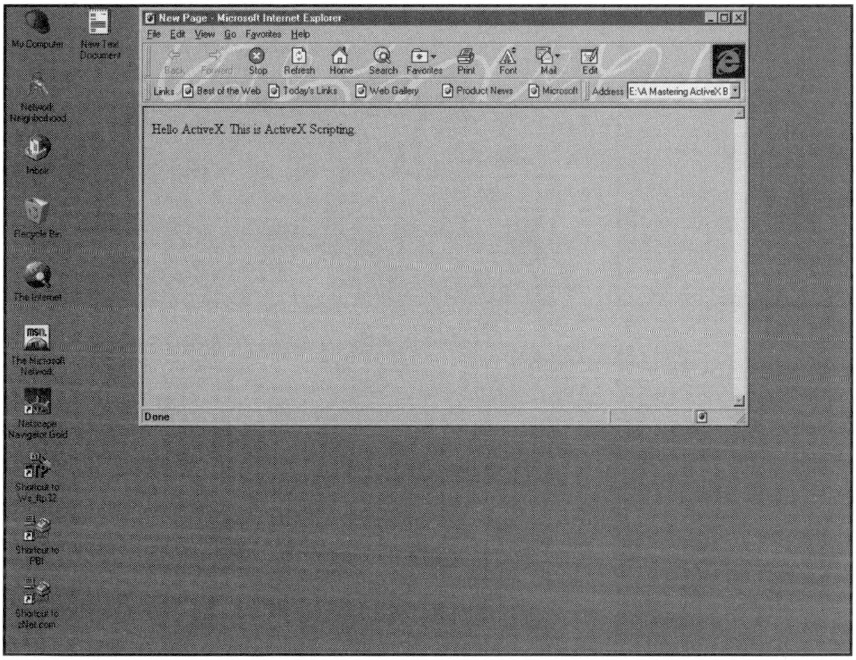

On the other hand, the following page:

```
<HTML>
<HEAD>
<TITLE>New Page</TITLE>
</HEAD>
<BODY>
This is ActiveX Scripting.
<script language="VBScript">
document.write ("Hello ActiveX.")
</script>
</BODY>
</HTML>
```

results in:

```
This is ActiveX Scripting. Hello ActiveX
```

as shown in Figure 5-3.

Figure 5-3
This is ActiveX Scripting

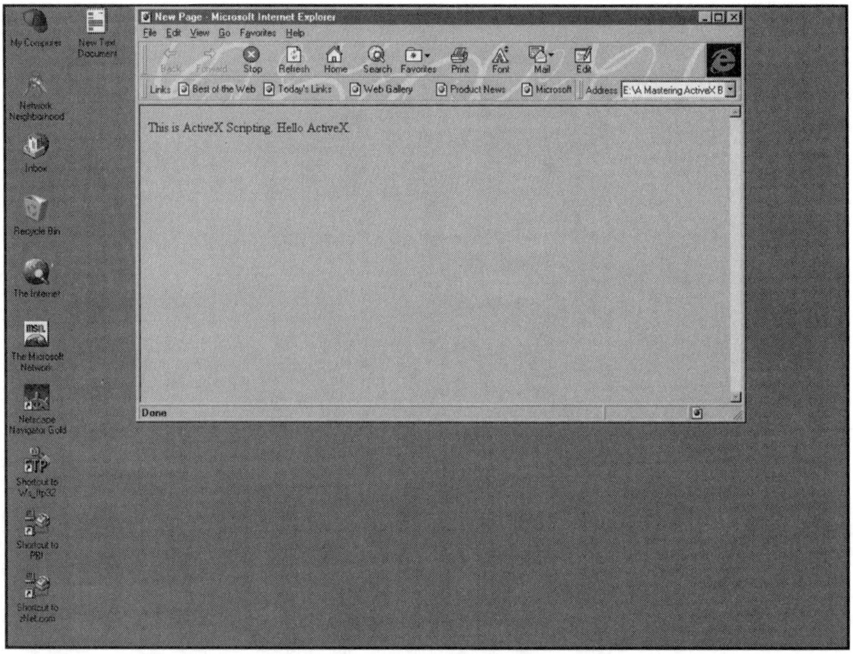

Attempts to reference objects that have not yet been loaded will fail because script statements are evaluated as the document is loaded. If these objects are defined by HTML elements that occur later in the document, they simply don't yet exist.

The Document object's write method can insert objects such as buttons using the INPUT tag, ActiveX controls using the OBJECT tag, and text.

Using Scripts as HTML Attributes

You can insert scripts as attributes to element tags in HTML. These attributes match events on the elements, and the script is executed when the event is fired. This method can be used for HTML intrinsic elements, such as forms, buttons, or links, but does not work for items inserted using the OBJECT tag.

The following example uses this syntax in VBButton to handle the `onClick` event. To demonstrate the ability to combine multiple scripting languages on the same page, the script for VBButton is implemented in VBScript, and that for JSButton in JScript.

```
<HTML>
<HEAD>
<TITLE>New Page</TITLE>
</HEAD>
<BODY>
<form name="Form1">
<input type="button" name="VBButton" value="Guess who I am! "
onClick="vbpress" language="VBScript">
<input type="button" name="JSButton" value="How About Me!"
onClick="jspress()" language="JScript">
</form>
<script language="VBSCRIPT">
sub vbpress
document.Form1.VBButton.value="I'm VBScript"
alert "Did you guess VBScript?"
end sub
</script>
<script language="JScript">
function jspress()
{
document.Form1.JSButton.value="I'm JScript"
alert("Did you guess and are you impressed?")
}
</script>
</BODY>
</HTML>
```

NOTE:
Use the language attribute on the input tag to indicate the script's language. If no language is specified, the script defaults to the language of the most recently encountered script block. If no script block has been encountered, the language defaults to JScript.

The result of running this code is shown in Figure 5-4

Figure 5-4 The Button script running

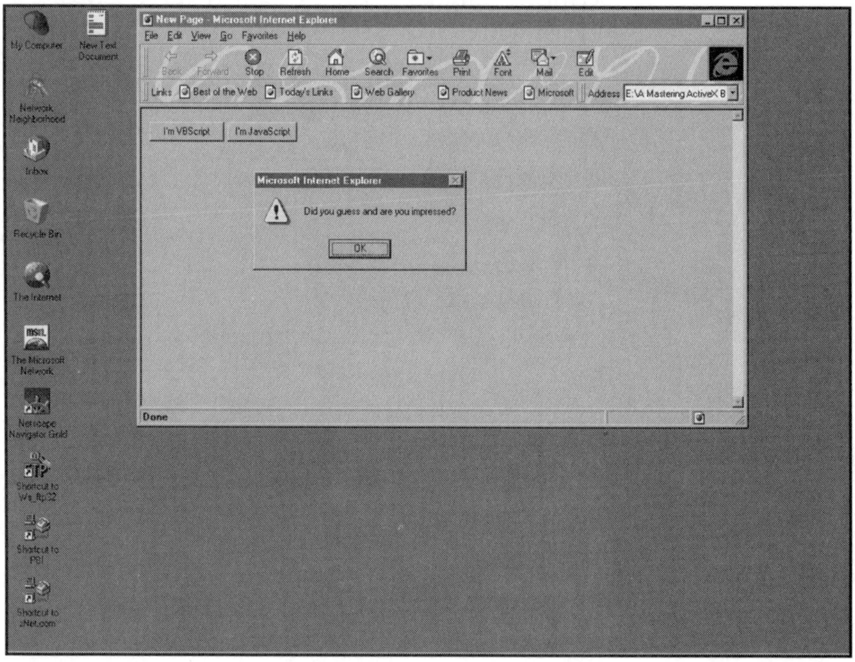

The elements FORM, INPUT, BODY, and A (anchor) support this syntax, but with differing events. The individual tags are discussed later in this chapter.

An Alternative Using SCRIPT

You can use the SCRIPT element with the `FOR="object" EVENT="eventname"` syntax. This method can be used for any named elements, and for any elements inserted using the OBJECT tag. The following example is similar to the previous "script" example, but it uses different syntax:

```
<form name="Form1">
<input type="button" name="VBButton" value="VBScript">
<script for="VBButton" event="onClick" language="VBScript">
alert "I'm VBScript again."
document.Form1.VBButton.value="Want to click me again?"
</script>
</form>
```

The result of running this script is shown in Figure 5-5.

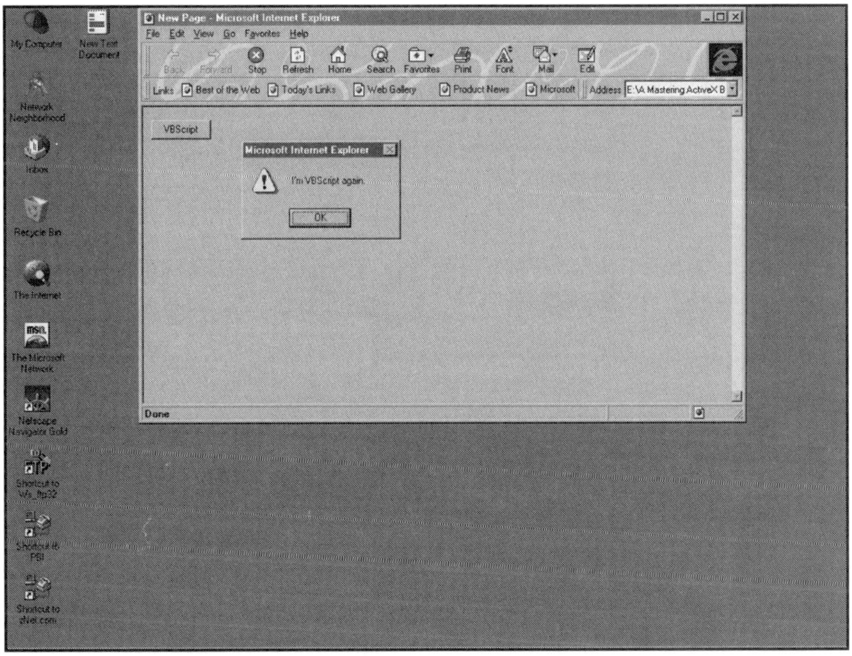

Figure 5-5
Another button script running

Using Scripts in URLs

The A (anchor) element can invoke scripts with a custom URL. In this way, a script will execute when the user clicks on a hyperlink. This URL type is valid in any context, but is most useful when used with the A element. For example:

```
<A HREF="JScript:alert('hi there')">Click me to see a message.<A>
```

displays an alert message box that contains the text `'hi there'`.

Syntax

```
script-engine:script-code
```

Executes the script code using the script engine when the URL is resolved. For example, to execute a script when the user clicks on a hyperlink, use:

```
<title>JScript example</title>
```

```
<A HREF=" JScript:alert(document.title)">Click here to see the
title of the current document..</A>
```

Notice that the script is executed in the context of the current page, which means that `document.title` evaluates to the document containing the script.

The result of running the three lines of code shown previously is shown in Figure 5-6.

Figure 5-6
Using scripting with URLs and the Anchor tag

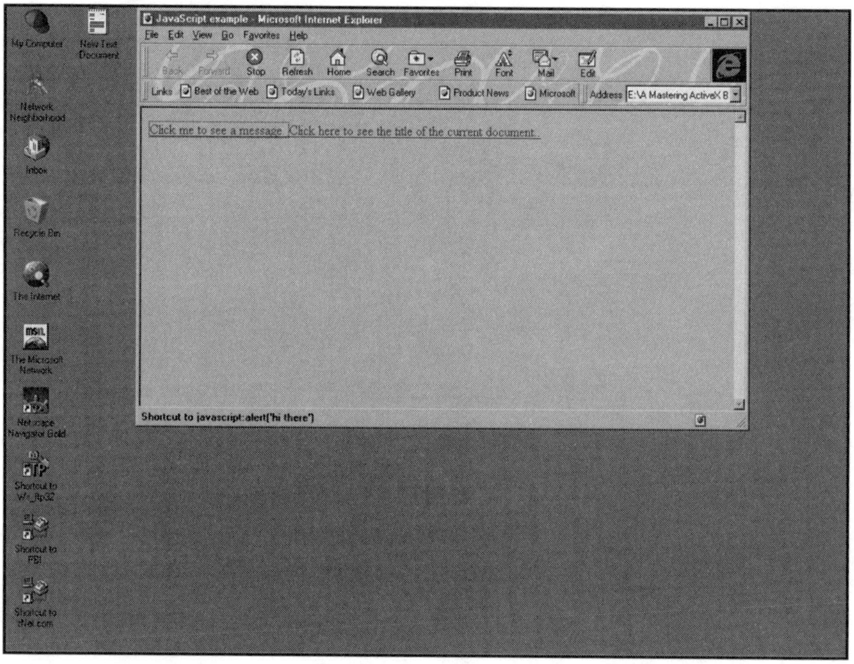

As you've seen, the scripting capabilities in Internet Explorer 3.0 are powerful. In addition to scripting HTML code and Internet Explorer objects, later I show you how to use this same capability to script ActiveX controls.

In the next pages, I cover, in alphabetical order, the objects, methods, functions, properties, events, and statements for Visual Basic Scripting Edition. I then show you the capabilities of the ActiveX Control Pad for helping with your scripting projects.

Visual Basic Scripting Edition

Table 5-3 lists the reserved words (key words) in VBScript.

Table 5-3 VBScript Reserved Word List

Abs	And	AppActivate	Array	Asc
Atn	Base	Beep	BOF	Boolean
Byte	Call	Case	Cbool	Cbyte
Ccur	Cdate	CDbl	ChDir	ChDrive
Choose	Chr	Cint	Circle	Clear
CLng	Close	Command	Compare	Const
Cos	CreateObject	CSng	CStr	CurDir
Currency	Cvar	CVErr	Date	DateAdd
DateDiff	DatePart	DateSerial	DateValue	DDB
Def	Dim	Dir	Do	DoEvents
Double	Each	Else	End	Environ
EOF	Eqv	Erase	Err	Error
Exit	Exp	Explicit	FileAttr	FileCopy
FileDateTime	FileLen	Fix	For	Format
FreeFile	Function	FV	Get	GetAttr
GetObject	GoSub	GoTo	Hex	Hour
If	Imp	Input	Instr	Int
Integer	IPmt	IRR	Is	IsArray
IsDate	IsEmpty	IsError	IsMissing	IsNull
IsNumeric	IsObject	Kill	Lbound	Lcase
Left	Len	Let	Like	Line
Loc	Lock	LOF	Log	Long
Loop	Lset	Ltrim	Me	Mid
Minute	MIRR	MkDir	Mod	Module
Month	Name	New	Next	Not
Now	Nper	NPV	Object	Oct
On	Open	Option	Or	Pmt
PPmt	Print	Private	Property	Pset
Public	Put	PV	QBColor	Raise
Randomize	Rate	ReDim	Reset	Resume
Return	RGB	Right	RmDir	Rnd

continues

Table 5-3 Continued

Rset	Rtrim	Second	Seek	Select
SendKeys	Set	SetAttr	Sgn	Shell
Sin	Single	SLN	Space	Spc
Sqr	Static	Stop	Str	StrComp
StrConv	String	Sub	Switch	SYD
Tab	Tan	Then	Time	Timer
TimeSerial	TimeValue	Trim	TypeName	Ubound
Ucase	Unlock	Val	Variant	VarType
Weekday	Wend	While	Width	With
Write	Xor	Year		

Objects

anchor (anchors array)

Syntax

```
<A [HREF = OptionalLocationObject]
NAME = "AnchorObjectName"
 [TARGET = "WindowObjectName"]>
TextForAnchor
</A>
```

Description

This is the standard HTML anchor for hypertext links.

Properties

Length Returns the number of anchors in a document.

Methods

None

Event Handlers

None

Property of

document

Examples

```
<HTML>
<HEAD><BODY BGCOLOR=WHITE TEXT=BLACK><TITLE>Color
Values</TITLE></HEAD>
<BODY>
<H1>Color Values</H1>
<P>
You can also use these string literals to set the color in the
HTML reflections of these properties.
</P>
<P>
<A HREF="clrchrt.htm#A">A</A> <A HREF="clrchrt.htm#B">B</A>
<A HREF="clrchrt.htm#C">C</A> <A HREF="clrchrt.htm#D">D</A>
<A HREF="clrchrt.htm#E">E</A> <A HREF="clrchrt.htm#F">F</A>
<A HREF="clrchrt.htm#G">G</A> <A HREF="clrchrt.htm#H">H</A>
<A HREF="clrchrt.htm#I">I</A> <A HREF="clrchrt.htm#J">J</A>
<A HREF="clrchrt.htm#K">K</A> <A HREF="clrchrt.htm#L">L</A>
<A HREF="clrchrt.htm#M">M</A> <A HREF="clrchrt.htm#N">N</A>
<A HREF="clrchrt.htm#O">O</A> <A HREF="clrchrt.htm#P">P</A>
<A HREF="clrchrt.htm#Q">Q</A> <A HREF="clrchrt.htm#R">R</A>
<A HREF="clrchrt.htm#S">S</A> <A HREF="clrchrt.htm#T">T</A>
<A HREF="clrchrt.htm#U">U</A> <A HREF="clrchrt.htm#V">U</A>
<A HREF="clrchrt.htm#W">W</A> <A HREF="clrchrt.htm#X">X</A>
<A HREF="clrchrt.htm#Y">Y</A> <A HREF="clrchrt.htm#Z">Z</A>
</P>
<PRE>
The following red, green, and blue values are in Decimal and
Hexadecimal.
            Decimal                   Hexadecimal
Color       R       G       B       R       G       B
</PRE>
<H1><A NAME="A">A</A></H1>
<PRE>
aliceblue               240       248       255       F0       F8       FF
</PRE>
<H1><A NAME="X">X</A></H1>
<P></P>
```

```
<H1><A NAME="Y">Y</A></H1>
<PRE>
yellow          255     255     0       FF      FF      00
</PRE>
<HR COLOR=yellow ALIGN=LEFT SIZE=15 WIDTH=50%>
<PRE>
yellowgreen     154     205     50      9A      CD      32
</PRE>
<HR COLOR=yellowgreen ALIGN=LEFT SIZE=15 WIDTH=50%>
<H1><A NAME="Z">Z</A></H1>
<P></P>
</BODY>
</HTML>
```

Related Items

Link (Object)

Anchors (method)

button (client)

Syntax

```
<INPUT TYPE = "BUTTON"
NAME = "ButtonObjectName"
VALUE = "ButtonObjectText"
[onClick = "EventHandlerObject"]>
```

Description

This defines a button on an HTML form.

Properties

name

value

Methods

click

Event Handlers

onClick

Property of

form

Examples

```
<INPUT TYPE="BUTTON" NAME="BttnReset" VALUE="Reset"
OnClick="resettower">
```

Related Items

form

reset

submit

checkbox (client)

Syntax

```
<INPUT TYPE = "CHECKBOX"
NAME = "CheckboxObjectName"
[CHECKED]
[onClick = "EventHandlerObject"]>
CheckboxObjectText
```

Description

This is an HTML form standard check box.

Properties

checked

defaultChecked

name

value

Methods

click

Event Handlers

onClick

Property of

form

Examples

```
<FORM>
<PRE>
Enter Your Name          <INPUT TYPE="TEXT" NAME="NAMEEMAIL"
SIZE="40" MAXLENGTH="40"><BR>
Enter Your Address       <INPUT TYPE="TEXT" NAME="ADDRESSSNAIL-
MAIL" SIZE="40" MAXLENGTH="40"><BR>
Enter Your City          <INPUT TYPE="TEXT" NAME="CITYEMAIL"
SIZE="40" MAXLENGTH="30"><BR>
Enter Your State         <INPUT TYPE="TEXT" NAME="STATEEMAIL"
SIZE="10" MAXLENGTH="6"><BR>
Enter Your Zip           <INPUT TYPE="TEXT" NAME="ZIPEMAIL"
SIZE="20" MAXLENGTH="10"><BR>
Enter Your Email Address <INPUT TYPE="TEXT" NAME="ADDRESSEMAIL"
SIZE="40" MAXLENGTH="40"><BR>
</PRE>
<P></P>
<INPUT TYPE="CHECKBOX" NAME="CBACTIVEX" CHECKED=TRUE>ActiveX<BR>
<INPUT TYPE="CHECKBOX" NAME="CBHTML">HTML 3.2<BR>
<INPUT TYPE="CHECKBOX" NAME="CBVBSCRIPT">VB Script<BR>
<INPUT TYPE="CHECKBOX" NAME="CBJSCRIPT">JScript<BR>
<P></P>
<INPUT TYPE="SUBMIT" NAME="CMDBSUBMIT">
<INPUT TYPE="RESET" NAME="CMDBRESET"><BR>
<P></P>
</FORM>
```

document

Syntax

```
<BODY
BACKGROUND = "imageobject"
BGCOLOR = "colorobject"
```

```
FGCOLOR = “colorobject”
LINK = “colorobjcct”
ALINK = “colorobject”
VLINK = “colorobject”
[onLoad = “eventcode”]
[onUnLoad = “eventcode”]>
</BODY>
```

Description

This is the standard HTML BODY statement.

Properties

alinkColor

anchors

bgColor

cookie

fgColor

forms

lastModified

linkColor

links

location

referrer

title

vlinkColor

Methods

clear

close

open

write

writeln

Event Handlers

None. The event handlers are actually associated with the windows object.

Property of

None

Examples

```
<BODY BGCOLOR = GOLDENROD TEXT = BLACK LINK = RED ALINK = BLUE
VLINK = VIOLET OnLoad="resettower">
```

Related Items

frame (object)

window (object)

elements (elements array)

Syntax

```
formobjectname.elements[index]

formobjectname.elements.length
```

Description

The elements array contains information about form elements.

Properties

length

Property of

form

Examples

```
<FORM NAME="MAILINFO">
<PRE>
```

```
Enter Your Name           <INPUT TYPE-"TEXT" NAME="NAMFFMAIL"
SIZE="40" MAXLENGTH="40"><BR>
Enter Your Address        <INPUT TYPE="TEXT" NAME="ADDRESSSNAIL-
MAIL" SIZE="40" MAXLENGTH="40"><BR>
Enter Your City           <INPUT TYPE="TEXT" NAME="CITYEMAIL"
SIZE="40" MAXLENGTH="30"><BR>
Enter Your State          <INPUT TYPE="TEXT" NAME="STATEEMAIL"
SIZE="10" MAXLENGTH="6"><BR>
Enter Your Zip            <INPUT TYPE="TEXT" NAME="ZIPEMAIL"
SIZE="20" MAXLENGTH="10"><BR>
Enter Your Email Address <INPUT TYPE="TEXT" NAME="ADDRESSEMAIL"
SIZE="40" MAXLENGTH="40"><BR>
</PRE>
<P></P>
<INPUT TYPE="CHECKBOX" NAME="CBACTIVEX" CHECKED=TRUE>ActiveX<BR>
<INPUT TYPE="CHECKBOX" NAME="CBHTML">HTML 3.2<BR>
<INPUT TYPE="CHECKBOX" NAME="CBVBSCRIPT">VB Script<BR>
<INPUT TYPE="CHECKBOX" NAME="CBJSCRIPT">JScript<BR>
<P></P>
<INPUT TYPE="SUBMIT" NAME="CMDBSUBMIT">
<INPUT TYPE="RESET" NAME="CMDBRESET"><BR>
<P></P>
</FORM>
<SCRIPT LANGUAGE="VBScript">
document.write(MAILINFO.elements.length)
</SCRIPT>
```

Related Items

form

Err (Object)

Syntax

```
Err[ {property|method}]
```

Description

This object contains information about runtime errors.

Properties

Description

HelpContext

HelpFile

LastDLLError

Number

Source

Methods

Clear

Raise

Event Handlers

On Error

Examples

```
On Error

document.write(Err.Number)

document.write(Err.Description)

Err.Clear
```

form (forms array)

Syntax

```
<FORM
NAME = "FormObjectName"
TARGET = "WindowObjectName"
ACTION = "ServerObjectURL"
METHOD = GET | POST
ENCTYPE = "MIMEEncodeType"
[onSubmit = "eventcode"]>
</FORM>
```

Description

This is the form tag, which allows you to create a form.

Properties

action

elements

encoding

method

target

Methods

submit

Event Handlers

onSubmit

Examples

```
<FORM NAME="MAILINFO" ACTION = "mailto:johndoe@anynet.net"
onSubmit = "SendInfo()">
<PRE>
Enter Your Name           <INPUT TYPE="TEXT" NAME="NAMEEMAIL"
SIZE="40" MAXLENGTH="40"><BR>
Enter Your Email Address <INPUT TYPE="TEXT" NAME="ADDRESSEMAIL"
SIZE="40" MAXLENGTH="40"><BR>
</PRE>
<P></P>
<INPUT TYPE="CHECKBOX" NAME="CBVBSCRIPT">VB Script<BR>
<INPUT TYPE="CHECKBOX" NAME="CBJSCRIPT">JScript<BR>
<P></P>
<INPUT TYPE="SUBMIT" NAME="CMDBSUBMIT">
<INPUT TYPE="RESET" NAME="CMDBRESET"><BR>
<P></P>
</FORM>
```

Related Items

elements (Property)

forms (Property)

frame (client)

Syntax

```
<FRAMESET
ROWS = "rowheight"
COLS = "colwidth">
FramesetDisplayText
[onLoad = "eventcode"]
[onUnload = "eventcode"]
[<FRAME NAME="frameobjectname" SRC="sourceobject">]
</FRAMESET>
```

Description

FRAMESET is used to define how the frames will be laid out on a page.

Properties

defaultStatus

frames

parent

self

status

top

window

Methods

close

MsgBox

open

InputBox

setTimeout

clearTimeout

Event Handlers

None. The event handlers are actually associated with the windows object.

Examples

```
<FRAMESET ROWS = 100 COLS = 100>
<FRAME NAME=”t1frame” SRC=”tempty.htm”>
<FRAME NAME=”t2frame” SRC=”tempty.htm”>
<FRAME NAME=”t3frame” SRC=”tempty.htm”>
</FRAMESET>
```

Related Items

document (Object)

window (Object)

frames (Property)

hidden (client)

Syntax

```
<INPUT
TYPE = “HIDDEN”
NAME = “hiddenobjectname”
[VALUE = “hiddentext”]>
```

Description

This is a text object that does not display.

Properties

defaultValue

name

value

Examples

```
<FORM>
<PRE>
Enter Your Name          <INPUT TYPE="TEXT" NAME="NAMEEMAIL"
SIZE="40" MAXLENGTH="40"><BR>
<INPUT TYPE="HIDDEN" NAME="HIDDENINFO">
Enter Your Email Address <INPUT TYPE="TEXT" NAME="ADDRESSEMAIL"
SIZE="40" MAXLENGTH="40"><BR>
</PRE>
<P></P>
<INPUT TYPE="SUBMIT" NAME="CMDBSUBMIT">
<INPUT TYPE="RESET" NAME="CMDBRESET"><BR>
<P></P>
</FORM>
```

Related Items

cookie (Property)

history (client)

Syntax

history.property

history.method

Description

This is used to return a list of the URLs that have been visited.

Properties

length

Methods

back

forward

go

Event Handlers

None

Property of

None

Examples

```
sub VBSBackUpOne
history.back
End Sub
```

Related Items

location (Object)

link (client)

Syntax

```
<A [NAME = "AnchorObjectName"]
HREF = OptionalLocationObject
TARGET = "WindowObjectName"
[onClick = "eventcode"]
[onMouseOver = "eventcode"]>
TextForLink
</A>
```

Description

This is the standard HTML link for hypertext links.

Properties

target

Methods

None

Event Handlers

onClick

onMouseOver

Property of

None

Examples

```
<HTML>
<HEAD><BODY BGCOLOR=WHITE TEXT=BLACK><TITLE>Color
Values</TITLE></HEAD>
<BODY>
<H1>Color Values</H1>
<P>
You can also use these string literals to set the color in the
HTML reflections of these properties.
</P>
<P>
<A HREF=”clrchrt.htm#A”>A</A> <A HREF=”clrchrt.htm#B”>B</A>
<A HREF=”clrchrt.htm#C”>C</A> <A HREF=”clrchrt.htm#D”>D</A>
<A HREF=”clrchrt.htm#E”>E</A> <A HREF=”clrchrt.htm#F”>F</A>
<A HREF=”clrchrt.htm#G”>G</A> <A HREF=”clrchrt.htm#H”>H</A>
<A HREF=”clrchrt.htm#I”>I</A> <A HREF=”clrchrt.htm#J”>J</A>
<A HREF=”clrchrt.htm#K”>K</A> <A HREF=”clrchrt.htm#L”>L</A>
<A HREF=”clrchrt.htm#M”>M</A> <A HREF=”clrchrt.htm#N”>N</A>
<A HREF=”clrchrt.htm#O”>O</A> <A HREF=”clrchrt.htm#P”>P</A>
<A HREF=”clrchrt.htm#Q”>Q</A> <A HREF=”clrchrt.htm#R”>R</A>
<A HREF=”clrchrt.htm#S”>S</A> <A HREF=”clrchrt.htm#T”>T</A>
<A HREF=”clrchrt.htm#U”>U</A> <A HREF=”clrchrt.htm#V”>U</A>
<A HREF=”clrchrt.htm#W”>W</A> <A HREF=”clrchrt.htm#X”>X</A>
<A HREF=”clrchrt.htm#Y”>Y</A> <A HREF=”clrchrt.htm#Z”>Z</A>
</P>
<PRE>
The following red, green, and blue values are in Decimal and
Hexadecimal.
                 Decimal                  Hexadecimal
Color                 R      G      B      R      G      B
</PRE>
<H1><A NAME=”A”>A</A></H1>
<PRE>
aliceblue240      248      255      F0      F8      FF
</PRE>
```

```
<H1><A NAME="X">X</A></H1>
<P></P>
<H1><A NAME="Y">Y</A></H1>
<PRE>
yellow                  255     255     0      FF     FF     00
</PRE>
<HR COLOR=yellow ALIGN=LEFT SIZE=15 WIDTH=50%>
<PRE>
yellowgreen             154     205     50     9A     CD     32
</PRE>
<HR COLOR=yellowgreen ALIGN=LEFT SIZE=15 WIDTH=50%>
<H1><A NAME="Z">Z</A></H1>
<P></P>
</BODY>
</HTML>
```

Related Items

anchors (Object)

link (Object)

location (client)

Syntax

```
location.property

location.method
```

Description

This object contains information about the current URL.

Properties

hash

host

hostname

href

pathname

port

protocol

search

Methods

assign

toString

Event Handlers

None

Property of

None

Examples

```
function WhereAmI()
{
IAmHere=location.href & " on " & location.hostname
End Sub
```

Related Items

history (Object)

location (Property)

navigator (client)

Syntax

```
navigator.property
```

Description

Contains Information about the browser being used.

Properties

appName

appVersion

appCodeName

userAgent

Methods

None

Event Handlers

None

Property of

None

Examples

```
Sub ReturnBrowserVersion()
BrowserVersion = navigator.appName & navigator.appVersion
End Sub
```

Related Items

links (Object)

anchors (Property)

password (client)

Syntax

```
<INPUT
TYPE = ""
NAME = ""
[VALUE = ""]
SIZE=integer>
```

Description

This defines a standard HTML form object

Properties

defaultValue

name

value

Methods

focus

blur

select

Event Handlers

None

Property of

None

Examples

```
<FORM>
<P></P>
Enter Your Password:<INPUT TYPE="PASSWORD" NAME="USERLOGON"
<P></P>
<INPUT TYPE="SUBMIT" NAME="CMDBSUBMIT">
<INPUT TYPE="RESET" NAME="CMDBRESET"><BR>
<P></P>
</FORM>
```

Related Items

form (Object)

text (Object)

radio (client)

Syntax

```
<INPUT
TYPE = "RADIO"
NAME = "radioobjectname"
VALUE = "radioobjectvalue"
[CHECKED]
[onClick = "eventcode"]>
radiobuttontext
```

Description

This is the form object for radio buttons.

Properties

checked

defaultChecked

index

length

name

value

Methods

click

Event Handlers

onClick

Property of

None

Examples

```
<FORM>
<P></P>
<INPUT TYPE="RADIO" NAME="RBACTIVEX" CHECKED=TRUE>ActiveX<BR>
<INPUT TYPE="RADIO" NAME="RBHTML">HTML 3.2<BR>
<INPUT TYPE="RADIO" NAME="RBVBSCRIPT">VB Script<BR>
<INPUT TYPE="RADIO" NAME="RBJSCRIPT">JScript<BR>
<P></P>
<INPUT TYPE="SUBMIT" NAME="CMDBSUBMIT">
<INPUT TYPE="RESET" NAME="CMDBRESET"><BR>
<P></P>
</FORM>
```

Related Items

checkbox (Object)

form (Object)

select (Object)

reset (client)

Syntax

```
<INPUT
TYPE = "RESET"
NAME = "resetobjectname"
VALUE = "resetobjecttext"
[onClick = "eventcode"]>
```

Description

This input type is one of the stock button types. This object resets a form to its initial state.

Properties

name

value

Methods

click

Event Handlers

onClick

Property of

None

Examples

```
<FORM>
<P></P>
<INPUT TYPE="RADIO" NAME="RBACTIVEX" CHECKED=TRUE>ActiveX<BR>
<INPUT TYPE="RADIO" NAME="RBHTML">HTML 3.2<BR>
<INPUT TYPE="RADIO" NAME="RBVBSCRIPT">VB Script<BR>
<INPUT TYPE="RADIO" NAME="RBJSCRIPT">JScript<BR>
<P></P>
```

```
<INPUT TYPE="SUBMIT" NAME="CMDBSUBMIT">
<INPUT TYPE="RESET" NAME="CMDBRESET"><BR>
<P></P>
</FORM>
```

Related Items

button (Object)

form (Object)

submit (Object)

select (client)

Syntax

```
<SELECT
NAME="selectobjectname"
[SIZE="integer"]
[MULTIPLE]
[onBlur=" eventcode "]
[onChange=" eventcode "]
[onFocus="eventcode"]>
<OPTION [SELECTED]> DisplayText [ ... <OPTION> DisplayText]
</SELECT>
```

Description

This object lets you place list boxes on a form.

Properties (Select)

length

name

options

selectedIndex

Properties (Option)

defaultSelected

index

selected

text

value

Methods

None

Event Handlers

onBlur

onChange

onFocus

Property of

None

Examples

```
<FORM>
<P>Choose a newsletter: <BR>
<SELECT NAME="newslettersingle">
<OPTION SELECTED> ActiveX
<OPTION> HTML 3.2
<OPTION> VB Script
<OPTION> JScript
</SELECT>
<P>Choose multiple newsletters: <BR>
<SELECT NAME="newslettermultiple" MULTIPLE>
<OPTION SELECTED> ActiveX
<OPTION> HTML 3.2
<OPTION> VB Script
<OPTION> JScript
</SELECT>
```

Related Items

form (Object

radio (Object)

options (Property)

string (common)

Syntax

```
estringobjectname.property
```

```
stringobjectname.method
```

Description

These methods and properties are used for string handling functions.

Properties

length

Methods

anchor

big

blink

bold

charAt

fixed

fontcolor

fontsize

indexOf

italics

lastIndexOf

link

small

strike

sub

substring

sup

LCase

UCase

Event Handlers

None

Property of

None

Examples

```
Sub MakeUpper(CnvrtString)
TempText = UCase(CnvrtString)
End Sub
Sub MakeLower(CnvrtString)
TempText = LCase(CnvrtString)
End Sub
```

Related Items

text (Object)

textarea (Object)

submit (client)

Syntax

```
<INPUT
TYPE = "SUBMIT"
NAME = "submitobjectname"
VALUE = "submitobjecttext"
[onClick = "eventcode"]>
```

Description

This input type is one of the stock button types. This object submits a form.

Properties

name

value

Methods

click

Event Handlers

onClick

Property of

None

Examples

```
<FORM>

<P></P>
<INPUT TYPE=”RADIO” NAME=”RBACTIVEX” CHECKED=TRUE>ActiveX<BR>
<INPUT TYPE=”RADIO” NAME=”RBHTML”>HTML 3.2<BR>
<INPUT TYPE=”RADIO” NAME=”RBVBSCRIPT”>VB Script<BR>
<INPUT TYPE=”RADIO” NAME=”RBJSCRIPT”>JScript<BR>
<P></P>
<INPUT TYPE=”SUBMIT” NAME=”CMDBSUBMIT”>
<INPUT TYPE=”RESET” NAME=”CMDBRESET”><BR>
<P></P>
</FORM>
```

Related Items

button (Object)

form (Object)

reset (Object)

submit (Method)

text (client)

Syntax

```
<INPUT
TYPE = "TEXT"
NAME = "textobjectname"
VALUE = "textobjectvalue"
SIZE = "integerlength"
[onBlur = "eventcode"]
[onChange = "eventcode"]
[onFocus = "eventcode"]
[onSelect = "eventcode"]>
```

Description

This is one of the standard HTML form objects. This allows entry of text.

Properties

defaultValue

name

value

Methods

focus

blur

select

Event Handlers

onBlur

onChange

onFocus

onSelect

Property of

None

Examples

```
<FORM>
<PRE>
Enter Your Name          <INPUT TYPE="TEXT" NAME="NAMEEMAIL"
SIZE="40" MAXLENGTH="40"><BR>
Enter Your Address       <INPUT TYPE="TEXT" NAME="ADDRESSSNAIL-
MAIL" SIZE="40" MAXLENGTH="40"><BR>
Enter Your City          <INPUT TYPE="TEXT" NAME="CITYEMAIL"
SIZE="40" MAXLENGTH="30"><BR>
Enter Your State         <INPUT TYPE="TEXT" NAME="STATEEMAIL"
SIZE="10" MAXLENGTH="6"><BR>
Enter Your Zip           <INPUT TYPE="TEXT" NAME="ZIPEMAIL"
SIZE="20" MAXLENGTH="10"><BR>
Enter Your Email Address <INPUT TYPE="TEXT" NAME="ADDRESSEMAIL"
SIZE="40" MAXLENGTH="40"><BR>
</PRE>
<P></P>
<INPUT TYPE="CHECKBOX" NAME="CBACTIVEX" CHECKED=TRUE>ActiveX<BR>
<INPUT TYPE="CHECKBOX" NAME="CBHTML">HTML 3.2<BR>
<INPUT TYPE="CHECKBOX" NAME="CBVBSCRIPT">VB Script<BR>
<INPUT TYPE="CHECKBOX" NAME="CBJSCRIPT">JScript<BR>
<P></P>
<INPUT TYPE="SUBMIT" NAME="CMDBSUBMIT">
<INPUT TYPE="RESET" NAME="CMDBRESET"><BR>
<P></P>
</FORM>
```

Related Items

form (Object)

password (Object)

string (Object)

textarea (Object)

textarea (client)

Syntax

```
<TEXTAREA
NAME = "textareaobjectname"
ROWS = "integerlength"
COLS = "integerlength"
[onBlur = "eventcode"]
[onChange = "eventcode"]
[onFocus = "eventcode"]
[onSelect = "eventcode"]>
displaytext
</TEXTAREA>
```

Description

This is one of the standard HTML form objects. This allows entry of text on multiple lines.

Properties

defaultValue

name

value

Methods

focus

blur

select

Event Handlers

onBlur

onChange

onFocus

onSelect

Property of

None

Examples

```
<FORM>
<PRE>
Enter Your Name          <INPUT TYPE="TEXT" NAME="NAMEEMAIL"
SIZE="40" MAXLENGTH="40"><BR>
Enter Your Address       <INPUT TYPE="TEXT" NAME="ADDRESSSNAIL-
MAIL" SIZE="40" MAXLENGTH="40"><BR>
Enter Your City          <INPUT TYPE="TEXT" NAME="CITYEMAIL"
SIZE="40" MAXLENGTH="30"><BR>
Enter Your State         <INPUT TYPE="TEXT" NAME="STATEEMAIL"
SIZE="10" MAXLENGTH="6"><BR>
Enter Your Zip           <INPUT TYPE="TEXT" NAME="ZIPEMAIL"
SIZE="20" MAXLENGTH="10"><BR>
Enter Your Email Address <INPUT TYPE="TEXT" NAME="ADDRESSEMAIL"
SIZE="40" MAXLENGTH="40"><BR>
Enter A Message          <TEXTAREA" NAME="OTHERNOTES" ROWS="10"
COLS="40"></TEXTAREA>
</PRE>
<P></P>
<INPUT TYPE="CHECKBOX" NAME="CBACTIVEX" CHECKED=TRUE>ActiveX<BR>
<INPUT TYPE="CHECKBOX" NAME="CBHTML">HTML 3.2<BR>
<INPUT TYPE="CHECKBOX" NAME="CBVBSCRIPT">VB Script<BR>
<INPUT TYPE="CHECKBOX" NAME="CBJSCRIPT">JScript<BR>
<P></P>
<INPUT TYPE="SUBMIT" NAME="CMDBSUBMIT">
<INPUT TYPE="RESET" NAME="CMDBRESET"><BR>
<P></P>
</FORM>
```

Related Items

form (Object)

password (Object)

string (Object)

text (Object)

window (client)

Syntax

```
windowobjectname=window.open(
"URL",
"windowname",
["windowoptions"])
```

Description

This is the topmost object in the VBScript object levels.

Properties

defaultStatus

frames

parent

self

status

top

window

Methods

close

open

setTimeout

clearTimeout

Event Handlers

onLoad

onUnload

Property of

None

Examples

```
<SCRIPT Language="VBScript">
window.open ( "new.htm", "new");
</SCRIPT>
```

Related Items

document (Object)

frame (Object)

frames (Property)

Methods and Functions

This section provides the methods and functions for Visual Basic Scripting Edition.

Abs (Function)

Syntax

```
Abs(numberobject)
```

Description

This method returns the absolute value of a number.

Examples

```
document.write (Abs(100))

document.write (Abs(-100))
```

anchor (Method)

Syntax

```
textobject.anchor(stringobject)
```

Description

This method generates an HTML anchor that is the target of a hypertext link.

Method of

string

Examples

```
tempstring="Index"

tempwindow=window.open("index.htm","tempwindow")
tempwindow.document.writeln(tempstring.anchor("indexanchor"))
tempwindow.document.close()
```

Related Items

link (Method)

Asc (Function)

Syntax

```
Asc(stringobject)
```

Description

This function returns the character code for the first character in a string.

Examples

```
document.write (Asc("V"))

document.write (Asc("B"))
```

Atn (Function)

Syntax

```
Atn(numberobject)
```

Description

This function returns in radians the arc tangent of a number.

Examples

```
document.write(Atn(1))

document.write(Atn(-1))
```

Related Items

cos (Function)

sin (Function)

tan (Function)

back (Method)

Syntax

```
history.back()
```

Description

Retrieves the previous entry in the history list and loads it.

Method of

History

Examples

```
Sub BackWards
history.back()
End Sub
```

Related Items

forward (Method)

go (Method)

big (Method)

Syntax

```
stringobject.big()
```

Description

The string object is displayed as if it had the HTML tag <BIG>.

Method of

string

Examples

```
temptext = "ActiveX and VBScript Rules"

document.write(temptext.big())
```

Related Items

fontsize (Method)

small (Method)

blink (Method)

Syntax

```
stringobject.blink()
```

Description

The string object is displayed as if it had the HTML tag <BLINK>.

Method of

string

Examples

```
temptext = "ActiveX and VBScript Rules"

document.write(temptext.blink())
```

Related Items

bold (Method)

italics (Method)

strike (Method)

blur (Method)

Syntax

```
object.blur
```

Description

This causes an object to no longer have the focus. Equivalent to lostFocus.

Method of

password

text

textarea

Examples

```
ADDRESSEMAIL.blur
```

Related Items

focus (Method)

select (Method)

bold (Method)

Syntax

```
stringobject.bold()
```

Description

The string object is displayed as if it had the HTML tag <B>.

Method of

string

Examples

```
temptext = "ActiveX and VBScript Rules"

document.write(temptext.bold())
```

Related Items

blink (Method)

italics (Method)

strike (Method)

CBool (Function)

Syntax

```
CBool(object)
```

Description

This function converts an object to a Boolean data type.

Examples

```
document.write (CBool(5=5))
```

```
document.write (CBool(5=4))
```

CByte (Function)

Syntax

```
CBool(object)
```

Description

This function converts an object to a Byte data type.

Examples

```
document.write (CByte("5+5"))
```

```
document.write (CByte("2+2"))
```

CDate (Function)

Syntax

```
CDate(object)
```

Description

This function converts an object to a Date data type.

Examples

```
document.write (CDate("June 17, 1996"))
```

CDbl (Function)

Syntax

```
CDbl(object)
```

Description

This function converts an object to a Double data type.

Examples

```
document.write (CDbl(299.645))
```

charAt (Method)

Syntax

```
stringobject.charAt(indexobject)
```

Description

This method returns the character at the indexobject.

Method of

string

Examples

```
temptext = "ActiveX and VBScript Rules"
document.write(temptext.charAt(0))
document.write(temptext.charAt(1))
document.write(temptext.charAt(2))
document.write(temptext.charAt(3))
document.write(temptext.charAt(4))
document.write(temptext.charAt(5))
document.write(temptext.charAt(6))
```

Related Items

indexOf (Method)

lastIndexOf (Method)

Chr (Function)

Syntax

```
Chr(numberobject)
```

Description

This function returns the character that corresponds to the character code.

Examples

```
document.write (Chr(68))
```

CInt (Function)

Syntax

```
CInt(object)
```

Description

This function converts an object to an Integer data type.

Examples

```
document.write (CInt(17.75))
```

clear (Method)

Syntax

```
document.clear()
```

Description

This method clears the document in a window.

Method of

document

Examples

```
mywindow.document.clear()
```

Related Items

close (Method)

open (Method)

write (Method)

writeln (Method)

Clear (Method)

Syntax

```
Err.Clear
```

Description

This method clears the error flag in the Err object.

Method of

Err

Examples

```
Err.Clear
```

clearTimeout (Method)

Syntax

```
clearTimeout(timeoutobject)
```

Description

This method clears a timeout that was set using a setTimeout method.

Method of

frame

window

Examples

```
mywindow.clearTimeout(mytimeout)
```

Related Items

setTimeout (Method)

click (Method)

Syntax

```
formelementobject.click()
```

Description

Generates a click event for the specified form element.

Method of

button

checkbox

radio

reset

submit

Examples

```
<FORM>
<P></P>
<INPUT TYPE="CHECKBOX" NAME="CBACTIVEX" CHECKED=TRUE>ActiveX<BR>
<INPUT TYPE="CHECKBOX" NAME="CBHTML">HTML 3.2<BR>
<INPUT TYPE="CHECKBOX" NAME="CBVBSCRIPT">VB Script<BR>
<INPUT TYPE="CHECKBOX" NAME="CBJSCRIPT">JScript<BR>
<P></P>
<INPUT TYPE="SUBMIT" NAME="CMDBSUBMIT">
<INPUT TYPE="RESET" NAME="CMDBRESET"><BR>
<P></P>
</FORM>
<SCRIPT LANGUAGE="VBScript">
CBHTML.click
CBJSCRIPT.click
</SCRIPT>
```

CLng (Function)

Syntax

```
CLng(object)
```

Description

This function converts an object to a Long data type.

Examples

```
document.write (CLng(17))
```

close (document object) (Method)

Syntax

```
document.close()
```

Description

This method closes a document stream and forces the layout to be displayed.

Method of

document

Examples

```
sub resettower
TO = "<BODY BACKGROUND = TO.JPG></BODY>"
T123 ="<BODY BACKGROUND = T123.JPG></BODY>"
parent.frames(0).document.write (T123)
parent.frames(0).document.close
parent.frames(1).document.write (TO)
parent.frames(1).document.close
parent.frames(2).document.write (TO)
parent.frames(2).document.close
End Sub
```

Related Items

clear (Method)

open (Method)

write (Method)

writeln (Method)

close (window object) (Method)

Syntax

```
windowobject.close()
```

Description

This method is used to close the window that is specified by the object.

Method of

window

Examples

```
mywindow.close()
```

Related Items

open (Method)

Cos (Method)

Syntax

```
Cos(numberobject)
```

Description

This method returns the cosine of a number that has a value between 1 and -1 based upon the numberobject that is in radians.

Method of

Math

Examples

```
document.write(Cos(100))
```

```
document.write(Cos(360))
```

Related Items

Atn (Method)

Sin (Method)

Tan (Method)

CreateObject (Function)

Syntax

```
CreateObject(object)
```

Description

This function is used to create an ActiveX object.

Examples

```
Set MyObject = CreateObject("Word.Document")
```

CSng (Function)

Syntax

```
CSng(object)
```

Description

This function converts an object to a Single data type.

Examples

```
document.write (CSng(1234.87))
```

CStr (Function)

Syntax

```
CStr(object)
```

Description

This function converts an object to a String data type.

Examples

```
document.write (CDate(2+2))
```

CVErr (Function)

Syntax

```
CVErr(numberobject)
```

Description

This function returns an error specified.

Examples

```
MyError = CVErr(171996)
```

Date (Function)

Syntax

```
dateobject = Date
```

Description

This is used to return the current system date.

Examples

```
<SCRIPT LANGUAGE="VBScript">
sub fancy_print(string)
document.write("<HR><P>" & string)
End Sub
AugsDate = Date
fancy_print(AugsDate)
</SCRIPT>
```

DateSerial (Function)

Syntax

```
dateobject = DateSerial(year, month, day)
```

Description

This is used to return the date for a year, month, and day.

Examples

```
<SCRIPT LANGUAGE="VBScript">
sub fancy_print(string)
document.write("<HR><P>" & string)
End Sub
AugsDate = DateSerial(1996, 6, 17)
fancy_print(AugsDate)
</SCRIPT>
```

DateValue (Function)

Syntax

```
dateobject = DateValue(datestring)
```

Description

This is used to return a date.

Examples

```
<SCRIPT LANGUAGE="VBScript">
sub fancy_print(string)
document.write("<HR><P>" & string)
End Sub
AugsDate = DateValue("June 17, 1996)
fancy_print(AugsDate)
</SCRIPT>
```

Day (Function)

Syntax

```
dateobject = Day(date)
```

Description

This is used to return the day of the month.

Examples

```
<SCRIPT LANGUAGE="VBScript">
sub fancy_print(string)
document.write("<HR><P>" & string)
End Sub
AugsDate = Day(Date)
fancy_print(AugsDate)
</SCRIPT>
```

Exp (Function)

Syntax

```
Exp(numberobject)
```

Description

This method returns the exponent of a number object.

Examples

```
document.write(Exp(1))
```

Related Items

Log (Function)

Fix (Function)

Syntax

```
Fix(numberobject)
```

Description

Fix is used to return the integer portion of a number. On negative numbers, Fix returns the Integer that is greater than the numberobject.

Examples

```
document.write(Fix(7.4))

document.write(Int(7.4))

document.write(Fix(-7.4))

document.write(Int(-7.4))
```

fixed (Method)

Syntax

```
stringobject.fixed()
```

Description

The string object is displayed as if it had the HTML tag <TT>. This is a fixed-pitch or monospace font.

Method of

string

Examples

```
temptext = "ActiveX and VBScript Rules"

document.write(temptext.fixed())
```

Related Items

fontcolor (Method)

Syntax

```
stringobject.fontcolor(colorobject)
```

Description

This method is used to set the font color. This can either be as a RGB color triplet or as a stringobject, as listed in the color value chart.

Method of

string

Examples

```
temptext = "ActiveX and VBScript Rules"

document.write(temptext.fontcolor("Teal"))

document.write(temptext.fontcolor(0128128))

document.write(temptext.fontcolor(008080))
```

fontsize (Method)

Syntax

```
stringobject.fontsize(sizeobject)
```

Description

This method is used to set the font size. This is an integer between 1 and 7.

Method of

string

Examples

```
temptext = "ActiveX and VBScript Rules"

document.write(temptext.fontsize(1))

document.write(temptext.fontsize(2))

document.write(temptext.fontsize(3))
```

```
document.write(temptext.fontsize(4))

document.write(temptext.fontsize(5))

document.write(temptext.fontsize(6))

document.write(temptext.fontsize(7))
```

Related Items

big (Method)

small (Method)

forward (Method)

Syntax

```
history.forward()
```

Description

Retrieves the next entry in the history list and loads it.

Method of

History

Examples

```
function For_Wards()
{
history.forward()
End Sub
```

Related Items

back (Method)

go (Method)

go (Method)

Syntax

```
history.go(relative|"full/partialURL")
```

Description

This method will load a URL from the history list, either by position or by a full or partial URL.

Method of

history

Examples

```
<INPUT TYPE=”button” VALUE=”Go” onClick=”history.go(msn.com’)”>
function BackTwo()
{
history.go(-2)
End Sub
```

Related Items

back (Method)

forward (Method)

Hex (Function)

Syntax

```
Hex(numberobject)
```

Description

Hex is used to return a hexadecimal number.

Examples

```
document.write(Hex(9))

document.write(Hex(10))

document.write(Hex(11))
```

Hour (Function)

Syntax

```
Hour(timeobject)
```

Description

This function returns the hours for the time object. This is a number between 0 and 23.

Examples

```
mydatentime = Time
document.write(Hour(mydatentime))
```

indexOf (Method)

Syntax

```
stringobject.indexOf(searchobject, [fromobject])
```

Description

This method returns an index value for the first occurrence of the search object in the string object.

Method of

string

Examples

```
temptext = "ActiveX and VBScript Rules"
document.write(temptext.indexOf("A"))
document.write(temptext.indexOf("R"))
document.write(temptext.indexOf("and"))
document.write(temptext.lastIndexOf("A"))
document.write(temptext.lastIndexOf("R"))
document.write(temptext.lastIndexOf("and"))
```

Related Items

charAt (Method)

lastIndexOf (Method)

InputBox (Function)

Syntax

```
InputBox(prompt [,title][,default][,xpos][,ypos][,helpfile,
context])
```

Description

The InputBox is used to display a message and accept user input.

Examples

```
Mystring = InputBox("Enter Your Name")
document.write(Mystring)
```

Int (Function)

Syntax

```
Int(numberobject)
```

Description

Int is used to return the integer portion of a number. On negative numbers, Int returns the Integer that is less than the numberobject.

Examples

```
document.write(Fix(7.4))

document.write(Int(7.4))

document.write(Fix(-7.4))

document.write(Int(-7.4))
```

IsArray (Function)

Syntax

```
IsArray(numberobject)
```

Description

IsArray returns a boolean whether the variable is an array.

Examples

```
Mytest = IsArray(test)
```

IsDate (Function)

Syntax

```
IsDate(dateobject)
```

Description

IsDate returns a boolean whether the variable can be converted to a date.

Examples

```
Mytest = IsDate(MyDate)
```

IsEmpty (Function)

Syntax

```
IsEmpty(object)
```

Description

IsEmpty returns a boolean whether the variable has been initialized.

Examples

```
Mytest = IsEmpty(NewVar)
```

IsError (Function)

Syntax

```
IsError(numberobject)
```

Description

IsError returns a boolean whether the variable is an error value.

Examples

```
Mytest = IsError(MyErrorCode)
```

IsNull (Function)

Syntax

```
IsNull(object)
```

Description

IsNull returns a boolean whether the variable has valid data.

Examples

```
Mytest = IsNull(NewVar)
```

IsNumeric (Function)

Syntax

```
IsNumeric(numberobject)
```

Description

IsNumeric returns a boolean whether the variable is a number.

Examples

```
Mytest = IsNumeric(NewVar)
```

IsObject (Function)

Syntax

```
IsObject(object)
```

Description

IsObject returns a boolean whether the object is a valid ActiveX object.

Examples

```
Mytest = IsObject(MyObject)
```

italics (Method)

Syntax

```
stringobject.italics()
```

Description

The string object is displayed as if it had the HTML tag <I>.

Method of

string

Examples

```
temptext = "ActiveX and VBScript Rules"
document.write(temptext.italics())
```

Related Items

blink (Method)

bold (Method)

strike (Method)

lastIndexOf (Method)

Syntax

```
stringobject.lastIndexOf(searchobject, [fromobject])
```

Description

This method returns an index value for the last occurrence of the search object in the string object.

Method of

string

Examples

```
temptext = "ActiveX and VBScript Rules"
document.write(temptext.indexOf("A"))
document.write(temptext.indexOf("R"))
document.write(temptext.indexOf("and"))
document.write(temptext.lastIndexOf("A"))
document.write(temptext.lastIndexOf("R"))
document.write(temptext.lastIndexOf("and"))
```

Related Items

charAt (Method)

indexOf (Method)

LBound (Function)

Syntax

```
LBound(arrayobject[, dimension])
```

Description

The function LBound is used to return the smallest subscript of an array.

Examples

```
document.write(LBound(MyArray))
```

LCase (Function)

Syntax

```
LCase(stringobject)
```

Description

LCase is used to convert the string object to lowercase.

Examples

```
temptext = "ActiveX and VBScript Rules"
document.write(LCase(temptext))
```

Left (Function)

Syntax

```
Left(stringobject, length)
```

Description

The Left function is used to return the leftmost characters up to length.

Examples

```
temptext = "ActiveX and VBScript Rules"
document.write(Left(temptext, 7))
```

Len (Function)

Syntax

```
Len(stringobject)
```

Description

The function Len is used to return the length of a string.

Examples

```
temptext = "ActiveX and VBScript Rules"
document.write(Len(temptext))
```

link (Method)

Syntax

```
linktextobject.link(hrefobject)
```

Description

Used to supply a link to a URL.

Method of

string

Examples

```
hotlink="Microsoft"
URL="http://www.msn.com"
document.open()
document.write("Click to return to " & hotText.link(URL))
document.close()
```

Related Items

anchor (Method)

Log (Function)

Syntax

```
Log(numberobject)
```

Description

This method returns the logarithm of the number object.

Examples

```
document.write(Log(1))
```

Related Items

Exp (Function)

LTrim (Function)

Syntax

```
LTrim(stringobject)
```

Description

The function LTrim is used to remove any spaces to the left of a string.

Examples

```
temptext = "    ActiveX and VBScript Rules    "
document.write(temptext)
document.write(LTrim(temptext))
```

Mid (Function)

Syntax

```
Mid(stringobject, startpos [,length])
```

Description

This function returns the characters from the start position to the length specified.

Examples

```
temptext = "ActiveX and VBScript Rules"
document.write(temptext)
document.write(Mid(temptext, 1, 7))
document.write(Mid(temptext, 13, 8))
```

Minute (Function)

Syntax

```
Minute(timeobject)
```

Description

This function returns the minutes for the time object. This is a number between 0 and 59.

Examples

```
mydatentime = Time
document.write(Minutes(mydatentime))
```

Month (Function)

Syntax

```
Month(dateobject)
```

Description

This function returns the month for the date object. This is a number between 1 and 12.

Examples

```
mydatentime = Date
document.write(Month(mydatentime))
```

MsgBox (Function)

Syntax

```
MsgBox(prompt [,buttons][,title][,helpfile, context])
```

Description

This function generates a dialog box that displays a prompt and buttons.

Examples

```
MsgBox("Invalid Input",0,"Error")

MsgBox("Invalid Input",1,"Error")
```

Related Items

InputBox (Method)

Now (Function)

Syntax

```
Now(dateobject)
```

Description

This function returns the current date and time according to your system.

Examples

```
mydatentime = Now
document.write(mydatentime)
```

Oct (Function)

Syntax

```
Oct(numberobject)
```

Description

This function returns the octal number for the number object.

Examples

```
document.write(Oct(7))

document.write(Oct(8))

document.write(Oct(9))
```

open (document object) (Method)

Syntax

```
document.open([“MIMEobject”])
```

Description

This method is used to open a document for input of write and writeln methods. The MIME objects are the following:

- text/html
- text/plain
- image/gif
- image/jpeg

- image/x-bitmap
- plug-in

Other MIME types that the browser supports are plug-in.

Method of

document

Examples

```
Sub resettower
T0 = "<BODY BACKGROUND = T0.JPG></BODY>"
T1 = "<BODY BACKGROUND = T1.JPG></BODY>"
T2 = "<BODY BACKGROUND = T2.JPG></BODY>"
T3 = "<BODY BACKGROUND = T3.JPG></BODY>"
T12 = "<BODY BACKGROUND = T12.JPG></BODY>"
T23 = "<BODY BACKGROUND = T23.JPG></BODY>"
T123 ="<BODY BACKGROUND = T123.JPG></BODY>"
parent.frames(0).document.open
parent.frames(0).document.write (T123)
parent.frames(0).document.close
parent.frames(1).document.open
parent.frames(1).document.write (T0)
parent.frames(1).document.close
parent.frames(2).document.open
parent.frames(2).document.write (T0)
parent.frames(2).document.close
End Sub
```

Related Items

clear (Method)

close (Method)

write (Method)

writeln (Method)

open (window object) (Method)

Syntax

```
[windowvariable=] [window].open("URL", "windowobject",
["windowoptions"])
```

Description

This method is used to start a new browser window. The window options are the following:

- toolbar[=yes|no]|[=1|0]
- location[=yes|no]|[=1|0]
- directories[=yes|no]|[=1|0]
- status[=yes|no]|[=1|0]
- menubar[=yes|no]|[=1|0]
- scrollbars[=yes|no]|[=1|0]
- resizable[=yes|no]|[=1|0]
- width=pixels
- height=pixels

Method of

windows

Examples

```
function windowOpener()
{
mywindow=window.open("","Display window","toolbar=no,
directories=no,menubar=no")
mywindow.document.write("<HEAD><TITLE>My window</TITLE></HEAD>")
mywindow.document.write("<CENTER><BIG><B>ActiveX and VBScript
Rule!</B></BIG></CENTER>")
}
```

Related Items

close (Method)

Raise (Method)

Syntax

```
Err.Raise(number, source, description, helpfile, helpcontext)
```

Description

This method is used to generate a runtime error.

Method of

Err

Examples

```
Err.Raise(655535, "My Error", "Test Error")
```

Right (Function)

Syntax

```
Right(stringobject, length)
```

Description

The Right function is used to return the rightmost characters up to length.

Examples

```
temptext = "ActiveX and VBScript Rules"
document.write(Right(temptext, 5))
```

Rnd (Function)

Syntax

```
Rnd(numberobject)
```

Description

This function is used to generate a random number between 0 and 1.

Examples

```
document.write(Rnd(1)*18)
```

RTrim (Function)

Syntax

```
RTrim(stringobject)
```

Description

The function RTrim is used to remove any spaces to the right of a string.

Examples

```
temptext = "    ActiveX and VBScript Rules     "
document.write(temptext)
document.write(RTrim(temptext))
```

Second (Function)

Syntax

```
Second(timeobject)
```

Description

This function returns the seconds for the time object. This is a number between 0 and 59.

Examples

```
mydatentime = Time
document.write(Second(mydatentime))
```

select (Method)

Syntax

```
formelementobject.select()
```

Description

This method is used to highlight the element object.

Method of

password

text

textarea

Examples

```
<FORM>
<PRE>
Enter Your Name          <INPUT TYPE="TEXT" NAME="NAMEEMAIL"
SIZE="40" MAXLENGTH="40"><BR>
Enter Your Email Address <INPUT TYPE="TEXT" NAME="ADDRESSEMAIL"
SIZE="40" MAXLENGTH="40"><BR>
</PRE>
<P></P>
<INPUT TYPE="SUBMIT" NAME="CMDBSUBMIT">
<INPUT TYPE="RESET" NAME="CMDBRESET"><BR>
<P></P>
</FORM>
<SCRIPT LANGUAGE="VBScript">
ADDRESSEMAIL.select()
</SCRIPT>
```

Related Items

blur (Method)

focus (Method)

Sgn (Function)

Syntax

```
Sgn(numberobject)
```

Description

This function returns an integer that indicates the sign of a number. The return values are the following:

- 1 Greater than zero
- 0 Equal to zero
- -1 Less than zero

Examples

```
document.write(Sgn(100))

document.write(Sgn(0))

document.write(Sgn(-100))
```

Sin (Function)

Syntax

```
Sin(numberobject)
```

Description

This method returns the sine of a number that has a value between 1 and -1 based upon the numberobject that is in radians.

Examples

```
document.write(Sin(100))

document.write(Sin(360))
```

Related Items

Atn (Method)

Cos (Method)

Tan (Method)

small (Method)

Syntax

```
stringobject.small()
```

Description

The string object is displayed as if it had the HTML tag <SMALL>.

Method of

string

Examples

```
temptext = "ActiveX and VBScript Rules"
document.write(temptext.small())
```

Related Items

big (Method)

fontsize (Method)

Space (Function)

Syntax

```
Space(numberobject)
```

Description

This function returns a string with the number of spaces specified.

Method of

Math

Examples

```
temptext = "ActiveX and"
temptext1 = "VBScript Rules"
document.write(temptext & temptext1)
document.write(temptext & Space(1) & temptext1)
document.write(temptext & Space(10) & temptext1)
```

Sqr (Function)

Syntax

```
Sqr(numberobject)
```

Description

This method returns the square root of a number object.

Examples

```
document.write(Sqr(1))

document.write(Sqr(2))

document.write(Sqr(3))
```

StrComp (Function)

Syntax

```
StrComp(string1, string2 [,compare])
```

Description

This function returns a value that indicates the result of a string comparison.

Examples

```
temptext0 = “ActiveX and”
temptext1 = “ActiveX and”
temptext2 = “VBScript Rules”
temptext3 = “VBScript Rules”
document.write(StrComp(temptext0 ,temptext1)
document.write(StrComp(temptext1 ,temptext2)
document.write(StrComp(temptext2 ,temptext3)
```

strike (Method)

Syntax

```
stringobject.strike()
```

Description

The string object is displayed as if it had the HTML tag <STRIKE>.

Method of

string

Examples

```
temptext = “ActiveX and VBScript Rules”
document.write(temptext.strike())
```

Related Items

blink (Method)

bold (Method)

italics (Method)

String (Function)

Syntax

```
String(length, character)
```

Description

This function returns a string with the number of characters specified in `length` and the character specified in `character`.

Examples

```
temptext = "ActiveX and"
temptext1 = "VBScript Rules"
document.write(temptext & String(2,"*") & temptext1)
document.write(temptext & String(5,"=") & temptext1)
document.write(temptext & String(5,61) & temptext1)
```

sub (Method)

Syntax

```
stringobject.sub()
```

Description

The string object is displayed as if it had the HTML tag <SUB> for subscript.

Method of

string

Examples

```
temptext = "ActiveX and VBScript Rules"
document.write(temptext.sub())
```

Related Items

sup (Method)

submit (Method)

Syntax

```
formnameobject.submit()
```

Description

This method is used to submit a form.

Method of

form

Examples

```
myform.submit()
```

Related Items

submit (Object)

onSubmit (Event Handler)

substring (Method)

Syntax

```
stringobject.substring(numberobject1, numberobject2)
```

Description

This method is used to return a subset of a string object.

Method of

string

Examples

```
temptext = "ActiveX and VBScript Rules"
document.write(temptext.substring(0,6))
document.write(temptext.substring(6,0))
document.write(temptext.substring(12,21))
document.write(temptext.substring(21,12))
```

Related Items

sup (Method)

Syntax

```
stringobject.sup()
```

Description

The string object is displayed as if it had the HTML tag <SUP> for superscript.

Method of

string

Examples

```
temptext = "ActiveX and VBScript Rules"
document.write(temptext.sup())
```

Related Items

sub (Method)

Tan (Function)

Syntax

```
Tan(numberobject)
```

Description

This method returns the tangent of a number. The number object is in radians.

Examples

```
document.write Tan(100)

document.write Tan(360)
```

Related Items

Atn (Function)

Cos (Function)

Sin (Function)

Time (Function)

Syntax

```
Time
```

Description

This is used to return time information.

Examples

```
MyDatenTime = Time
document.write(MyDatenTime)
```

TimeSerial (Function)

Syntax

```
TimeSerial(hour, minute, second)
```

Description

This is used to return time information.

Examples

```
MyDatenTime = TimeSerial(13, 33, 40)
document.write(MyDatenTime)
```

TimeValue (Function)

Syntax

```
TimeValue(time)
```

Description

This is used to return time information.

Examples

```
MyDatenTime = TimeValue("1:33:40 PM")
document.write(MyDatenTime)
```

toLowerCase (Method)

Syntax

```
stringobject.toLowerCase()
```

Description

This method is used to convert a string object to all lowercase letters.

Method of

string

Examples

```
temptext = "ActiveX and VBScript Rules"
document.write(temptext.toLowerCase())
document.write(temptext.toUpperCase())
```

Related Items

toUpperCase (Method)

toUpperCase (Method)

Syntax

```
stringobject.toUpperCase()
```

Description

This method is used to convert a string object to all uppercase letters.

Method of

string

Examples

```
temptext = "ActiveX and VBScript Rules"
document.write(temptext.toLowerCase())
document.write(temptext.toUpperCase())
```

Related Items

toUpperCase (Method)

Trim (Function)

Syntax

```
Trim(stringobject)
```

Description

The function Trim is used to remove any spaces to the left and the right of a string.

Examples

```
temptext = "    ActiveX and VBScript Rules    "
document.write(temptext)
document.write(Trim(temptext))
```

UBound (Function)

Syntax

```
UBound(arrayobject[, dimension])
```

Description

The function UBound is used to return the largest subscript of an array.

Examples

```
document.write(UBound(MyArray))
```

UCase (Function)

Syntax

```
UCase(stringobject)
```

Description

UCase is used to convert the string object to uppercase.

Examples

```
temptext = "ActiveX and VBScript Rules"
document.write(UCase(temptext))
```

VarType (Function)

Syntax

```
VarType(varname)
```

Description

The function is used to return a value that specifies the variable type. The return types are the following:

- 0 Empty
- 1 Null
- 2 Integer
- 3 Long
- 4 Single
- 5 Double
- 6 Currency
- 7 Date
- 8 String
- 9 ActiveX Object
- 10 Error
- 11 Boolean
- 12 Variant
- 13 Non-ActiveX Object

Examples

```
MyVar0 = ""
MyVar1 = "VBScript"
MyVar2 = Now
MyVar3 = "123"
MyVar4 = "123.33"
```

```
document.write(VarType(MyVar0))
document.write(VarType(MyVar1))
document.write(VarType(MyVar2))
document.write(VarType(MyVar3))
document.write(VarType(MyVar4))
```

Weekday (Function)

Syntax

```
Weekday(date[,firstdayofweek])
```

Description

This function returns the day of the week for the date object. This is a number between 1 and 7.

Examples

```
mydatentime = Date
document.write(Weekday(mydatentime))
```

write (Method)

Syntax

```
write(object1, [,object2], ...[,objectN])
```

Description

This method is used to write HTML to a document.

Method of

document

Examples

```
function resettower()
{
T0 = "<BODY BACKGROUND = T0.JPG></BODY>"
T123 ="<BODY BACKGROUND = T123.JPG></BODY>"
parent.frames(0).document.write (T123)
parent.frames(0).document.close
parent.frames(1).document.write (T0)
parent.frames(1).document.close
```

```
parent.frames(2).document.write (T0)
parent.frames(2).document.close
End Sub
```

Related Items

close (Method)

clear (Method)

open (Method)

writeln (Method)

writeln (Method)

Syntax

```
writeln(object1, [,object2], ...[,objectN])
```

Description

This method is used to write HTML to a document. This method is different from write because it appends a newline character at the end of the line.

Method of

document

Examples

```
function resettower()
{
T0 = "<BODY BACKGROUND = T0.JPG></BODY>"
T123 ="<BODY BACKGROUND = T123.JPG></BODY>"
parent.frames(0).document.writeln (T123)
parent.frames(0).document.close
parent.frames(1).document.writeln (T0)
parent.frames(1).document.close
parent.frames(2).document.writeln (T0)
parent.frames(2).document.close
End Sub
```

Related Items

close (Method)

clear (Method)

open (Method)

write (Method)

Year (Function)

Syntax

```
Year(dateobject)
```

Description

This function returns the year for the date object.

Examples

```
mydatentime = Date
document.write(Year(mydatentime))
```

Properties

This section describes the properties used in the Visual Basic Scripting Edition.

action

Syntax

```
formobject.action
```

Description

This property is used to return or set the URL that a forms elements are sent to.

Applies to

form

Examples

```
document.myform.action=myformreceipt
```

Related Items

method (Property)

target (Property)

alinkColor

Syntax

```
document.alinkColor=colorobject
```

Description

This property sets or returns the color of an active link. This color shows up when you do a mouse-down, but before the mouse-up.

Applies to

document

Examples

```
document.bgColor="ffffff"
document.fgColor="000000"
document.alinkColor="Teal"
document.linkColor="Red"
document.vlinkColor="Blue"
```

Related Items

bgColor (Property)

fgColor (Property)

linkColor (Property)

vlinkColor (Property)

anchors

Syntax

```
document.anchor
```

Description

This property is used to set or return information about the anchors in a document.

Applies to

document

Examples

```
numanchorsdocument=document.anchors.length
```

Related Items

links (Property)

length (Property)

appCodeName

Syntax

```
navigator.appCodeName
```

Description

This property returns the code name of the browser being used. This property is read-only.

Applies to

navigator

Examples

```
document.write(navigator.appCodeName)
document.write(navigator.appName)
document.write(navigator.appVersion)
document.write(navigator.userAgent)
```

Related Items

appName (Property)

appVersion (Property)

userAgent (Property)

appName

Syntax

```
navigator.appName
```

Description

This property returns the name of the browser being used. This property is read-only.

Applies to

navigator

Examples

```
document.write(navigator.appCodeName)
document.write(navigator.appName)
document.write(navigator.appVersion)
document.write(navigator.userAgent)
```

Related Items

appCodeName (Property)

appVersion (Property)

userAgent (Property)

appVersion

Syntax

```
navigator.appVersion
```

Description

This property returns the version information of the browser being used. This property is read-only.

Applies to

navigator

Examples

```
document.write(navigator.appCodeName)
document.write(navigator.appName)
document.write(navigator.appVersion)
document.write(navigator.userAgent)
```

Related Items

appCodeName (Property)

appName (Property)

userAgent (Property)

bgColor

Syntax

```
document.bgColor=colorobject
```

Description

This property sets or returns the color of document background.

Applies to

document

Examples

```
document.bgColor=”ffffff”
document.fgColor=”000000”
document.alinkColor=”Teal”
document.linkColor=”Red”
document.vlinkColor=”Blue”
```

Related Items

alinkColor (Property)

fgColor (Property)

linkColor (Property)

vlinkColor (Property)

checked

Syntax

```
formelement.checked
```

Description

This property sets or returns whether a check box or a radio button is checked. You can use this property to set an item checked.

Applies to

checkbox

radio

Examples

```
document.write(myform.myrb.checked)
```

Related Items

defaultChecked (Property)

cookie

Syntax

```
document.cookie
```

Description

This property returns or sets the value that the navigator object stores in the cookies.txt file.

Applies to

document

Examples

```
document.write(document.cookie)
```

Related Items

hidden (Object)

defaultChecked

Syntax

```
formelement.defaultChecked
```

Description

This property sets or returns whether a check box or a radio button has the default checked. You can use this property to set an item to be the default checked.

Applies to

checkbox

radio

Examples

```
document.write(myform.myrb.defaultChecked)
myform.myrb.defaultChecked=true
```

Related Items

checked (Property)

defaultSelected

Syntax

```
selectelement.options.defaultSelected
```

Description

This property sets or returns whether a select item is the default. You can use this property to set an item to be the default selected.

Applies to

options

Examples

```
document.write(myselect.options.defaultSelected)
myselect.options.defaultSelected=true
```

Related Items

defaultSelected (Property)

index (Property)

selected (Property)

selectedIndex (Property)

defaultStatus

Syntax

```
windowobject.defaultStatus
```

Description

This property is used to set or return the message that is displayed at the bottom of the browser window in the status bar.

Applies to

window

Examples

```
Sub ToolTip
window.defaultStatus="Link to a cool site"
window.status="Cool site"
End Sub
<A HREF="http://www.coolsite.com" onMouseOver="ToolTip">
Cool Site</A>
```

Related Items

status (Property)

defaultValue

Syntax

```
textobject.defaultValue
```

Description

This is used to set or return the default value for a text object.

Applies to

hidden

password

text

textarea

Examples

```
ADDRESSEMAIL.defaultValue="yourname@your.server"
```

Related Items

defaultValue (Property)

value (Property)

Description

Syntax

```
Err.Description
```

Description

This property sets or returns the description for an error.

Applies to

Err

Examples

```
document.write(Err.Description)
```

Related Items

HelpContext (Property)

HelpFile (Property)

LastDLLError(Property)

Number (Property)

Source (Property)

elements

Syntax

```
formobject.elements
```

Description

This property allows you to set and return information about a form array.

Applies to

form

Examples

```
document.write(myform.elements[0].name)
```

Related Items

encoding

Syntax

```
formobject.encoding
```

Description

This property is used to return the MIME encoding for a form object.

Applies to

form

Examples

```
document.write(myform.encoding)
```

fgColor

Syntax

```
document.fgColor=colorobject
```

Description

This property sets the color for the foreground text.

Applies to

document

Examples

```
document.bgColor="ffffff"
document.fgColor="000000"
document.alinkColor="Teal"
document.linkColor="Red"
document.vlinkColor="Blue"
```

Related Items

alinkColor (Property)

bgColor (Property)

linkColor (Property)

vlinkColor (Property)

forms

Syntax

```
document.forms
```

Description

This property allows you to return and set information about a forms array.

Applies to

document

Examples

```
document.write(document.forms.length)
document.write(document.forms[0].elements.length)
```

Related Items

length (Property)

frames

Syntax

```
window.frames
```

Description

This property allows you to return and set information about a frames array.

Applies to

window

Examples

```
document.write(window.frames.length)
```

Related Items

length (Property)

hash

Syntax

```
location.hash
```

Description

This property returns the anchor name portion of a URL that begins with the hash mark (#).

Applies to

location

Examples

```
document.write(location.hash)
document.write(location.host)
document.write(location.hostname)
document.write(location.href)
document.write(location.pathname)
document.write(location.port)
document.write(location.protocol)
document.write(location.search)
```

Related Items

host (Property)

href (Property)

pathname (Property)

port (Property)

protocol (Property)

search (Property)

HelpContext

Syntax

```
Err.HelpContext
```

Description

This property sets or returns the help context id for a topic in an MS Windows help file.

Applies to

Err

Examples

```
document.write(Err.HelpContext)
```

Related Items

Description (Property)

HelpFile (Property)

LastDLLError(Property)

Number (Property)

Source (Property)

HelpFile

Syntax

```
Err.HelpFile
```

Description

This property sets or returns the qualified path to an MS Windows help file.

Applies to

Err

Examples

```
document.write(Err.HelpFile)
```

Related Items

Description (Property)

HelpContext (Property)

LastDLLError(Property)

Number (Property)

Source (Property)

host

Syntax

```
location.host
```

Description

This property returns the hostname:port portion of a URL.

Applies to

location

Examples

```
document.write(location.hash)
document.write(location.host)
document.write(location.hostname)
document.write(location.href)
document.write(location.pathname)
document.write(location.port)
document.write(location.protocol)
document.write(location.search)
```

Related Items

hash (Property)

href (Property)

pathname (Property)

port (Property)

protocol (Property)

search (Property)

hostname

Syntax

```
location.hostname
```

Description

This property returns the domain name or IP address portion of a URL.

Applies to

location

Examples

```
document.write(location.hash)
document.write(location.host)
document.write(location.hostname)
document.write(location.href)
document.write(location.pathname)
document.write(location.port)
document.write(location.protocol)
document.write(location.search)
```

Related Items

hash (Property)

host (Property)

href (Property)

pathname (Property)

port (Property)

protocol (Property)

search (Property)

href

Syntax

```
location.href
```

Description

This property returns the complete URL.

Applies to

location

Examples

```
document.write(location.hash)
document.write(location.host)
document.write(location.hostname)
document.write(location.href)
document.write(location.pathname)
document.write(location.port)
document.write(location.protocol)
document.write(location.search)
```

Related Items

hash (Property)

host (Property)

pathname (Property)

port (Property)

protocol (Property)

search (Property)

index

Syntax

```
radioobject.index

selectobject.options.index
```

Send Us YOUR COMMENTS

Dear Reader:

Thank you for buying this book. In order to offer you more quality books on the topics ***you*** would like to see, we need your input. At Prima Publishing, we pride ourselves on timely responsiveness to our readers' needs. If you complete and return this brief questionnaire, ***we will listen!***

Name (First) ____ (M.I.) ____ (Last) ____

Company ____ Type of business ____

Address ____ City ____ State ____ ZIP ____

Phone ____ Fax ____ E-mail address: ____

May we contact you for research purposes? ❑ Yes ❑ No

(If you participate in a research project, we will supply you with the Prima computer book of your choice.)

❶ How would you rate this book, overall?

- ❑ Excellent
- ❑ Very good
- ❑ Good
- ❑ Fair
- ❑ Below average
- ❑ Poor

❷ Why did you buy this book?

- ❑ Price of book
- ❑ Content
- ❑ Author's reputation
- ❑ Prima's reputation
- ❑ CD-ROM/disk included with book
- ❑ Information highlighted on cover
- ❑ Other (please specify): ____

❸ How did you discover this book?

- ❑ Found it on bookstore shelf
- ❑ Saw it in Prima Publishing catalog
- ❑ Recommended by store personnel
- ❑ Recommended by friend or colleague
- ❑ Saw an advertisement in: ____
- ❑ Read book review in: ____
- ❑ Saw it on Web site: ____
- ❑ Other (please specify): ____

❹ Where did you buy this book?

- ❑ Bookstore (name): ____
- ❑ Computer store (name): ____
- ❑ Electronics store (name): ____
- ❑ Wholesale club (name): ____
- ❑ Mail order (name): ____
- ❑ Direct from Prima Publishing
- ❑ Other (please specify): ____

❺ Which computer periodicals do you read regularly? ____

❻ Would you like to see your name in print?

May we use your name and quote you in future Prima Publishing books or promotional materials?

❑ Yes ❑ No

❼ Comments & suggestions: ____

TAPE HERE

❽ I am interested in seeing more computer books on these topics

- ❑ Word processing
- ❑ Desktop publishing
- ❑ Databases/spreadsheets
- ❑ Web site development
- ❑ Networking
- ❑ Internetworking
- ❑ Programming
- ❑ Intranetworking

❾ How do you rate your level of computer skills?

- ❑ Beginner
- ❑ Intermediate
- ❑ Advanced

❿ What is your age?

- ❑ Under 18
- ❑ 18–29
- ❑ 30–39
- ❑ 40–49
- ❑ 50–59
- ❑ 60–over

SAVE A STAMP

Visit our Web site at **http://www.primapublishing.com**

and simply fill out one of our online response forms.

PLEASE
PLACE
STAMP
HERE

PRIMA PUBLISHING
Computer Products Division
701 Congressional Blvd., Suite 350
Carmel, IN 46032

Description

This property sets or returns the index for either a group of radio objects or an option in a selectobject.

Applies to

radio

options

Examples

```
document.write(myselect.options.index)
```

Related Items

defaultSelected (Property)

selected (Property)

selectedIndex (Property)

LastDLLError

Syntax

```
Err.LastDLLError
```

Description

This property returns a value whether a call to a DLL was successful or not.

Applies to

Err

Example

```
document.write(Err.Description)
```

Related Items

Description (Property)

HelpContext (Property)

HelpFile (Property)

Number (Property)

Source (Property)

lastModified

Syntax

```
document.lastModified
```

Description

This returns the date that a document was last modified. This property is read-only.

Applies to

document

Example

```
document.write(mydocument.lastModified)
```

length

Syntax

```
object.length
```

Description

This property returns the length of an object.

Applies to

history

radio

select

string

anchors

forms

frames

links

options

Examples

```
temptext="ActiveX and VBScript Rules"
document.write(temptext.length)
document.write(document.forms.length)
document.write(document.forms[0].elements.length)
document.write(window.frames.length)
```

linkColor

Syntax

```
document.linkColor=colorobject
```

Description

This property sets or returns the color of a link.

Applies to

document

Examples

```
document.bgColor="ffffff"
document.fgColor="000000"
document.alinkColor="Teal"
document.linkColor="Red"
document.vlinkColor="Blue"
```

Related Items

alinkColor (Property)

bgColor (Property)

fgColor (Property)

vlinkColor (Property)

links

Syntax

```
document.links
```

Description

This is an array of links on a document.

Applies to

document

Examples

```
document.write(document.links.length)
```

```
document.write(document.links[0].href)
```

Related Items

anchors (Property)

length (Property)

location

Syntax

```
document.location
```

Description

This property returns the complete URL for the document.

Applies to

document

Example

```
document.write(document.location)
```

Related Items

location (Object)

method

Syntax

formobject.method

Description

This property is used to set or return how the form object information is sent to the server.

Applies to

form

Examples

```
document.write(myform.method)
myform.method="post"
```

Related Items

action (Property)

target (Property)

name

Syntax

```
object.name
```

Description

This property is used to set or return the name for an object.

Applies to

button

checkbox

hidden

password

radio

reset

select

submit

text

textarea

Example

```
document.write(submit.name)
```

Number

Syntax

```
Err.Number
```

Description

This property returns the number for an error.

Applies to

Err

Example

```
document.write(Err.Number)
```

Related Items

Description (Property)

HelpContext (Property)

HelpFile (Property)

LastDLLError(Property)

Source (Property)

value (Property)

options

Syntax

```
selectobject.option
```

Description

This is an array of options for a select object.

Applies to

select

defaultSelected

index

text

value

Examples

```
document.write(myselect.length)
```

```
document.write(myselect.options[0].value)
```

Related Items

length (Property)

parent

Syntax

```
window.parent
```

Description

This returns information concerning the topmost window for an object.

Applies to

window

Examples

```
document.write(window.parent.name)
```

pathname

Syntax

```
location.pathname
```

Description

This property returns the path name portion of a URL.

Applies to

location

Examples

```
document.write(location.hash)
document.write(location.host)
document.write(location.hostname)
document.write(location.href)
document.write(location.pathname)
document.write(location.port)
document.write(location.protocol)
document.write(location.search)
```

Related Items

hash (Property)

host (Property)

href (Property)

port (Property)

protocol (Property)

search (Property)

port

Syntax

```
location.port
```

Description

This property returns the port number portion, if available, of a URL.

Applies to

location

Examples

```
document.write(location.hash)
document.write(location.host)
document.write(location.hostname)
document.write(location.href)
document.write(location.pathname)
document.write(location.port)
document.write(location.protocol)
document.write(location.search)
```

Related Items

hash (Property)

host (Property)

href (Property)

pathname (Property)

protocol (Property)

search (Property)

protocol

Syntax

```
location.protocol
```

Description

This property returns the protocol portion of a URL.

Applies to

location

Examples

```
document.write(location.hash)
document.write(location.host)
document.write(location.hostname)
document.write(location.href)
document.write(location.pathname)
```

```
document.write(location.port)
document.write(location.protocol)
document.write(location.search)
```

Related Items

hash (Property)

host (Property)

href (Property)

pathname (Property)

port (Property)

search (Property)

reffer

Syntax

```
document.reffer
```

Description

This property contains information about the document that linked to the current document.

Applies to

document

```
Exampledocument.write(document.reffer)
```

search

Syntax

```
location.search
```

Description

This property returns the search portion of a URL that begins with the question mark (?).

Applies to

location

Examples

```
document.write(location.hash)
document.write(location.host)
document.write(location.hostname)
document.write(location.href)
document.write(location.pathname)
document.write(location.port)
document.write(location.protocol)
document.write(location.search)
```

Related Items

hash (Property)

host (Property)

href (Property)

pathname (Property)

port (Property)

protocol (Property)

selected

Syntax

```
selectelement.options.selected
```

Description

This property sets or returns a select item. You can use this property to set an item to be selected.

Applies to

options

Examples

```
document.write(myselect.options.selected)

myselect.options.selected=true
```

Related Items

defaultSelected (Property)

selectedIndex

Syntax

```
selectelement.selectedIndex
```

Description

This property sets or returns an index for a select item.

Applies to

select

Example

```
document.write(myselect.selectedIndex)
```

Related Items

defaultSelected (Property)

index (Property)

selected (Property)

self

Syntax

```
self
```

Description

This property refers to the current window.

Applies to

window

Example

```
document.write(self.name)
```

Related Items

window (Property)

Source

Syntax

```
Err.Source
```

Description

This property sets or returns the name of the application or object that generated the error.

Applies to

Err

Example

```
document.write(Err.Source)
```

Related Items

Description (Property)

HelpContext (Property)

HelpFile (Property)

LastDLLError(Property)

Number (Property)

status

Syntax

```
windowobject.status
```

Description

This property is used to set or return the message that is displayed at the bottom of the browser window in the status bar.

Applies to

window

Examples

```
Sub ToolTip
window.defaultStatus="Link to a cool site"
```

```
window.status="Cool site"
End Sub
<A HREF="http://www.coolsite.com" onMouseOver="ToolTip()">
Cool Site</A>
```

Related Items

defaultStatus (Property)

target

Syntax

```
formobject.target

linkobject.target
```

Description

This is used to specify the window for responses.

Applies to

form

link

Example

```
mydocument.myform.target="ConfirmationWindow"
```

Related Items

action (Property)

method (Property)

text

Syntax

```
selectobject.text
```

Description

This returns the string stored for the select object.

Applies to

select

Examples

```
document.write(myselect.text)
```

Related Items

title

Syntax

```
document.title
```

Description

This property is used to return or set the title for a document.

Applies to

document

Example

```
document.title="ActiveX and VBScript"
```

Related Items

top

Syntax

```
top
```

Description

This property refers to the topmost window. This window is its own parent.

Applies to

window

Example

```
document.write(top.name)
```

Related Items

userAgent

Syntax

```
navigator.userAgent
```

Description

This property returns the user-agent header that is sent in the HTTP protocol. This property is read-only.

Applies to

navigator

Examples

```
document.write(navigator.appCodeName)
document.write(navigator.appName)
document.write(navigator.appVersion)
document.write(navigator.userAgent)
```

Related Items

appCodeName (Property)

appName (Property)

appVersion (Property)

value

Syntax

```
object.value
```

Description

This is used to set or return the value for an object.

Applies to

button

checkbox

hidden

password

radio

reset

select

submit

text

textarea

Examples

```
ADDRESSEMAIL.value="yourname@your.server"
document.write(ADDRESSEMAIL.value)
```

Related Items

defaultValue (Property)

vlinkColor

Syntax

```
document.vlinkColor=colorobject
```

Description

This property sets the color of visited links.

Applies to

document

Examples

```
document.bgColor="ffffff"
document.fgColor="000000"
document.alinkColor="Teal"
document.linkColor="Red"
document.vlinkColor="Blue"
```

Related Items

alinkColor (Property)

bgColor (Property)

fgColor (Property)

linkColor (Property)

window

Syntax

```
window
```

Description

This is used to separate a window object from the window property. The window property refers to the current window.

Applies to

window

Example

```
document.write(window.name)
```

Related Items

self (Property)

Events

This section describes the events used in Visual Basic Scripting Edition.

onBlur

Description

This event is generated when an object loses the focus.

Event Handler of

select

text

textarea

Example

```
<INPUT TYPE="TEXT" VALUE="" NAME="USEREMAIL"
onBlur="CovertToLower">
```

Related Items

onChange (Event Handler)

onFocus (Event Handler)

onChange

Description

This event is generated when an object changes.

Event Handler of

select

text

textarea

Example

```
<INPUT TYPE="TEXT" VALUE="" NAME="USEREMAIL"
onChange="CovertToLower">
```

Related Items

onBlur (Event Handler)

onFocus (Event Handler)

onClick

Description

This event is generated when an object is clicked.

Event Handler of

button

checkbox

radio

link

reset

submit

Example

```
<INPUT TYPE="BUTTON" VALUE="Send" NAME="SENDUSEREMAIL"
onClick="SendInformation">
```

onFocus

Description

This event is generated when an object receives the focus.

Event Handler of

select

text

textarea

Example

```
<INPUT TYPE="TEXT" VALUE="" NAME="USEREMAIL" onFocus="
displayhelp">
```

Related Items

onBlur (Event Handler)

onChange (Event Handler)

onLoad

Description

This event is generated when an object is loaded.

Event Handler of

window

Example

```
<BODY onLoad="Greetings">
```

Related Items

onUnload (Event Handler)

onMouseOver

Description

This event is generated when the cursor passes over an object.

Event Handler of

link

Examples

```
Sub ToolTip
window.defaultStatus="Link to a cool site"
window.status="Cool site"
End Sub
<A HREF="http://www.coolsite.com" onMouseOver="ToolTip()">
Cool Site</A>
```

Related Items

onSelect

Description

This event is generated when an object text is selected.

Event Handler of

text

textarea

Example

```
<INPUT TYPE="TEXT" VALUE="" NAME="USEREMAIL" onSelect="
selecttext">
```

Related Items

onUnload (Event Handler)

onSubmit

Description

An onSubmit event is generated when a user clicks the Submit button.

Event Handler of

form

Examples

```
<FORM NAME="myform">
<PRE>
Enter Your Name          <INPUT TYPE="TEXT"
NAME="NAMEEMAIL" SIZE="40" MAXLENGTH="40"><BR>
Enter Your Address       <INPUT TYPE="TEXT"
NAME="ADDRESSSNAILMAIL" SIZE="40" MAXLENGTH="40"><BR>
Enter Your City          <INPUT TYPE="TEXT"
NAME="CITYEMAIL" SIZE="40" MAXLENGTH="30"><BR>
Enter Your State         <INPUT TYPE="TEXT"
NAME="STATEEMAIL" SIZE="10" MAXLENGTH="6"><BR>
Enter Your Zip           <INPUT TYPE="TEXT"
NAME="ZIPEMAIL" SIZE="20" MAXLENGTH="10"><BR>
Enter Your Email Address <INPUT TYPE="TEXT"
NAME="ADDRESSEMAIL" SIZE="40" MAXLENGTH="40"><BR>
</PRE>
<P></P>
<INPUT TYPE="CHECKBOX" NAME="CBACTIVEX" CHECKED=TRUE>ActiveX<BR>
<INPUT TYPE="CHECKBOX" NAME="CBHTML">HTML 3.2<BR>
<INPUT TYPE="CHECKBOX" NAME="CBVBSCRIPT">VB Script<BR>
<INPUT TYPE="CHECKBOX" NAME="CBJSCRIPT">JScript<BR>
<P></P>
<INPUT TYPE="SUBMIT" NAME="CMDBSUBMIT">
<INPUT TYPE="RESET" NAME="CMDBRESET"><BR>
<P></P>
</FORM>
<SCRIPT LANGUAGE="VBScript">
myform.onSubmit="SendInformation"
</SCRIPT>
```

Related Items

submit (Object)

submit (Method)

onUnload

Description

This event is generated when an object is unloaded.

Event Handler of

window

Example

```
<BODY onUnload="Goodbye">
```

Related Items

onLoad (Event Handler)

Statements

This section describes the statements used in Visual Basic Scripting Edition.

Call

Syntax

```
Call procedure
```

Description

This statement is used to call a DLL procedure a Sub procedure or a Function procedure.

Examples

```
sub myfunc
Call myfunc1
document.write("ActiveX")
End Sub
sub myfunc1
```

```
document.write("VBScript")
End Sub
```

comment

Syntax

```
rem VBScript comment

' VBScript comment
```

Description

This is used to comment source code for greater readability.

Examples

```
rem VBScript

' VBScript
```

Date (Statement)

Syntax

```
Date = dateobject
```

Description

This is used to set the current system date.

Examples

```
MyDatenTime = "June 17, 1996"
Date = MyDatenTime
```

Dim

Syntax

```
Dim variable[([subscripts])][,variable][...,variable]
```

Description

This statement is used to declare variables and allocate space.

Examples

```
Sub myfunc
```

```
Dim MyDate, MyArray(10), Count
document.write(MyDate)
For Count = 0 to 10
document.write(MyArray(Count))
Next Count
End Sub
```

Do Loop

Syntax

```
Do While(condition)
...statements
Loop
```

Or

```
Do
...statements
Loop While(condition)
```

Description

This statement is used to loop through a series of statements until the condition is true.

Examples

```
Sub myfunc
Count = 0
Do While Count < 10
Count = Count + 1
document.write(Count)
Loop
Count = 0
Do
Count = Count + 1
document.write(Count)
Loop While Count < 10
End Sub
```

End Function

Syntax

```
End Function
```

Description

This statement is used to end a Function block.

Examples

```
Funtion myfunc
Count = 0
Do While Count < 10
Count = Count + 1
document.write(Count)
Loop
Count = 0
Do
Count = Count + 1
document.write(Count)
Loop While Count < 10
End Function
```

End Sub

Syntax

```
End Sub
```

Description

This statement is used to end a Sub block.

Examples

```
Sub myfunc
Count = 0
Do While Count < 10
Count = Count + 1
document.write(Count)
Loop
Count = 0
```

```
Do
Count = Count + 1
document.write(Count)
Loop While Count < 10
End Sub
```

Erase

Syntax

```
Erase array
```

Description

This statement is used to reset the values of a fixed array or release dynamic array storage.

Examples

```
Sub myfunc
Dim MyDate, MyArray(10), Count
document.write(MyDate)
For Count = 0 to 10
document.write(MyArray(Count))
Next Count
Erase MyArray
End Sub
```

Exit Function

Syntax

```
Exit Function
```

Description

This statement is used to break out of a Function.

Examples

```
Funtion myfunc
Count = 0
Do While Count < 10
Count = Count + 1
If Count = 5 Then Exit Function
```

```
document.write(Count)
Loop
Count = 0
Do
Count = Count + 1
document.write(Count)
Loop While Count < 10
End Function
```

Exit Sub

Syntax

```
Exit Sub
```

Description

This statement is used to break out of a Sub.

Examples

```
Sub myfunc
Count = 0
Do While Count < 10
Count = Count + 1
If Count = 5 Then Exit Sub
document.write(Count)
Loop
Count = 0
Do
Count = Count + 1
document.write(Count)
Loop While Count < 10
End Sub
```

For Next

Syntax

```
For variable = startnum To endnum Step stepnum
...Statements
Next variable
```

Description

The For Next loop is used to execute a block of statements from the start number to the end number.

Examples

```
Sub myfunc
Dim Count
For Count = 0 to 10
document.write(Count)
Next Count
For Count = 0 to 10 Step 2
document.write(Count)
Next Count
For Count = 1 to 10 Step 2
document.write(Count)
Next Count
End Sub
```

Function

Syntax

```
Function
```

Description

This statement is used to start a Function block.

Examples

```
Funtion myfunc
Count = 0
Do While Count < 10
Count = Count + 1
document.write(Count)
Loop
Count = 0
Do
Count = Count + 1
document.write(Count)
```

```
Loop While Count < 10
End Function
```

If Then Else

Syntax

```
If (condition) Then
...statements
else
...else statements
End If
```

Description

This statement is used to test for a condition, and if true, executes the statements. If the else is specified and the condition is false, those statements are executed.

Examples

```
temp = "VBScript"
temp1 = "VBScript"
If temp = temp1 Then
document.write(temp & " equals " & temp1)
else
document.write(temp & " does not equal " & temp1)
End If
temp = "ActiveX"
temp1 = "VBScript"
If temp = temp1 Then
document.write(temp & " equals " & temp1)
else
document.write(temp & " does not equal " & temp1)
End If
```

Let

Syntax

```
Let variable=expression
```

Description

This lets you assign the value of an expression to a variable. Let is an optional word and is not required.

Examples

```
Let temp = "VBScript"

temp = "VBScript"
```

Mid (Statement)

Syntax

```
Mid(stringobject, startpos [,length])
```

Description

This function returns the characters from the start position to the length specified.

Examples

```
temptext = "OLE and VBScript Rules"
document.write(temptext)
document.write(Mid(temptext, 1, 3)="ActiveX")
```

On Error

Syntax

```
On Error
```

Description

This statement is used to trigger an error handler when an error occurs.

Examples

```
On Error GoTo ErrorHandler
```

Option Explicit

Syntax

```
Option Explicit
```

Description

This forces the explicit declarations of variables.

Examples

```
Option Explicit
```

Private

Syntax

```
Private variablenames
```

Description

This statement is similar to the Dim statement except that the scope of the variable is restricted to the module level.

Examples

```
Private temptext
```

Randomize

Syntax

```
Randomize
```

Description

This statement is used to seed the random number generator.

Example

```
Randomize
```

ReDim

Syntax

```
ReDim
```

Description

This statement is used to redimension an array.

Examples

```
Sub myfunc
```

```
Dim MyDate, MyArray(10), Count
document.write(MyDate)
For Count = 0 to 10
document.write(MyArray(Count))
Next Count
ReDim MyArray(20)
End Sub
```

Resume

Syntax

```
Resume
```

Description

This statement is used to resume execution after an error.

Examples

```
Sub MyErrorHandler
' Handle error
Resume
End Sub
```

Select Case

Syntax

```
Select Case variable
Case
End Select
```

Description

This statement is used to select one item from a list of items.

Examples

```
Select Case ButtonPressed
Case 1
document.write("Button 1 was pressed")
Case 2
document.write("Button 2 was pressed")
Case 3
```

```
document.write("Button 3 was pressed")
Case Else
document.write("No button was pressed")
End Select
```

Set

Syntax

```
Set variable = object
```

Description

This statement is used to set an object reference to a variable.

Example

```
Set MyDate = Date
```

Static

Syntax

```
Static variable
```

Description

This statement is used to preserve variable content.

Examples

```
Sub myfunc
Static MyDate, MyArray(10), Count
document.write(MyDate)
For Count = 0 to 10
document.write(MyArray(Count))
Next Count
ReDim MyArray(20)
End Sub
```

Sub

Syntax

```
Sub
```

Description

This statement is used to start a Sub block.

Examples

```
Sub myfunc
Count = 0
Do While Count < 10
Count = Count + 1
document.write(Count)
Loop
Count = 0
Do
Count = Count + 1
document.writc(Count)
Loop While Count < 10
End Sub
```

Time (Statement)

Syntax

```
Time = timeobject
```

Description

This is used to set the current system time.

Examples

```
MyDatenTime = "13:30:00"
Time - MyDatenTime
```

While Wend

Syntax

```
while (condition)
...statements
Wend
```

Description

The while statement is used to loop through statements until condition is reached.

Examples

```
Sub Myfunc
while (templ < 10)
document.write(templ)
templ = templ + 1
Wend
End Sub
```

Visual Basic Scripting Edition is a subset of Visual Basic and Visual Basic for Applications. It adds functionality, however, to handle things in the world of HTML and the World Wide Web. It also provides the functionality to make use of ActiveX controls, as you will see in the next pages.

Installing the ActiveX Control Pad

The ActiveX Control Pad is a standard Wizard install. If you have installed the Internet Explorer 3.0 final release, the HTML Layout Control and a number of other ActiveX controls will have been installed with Internet Explorer and are used by ActiveX Control Pad.

HTML Layout Control

Because the functionality provided by the HTML Layout Control is not part of any completed W3C standard, the code generated for this control is stored in .ALX files. These files are called and loaded from the main HTML document. The HTML Layout Control allows full control over regions in 2-D space. Actually, for those familiar with Visual Basic, it looks much like the Toolbox, Form, and Properties as they appear in Visual Basic. And Scripting Wizard provides the code-building part.

Using ActiveX Control Pad

You can start the ActiveX Control Pad from the Start menu or by double-clicking its icon in Explorer. The start-up screen is shown in Figure 5-7 with the HTML code page maximized. Notice that you are provided with skeleton HTML code. As mentioned earlier, this application is deceptively simple in appearance but you need to look at several menu selections. You can also right-click on any HTML file icon and choose Edit with ActiveX Control Pad to start the ActiveX Control Pad.

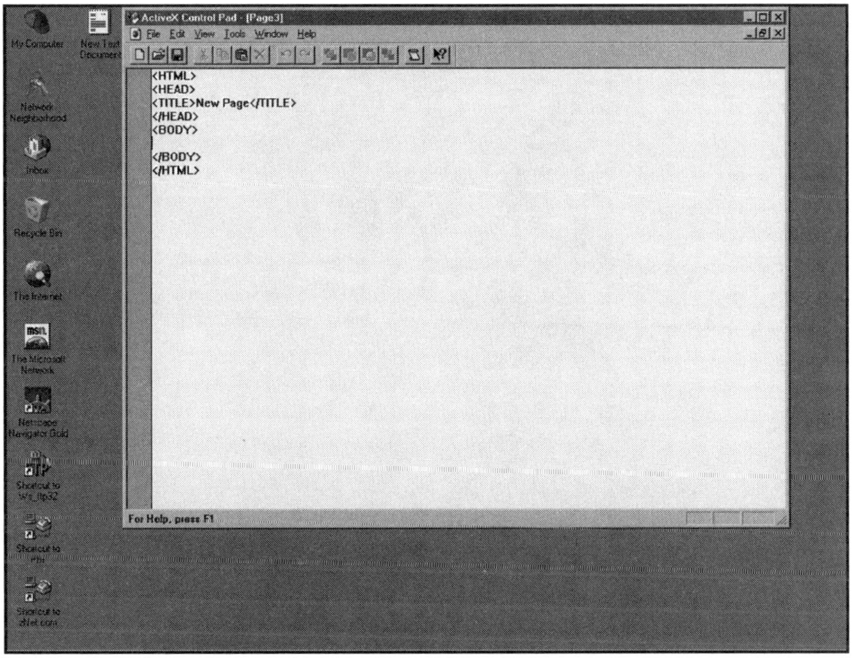

Figure 5-7 The ActiveX Control Pad

Menus

Toolbar, menus, and status bar are available by default. Menus include File, Edit, View, Tools, Window, and Help.

File Menu

In addition to the standard Open..., Close, Save, Save As..., Save All, and Print selections, you will see New HTML and New HTML Layout. The New HTML selection will display a new page in the HTML Editor window. The New HTML Layout will start the HTML Layout Control. I cover this a little later. The menu is shown in Figure 5-8.

Edit Menu

The Edit menu has Undo, Redo, Cut, Copy, Paste, Delete, and Select All. The Insert ActiveX Control... selection allows you to insert an ActiveX control at the cursor location in the open HTML page. I cover that in detail later. Insert HTML Layout... brings up a standard file dialog with the default set to .alx to allow the insertion of an .ALX file. The bottom menu selection changes to match the context in the HTML code window. The menu is shown in Figure 5-9.

Figure 5-8
The File menu

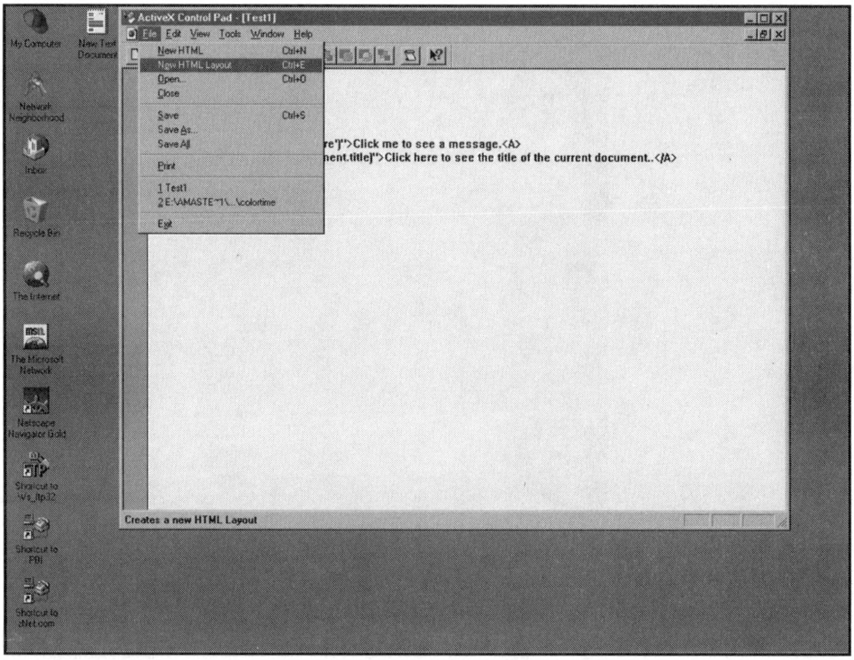

Figure 5-9
The Edit menu

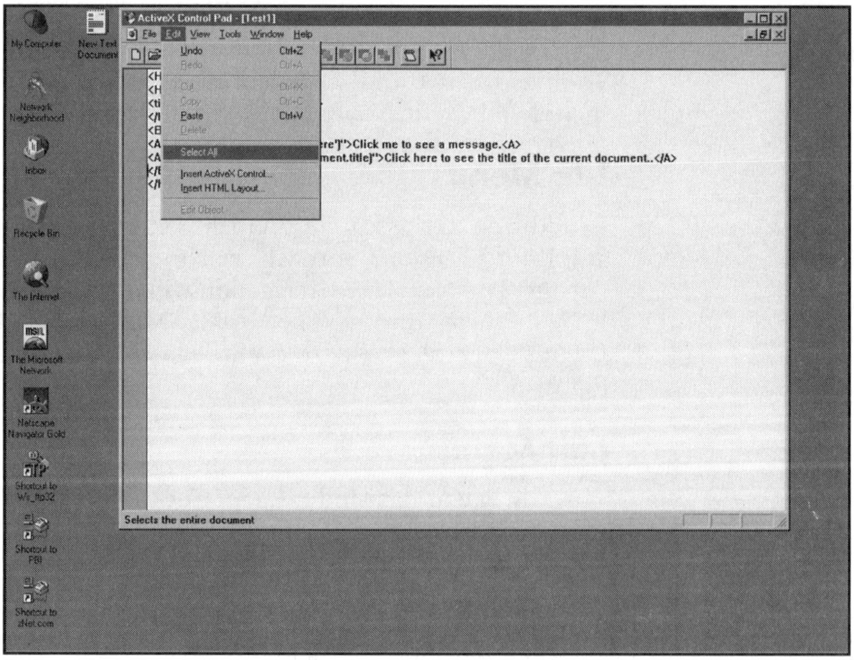

View Menu

The View menu, shown in Figure 5-10, allows you to enable or disable the display of the toolbar and status bar. It presents a different set of items with other parts of the ActiveX Control Pad running.

Fig. 5-10
The View menu

Tools Menu

The Tools menu (Figure 5-11) allows you to start the Script Wizard..., to be covered in more detail. The Options flyout allows you to set up options for the HTML Layout... and Script... displays.

Window Menu

The Windows menu shown in Figure 5-12 has the usual Cascade and Tile selections. It also maintains a list of open HTML pages.

Help menu

The Help menu is shown in Figure 5-13. Control Pad Help Topics presents a standard Windows help file. The *HTML Reference* and *VBScript Reference* will start Internet Explorer and display help as HTML documents. If help is not available on your machine, Internet Explorer will attempt a connection to the Web to obtain the latest help files.

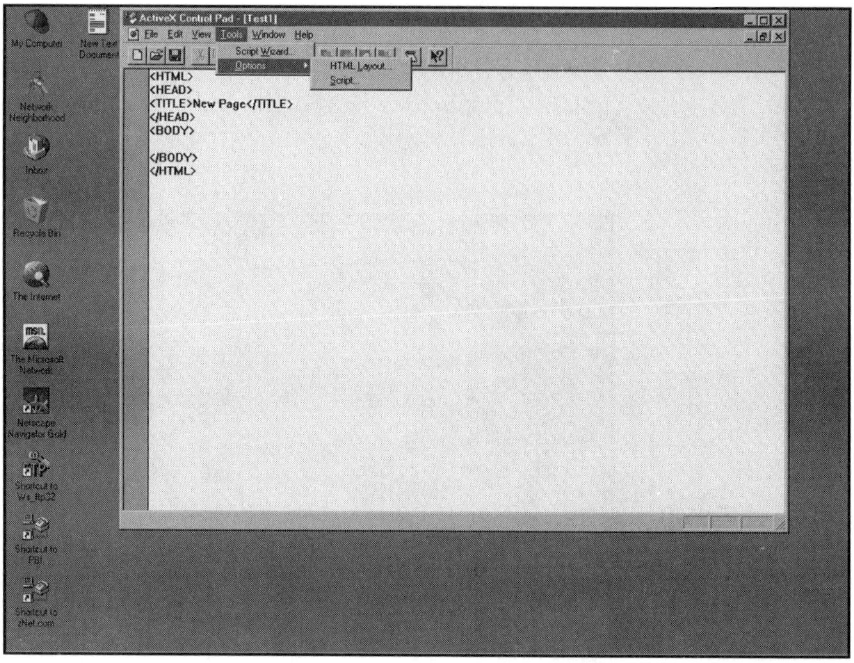

Figure 5-11
The Tools menu

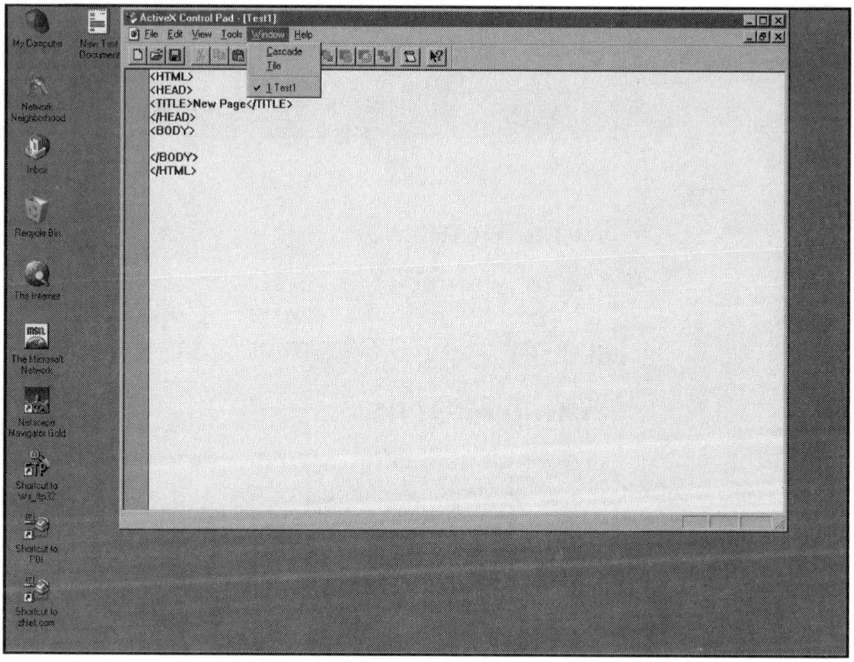

Figure 5-12
The Window menu

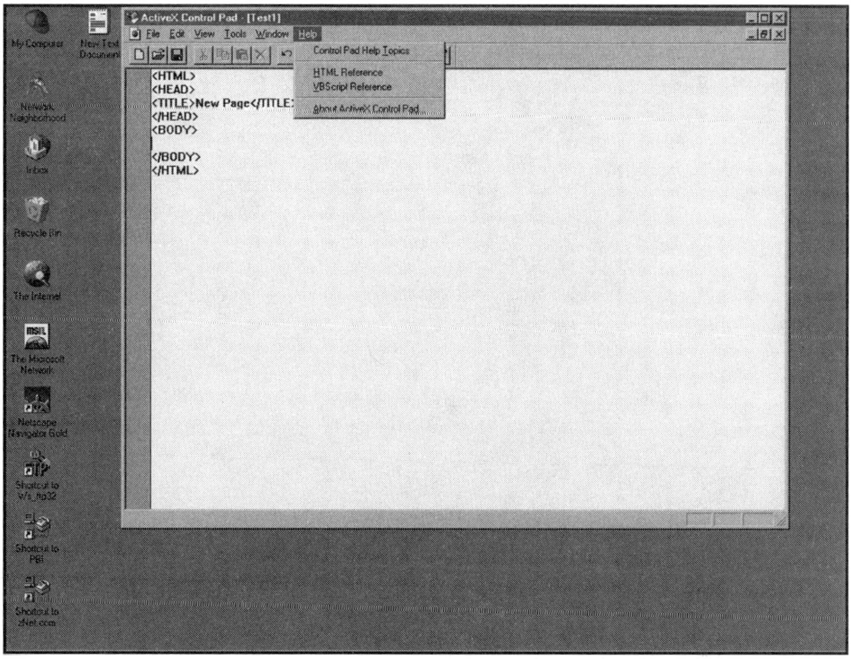

Figure 5-13
The Help menu

Going back, for a moment, to the Tools menu, Figure 5-14 shows the HTML Layout options available. The Grid settings Vertical and Horizontal Spacing default is 8 points. A finer-grain display is 4 points. You can set this to any value that suits. You can also elect Show Grid and Snap to Grid.

Figure 5-15 shows the Script Options dialog box (from the Tools menu flyout). You will understand the selections available after covering the Script Wizard.

Inserting Controls

Before embarking on what may be an adventure into the HTML Layout Control and Visual Basic Scripting, you should try the Insert ActiveX Control... selection from the Edit menu. When you select this option, the Insert ActiveX Control dialog shown box in Figure 5-16 is displayed. The amount of content will depend on how many .OCX (the extension for ActiveX controls) files are on your computer. These files are provided by a large number of development systems and applications in Office 95, for example. Scroll down the list to find controls whose names start with Microsoft Forms 2.0... and select Microsoft Forms 2.0 CommandButton. Click OK.

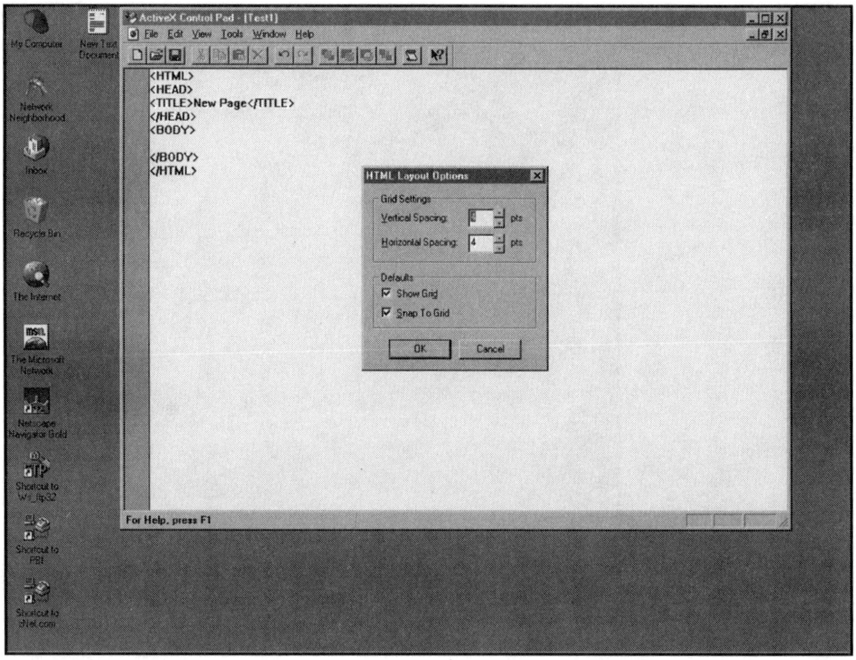

Figure 5-14
The HTML Layout Options dialog box

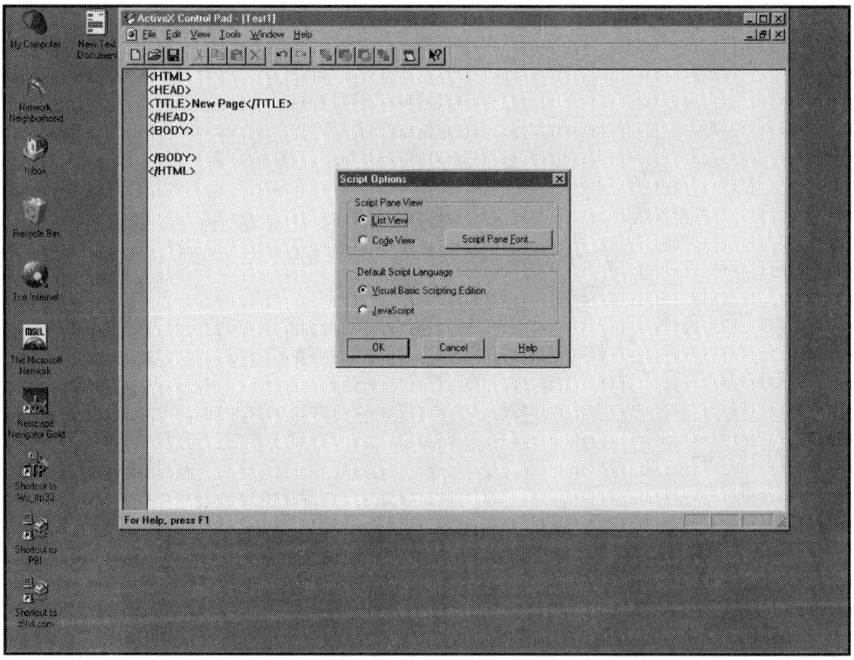

Figure 5-15
The Script Options dialog box

Your computer may take some time to sort everything out, but after a reasonable amount of time, you should see the Edit ActiveX Control and Properties dialogs as shown in Figure 5-17. The CommandButton displayed in the Edit ActiveX Control dialog is the control that will be placed in your HTML code, and the Prop-erties dialog box shows all the properties available for this control. Again, the resemblance to the Visual Basic development environment is there.

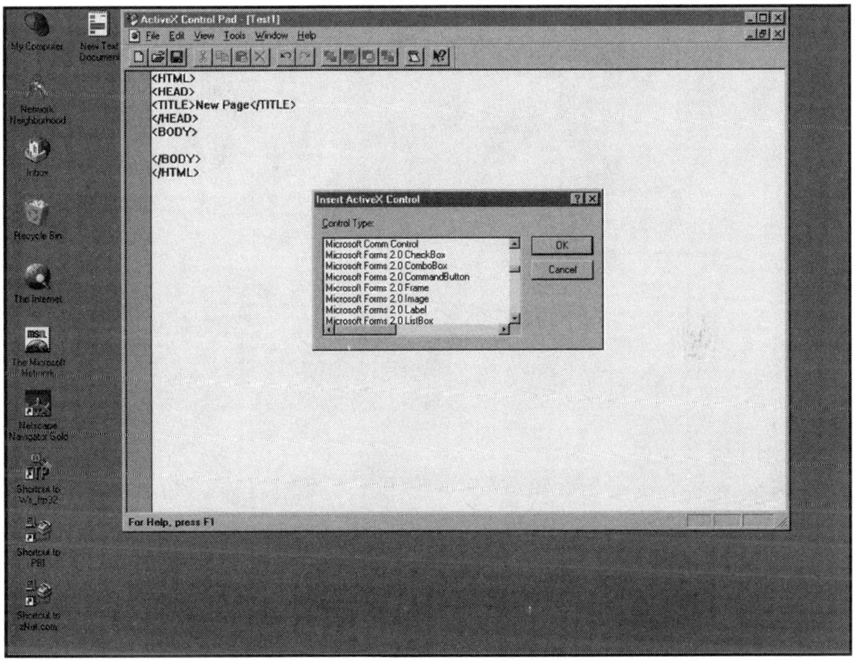

Figure 5-16
The Insert ActiveX Control dialog box

I'm going to change just the Caption property. You can change this property by entering a new caption directly on the control (just click the CommandButton) or by entering it in the Caption field in the Properties dialog. However you do the editing, the new Caption will show up in both fields as shown in Figure 5-18. You can, if you choose, set any other properties at this time. When you're finished, click the close (x) in the upper-right corner of the Edit ActiveX Control dialog box.

The code for the new button will be inserted at the cursor in the HTML code page shown in Figure 5-19. Notice that a small 3-D cube appears in the left border. You can edit this control at any time by clicking the cube icon.

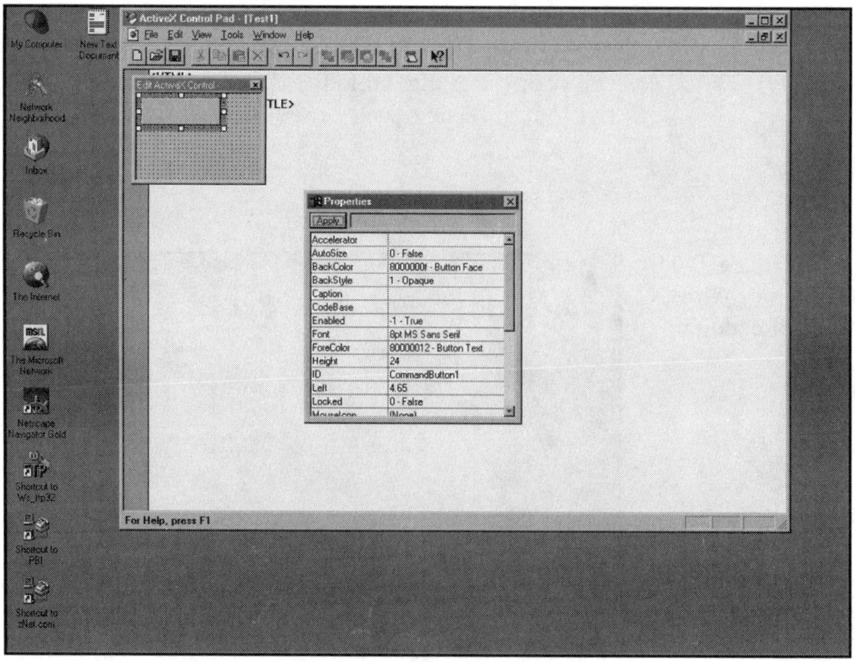

Figure 5-17 The display for editing a CommandButton

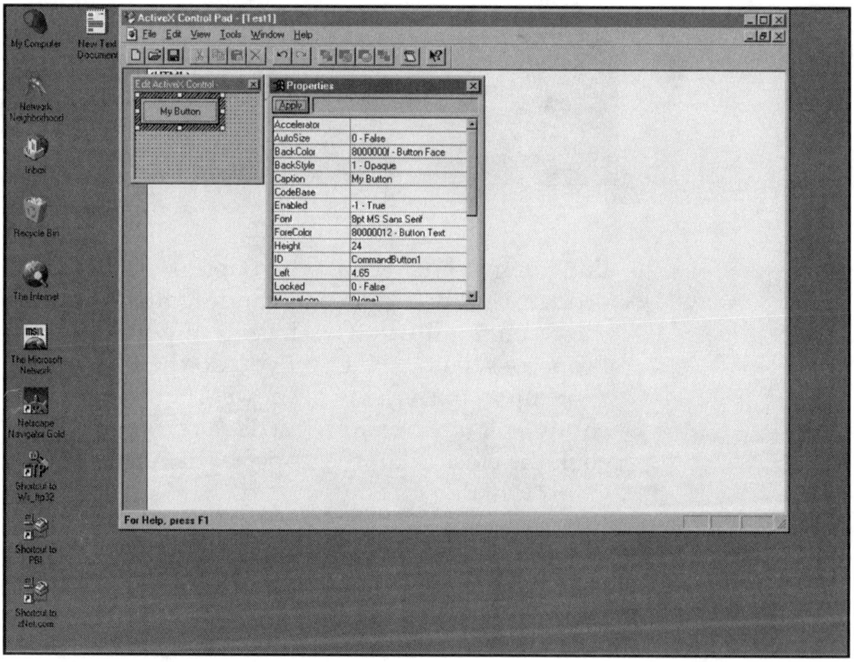

Figure 5-18 The Edited caption

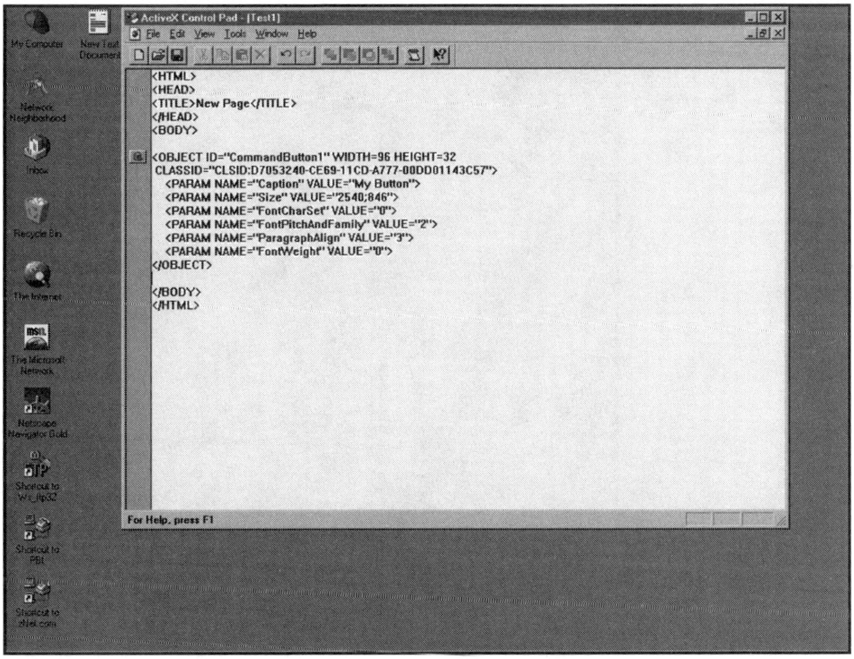

Figure 5-19
The button oject code inserted

Now save the Test1 code and double-click the Test1 icon in Explorer to bring up Internet Explorer and display the page shown in Figure 5-20. You have just completed your first ActiveX programming using ActiveX controls.

The HTML Layout Control

The HTML Layout Control is provided with the latest Internet Explorer 3.0. You should install it when you install Internet Explorer so that you can use it with the ActiveX Control Pad. To start the HTML Layout Control in design mode, select New HTML Layout from the Files menu. Your system may take some time to display the content shown in Figure 5-21. As shown in the figure, elements have been resized and repositioned. The Properties dialog is also running.

> **NOTE:**
> **For users of Visual Basic, the interface should look quite familiar, but keep the following in mind: This application is very pop-up menu intense. It also changes the contents of menus on the main application, depending on the piece that is running.**

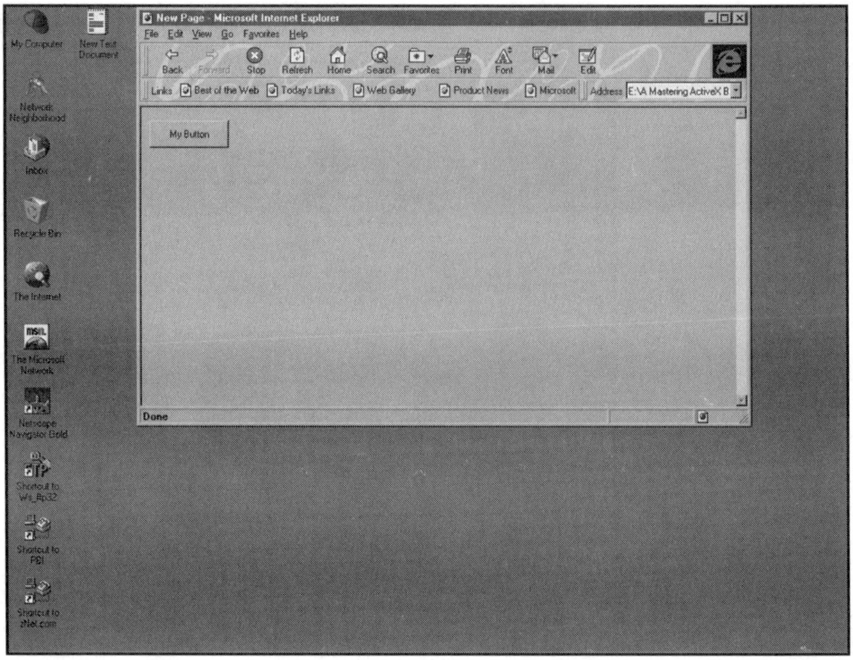

Figure 5-20 The button object running in Internet Explorer

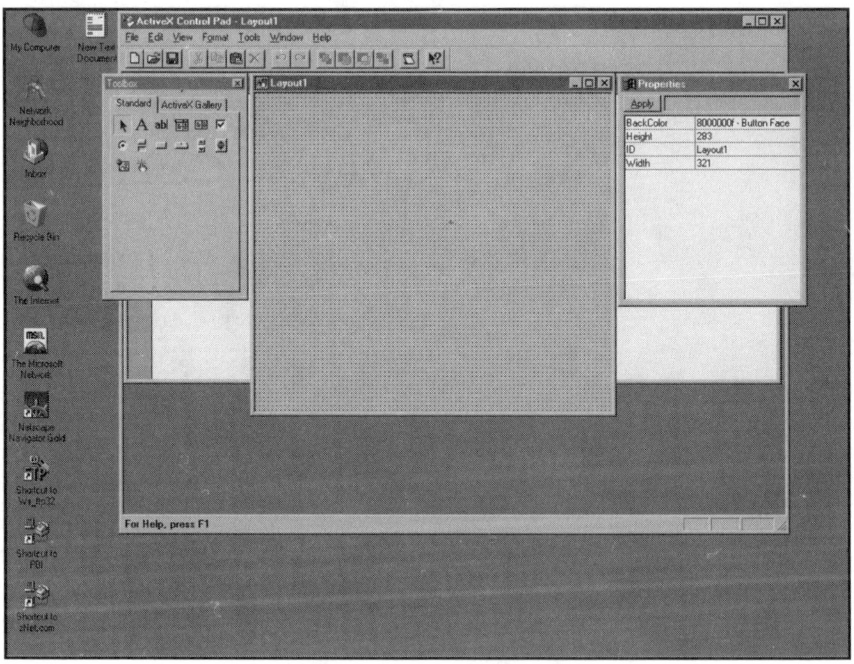

Figure 5-21 The HTML layout control

I'll begin with the menu changes. Figure 5-22 shows the View menu. It now provides toggles for the Grid, Toolbox, and Properties dialog boxes. Also, a Format menu item has been added. This menu is shown in Figure 5-23. The top-five flyout menus provide for aligning, making the same size, sizing, and horizontal and vertical spacing. The functionality is evident when you select a group of components on the layout and activate the menu. The bottom four elements allow the z-order positioning of elements on the screen. Remember, the HTML Layout control is designed to allow 2-D positioning of images and other content. Images can be opaque or transparent and can be overlapped on the display surface to provide interesting effects.

Figure 5-22
The New View menu

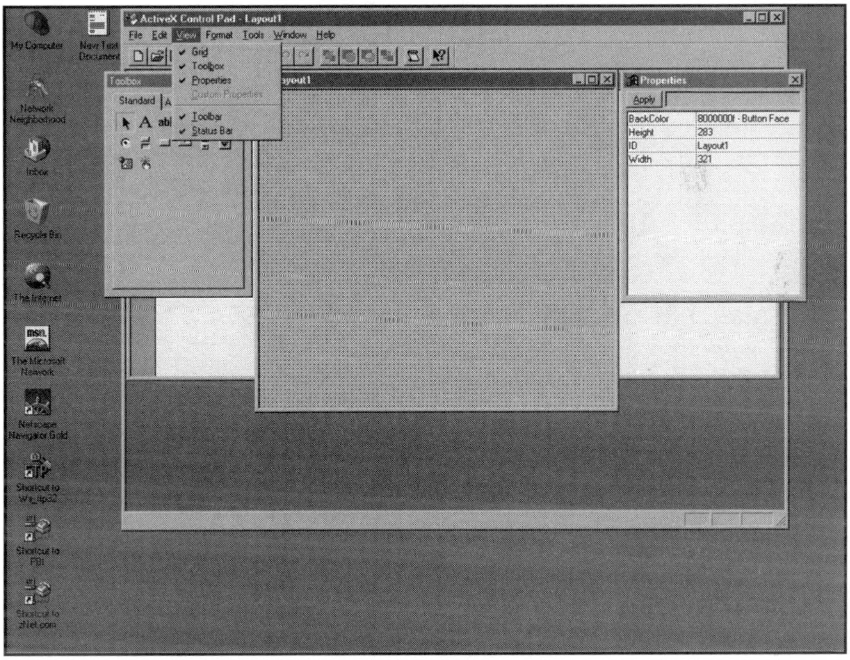

The multitude of pop-up menus is illustrated in the next few pages. First, Figure 5-24 shows the pop-up displayed when you right-click the tabs on the toolbox. You can add a New Page (actually, a new tab) as with the ActiveX Gallery tab), Delete Page, Rename the Page (tab), and Move the Page. You can also Import and Export Pages. This means that you can have different control sets for different projects and install them as you need them. When you add a page, the page will have its own pointer.

Right-clicking on the body of the page allows you to add Additional Controls to the page, as in Figure 5-25, and right-clicking on a control icon will allow you to Delete a control from the page or

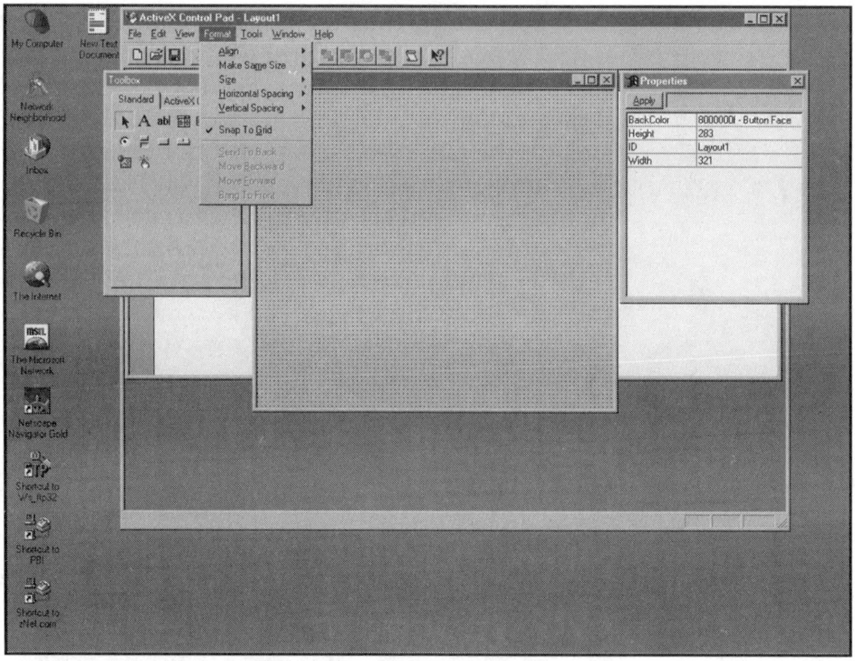

Figure 5-23
The newly installed Format menu

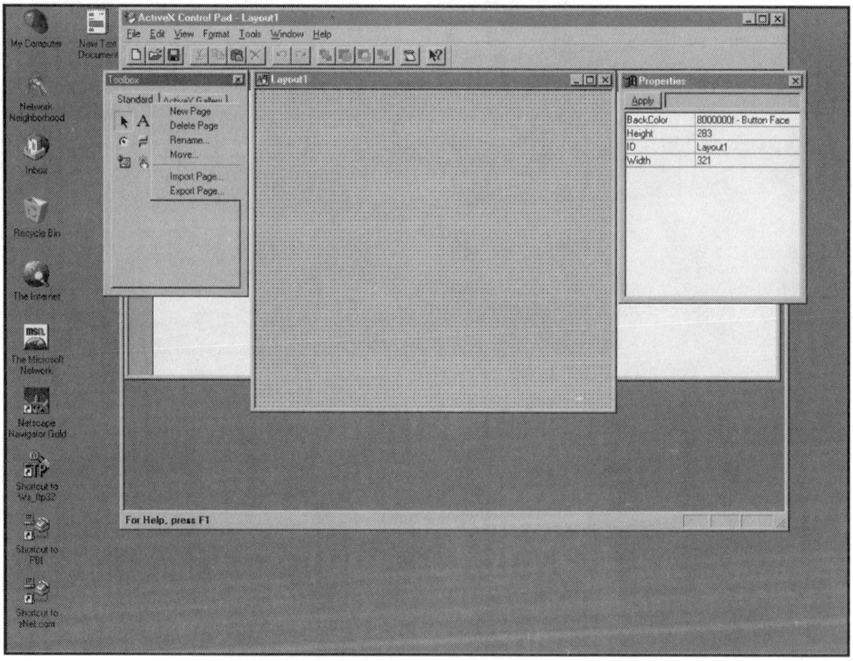

Figure 5-24
The toolbox tab pop-up

Customize it as shown in Figure 5-26. The Customize Control dialog box is shown in Figure 5-27. This all results in very complete control of the ActiveX controls that you use in projects.

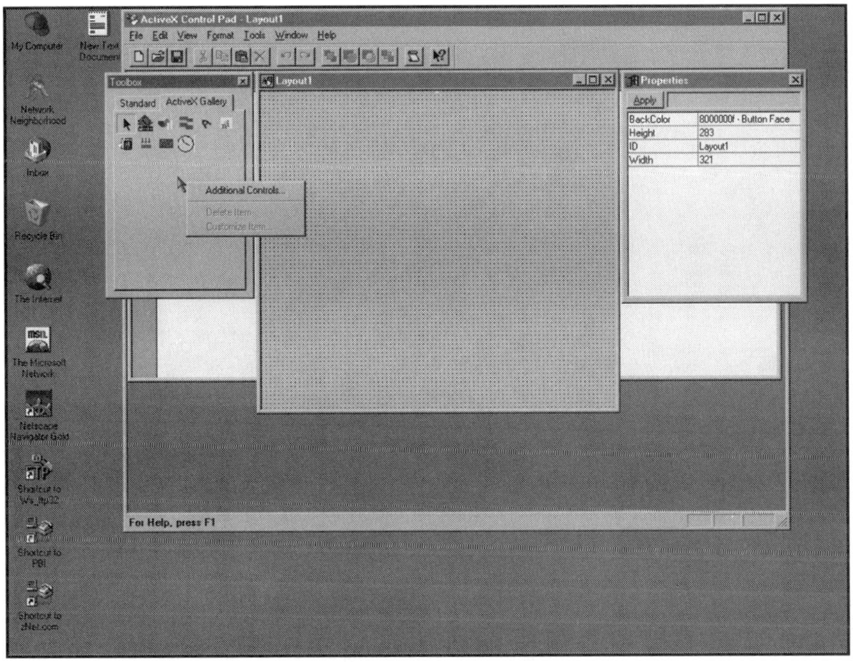

Figure 5-25 The Additional Controls pop-up

The last pop-up that I consider now is the one shown in Figure 5-28. This pop-up is associated with the Layout form itself. Besides Undo, Redo, Paste, and Select All, this pop-up provides a selection to start the Script Wizard View Source Code, and activate the Properties dialog. The top items are self-explanatory. The Script Wizard allows you to script elements in the .ALX control code. Electing to View Source Code will bring up a dialog box advising you that the HTML Layout Control will save your source and close if you want to continue.

In Figure 5-29, I've added three Label controls, three TextBox controls, and a CommandButton control. You can easily duplicate this arrangement. I'm not scripting the Change Color button right now.

Select Save As... from the main File menu and save the file as LAYOUT1.ALX in the directory containing the Test1 HTML file. After it's saved, you can close the HTML Layout Control.

Select the Insert HTML Layout... from the main Edit menu. From the File Open dialog box, select the LAYOUT1.ALX that you just finished and click OK. The result will be the insertion of an object (the HTML

Figure 5-26
The Control pop-up

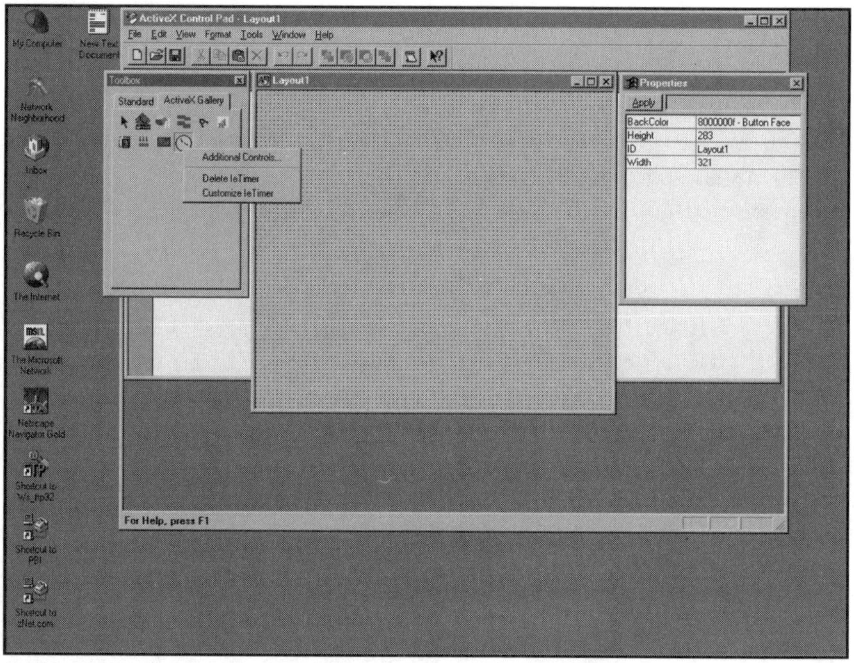

Figure 5-27
The Customize Control dialog box

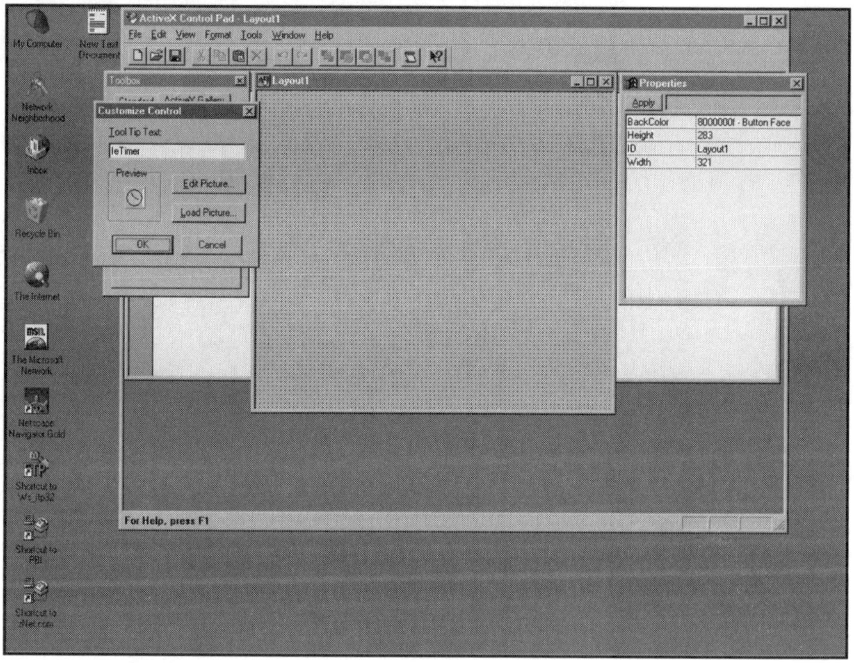

Figure 5-28
The Layout Control pop-up

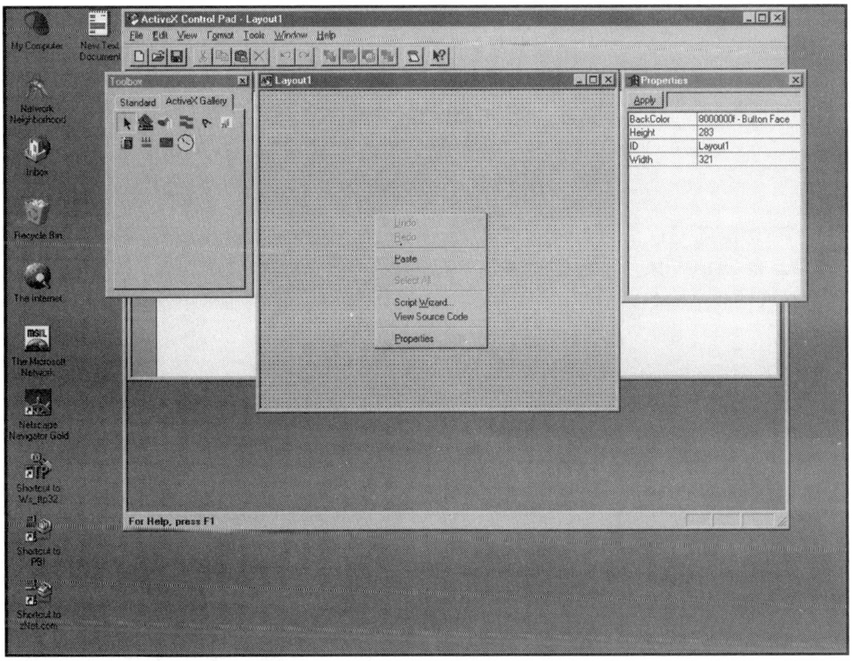

Figure 5-29
The new layout

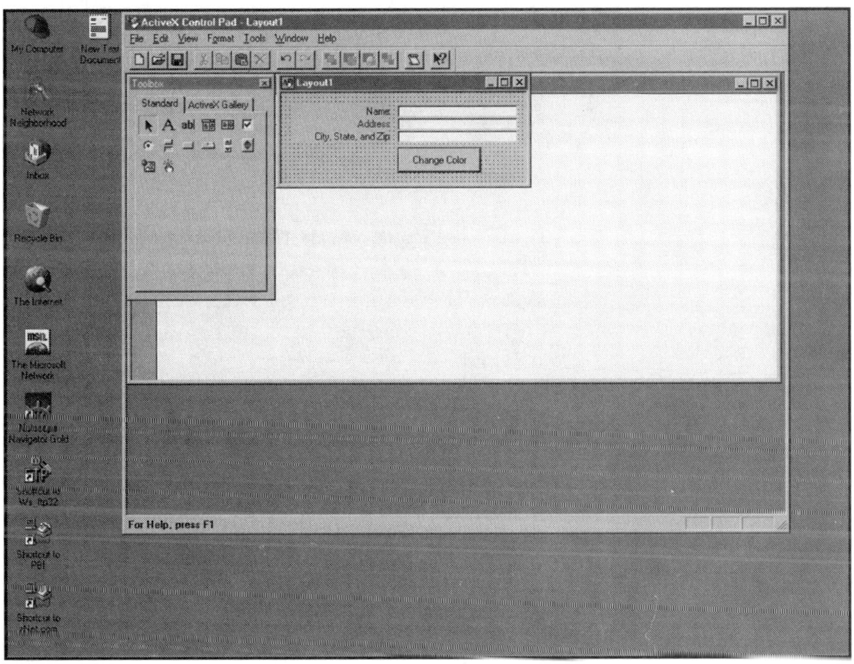

Layout control object) in the HTML source window, as shown in Figure 5-30. Notice that a small icon is inserted in the border to indicate that this is an HTML Layout control object. You can edit the .ALX file at any time by clicking this icon. Figure 5-31 shows what the new code looks like in Internet Explorer.

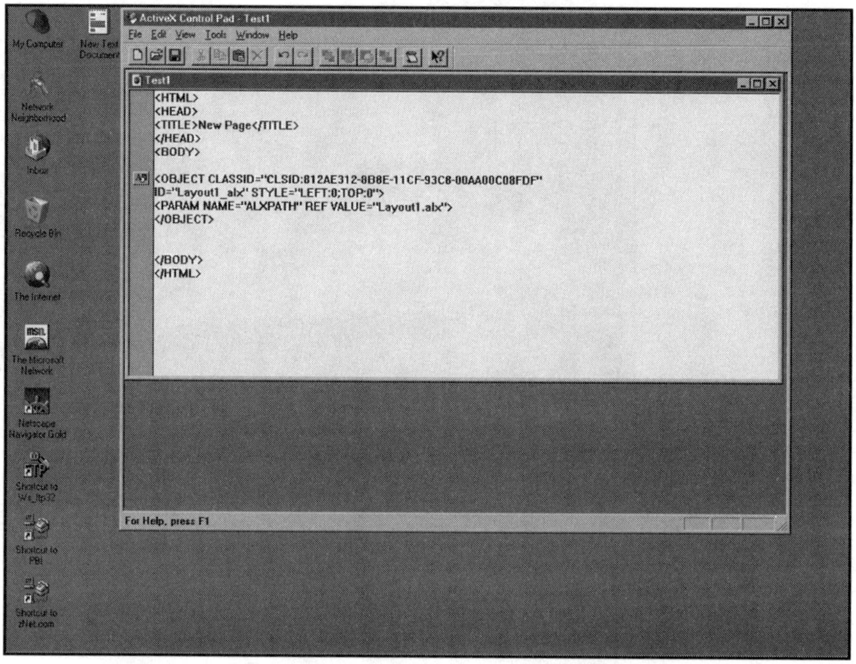

Figure 5-30 The object inserted in the HTML page

It should be obvious that the possibilities are almost endless. Thousands of vendors are at work making their components available for use on the Internet, and a substantial number of controls already exist. The remaining piece here is the Script Wizard.

The Script Wizard

The Script Wizard is the Visual Basic equivalent of View Code. It allows you to write the necessary VBScript or JScript applications to achieve the results you want. Windows is an event driven environment. A keypress, a mouse click, a timer, or any number of other things can generate events. A generated event usually means that the user or the system wants some action to occur. In Script Wizard, you select an event, and then select the action that the event should cause. Figure 5-32 is the List View that you will see when you start Script Wizard from the HTML editor.

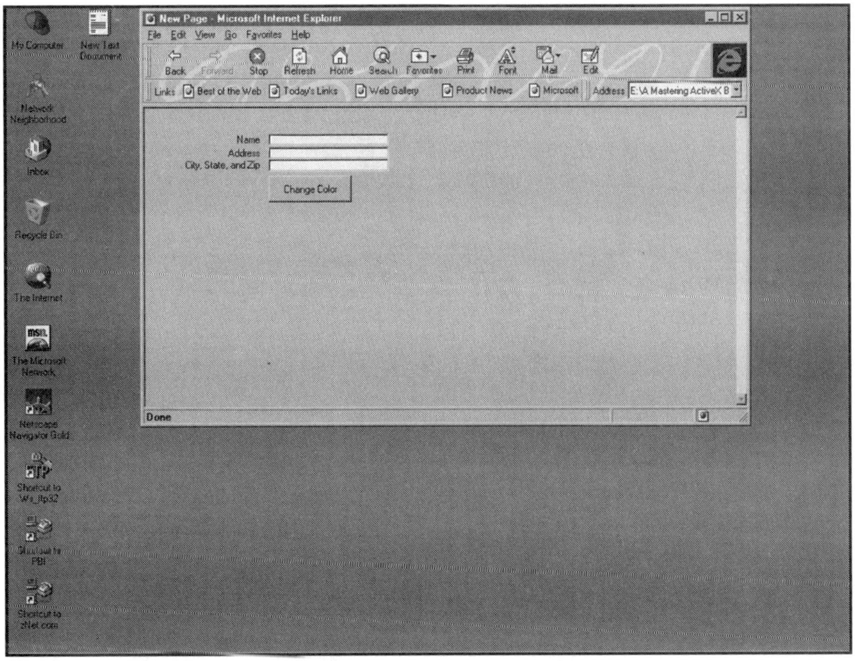

Figure 5-31 The result in Internet Explorer

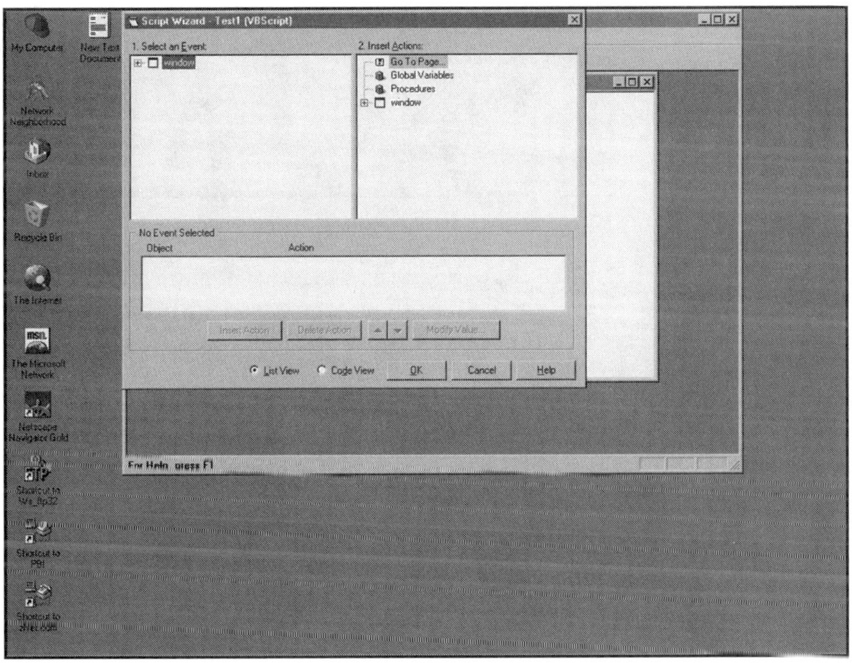

Figure 5-32 The Script Wizard window

You can see in Figure 5-33 that I have expanded the 1. Select an Event: and 2. Insert Action: outline views by clicking the associated +

signs. The events available under the Window icon are `onLoad` and `onUnload`. Events will always be preceded with an open diamond icon if no action has been selected. If an action has been selected, the diamond icon will be filled. Possible actions are shown in the actions pane preceded by a yellow filled box with an exclamation point. Properties are preceded by an icon that looks like blue text.

Figure 5-33
The Script Wizard events and actions expanded

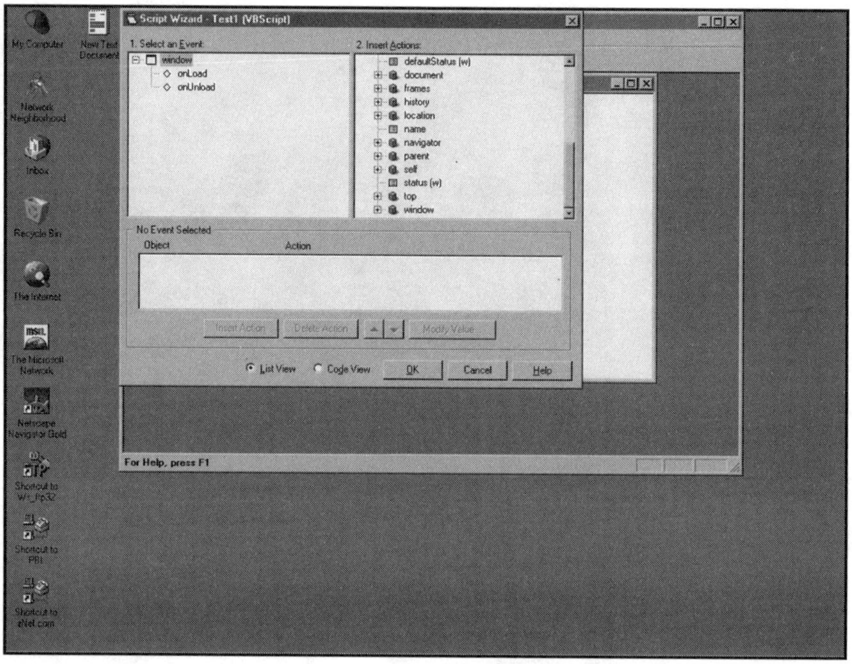

Notice that the 2. Insert Actions: pane shows the various objects (preceded by a cube) that I discussed earlier in this chapter under the scripting object model. As suggested there, you can write scripts to manipulate these items.

In List View, you select an event in the left pane, and then select an appropriate action in the right pane. The List View is provided for those not acquainted with programming. In Code View, you work in a somewhat similar manner, but the view is more in keeping with what a programmer might prefer to see. The pane below the Event and Actions panes is where the various actions you enter will be placed. The buttons across the bottom are mostly self-explanatory.

Scripting in the HTML Layout View

When you open the Script Wizard from the HTML Layout Control, the items that you added to the layout are presented for scripting, as shown in Figure 5-34. I'm scripting a Click event to change the color of CommandButton1 when the mouse is clicked. I'm also scripting the click event of CommandButton1 to change the background color of all TextBoxes. These are not earth shattering scripting actions, but will serve to demonstrate.

> **NOTE:**
> **In the process of building this script, an `invalid property value` error was generated in Internet Explorer when the script was run. The fix was to place double quotation marks around the color values as shown in the code a little later. Any time you have a problem with almost any value, the answer is frequently as simple as adding double quotation marks.**

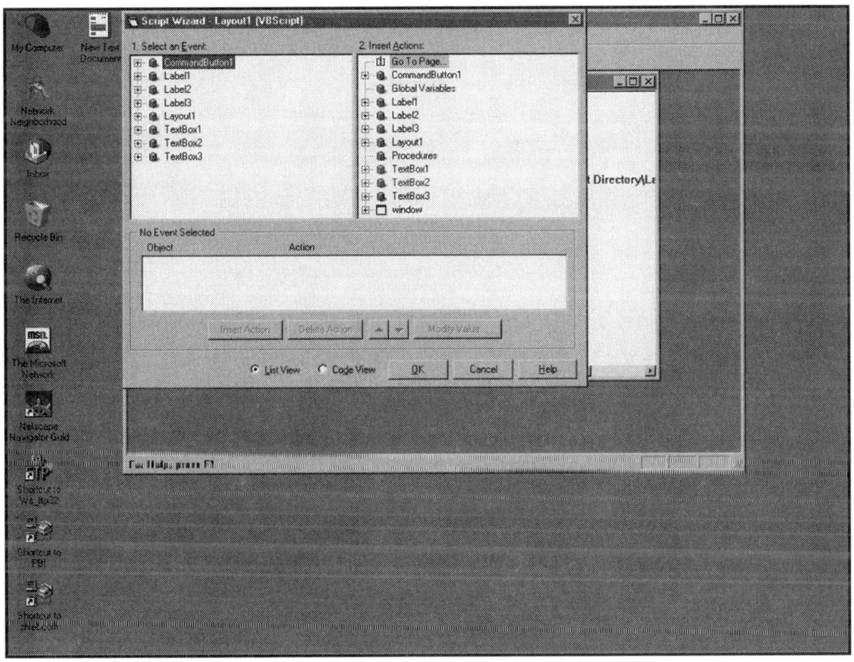

Figure 5-34
Scripting the HTML layout

The HTML Code

The HTML code in the ActiveX Control Pad contains the instructions necessary to cause Internet Explorer to read the .ALX file.

```
<HTML>
<HEAD>
<TITLE>New Page</TITLE>
</HEAD>
<BODY>
<OBJECT CLASSID="CLSID:812AE312-8B8E-11CF-93C8-00AA00C08FDF"
ID="Layout1_alx" STYLE="LEFT:0;TOP:0">
<PARAM NAME="ALXPATH" REF VALUE="file:E:\A Mastering ActiveX
Book\A Test Directory\Layout1.alx">
</OBJECT>
</BODY>
</HTML>
```

The .ALX file listing is as follows:

```
<SCRIPT LANGUAGE="VBScript">
<!—
Sub CommandButton1_Enter()
CommandButton1.BackColor = &H000000FF
end sub
Sub CommandButton1_Click()
TextBox1.BackColor = "&H0000FFFF"
TextBox3.BackColor = "&H0000FFFF"
TextBox2.BackColor = "&H0000FFFF"
end sub
—>
</SCRIPT>
<DIV ID="Layout1" STYLE="LAYOUT:FIXED;WIDTH:221pt;HEIGHT:80pt;">
<OBJECT ID="Label1"
CLASSID="CLSID:978C9E23-D4B0-11CE-BF2D-00AA003F40D0"
STYLE="TOP:11pt;LEFT:11pt;WIDTH:86pt;HEIGHT:11pt;ZINDEX:0;">
<PARAM NAME="Caption" VALUE="Name">
<PARAM NAME="Size" VALUE="3034;388">
<PARAM NAME="FontCharSet" VALUE="0">
<PARAM NAME="FontPitchAndFamily" VALUE="2">
<PARAM NAME="ParagraphAlign" VALUE="2">
<PARAM NAME="FontWeight" VALUE="0">
</OBJECT>
```

```
<OBJECT ID="Label2"
CLASSID="CLSID:978C9E23-D4B0-11CE-BF2D-00AA003F40D0"
STYLE="TOP:23pt;LEFT:11pt;WIDTH:86pt;HEIGHT:11pt;ZINDEX:1;">
<PARAM NAME="Caption" VALUE="Address">
<PARAM NAME="Size" VALUE="3034;388">
<PARAM NAME="FontCharSet" VALUE="0">
<PARAM NAME="FontPitchAndFamily" VALUE="2">
<PARAM NAME="ParagraphAlign" VALUE="2">
<PARAM NAME="FontWeight" VALUE="0">
</OBJECT>
<OBJECT ID="Label3"
CLASSID="CLSID:978C9E23-D4B0-11CE-BF2D-00AA003F40D0"
STYLE="TOP:34pt;LEFT:11pt;WIDTH:86pt;HEIGHT:11pt;ZINDEX:2;">
<PARAM NAME="Caption" VALUE="City, State, and Zip">
<PARAM NAME="Size" VALUE="3034;388">
<PARAM NAME="FontCharSet" VALUE="0">
<PARAM NAME="FontPitchAndFamily" VALUE="2">
<PARAM NAME="ParagraphAlign" VALUE="2">
<PARAM NAME="FontWeight" VALUE="0">
</OBJECT>
<OBJECT ID="TextBox1"
CLASSID="CLSID:8BD21D10-EC42-11CE-9E0D-00AA006002F3"
STYLE="TOP:11pt;LEFT:105pt;WIDTH:109pt;HEIGHT:11pt;TABINDEX:3;
ZINDEX:3;">
<PARAM NAME="VariousPropertyBits" VALUE="746604571">
<PARAM NAME="Size" VALUE="3845;388">
<PARAM NAME="FontCharSet" VALUE="0">
<PARAM NAME="FontPitchAndFamily" VALUE="2">
<PARAM NAME="FontWeight" VALUE="0">
</OBJECT>
<OBJECT ID="TextBox2"
CLASSID="CLSID:8BD21D10-EC42-11CE-9E0D-00AA006002F3"
STYLE="TOP:23pt;LEFT:105pt;WIDTH:109pt;HEIGHT:11pt;TABINDEX:4;
ZINDEX:4;">
<PARAM NAME="VariousPropertyBits" VALUE="746604571">
<PARAM NAME="Size" VALUE="3845;388">
<PARAM NAME="FontCharSet" VALUE="0">
<PARAM NAME="FontPitchAndFamily" VALUE="2">
```

```
<PARAM NAME="FontWeight" VALUE="0">
</OBJECT>
<OBJECT ID="TextBox3"
CLASSID="CLSID:8BD21D10-EC42-11CE-9E0D-00AA006002F3"
STYLE="TOP:34pt;LEFT:105pt;WIDTH:109pt;HEIGHT:11pt;TABINDEX:5;
ZINDEX:5;">
<PARAM NAME="VariousPropertyBits" VALUE="746604571">
<PARAM NAME="Size" VALUE="3845;388">
<PARAM NAME="FontCharSet" VALUE="0">
<PARAM NAME="FontPitchAndFamily" VALUE="2">
<PARAM NAME="FontWeight" VALUE="0">
</OBJECT>
<OBJECT ID="CommandButton1"
CLASSID="CLSID:D7053240-CE69-11CD-A777-00DD01143C57"
STYLE="TOP:49pt;LEFT:105pt;WIDTH:75pt;HEIGHT:23pt;TABINDEX:6;
ZINDEX:6;">
<PARAM NAME="Caption" VALUE="Change Color">
<PARAM NAME="Size" VALUE="2646;811">
<PARAM NAME="FontCharSet" VALUE="0">
<PARAM NAME="FontPitchAndFamily" VALUE="2">
<PARAM NAME="ParagraphAlign" VALUE="3">
<PARAM NAME="FontWeight" VALUE="0">
</OBJECT>
</DIV>
```

You can duplicate the preceding code by entering it into a text editor, or you can use the ActiveX Control Pad to experiment. I have not provided a figure because the color changes simply wouldn't show.

Summary

This chapter contains a large amount of information. It is also a handy reference in the absence of much written material on some of the items covered. I cover cascading style sheets in the next chapter, and then give you some additional scripting examples in the following chapter. At that point, you should be quite expert at most of the ActiveX-related business.

Chapter 6

Understanding Cascading Style Sheets

In preceding chapters, I have covered most of the elements that go into presenting information on a Web site. HTML is at the top of the list (a complete HTML 3.2 reference is provided in Appendix 2). It is the basic language used to format and present information. Scripting and ActiveX controls can be used to present information in totally new ways. In every scenario, the idea is to keep the amount of information traveling over the network as small as possible. Graphics files can get quite large, as can many other types of content.

One approach is to have as much content as possible in text. With standard HTML, however, the possible ways to present text are quite limited. The default is two type faces—proportional and fixed—and about seven sizes. This does not leave much room for enhancements. But now, things are different. The World Wide Web Consortium has introduced draft standards for Cascading Style Sheets, Level 1 (CSS1). The cascading part simply means that styles can be added at a number of levels in a document. They can be provided in the form of a .css file, they can be imbedded in a document, or they can be placed in line with code. Level 1 might be considered a version number. You're left with style sheets.

The publishing industry has long used style sheets to tell composition or word processing software how to format text elements in a document. CSS1 is little different. The syntax is more in keeping with HTML and the Web. I am going to give you a start here. For the latest version of the CSS1 specification, browse to `http://www.w3.org/pub/WWW/TR/WD-css1.html`.

Internet Explorer 3.0 and Netscape Navigator 3.0 both support Cascading Style Sheets.

Adding Style Sheets to Web Pages

Style sheets are not particularly difficult. If you want, for example, to change the color of Heading 1 (H1) elements, you would write:

```
<STYLE>
<!–
H1 { color: red }
–>
</STYLE>
```

An HTML page demonstrating this change is shown here:

```
<HTML>
<HEAD>
<TITLE>New Page</TITLE>
<STYLE>
<!–
H1 { color: red }
–>
</STYLE>
</HEAD>
<BODY>
<H1>This text should be in red.</H1>
</BODY>
</HTML>
```

The `H1 { color: red }` is called a *rule*. A rule consists of two parts: a selector (in this case, `H1`) and one or more declarations (in this case, `color: red`). The declaration also consists of two parts: a property (in this case, `color`) and a value (in this case, `red`), separated by a colon. The white space (spaces between elements) is used for readability; browsers will parse the information correctly with or without spaces.

Notice the use of the <!– and –> comment markers surrounding the style definition. Browsers that don't understand styles will ignore the unrecognized tags (<STYLE></STYLE>) but would most likely print the definition as plain text if the comment markers are not used.

You can:

1. LINK an external style sheet
2. Put a style element inside the HEAD
3. Import a style sheet using @import
4. Embed a style statement in-line

The following code shows how:

```
<HTML>
<HEAD>
<TITLE>Containing Style Sheets</TITLE>
<LINK REL=STYLESHEET TYPE="text/css"
HREF="http://www.someone.com/mystyle" TITLE="mystyle"> (1)
<STYLE TYPE="text/css">
@import url(http://www.someone.com/mystyle); (2)
H1 { color: burlywood} (3)
</STYLE>
</HEAD>
<BODY>
<H1>This text should be in the color called burlywood.</H1>
<P STYLE="color: goldenrod">This paragraph will be goldenrod. (4)
</BODY>
</HTML>
```

The following reference material will provide you with some material with which to experiment. The Cascading Style Sheets Working Draft from the URL given earlier will provide much additional information.

Note: You might ask, "So what does this have to do with ActiveX Controls?" My answer would be, "Nothing directly." The fact is, Web technology is going to be expanding at near light speed over the next year or so. Cascading Style Sheets are going to be very important to this technology in making Web sites faster and more attractive. You might even find that you can work Cascading Style Sheets into ActiveX Controls that you develop. Setting fonts, font sizes, font styles, colors, and other attributes dynamically might well provide that last ounce of sizzle you're looking for.

It should be pointed out that, as of today, the only browser that understands Cascading Style Sheets is Internet Explorer 3.0. Netscape has indicated that it will support style sheets next year but, here again, following proprietary venues instead of defining and using standards across all platforms is not working well yet. So, if you use Cascading Style Sheets, be sure to provide alternative content in your pages for browsers that do not understand style sheets.

A Style Reference Guide and Tutorial

This section goes into more detail about the options for style sheets. I have also provided a number of examples to illustrate the possibilities. Keep in mind that these will look as they should only if you use Internet Explorer 3.0 or 4.0 until Netscape and others provide support.

Quick Reference

Table 6-1 serves as a quick reference for many of the capabilities of style sheets.

Table 6-1
Style sheet capabilities

Property	Use	Type	Example
font-size	Sets size	px	{font-size:14pt}
		cm	
		in	
		pt	

Property	Use	Type	Example
font-family	Sets face	family	{font-family:Arial}
font-weight	Sets weight	normal	{font-weight:bold}
		bold	
font-style	Sets style	normal	{font-style:italic}
		italic	
line-height	Sets height	px	{line-height:18pt}
		cm	
		in	
		pt	
color	Sets color	colorname	{color:Black}
		RGB	
text-decoration	Sets decoration	none	{text-decoration:none}
		underline	
		italic	
		line-through	
margin-left	Sets margin left	px	{margin-left:.5in}
		cm	
		in	
		pt	
margin-right	Sets margin right	px	{margin-right:.5in}
		cm	
		in	
		pt	
text-align	Sets alignment	left	{text-align:left}
		center	
		right	
text-indent	Sets indent	px	{text-indent:1in}
		cm	
		in	
		pt	
background	Sets background	colorname	{background:white}
		RGB	
		URL	

Point size

With the font-size property, set the size of the font for the tag that you are defining. This property can be set in the following units:

- centimeters (cm)
- inches (in)
- pixels (px)
- points (pt)
- percentage (%)

Example

```
<HTML>
<HEAD>
<TITLE>Cascading Style Sheet Demo</TITLE>
<style type="text/css">
<!—
H1{font-size: 16pt}
—>
</STYLE>
</HEAD>
<BODY>
<H1>This is 16 point type.</H1>
</BODY>
</HTML>
```

This example displays the page shown in Figure 6-1.

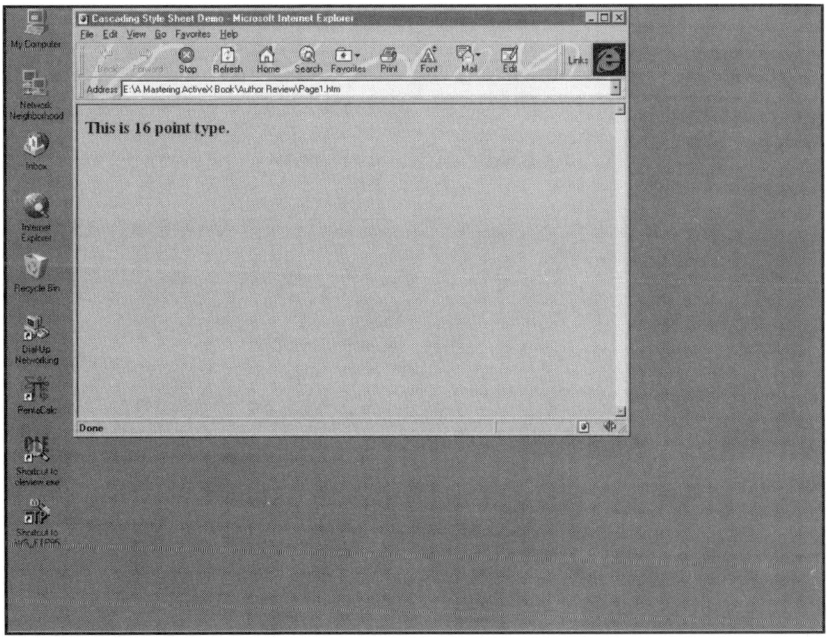

Figure 6-1
Setting point size

Typeface

Set the name of the font for the tag you are defining with the font-family property. Multiple declarations can be made. In the following example, I have included font-size: 16pt, and font-family: Verdana. A semicolon is used to terminate the first declaration, and both are included within the curly brackets. Also, I can use Verdana because that font exists on my computer.

Examples

```
<HTML>
<HEAD>
<TITLE>Cascading Style Sheet Demo</TITLE>
<style typc–"tcxt/css">
<!–
H1{font-size: 16pt;
   font-family: Verdana}
–>
</STYLE>
</HEAD>
<BODY>
```

```
<H1>This is 16 point Verdana.</H1>
</BODY>
</HTML>
```

The result of running this page is shown in Figure 6-2.

Figure 6-2
Setting the font name

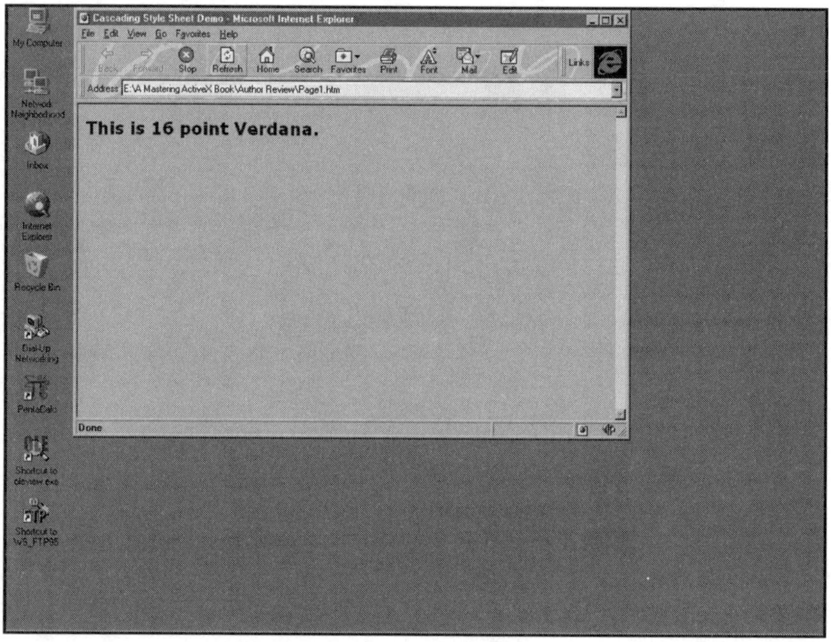

Not all machines will have the fonts that you specify installed. The following generic fonts are used by default in most browsers:

- serif
- sans-serif
- monospace

Times Roman is a serif font example; Arial is a sans-serif font example; and Courier is a monospace font example. To accommodate the greatest number of browsers, you might change the font-family to look like this:

```
H1{font-size: 16pt;
font-family: Verdana, Arial, sans-serif}
```

You can have up to three alternate fonts described.

Weight

Set the weight of the font for the tag you are defining with the font-weight property. This property can be set in the following weights:

- bold
- normal

Examples

```
<HTML>
<HEAD>
<TITLE>Cascading Style Sheet Demo</TITLE>
<style type="text/css">
<!—
H1{font-size: 16pt;
   font-family: Verdana}

p {font-size: 12pt;
   font-family: Comic Sans MS;
   font-weight: bold}
—>
</STYLE>
</HEAD>
<BODY>
<H1>This is 16 point Verdana.</H1>
<p>and this is Comic Sans Bold
</BODY>
</HTML>
```

In this example, I've added the <p> or paragraph tag as a selector and made it 12-point, Comic Sans MS with font-weight set to bold. The result in a browser is shown in Figure 6-3.

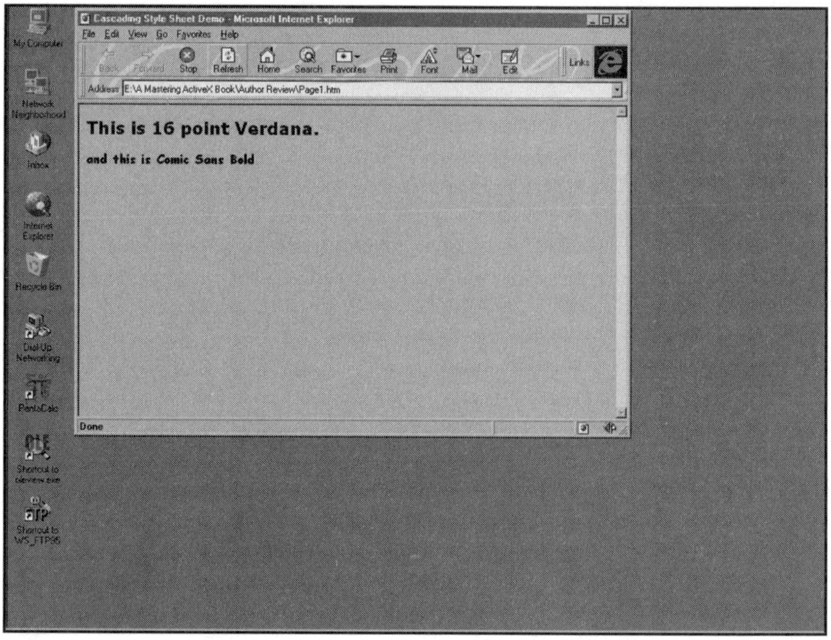

Figure 6-3
Setting the font weight to bold

Here are some other possibilities.

```
H1{font-size: 16pt;
   font-family: Arial;
   font-weight: bold}

H1{font-size: 16pt;
   font-family: Arial;
   font-weight: normal}
```

Style

Set the style of the font for the tag you are defining using the font-style property. This property can be set in the following styles:

- italic
- normal

Examples

```
H1{font-size: 16pt;
   font-family: Arial;
   font-weight: bold;
```

```
    font-style: normal}

H1{font-size: 16pt;
    font-family: Arial;
    font-weight: normal;
    font- style: italic}
```

It should be clear from what I've just covered that Cascading Style Sheets allow some impressive improvements to Web pages. In many instances, as I show later in this chapter, this capability can be used in place of graphics. The result is a much faster download of the pages from the server to the client, and a much cleaner display.

Leading

Set the line height or leading of the font for the tag you are defining using the line-height property. This property can be set in the following measurement units:

- centimeters (cm)
- inches (in)
- pixels (px)
- points (pt)

Leading is the typesetting term for the distance between the baselines of two lines of text.

Example

```
<HTML>
<HEAD>
<TITLE>Cascading Style Sheet Demo</TITLE>
<style type="text/css">
<!—
H1{font-size: 16pt;
        font-family: Verdana;
        line-height: 10pt}

p {font-size: 12pt;
     font-family: Comic Sans MS;
      font-weight: bold}
```

```
-->
</STYLE>
</HEAD>
<BODY>
<H1>This is 16 point Verdana.<br>
This is 16 point Verdana with line-height set to 10 points.</H1>
<p>and this is Comic Sans Bold
</BODY>
</HTML>
```

In the preceding example, I've set the line height for the H1 selector to 10 point. The font is set to 16 point. Using the <br> or break tag, the lines overlap as you might expect. The effect is shown in Figure 6-4.

Figure 6-4
Setting line height to cause overlap

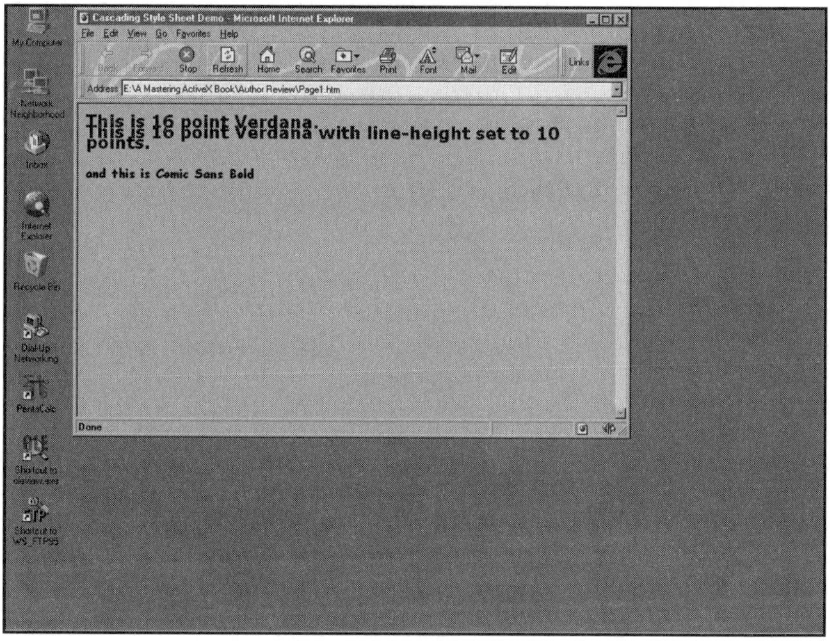

The very best way to gain a better understanding of Cascading Style Sheets is to use the preceding examples and experiment. You can't break anything and you may discover tricks that I haven't mentioned here.

Grouping Font Attributes

The attributes covered previously are the most commonly used attributes. The Cascading Style Sheet specification has a short cut that allows more compact style sheets. The attributes so far are grouped into a single attribute called `font`.

Example

So, this:

```
H1{font-size: 16pt;
   font-family: Arial, sans-serif;
   font-weight: bold;
   font-style: normal;
   line-height: 20pt}
```

Becomes this:

```
H1{font: "Arial, sans-serif" 16pt/20pt bold normal}
```

Colors

Set the color of the font for the tag you are defining with the color property. This property can be set in the following styles:

- RGB triplet
- colorname

A complete color chart is available in Appendix B.

Example

```
H1{font-size: 16pt "Arial";
   font-weight: bold;
   color: Red}
```

Special Text Effects

Set any special effects of the font for the tag you are defining using the text-decoration property. This property can be set in the following styles:

- none
- underline
- italic
- line-through

Examples

```
H1{font-size: 16pt "Arial";
   font-weight: bold;
   text-decoration: none;
   color: Red}

H1{font-size: 16pt "Arial";
   font-weight: bold;
   text-decoration: underline;
   color: Red}

H1{font-size: 16pt "Arial";
   font-weight: bold;
   text-decoration: italic;
   color: Red}

H1{font-size: 16pt "Arial";
   font-weight: bold;
   text-decoration: line-through;
   color: Red}
```

Margins

Set the left margin of the font for the tag you are defining using the margin-left property. This property can be set in the following measurement units:

- centimeters (cm)
- inches (in)
- pixels (px)
- points (pt)

Set the right margin of the font for the tag you are defining using the margin-right property. This property can be set as shown previously.

Example

```
H1{font-size: 16pt "Arial";
   font-weight: bold;
   text-decoration: none;
   margin-left: 1in;
   margin-right: 1in;
   color: Red}
```

Alignment

Set the alignment of the font for the tag you are defining using the text-align property. This property can be set in the following styles:

- left
- right
- center

Examples

```
H1{font-size: 16pt "Arial";
   font-weight: bold;
   text-align: left}

H1{font-size: 16pt "Arial";
   font-weight: bold;
   text-align: right}

H1{font-size: 16pt "Arial";
   font-weight: bold;
   text-align: center}
```

Indentation

Set the indent of the font for the tag you are defining using the text-indent property. This property can be set in the following measurement units:

- centimeters (cm)
- inches (in)
- pixels (px)
- points (pt)

Example

```
H1{font-size: 16pt "Arial";
   font-weight: bold;
   text-indent: 2in}
```

Background Color and Images

Set the background color of the font for the tag you are defining using the background property. This property can be set in the following styles:

- RGB triplet
- colorname
- URL

For the colorname and RGB triplet, see the section on color. A URL must be enclosed by parentheses ().

Example

```
H1{font-size: 16pt "Arial";
   font-weight: bold;
   color: black;
   background: white}

H1{font-size: 16pt "Arial";
   font-weight: bold;
   color: black;
   background: URL(http://www.mysite.com/clouds.gif)}
```

Using TrueType Fonts on the Web

TrueType fonts and Cascading Style Sheets go hand in hand. To that end, Microsoft has made both fonts and style sheets available on its Web site. First, look at the following URL for the latest in available fonts for the Web:

```
http://www.microsoft.com/truetype/
```

Look at the following sites for much additional information on style sheets plus other free style sheets designed for different purposes that you can download and use.

```
http://www.microsoft.com/gallery/files/styles/
http://www.microsoft.com/truetype/css/gallery/entrance.htm
http://www.microsoft.com/truetype/css/content.htm
```

One technique that simply must be expanded on here is a layering technique, called *typespotting*, that Microsoft uses to produce some spectacular results using text with no graphics. As the following HTML illustrates, several CLASS definitions named `.layer1` through `.layer5` are defined. Each layer name changes the font color, shifts the left and top margin, and makes other small changes. Text is printed five times for each version, with the layers called one after the other enclosed in <DIV></DIV> tags. The result of the code that follows is shown in Figure 6-5.

```
<HTML>
<HEAD>
<TITLE>Typespotting - Times New Roman </TITLE>
<STYLE  TYPE="text/css">
<!—
BODY { background: darkgreen }
.copy {      margin-left: 80px;
      margin-right: 60px;
      color: black;
      font-size: 18px;
      font-family: Times New Roman }
.topline { color: black;
      font-size: 10px;
      font-family: Times New Roman }
P {      color: black;
```

```
     font-size: 14px;
     font-family: Times New Roman }
.layer1 {      color: orange;
     font-size: 40px;
     font-family: Times New Roman }
.layer2 { margin-top: -47px;
     margin-left: 4px;
     color: gray;
     font-size: 40px;
     font-family: Times New Roman }
.layer3 { margin-top: -48px;
     margin-left: 2px;
     color: yellow;
     font-size: 40px;
     font-family: Times New Roman }
.layer4 { margin-top: -45px;
     margin-left: 2px;
     color: darkorange;
     font-size: 40px;
     font-family: Times New Roman }
.layer5 { margin-top: -48px;
     margin-left: 2px;
     color: gold;
     font-size: 40px;
     font-family: Times New Roman }
->
</STYLE>
</HEAD>
<BODY>
<CENTER>
     <DIV ALIGN=CENTER CLASS=layer1><B>Hotel Times New
➥Roman</B></DIV>
     <DIV ALIGN=CENTER CLASS=layer2><B>Hotel Times New
➥Roman</B></DIV>
     <DIV ALIGN=CENTER CLASS=layer3><B>Hotel Times New
➥Roman</B></DIV>
     <DIV ALIGN=CENTER CLASS=layer4><B>Hotel Times New
➥Roman</B></DIV>
```

```
    <DIV ALIGN=CENTER CLASS=layer5><B>Hotel Times New
➥Roman</B></DIV>
<BR><BR>
    <DIV ALIGN=CENTER CLASS=layer1><B>&#183;
➥Sparrowchester &#183;</B></DIV>
    <DIV ALIGN=CENTER CLASS=layer2><B>&#183;
➥Sparrowchester &#183;</B></DIV>
    <DIV ALIGN=CENTER CLASS=layer3><B>&#183;
➥Sparrowchester &#183;</B></DIV>
    <DIV ALIGN=CENTER CLASS=layer4><B>&#183;
➥Sparrowchester &#183;</B></DIV>
    <DIV ALIGN=CENTER CLASS=layer5><B>&#183;
➥Sparrowchester &#183;</B></DIV>
</CENTER>
</BODY>
</HTML>
```

Figure 6-5
A novel approach to style sheets

It should be clear from this that Cascading Style Sheets, Level 1 holds significant promise for the future of the Internet. The Internet URLs given throughout this chapter should give you a wealth of additional information.

Summary

The Web and the tools to improve the appearance of Web pages are both growing swiftly. It will likely take some time for Cascading Style Sheets to find their way into general use, but with these and what you've learned previously, Web authoring will become more and more time consuming and require using every new tool at your disposal. All of this falls under the umbrella of ActiveX and the Active initiative generally. In the next chapter, I give you more on scripting by using what might be a live site. I then get into building ActiveX controls using the ActiveX SDK.

Chapter 7

Building Web Pages with Scripting

In this chapter, I expand on scripting and provide additional information on available ActiveX controls. The example is based on a live Web site. The content can be found at:

`http://www.checkmaster.com/activex/`

You are welcome to use the images in the image directory there, and welcome to use or expand on the HTML and scripts at that location.

I cover a little additional information about JScript support, and take a look at some controls available from Microsoft's Web site. I show you a little about using these controls, and then take you through some working HTML, using controls and scripting. This chapter should tie up all of the loose ends and summarize everything that you've learned.

Java Support with ActiveX

Microsoft provides heavy support for Java. Java applets can be built using the new Visual J++ to take advantage of the COM model in ActiveX. The Java VM provided with Internet Explorer is very powerful using the JIT (Just In Time) compiler. Java can be provided to cross-platform browsers because the bytecode in Java provide cross-platform capabilities.

You can develop ActiveX controls using Visual J++, Visual Basic, Visual C++, and a number of other languages. You can bring your Web pages to life using these controls and VBScript of JScript.

VB Script Coding Conventions

You will find additional information about coding conventions in a number of sources. A few of the more common ones are covered here. Coding conventions are especially helpful in large projects, and you might like to simply build your own coding conventions list if you haven't done so already.

Constant Naming

Constant names should be in uppercase letters with underscore separators. Examples are as follows:

```
NEW_LINE

CARRIAGE_RETURN_LINE_FEED

MAX_NUMBER

MAX_ITEMS
```

Variable Naming

Variable naming conventions help identify various data types in code. The more common ones are listed here. You may also want to develop additional conventions to indicate scope.

Subtype	Prefix
Boolean	bln
Byte	byt
Date/time	dtm
Double	dbl
Error	err
Integer	int
Long	lng
Object	obj
Single	sng
String	str

Object Naming

Table 7-1 shows a few of the recommended conventions for naming objects and controls in your code.

Table 7-1 Conventions for naming objects and controls

Subtype	Prefix
3D Panel	pnl
Animated button	ani
Check box	chk
Combo box, drop down list	cbo
Command button	cmd
Common dialog	dlg
Frame	fra
Horizontal scroll bar	hsb
Image	img
Label	lbl
Line	lin
List Box	lst
Spin	spn
Text box	txt
Vertical scroll bar	vsb
Slider	sld

There are a number of other conventions in manuals relating to programming that you might like to incorporate into your conventions.

The ActiveX Component Gallery

You may want to download the available controls at Microsoft's Web sites. Two URLs of interest are shown here, followed by a description and information on each of the controls in the ActiveX gallery.

```
http://www.microsoft.com/gallery/default.htm
http://www.microsoft.com/activex/gallery/
```

Animated Button Control

When you copy files in Windows 95, the screen shows an image of paper flying from one folder to another. This is one possibility for the Animated Button control. There are obviously hundreds of other applications.

States

The Animated Button control has four possible states:

State	Action
Down	Left-button down (click)
Focus	Focus is on the control
Mouseover	The mouse moves over the control
Default	Neither the mouse cursor nor focus

NOTE:
The states are mutually exclusive. The Down state has precedence over all other states. The Default state has the least precedence. The Mouseover state has precedence over Focus. If a control has focus and the mouse moves over it, the control goes to the Mouseover state.

Properties

URL	URL location for the AVI to used
DefaultFrStart	Start frame for the Default state
DefaultFrEnd	End frame for the Default state
MouseoverFrStart	Start frame for the Mouseover state
MouseoverFrEnd	End frame for the Mouseover state
FocusFrStart	Start frame for the Focus state
FocusFrEnd	End frame for the Focus state
DownFrStart	Start frame for the Down state
DownFrEnd	End frame for the Down state

Methods

`AboutBox`	Displays the About dialog box Events
`ButtonEvent_Click`	Fires when the button is clicked
`ButtonEvent_DblClick`	Fires when the button is double-clicked
`ButtonEvent_Focus`	Fires when the button gets focus
`ButtonEvent_Enter`	Fires when the mouse enters the button area
`ButtonEvent_Leave`	Fires when the mouse leaves the button area

Sample HTML

```
<HTML>
<HEAD>
<TITLE>Anibutton</TITLE>
</HEAD>
<BODY>

<OBJECT CLASSID="CLSID:812AE312-8B8E-11CF-93C8-00AA00C08FDF"
ID="Anibtn_alx" STYLE="LEFT:0;TOP:0">
<PARAM NAME="ALXPATH" REF VALUE="file:Anibtn.alx">
</OBJECT>

</BODY>
</HTML>
```

Sample ALX

```
<DIV ID="Layout1" STYLE="LAYOUT:FIXED;WIDTH:400pt;HEIGHT:300pt;">
    <OBJECT ID="anbtn1"
     CLASSID="CLSID:0482B100-739C-11CF-A3A9-00A0C9034920"
STYLE="TOP:19pt;LEFT:19pt;WIDTH:56pt;HEIGHT:30pt;TABINDEX:0;ZIN-
DEX:0;">
        <PARAM NAME="_ExtentX" VALUE="1984">
        <PARAM NAME="_ExtentY" VALUE="1058">
        <PARAM NAME="defaultfrstart" VALUE="0">
        <PARAM NAME="defaultfrend" VALUE="-1">
        <PARAM NAME="mouseoverfrstart" VALUE="0">
        <PARAM NAME="mouseoverfrend" VALUE="-1">
        <PARAM NAME="focusfrstart" VALUE="0">
        <PARAM NAME="focusfrend" VALUE="-1">
        <PARAM NAME="downfrstart" VALUE="0">
        <PARAM NAME="downfrend" VALUE="-1">
    </OBJECT>
</DIV>
```

Chart Control

This control allows charts to be generated on the Internet. Using server side operations the values for the chart could be updated at some regular interval to provide real time charting.

Chart Types

The Chart control provides the following charts:

- Pie chart
- Point chart
- Line chart
- Area chart
- Bar chart
- Column chart
- Stocks chart

Properties

Rows	The number of rows
Columns	The number of columns
HorizontalGrid	Horizontal grids
VerticalGrid	Vertical grids
ChartType	Type of chart; possible values are the following: Simple Pie - 0 Pie with wedge out - 1 Simple Point Chart - 2 Stacked Point Chart - 3 Full Point Chart - 4 Simple Line Chart - 5 Stacked Line Chart - 6 Full Line Chart - 7 Simple Area Chart - 8 Stacked Area Chart - 9 Full Area Chart - 10 Simple Column Chart - 11 Stacked Column Chart - 12 Full Column Chart - 13 Simple Bar Chart - 14 Stacked Bar Chart - 15 Full Bar Chart - 16 HLC Stock Chart - 17 HLC Stock Chart WSJ - 18 OHLC Stock Chart - 19 OHLC Stock Chart WSJ - 20
RowIndex	The row index

Properties

ColumnIndex	The column index
DataItem	A data value identified by RowIndex and ColumnIndex
ColorScheme	Predefined set of colors to use; used to fill regions; values can be 0, 1, or 2.
BackStyle	Transparent or opaque background; values can be the following: Transparent - 0 Opaque - 1
Scale	The percentage scaling factor defaults to 100 percent scaling; value should lie between 1 to 100 or default is used
RowName	Used with RowIndex to specify a name to be used in legends and labels; on the HTML page, row names are specified using the RowNames <PARAM> tag: `<param name="RowNames" value="Nov Dec">`
ColumnName	Used with ColumnIndex to specify a name to be used in legends and labels; on the HTML page, column names are specified using the ColumnNames <param> tag: `<param name="ColumnNames" value="Windows WindowsNT OS2">`
DisplayLegend	View or hide the legend; values are the following: Show Legend - 1 Hide Legend - 0
GridPlacement	Controls how the grids are drawn; grid lines can be over the chart or below the chart; values are the following: Grid lines in the background - 0 Grid lines in the foreground - 1
Data param tags	Data param tags are used to specify data values for the chart; to specify data values for row x, use the following syntax: `<param name="data[x]" value="num1 num2 num3">`
URL	This property allows you to specify a data file using a URL; the Chart control will use the data specified in the data file to draw the chart

Methods

AboutBox	Displays the About box
Reload	Forces the data in the URL to be downloaded

Events

None.

Sample HTML

```
<HTML>
<HEAD>
<TITLE>Pie Chart</TITLE>
</HEAD>
<BODY>

<OBJECT CLASSID="CLSID:812AE312-8B8E-11CF-93C8-00AA00C08FDF"
ID="Chart_alx" STYLE="LEFT:0;TOP:0">
<PARAM NAME="ALXPATH" REF VALUE="Chart.alx">
 </OBJECT>



</BODY>
</HTML>
```

Sample ALX

```
<DIV ID="Layout2" STYLE="LAYOUT:FIXED;WIDTH:400pt;HEIGHT:300pt;">
    <OBJECT ID="iechart1"
     CLASSID="CLSID:FC25B780-75BE-11CF-8B01-444553540000"
STYLE="TOP:34pt;LEFT:94pt;WIDTH:154pt;HEIGHT:124pt;ZINDEX:0;">
         <PARAM NAME="_ExtentX" VALUE="5424">
         <PARAM NAME="_ExtentY" VALUE="4366">
         <PARAM NAME="Rows" VALUE="4">
         <PARAM NAME="Columns" VALUE="3">
         <PARAM NAME="ChartType" VALUE="0">
         <PARAM NAME="Data[0][0]" VALUE="9">
         <PARAM NAME="Data[0][1]" VALUE="10">
         <PARAM NAME="Data[0][2]" VALUE="11">
         <PARAM NAME="Data[1][0]" VALUE="7">
         <PARAM NAME="Data[1][1]" VALUE="11">
         <PARAM NAME="Data[1][2]" VALUE="12">
         <PARAM NAME="Data[2][0]" VALUE="6">
         <PARAM NAME="Data[2][1]" VALUE="12">
```

```
        <PARAM NAME=”Data[2][2]” VALUE=”13”>
        <PARAM NAME=”Data[3][0]” VALUE=”11”>
        <PARAM NAME=”Data[3][1]” VALUE=”13”>
        <PARAM NAME=”Data[3][2]” VALUE=”14”>
        <PARAM NAME=”HorizontalAxis” VALUE=”0”>
        <PARAM NAME=”VerticalAxis” VALUE=”0”>
        <PARAM NAME=”hgridStyle” VALUE=”1”>
        <PARAM NAME=”vgridStyle” VALUE=”0”>
        <PARAM NAME=”ColorScheme” VALUE=”0”>
        <PARAM NAME=”BackStyle” VALUE=”1”>
        <PARAM NAME=”Scale” VALUE=”100”>
        <PARAM NAME=”DisplayLegend” VALUE=”0”>
        <PARAM NAME=”BackColor” VALUE=”16777215”>
        <PARAM NAME=”ForeColor” VALUE=”32768”>
    </OBJECT>
</DIV>
```

Figure 7-1 shows the result of running this code.

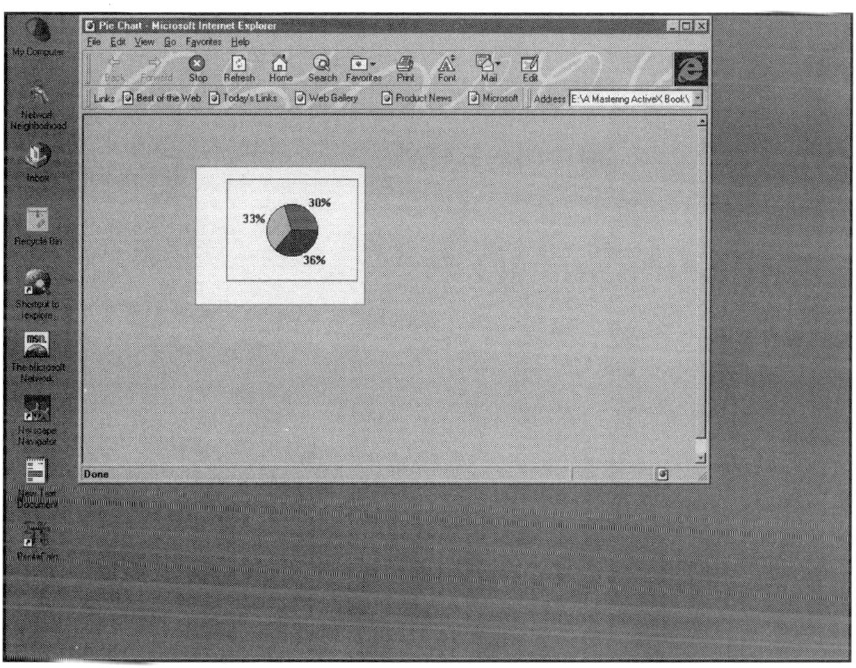

Figure 7-1 The ActiveX Gallery chart

Gradient Control

The gradient control allows the active generation of interesting graphics without the attendant download cost of these graphics.

Properties

StartColor	The color with which the transition starts
EndColor	The color with which the transition ends
	Direction of color transition: 0 - horizontal 1 - vertical 2 - toward the center 3 - toward the corner 4 - across diagonal down 5 - across diagonal up 6 - around the point specified in StartPoint 7 - across the line joining StartPoint and EndPoint
StartPoint	Start point coordinates in the format (x,y)
EndPoint	End point coordinates in the format (x,y)

Methods

AboutBox	Displays About box

Events

None

Sample HTML

```
<HTML>
<HEAD>
<TITLE>New Page</TITLE>
</HEAD>
<BODY>

<OBJECT CLASSID=”CLSID:812AE312-8B8E-11CF-93C8-00AA00C08FDF”
ID=”Gradient_alx” STYLE=”LEFT:0;TOP:0”>
<PARAM NAME=”ALXPATH” REF VALUE=”Gradient.alx”>
 </OBJECT>
```

```
</BODY>
</HTML>
```

Sample ALX

```
<DIV ID="Layout1" STYLE="LAYOUT:FIXED;WIDTH:400pt;HEIGHT:300pt;">
    <OBJECT ID="iegrad1"
     CLASSID="CLSID:017C99A0-8637-11CF-A3A9-00A0C9034920"
STYLE="TOP:11pt;LEFT:11pt;WIDTH:132pt;HEIGHT:91pt;ZINDEX:0;">
        <PARAM NAME="_ExtentX" VALUE="4657">
        <PARAM NAME="_ExtentY" VALUE="3201">
        <PARAM NAME="StartColor" VALUE="#0000FF">
        <PARAM NAME="EndColor" VALUE="#000014">
        <PARAM NAME="Direction" VALUE="0">
        <PARAM NAME="StartPoint" VALUE="(0,0)">
        <PARAM NAME="EndPoint" VALUE="(100,50)">
    </OBJECT>
</DIV>
```

Label Control

The Label control allows items on a display to be labeled.

Properties

Caption	Specifies text to be displayed
Angle	Specifies angle (counter-clockwise rotation) in degrees
Alignment	Specifies text alignment; values are the following: 0 left, top 1 center, top 2 right, top 3 left, centered 4 centered, centered 5 right, centered 6 left, bottom 7 centered, bottom 8 right, bottom
BackStyle	Control background: 0 Transparent 1 Opaque
FontName	TrueType font name

FontSize	Font size in points
FontItalic	Italics
FontBold	Bold
FontUnderline	Underline
FontStrikeout	Strikeout
Mode	Mode to render text: 0 Normal 1 Normal text with rotation 2 apply the user specified lines while rendering without rotation 3 apply the user specified lines while rendering, allow rotation

Methods

AboutBox	About box

Events

Click	Label click
Change	Caption change
DblClick	Label double-click
MouseDown	Mouse button press
MouseMove	Mouse move while over the label
MouseUp	Mouse button release

Sample HTML

```
<HTML>
<HEAD>
<TITLE>Label Control</TITLE>
</HEAD>
<BODY>

<OBJECT CLASSID="CLSID:812AE312-8B8E-11CF-93C8-00AA00C08FDF"
ID="Label_alx" STYLE="LEFT:0;TOP:0">
<PARAM NAME="ALXPATH" REF VALUE="file:E:\A Mastering ActiveX
Book\Mastering ActiveX\Part 2 Using Authoring and Scripting
```

```
Tools\Chapter 8 Building Web Pages with
Scripting\other\Label.alx”>
 </OBJECT>


</BODY>
</HTML>
```

Sample ALX

```
<DIV ID=”Layout1” STYLE=”LAYOUT:FIXED;WIDTH:400pt;HEIGHT:300pt;”>
    <OBJECT ID=”IeLabel1”
     CLASSID=”CLSID:99B42120-6EC7-11CF-A6C7-00AA00A47DD2”
STYLE=”TOP:15pt;LEFT:11pt;WIDTH:124pt;HEIGHT:120pt;ZINDEX:0;”>
        <PARAM NAME=”_ExtentX” VALUE=”4366”>
        <PARAM NAME=”_ExtentY” VALUE=”4233”>
        <PARAM NAME=”Caption” VALUE=”Rotating Label”>
        <PARAM NAME=”Angle” VALUE=”45”>
        <PARAM NAME=”Alignment” VALUE=”4”>
        <PARAM NAME=”Mode” VALUE=”1”>
        <PARAM NAME=”FillStyle” VALUE=”0”>
        <PARAM NAME=”FillStyle” VALUE=”0”>
        <PARAM NAME=”ForeColor” VALUE=”#000000”>
        <PARAM NAME=”BackColor” VALUE=”#D8CCB8”>
        <PARAM NAME=”FontName” VALUE=”Arial”>
        <PARAM NAME=”FontSize” VALUE=”12”>
        <PARAM NAME=”FontItalic” VALUE=”0”>
        <PARAM NAME=”FontBold” VALUE=”0”>
        <PARAM NAME=”FontUnderline” VALUE=”0”>
        <PARAM NAME=”FontStrikeout” VALUE=”0”>
        <PARAM NAME=”TopPoints” VALUE=”0”>
        <PARAM NAME=”BotPoints” VALUE=”0”>
    </OBJECT>
</DIV>
```

Figure 7-2 shows the result of running this code.

Figure 7-2
The ActiveX Gallery
Rotating Label

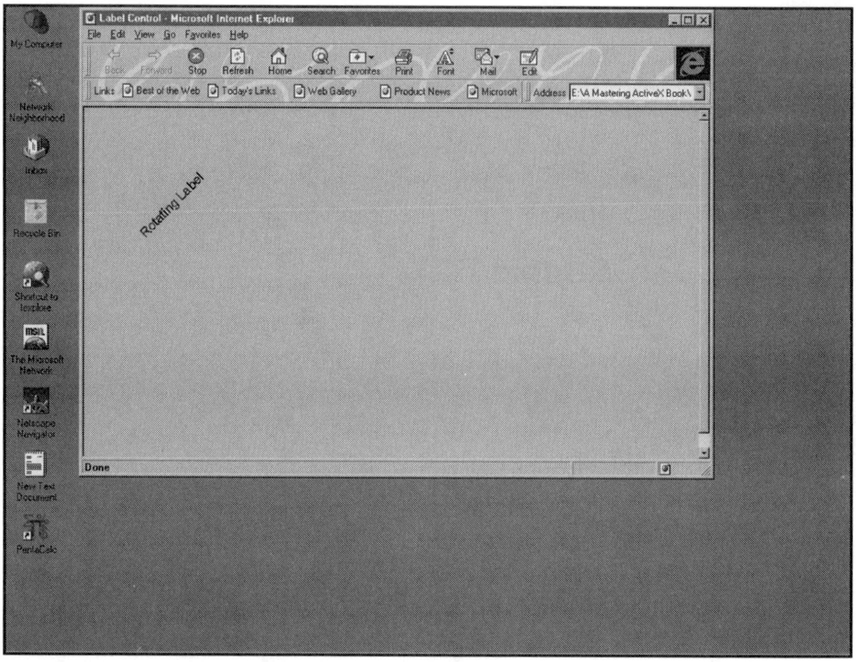

Marquee Control

The marquee allows a Web designer to include a scrolling marquee in Web pages.

Properties

ScrollStyleX	Horizontal scroll style; values are Bounce and Circular (default)
ScrollStyleY	Vertical scroll style; values are Bounce and Circular (default)
ScrollDelay	Time in milliseconds for each movement of the URL; values are positive integers (default is 100)
LoopsX	Times the image scrolls horizontally if ScrollStyleX is Circular, or bounces if ScrollStyleX is Bounce; values are integers above or equal to -1; zero indicates a horizontal slide, -1 indicates an infinite loop (default is -1)
LoopsY	Times the image scrolls vertically if ScrollStyleY is Circular, or bounces if ScrollStyleY is Bounce; values are integers above or equal to -1; zero indicates a horizontal slide, -1 indicates an infinite loop (default is -1)

ScrollPixelsX	Number of pixels to move horizontally each ScrollDelay millisecond; values are integers; default is 75 pixels
ScrollPixelsY	Number of pixels to move vertically each ScrollDelay millisecond; values are integers; default is zero
szURL	The URL to scroll
DrawImmediately	Progressively render; values are 1 (true) or 0 (false); the default is 1
Whitespace	Whitespace between URLs and/or images; values are integers; default is zero
PageFlippingOn	Marquee flips between multiple URLs instead of scrolling when the user presses the right mouse button or via the put_CurrentURL automation function; values are 1 (true) or 0 (false); default is 0
Zoom	Percentage of original size; values are positive integers; default is 100
WidthOfPage	Width in pixels; values are positive integers; default is 640

Methods

AboutBox	About box
Pause	Stops scrolling
Resume	Restarts scrolling

Events

void OnStartOfImage(void)	Issued before the URL appears in the marquee window.
void OnEndOfImage (int HorizontalOrVertical)	Issued when completely scrolled.
OnBounce (int SideBouncedOff)	Fired only in bounce mode when the image bounces off a side. SideBouncedOff returns "L" for left, "R" for right, "T" for top, and "B" for bottom.
void OnScroll (int HorizontalOrVertical)	Issued when the control is about to scroll. HorizontalOrVertical indicates whether horizontal or vertical scrolling is about to begin again (returns "H" for horizontal, "V" for vertical). This event is not fired for bounces or slides; nor is it fired the first time the image is scrolled.
void OnLMouseClick(void)	Fired when the user presses the left mouse button in the marquee window.

Sample HTML

Samples are shown later.

Menu Control

The Menu control allows the display of Windows style menus on Web pages.

Properties

ItemCount	Number items in the current menu (read only)
Caption	Caption to display

Paramater Tags

Menuitem[]	Menu item to display
Caption	Caption to display

Methods

AboutBox	About box.
PopUp	Pops up the menu. If no X or Y position is passed, the current ([in] int x, [in] int y) mouse position is used for the pop-up. x and y values are relative to the window.
Clear	Clears all menu items.
RemoveItem ([in] int index)	Removes an item. If no menu item exists, nothing is done.
Additem ([in] String, [in/optional] int index)	Adds String as a menu item at the index. If no index, the item is appended.

Events

Select(int item)	Item indicates the menu item selected.
Click	No menu items were present, and the button was clicked.

Sample HTML

```
<OBJECT
id=menu2
classid="clsid:52DFAE60-CEBF-11CF-A3A9-00A0C9034920"
width=80
height=25
align=middle
>
```

```
<param NAME="Menuitem[0]" value="MyMenu1">
<param NAME="Menuitem[1]" value="MyMenu2">
<param NAME="Menuitem[2]" value="MyMenu3">
<param NAME="Menuitem[3]" value="MyMenu4">
<param NAME="Menuitem[4]" value="">
<param NAME="Menuitem[5]" value="MyMenu6">
<param NAME="Caption" value="My Menu">
</OBJECT>
```

Pop-up Menu Control

The Pop-up menu normally associated with a right click makes an excellent way to add navigational systems to your Web pages.

Properties

ItemCount	The number of menu items in the current menu (read only)

Parameter Tags

Menuitem[]	The menu item to be displayed

Methods

AboutBox	Displays the About dialog box.
PopUp ([in] int x, [in] int y)	Pop the menu. If no X or Y position is passed, the current mouse position is used to display the pop-up menu. x and y values are relative to the window.
Clear	Clear all menu items.
RemoveItem ([in] int index)	Remove the specified item.
Additem ([in] String, [in/optional] int index)	Add String menu item at the Index. If index is omitted, the item is appended.

Events

Click(int item)	Item clicked is one of the parameters passed

Sample HTML

```
<HTML>
<HEAD>
<TITLE>Popup Menu</TITLE>
</HEAD>
<BODY>
```

```
<OBJECT CLASSID="CLSID:812AE312-8B8E-11CF-93C8-00AA00C08FDF"
ID="Popup_alx" STYLE="LEFT:0;TOP:0">
<PARAM NAME="ALXPATH" REF VALUE="file:E:\A Mastering ActiveX
Book\Mastering ActiveX\Part 2 Using Authoring and Scripting
Tools\Chapter 8 Building Web Pages with
Scripting\other\Popup.alx">
</OBJECT>

</BODY>
</HTML>
```

Sample ALX

```
<DIV ID="Layout2" STYLE="LAYOUT:FIXED;WIDTH:244pt;HEIGHT:183pt;">
    <OBJECT ID="pmenu1"
     CLASSID="CLSID:52DFAE60-CEBF-11CF-A3A9-00A0C9034920"
STYLE="TOP:8pt;LEFT:8pt;WIDTH:74pt;HEIGHT:17pt;TABINDEX:0;ZIN-
DEX:0;">
        <PARAM NAME="_ExtentX" VALUE="2619">
        <PARAM NAME="_ExtentY" VALUE="609">
        <PARAM NAME="Caption" VALUE="Popup Menu">
        <PARAM NAME="Menuitem[0]" VALUE="Windows 95">
        <PARAM NAME="Menuitem[1]" VALUE="Windows NT">
        <PARAM NAME="Menuitem[2]" VALUE="ActiveX Control">
        <PARAM NAME="Menuitem[3]" VALUE="Huh????">
        <PARAM NAME="Menuitem[4]" VALUE="Number 5">
    </OBJECT>
</DIV>
```

Figure 7-3 shows the result of running this code.

Pop-up Window Control

The Pop-up window allows the display of information on a Web page.

Properties

None.

Figure 7-3
The ActiveX Gallery pop-up menu

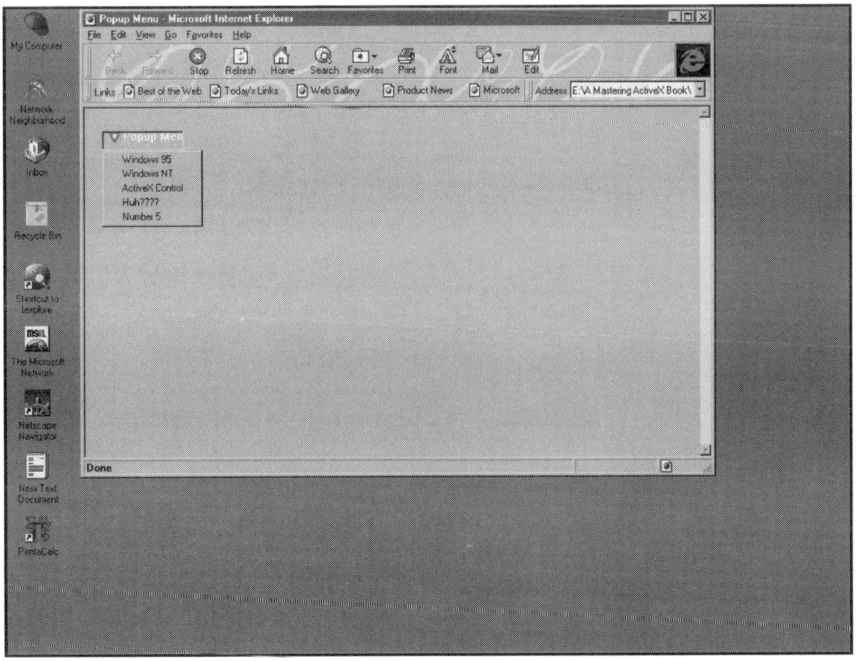

Methods

AboutBox	About box.	
Display the Pop-up window using the following parameter:		
	URL	The URL location of the HTML page.
Scale	[optional] True False Dismiss	Boolean values: Scale the display to fit the Pop-up window. Clip display to fit in the Pop-up window. Remove the popup.

Events

None.

Sample HTML

```
<OBJECT
classid=”clsid:A23D7C20-CABA-11CF-A5D4-00AA00A47DD2”
id=PopObj
</OBJECT>
```

Preloader Control

Properties

URL	URL to be downloaded
Enable	Enables (Enable=1) or disables (Enable=0) the control
CacheFile	File name of the local cached file (read only)
Bytes	The amount of data read so far in bytes (read only)
Percentage	The amount of data read so far in percentage (read only)

Methods

AboutBox	Displays the About dialog box

Events

Complete	Fired when the download has been completed
Error	Fired when the download could not be completed

Sample HTML

```
<OBJECT
id=Preload1
classid="clsid:16E349E0-702C-11CF-A3A9-00A0C9034920"
width=1
height=1
>
<PARAM NAME="URL" value="iepreld.htm">
<PARAM NAME="enable" value="0">
</OBJECT>
```

Timer Control

Properties

Enabled	Enables or disables the timer: True - Enabled state False - Disabled state
Interval	Interval for timer trigger in milliseconds

Methods

AboutBox	Displays the About dialog box

Events

Timer	This event is triggered when the timer is enabled and has a positive interval

Sample HTML

```
<OBJECT
classid="clsid:59CCB4A0-727D-11CF-AC36-00AA00A47DD2"
id=timer1
align=middle
>
<param name="Interval" value="1000">
<param name="Enabled" value="True">
</OBJECT>
```

View Tracker Control

Properties

Image	URL specifying an image for the control

Methods

AboutBox	Displays the About dialog box

Events

OnShow	Control falls within the view area
OnHide	Control scrolls off the view area

Web Pages with Scripting

The following code pages are all available at:

```
http://www.checkmaster.com/activex/
```

In addition to using several controls, they also show scripting in both JScript and VBScript. You can use the ActiveX Control Pad or a text editor to enter the code that follows. What I can't supply on paper is available at the Web site listed previously.

INDEX.HTM

This is the main index to the site. It uses a significant number of the new HTML tags and controls. It gives you the time and date in both

JScript and VBScript. It has a marquee running. It uses a rotating label control. It uses frames and floating frames and a table for selections.

The VBScript, JScript, and Other buttons contain the additional content for this site. The Web page is shown in Figure 7-4.

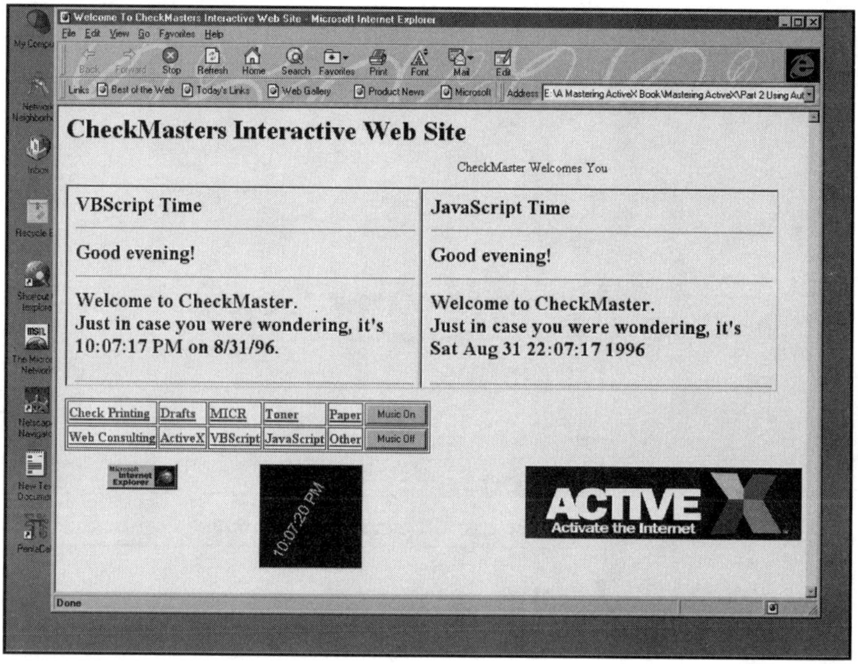

Figure 7-4 An Interactive Web Site for Demonstration

```
<HTML>
<HEAD><TITLE>Welcome To CheckMasters Interactive Web
Site</TITLE></HEAD>
<BODY BGCOLOR="beige" TOPMARGIN=8>
<SCRIPT LANGUAGE="VBScript">
Sub MusicOn
  parent.frames(3).document.write "<BGSOUND
src=music\mgcmmnt.mid>"
  parent.frames(3).document.close
End Sub
Sub MusicOff
  parent.frames(3).document.write "<BGSOUND src=>"
  parent.frames(3).document.close
End Sub
```

```
</SCRIPT>
<H1>CheckMasters Interactive Web Site</H1>
<MARQUEE BGCOLOR="beige" DIRECTION=LEFT BEHAVIOR=SCROLL
LOOP=INFINITE SCROLLAMOUNT=10 SCROLLDELAY=200>
CheckMaster Welcomes You</MARQUEE>
<P></P>
<IFRAME NAME="timevbsframe" SRC="timevbs.htm" WIDTH=430
HEIGHT=240 SCROLLING=NO FRAMEBORDER=10>
</IFRAME>
<IFRAME NAME="timejsframe" SRC="timejs.htm" WIDTH=430 HEIGHT=240
SCROLLING=NO FRAMEBORDER=10>
</IFRAME>
<P></P>
<TABLE BORDER BORDERCOLOR=maroon>
<TR>
<TD BGCOLOR="white"><A HREF="test.htm"><B>Check
Printing</B></A></TD>
<TD BGCOLOR="white"><A HREF="test.htm"><B>Drafts</B></A></TD>
<TD BGCOLOR="white"><A HREF="test.htm"><B>MICR</B></A></TD>
<TD BGCOLOR="white"><A HREF="test.htm"><B>Toner</B></A></TD>
<TD BGCOLOR="white"><A HREF="test.htm"><B>Paper</B></A></TD>
<TD BGCOLOR="white"><INPUT TYPE="BUTTON" VALUE="Music On"
onclick=MusicOn></TD>
</TR>
<TR>
<TD BGCOLOR="white"><A HREF="test.htm"><B>Web
Consulting</B></A></TD>
<TD BGCOLOR="white"><A HREF="test.htm"><B>ActiveX</B></A></TD>
<TD BGCOLOR="white"><A HREF="vbs.htm"><B>VBScript</B></A></TD>
<TD BGCOLOR="white"><A HREF="js.htm"><B>JScript</B></A></TD>
<TD BGCOLOR="white"><A HREF="other.htm"><B>Other</B></A></TD>
<TD BGCOLOR="white"><INPUT TYPE="BUTTON" VALUE="Music Off"
onclick=MusicOff></TD>
</TR>
</TABLE>
<P></P>
<IMG SRC="images\ie_ani.gif" ALIGN="left" HSPACE=50>
<IMG SRC="images\msactive.jpg" ALIGN="right">
<IFRAME NAME="timespinframe" SRC="zrottime.htm" WIDTH=125
```

```
HEIGHT=125 SCROLLING=NO FRAMEBORDER=10>
</IFRAME>
<IFRAME NAME="music" SRC="music.htm" WIDTH=1 HEIGHT=1>
</IFRAME>
</BODY>
</HTML>
```

TEST.HTM

This is a filler page.

```
<HTML>
<HEAD><BODY BGCOLOR=WHITE TEXT=BLACK><TITLE>Augs Test
Page</TITLE></HEAD>
<BODY>
<H1>Augs Test Page</H1>
<H2>
<A HREF="index.html">Home</A>
</H2>
</BODY>
</HTML>
```

VBS.HTM

This page, shown in Figure 7-5, is a simple hyperlink table of contents for the VBScript examples.

```
<HTML>
<HEAD><BODY BGCOLOR=WHITE
TEXT=BLACK><TITLE>VBScript</TITLE></HEAD>
<BODY>
<H1>Augs VBScript Sample Page</H1>
<H2>
<A HREF="towervbs.htm"><B>Tower of Hanoi</B></A><BR>
<A HREF="ohmvbs.htm"><B>Ohms Law Calculator</B></A><BR>
<A HREF="deckcalc.htm"><B>Deck Calculator</B></A><BR>
<A HREF="tilecalc.htm"><B>Tile Calculator</B></A><BR>
<A HREF="timevbs.htm"><B>Time Display</B></A><BR>
<A HREF="zrottime.htm"><B>Rotating Object</B></A><BR>
<A HREF="grphview.htm"><B>Graphic Viewer</B></A><BR>
<A HREF="bckgrnd.htm"><B>Backgrounds</B></A><BR><BR>
```

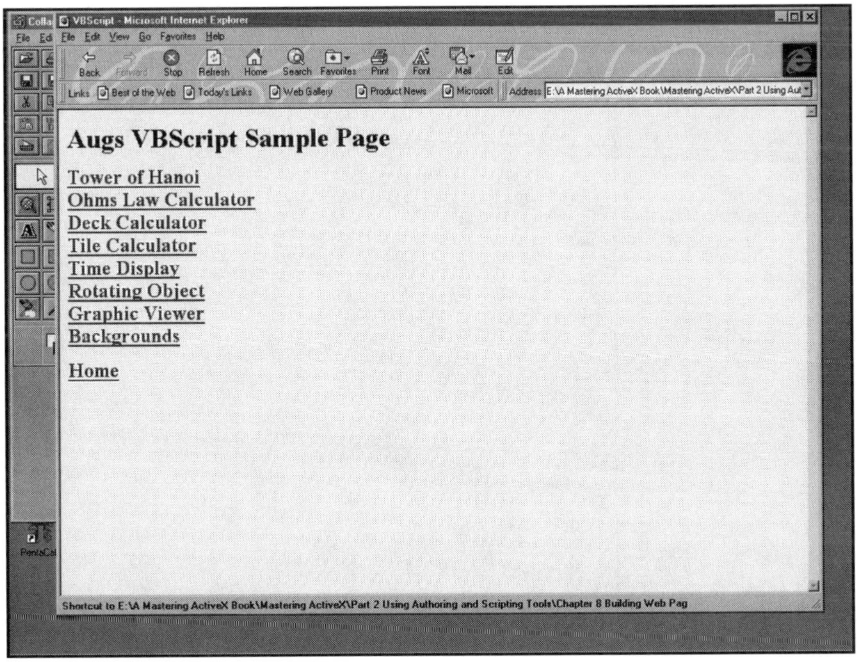

Figure 7-5
A Table of Contents for VBScript

```
<A HRFF="index.html"><B>Home</B></A><BR>
</H2>
</BODY>
</HTML>
```

JS.HTM

This page, shown in Figure 7-6, is a simple hyperlink table of contents for the JScript examples.

```
<HTML>
<HEAD><BODY BGCOLOR=WHITE
TEXT=BLACK><TITLE>JScript</TITLE></HEAD>
<BODY>
<H1>Augs JScript Sample Page</H1>
<H2>
<A HREF="towerjs.htm"><B>Tower of Hanoi</B></A><BR>
<A HRFF="ohmjs.htm"><B>Ohms Law Calculator</B></A><BR>
<A HREF="timejs.htm"><B>Time Display</B></A><BR><BR>
<A HREF="index.html"><B>Home</B></A><BR>
</H2>
</BODY>
</HTML>
```

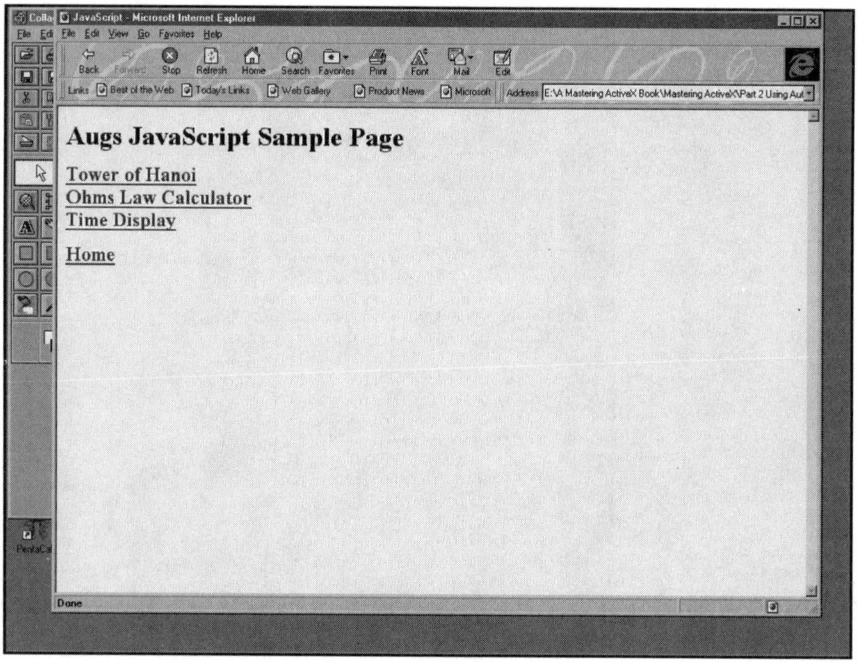

Figure 7-6
A Table of Contents for JScript

TOWERVBS.HTM

Figure 7-7 shows the Web page generated by the following script. It is not a Tower of Hanoi solver; it simply steps through one solution and demonstrates additional methods for activating Web pages.

```
<HTML>
<HEAD><TITLE>Tower Of Hanoi (VBScript)</TITLE></HEAD>
<BODY BGCOLOR=BEIGE TEXT=BLACK LINK=RED VLINK=BLACK
LANGUAGE=”VBScript” OnLoad=”resettower”>
<H1>Tower Of Hanoi (VBScript)</H1>
<SCRIPT LANGUAGE=”VBScript”>
sub resettower
  parent.frames(0).document.write “<BODY
BACKGROUND=images\T123.JPG></BODY>”
  parent.frames(0).document.close
  parent.frames(1).document.write “<BODY
BACKGROUND=images\T0.JPG></BODY>”
  parent.frames(1).document.close
  parent.frames(2).document.write “<BODY
BACKGROUND=images\T0.JPG></BODY>”
```

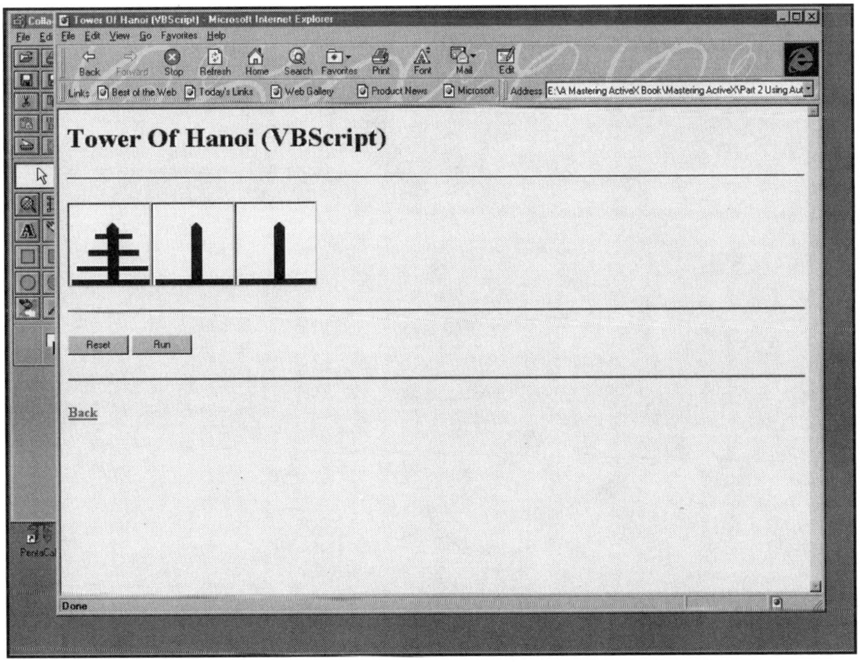

Figure 7-7 A Tower of Hanoi solution

```
  parent.frames(2).document.close
end sub
sub messageboxtimer
  MSGBOX “Next”,15,”Tower”
end sub
sub runtower
  parent.frames(0).document.write “<BODY
BACKGROUND=images\T23.JPG></BODY>”
  parent.frames(0).document.close
  parent.frames(1).document.write “<BODY
BACKGROUND=images\T0.JPG></BODY>”
  parent.frames(1).document.close
  parent.frames(2).document.write “<BODY
BACKGROUND=images\T1.JPG></BODY>”
  parent.frames(2).document.close
  messageboxtimer
  parent.frames(0).document.write “<BODY
BACKGROUND=images\T3.JPG></BODY>”
  parent.frames(0).document.close
  parent.frames(1).document.write “<BODY
```

```
BACKGROUND=images\T2.JPG></BODY>"
  parent.frames(1).document.close
  parent.frames(2).document.write "<BODY
BACKGROUND=images\T1.JPG></BODY>"
  parent.frames(2).document.close
  messageboxtimer
  parent.frames(0).document.write "<BODY
BACKGROUND=images\T3.JPG></BODY>"
  parent.frames(0).document.close
  parent.frames(1).document.write "<BODY
BACKGROUND=images\T12.JPG></BODY>"
  parent.frames(1).document.close
  parent.frames(2).document.write "<BODY
BACKGROUND=images\T0.JPG></BODY>"
  parent.frames(2).document.close
  messageboxtimer
  parent.frames(0).document.write "<BODY
BACKGROUND=images\T0.JPG></BODY>"
  parent.frames(0).document.close
  parent.frames(1).document.write "<BODY
BACKGROUND=images\T12.JPG></BODY>"
  parent.frames(1).document.close
  parent.frames(2).document.write "<BODY
BACKGROUND=images\T3.JPG></BODY>"
  parent.frames(2).document.close
  messageboxtimer
  parent.frames(0).document.write "<BODY
BACKGROUND=images\T1.JPG></BODY>"
  parent.frames(0).document.close
  parent.frames(1).document.write "<BODY
BACKGROUND=images\T2.JPG></BODY>"
  parent.frames(1).document.close
  parent.frames(2).document.write "<BODY
BACKGROUND=images\T3.JPG></BODY>"
  parent.frames(2).document.close
  messageboxtimer
  parent.frames(0).document.write "<BODY
BACKGROUND=images\T1.JPG></BODY>"
  parent.frames(0).document.close
```

```
  parent.frames(1).document.write "<BODY
BACKGROUND=images\T0.JPG></BODY>"
  parent.frames(1).document.close
  parent.frames(2).document.write "<BODY
BACKGROUND=images\T23.JPG></BODY>"
  parent.frames(2).document.close
  messageboxtimer
  parent.frames(0).document.write "<BODY
BACKGROUND=images\T0.JPG></BODY>"
  parent.frames(0).document.close
  parent.frames(1).document.write "<BODY
BACKGROUND=images\T0.JPG></BODY>"
  parent.frames(1).document.close
  parent.frames(2).document.write "<BODY
BACKGROUND=images\T123.JPG></BODY>"
  parent.frames(2).document.close
end sub
</SCRIPT>
<P>
<HR COLOR=GREEN><BR></P>
<IFRAME NAME="t1frame" SRC="tempty.htm" WIDTH=100 HEIGHT=100
SCROLLING=NO FRAMEBORDER=5>
</IFRAME>
<IFRAME NAME="t2frame" SRC="tempty.htm" WIDTH=100 HEIGHT=100
SCROLLING=NO FRAMEBORDER=5>
</IFRAME>
<IFRAME NAME="t3frame" SRC="tempty.htm" WIDTH=100 HEIGHT=100
SCROLLING=NO FRAMEBORDER=5>
</IFRAME>
<P>
<HR COLOR=GREEN><BR></P>
<P></P>
<INPUT TYPE="BUTTON" VALUE="Reset" OnClick="resettower()">
<INPUT TYPE="BUTTON" VALUE="Run" OnClick="runtower()">
<P></P>
<P>
<HR COLOR=GREEN><BR></P>
<P><B><A HREF="vbs.htm">Back</A></B></P>
<IMG SRC="images\t0.jpg" HEIGHT=1 WIDTH=1>
```

```
<IMG SRC="images\t1.jpg" HEIGHT=1 WIDTH=1>
<IMG SRC="images\t2.jpg" HEIGHT=1 WIDTH=1>
<IMG SRC="images\t3.jpg" HEIGHT=1 WIDTH=1>
<IMG SRC="images\t12.jpg" HEIGHT=1 WIDTH=1>
<IMG SRC="images\t23.jpg" HEIGHT=1 WIDTH=1>
<IMG SRC="images\t123.jpg" HEIGHT=1 WIDTH=1>
</BODY>
</HTML>
```

OHMVBS.HTM

Ohm's Law is seldom used in this age of electronics, but here is another example of scripting. Figure 7-8 shows the page, and you can calculate Volts, Amps, or Resistance by entering values for the other two items.

Figure 7-8 An Ohm's Law calculator

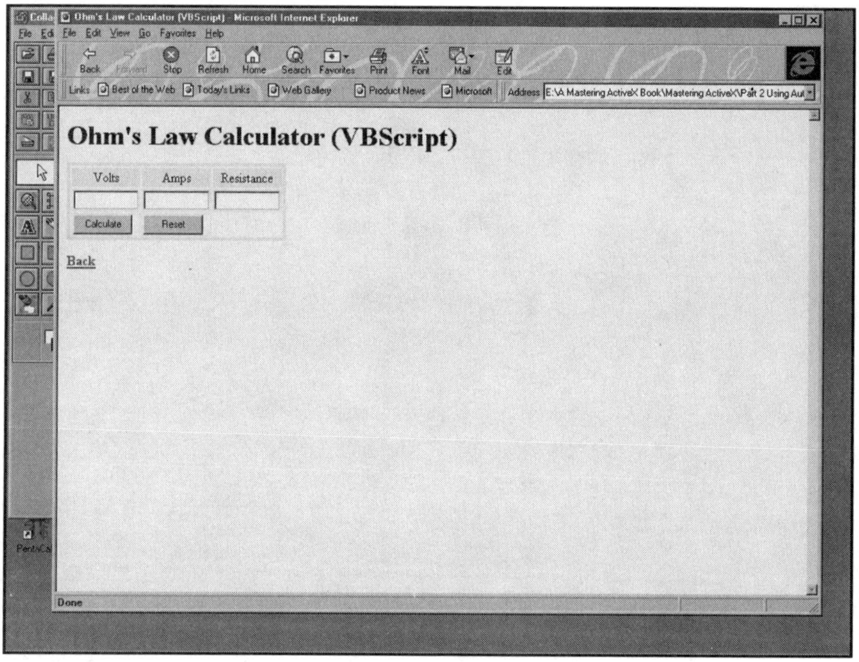


```
<HTML>
<HEAD><TITLE>Ohm's Law Calculator (VBScript)</TITLE></HEAD>
<BODY  BGCOLOR=BEIGE>
<SCRIPT LANGUAGE="VBScript">
sub calcvalues
```

```
  dim MyForm
  set MyForm = Document.Ohms
  if MyForm.evolt.value = "" then
    MyForm.evolt.value = MyForm.iamps.value * MyForm.rres.value
    exit sub
  end if
  if MyForm.iamps.value = "" then
    MyForm.iamps.value = MyForm.evolt.value / MyForm.rres.value
    exit sub
  end if
  if MyForm.rres.value = "" then
    MyForm.rres.value = MyForm.evolt.value / MyForm.iamps.value
    exit sub
  end if
end sub
sub clearvalues
  dim MyForm1
  set MyForm1 = Document.Ohms
  MyForm1.evolt.value = ""
  MyForm1.iamps.value = ""
  MyForm1.rres.value = ""
end sub
</SCRIPT>
<H1>Ohm's Law Calculator (VBScript)</H1>
<P>
<FORM NAME=Ohms>
<TABLE BORDER=4 BORDERCOLOR=BISQUE BGCOLOR=BEIGE>
<TR>
<TD BGCOLOR=BISQUE><DIV ALIGN=CENTER>Volts</DIV></TD>
<TD BGCOLOR=BISQUE><DIV ALIGN=CENTER>Amps</DIV></TD>
<TD BGCOLOR=BISQUE><DIV ALIGN=CENTER>Resistance</DIV></TD>
</TR>
<TR>
<TD><INPUT TYPE=TEXT NAME=evolt SIZE=12> </TD>
<TD><INPUT TYPE=TEXT NAME=iamps SIZE=12> </TD>
<TD><INPUT TYPE=TEXT NAME=rres SIZE=12> </TD>
</TR>
```

```
<TR>
<TD><INPUT TYPE="button" VALUE="Calculate" onClick="calcval-
ues"></TD>
<TD><INPUT TYPE="button" VALUE="Reset"
onClick="clearvalues"></TD>
</TR>
</TABLE>
</FORM>
<A HREF="vbs.htm"><B>Back</B></A><BR>
</BODY>
</HTML>
```

DECKCALC.HTM

If you ever want to build a deck, the Deck Calculator will help you determine how much material is required for your project. Figure 7-9 shows the calculator and the options. For a project, extend it to add capabilities.

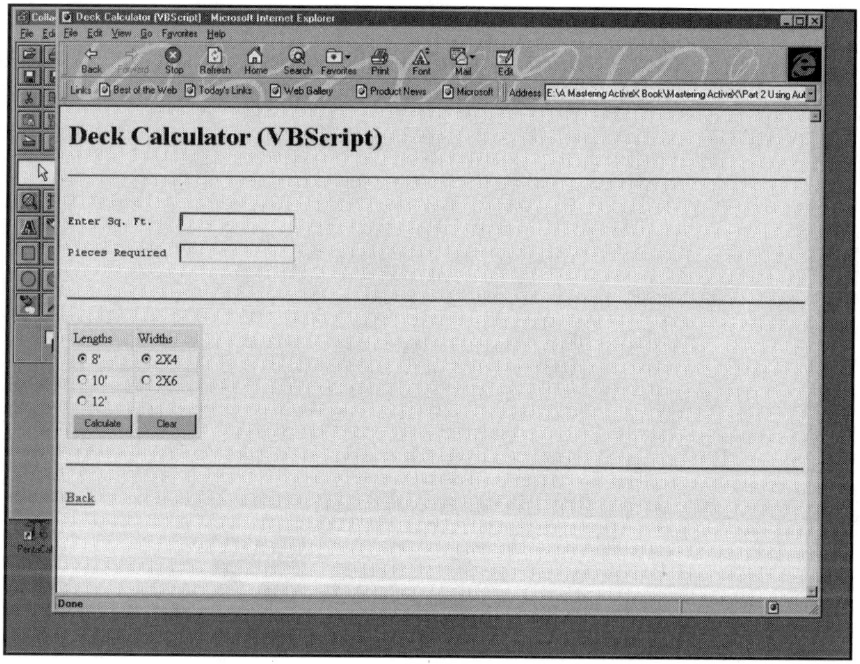

Figure 7-9
A Deck calculator

```
<HTML>
<HEAD><TITLE>Deck Calculator (VBScript)</TITLE></HEAD>
<BODY BGCOLOR=BEIGE TEXT=BLACK LINK=RED VLINK=BLACK
LANGUAGE="VBScript">
<SCRIPT LANGUAGE="VBScript">
Sub ClearFields
  dim MyForm1
  set MyForm1 = Document.WoodType
  SquareFeet.value = ""
  DisplayText.value = ""
  MyForm1.elements(0).checked = true
  MyForm1.elements(1).checked = true
End Sub
Sub RunCompute
  dim woodlength
  dim woodwidth
  dim sqrefeet
  dim temphold0, temphold1, temphold2
  dim MyForm
  set MyForm = Document.WoodType
  if MyForm.elements(0).checked then
    woodlength = 8
  end if
  if MyForm.elements(1).checked then
    woodwidth = 4
  end if
  if MyForm.elements(2).checked then
    woodlength = 10
  end if
  if MyForm.elements(3).checked then
    woodwidth = 6
  end if
  if MyForm.elements(4).checked then
    woodlength = 12
  end if
```

```
  sqrefeet = SquareFeet.value
  temphold0 = sqrefeet * 144
  temphold1 = woodwidth * (woodlength * 12)
  temphold2 = int(temphold0 / temphold1) + 1
  DisplayText.value = temphold2
End Sub
</SCRIPT>
<H1>Deck Calculator (VBScript)</H1>
<HR COLOR=GREEN><BR>
<PRE>
Enter Sq. Ft.     <INPUT TYPE=TEXT NAME="SquareFeet" SIZE=24><BR>
Pieces Required  <INPUT TYPE=TEXT NAME="DisplayText" SIZE=24><BR>
</PRE>
<HR COLOR=GREEN><BR>
<FORM NAME=WoodType>
<TABLE BORDER=4 BORDERCOLOR=BISQUE BGCOLOR=BEIGE>
<TR>
<TD BGCOLOR=BISQUE>Lengths</TD>
<TD BGCOLOR=BISQUE>Widths</TD>
</TR>
<TR>
<TD><INPUT TYPE=RADIO NAME="length1" CHECKED=TRUE>8'</TD>
<TD><INPUT TYPE=RADIO NAME="width1" CHECKED=TRUE>2X4</TD>
</TR>
<TR>
<TD><INPUT TYPE=RADIO NAME="length1">10'</TD>
<TD><INPUT TYPE=RADIO NAME="width1">2X6</TD>
</TR>
<TR>
<TD><INPUT TYPE=RADIO NAME="length1">12'</TD>
</TR>
<TR>
<TD><INPUT TYPE="BUTTON" VALUE="Calculate"
onclick=RunCompute></TD>
<TD><INPUT TYPE="BUTTON" VALUE="Clear" onclick=ClearFields></TD>
</TR>
</TABLE>
```

```
</FORM>
<P>
<HR COLOR=GREEN><BR></P>
<P><B><A HREF="vbs.htm">Back</A></B></P>
</BODY>
</HTML>
```

BCKGRND.HTM

```
<HTML>
<HEAD><TITLE>Backgrounds (VBScript)</TITLE></HEAD>
<BODY BGCOLOR=BEIGE TEXT=BLACK LINK=RED VLINK=BLACK
LANGUAGE="VBScript">
<SCRIPT LANGUAGE="VBScript">
Sub ClearGraphic
  parent.frames(0).document.write "<BODY></BODY>"
  parent.frames(0).document.close
End Sub
Sub RunGraphic
  dim temptext
  dim imagename
  dim MyForm
  set MyForm = Document.BackGround
  if MyForm.elements(0).checked then
    imagename="images\bckwood1.jpg"
  end if
  if MyForm.elements(1).checked then
    imagename="images\bckline1.jpg"
  end if
  if MyForm.elements(2).checked then
    imagename="images\bckwood2.jpg"
  end if
  if MyForm.elements(3).checked then
    imagename="images\bckline2.jpg"
  end if
  if MyForm.elements(4).checked then
    imagename="images\bckwood3.jpg"
  end if
```

```
  if MyForm.elements(5).checked then
    imagename="images\bckline3.jpg"
  end if
  temptext="<BODY BACKGROUND = " & chr(34) & trim(imagename) &
chr(34) &"></BODY>"
  parent.frames(0).document.write temptext
  parent.frames(0).document.close
End Sub
</SCRIPT>
<H1>Backgrounds (VBScript)</H1>
<P>
<HR COLOR=GREEN><BR></P>
<IFRAME NAME="t1frame" SRC="tempty.htm" WIDTH=300 HEIGHT=200
FRAMEBORDER=5></IFRAME>
<P>
<HR COLOR=GREEN><BR></P>
<P>Background Type</P>
<FORM NAME=BackGround>
<INPUT TYPE=RADIO NAME="bckgnd1" CHECKED=TRUE>Wood 1
<INPUT TYPE=RADIO NAME="bckgnd1">Line 1<BR>
<INPUT TYPE=RADIO NAME="bckgnd1">Wood 2
<INPUT TYPE=RADIO NAME="bckgnd1">Line 2<BR>
<INPUT TYPE=RADIO NAME="bckgnd1">Wood 3
<INPUT TYPE=RADIO NAME="bckgnd1">Line 3<BR><BR>
<INPUT TYPE="BUTTON" VALUE="Display" onclick=RunGraphic>
<INPUT TYPE="BUTTON" VALUE="Clear" onclick=ClearGraphic>
</FORM>
<P>
<HR COLOR=GREEN><BR></P>
<P><B><A HREF="vbs.htm">Back</A></B></P>
</BODY>
</HTML>
```

GRPHVIEW.HTM

```
<HTML>
<HEAD><TITLE>Graphic Viewer (VBScript)</TITLE></HEAD>
<BODY BGCOLOR=BEIGE TEXT=BLACK LINK=RED VLINK=BLACK
LANGUAGE="VBScript">
```

```
<SCRIPT LANGUAGE="VBScript">
Sub ClearGraphic
  parent.frames(0).document.write "<BODY></BODY>"
  parent.frames(0).document.close
  GraphicName.Value = ""
End Sub
Sub RunGraphic
  dim temptext
  temptext="<BODY><IMG SRC=" & trim(GraphicName.Value) &
"></BODY>"
  parent.frames(0).document.write temptext
  parent.frames(0).document.close
End Sub
</SCRIPT>
<H1>Graphic Viewer (VBScript)</H1>
<P>
<HR COLOR=GREEN><BR></P>
<IFRAME NAME="t1frame" SRC="tempty.htm" WIDTH=500 HEIGHT=250
SCROLLING="Yes" FRAMEBORDER=5>
</IFRAME>
<P>
<HR COLOR=GREEN><BR></P>
<P></P>
<INPUT TYPE=TEXT NAME="GraphicName" SIZE=24><BR><BR>
<INPUT TYPE="BUTTON" VALUE="Show" onclick="RunGraphic">
<INPUT TYPE="BUTTON" VALUE="Clear" onclick="ClearGraphic">
<P></P>
<P>
<HR COLOR=GREEN><BR></P>
<P><B><A HREF="vbs.htm">Back</A></B></P>
</BODY>
</HTML>
```

MUSIC.HTM

```
<HTML>
<HEAD><TITLE>Music</TITLE></HEAD>
<BODY BGCOLOR="beige" TOPMARGIN=8>
```

```
<BGSOUND src="music\mgcmmnt.mid">
</BODY>
</HTML>
```

OHMJS.HTM

```
<HTML>
<HEAD>
<TITLE>Ohm's Law Calculator (JScript)</TITLE>
<SCRIPT LANGUAGE="JScript">
function calcvalues(form)
{
    if ((form.evolt.value == null || form.evolt.value.length ==
0)) {
        form.evolt.value = form.iamps.value * form.rres.value;
        return;
    }
    if ((form.iamps.value == null || form.iamps.value.length ==
0)) {
        form.iamps.value = form.evolt.value / form.rres.value;
        return;
    }
    if ((form.rres.value == null || form.rres.value.length ==
0)) {
        form.rres.value = form.evolt.value / form.iamps.value;
        return;
    }
}
function clearvalues(form)
{
    form.evolt.value = "";
    form.iamps.value = "";
    form.rres.value = "";
}
</SCRIPT>
</HEAD>
<BODY  BGCOLOR=BEIGE>
<H1>Ohm's Law Calculator (JScript)</H1>
```

```
<P>
<FORM method=POST>
<TABLE BORDER=4 BORDERCOLOR=BISQUE BGCOLOR=BEIGE>
<TR>
<TD BGCOLOR=BISQUE><DIV ALIGN=CENTER>Volts</DIV></TD>
<TD BGCOLOR=BISQUE><DIV ALIGN=CENTER>Amps</DIV></TD>
<TD BGCOLOR=BISQUE><DIV ALIGN=CENTER>Resistance</DIV></TD>
</TR>
<TR>
<TD><INPUT TYPE=TEXT NAME=evolt  SIZE=12> </TD>
<TD><INPUT TYPE=TEXT NAME=iamps  SIZE=12> </TD>
<TD><INPUT TYPE=TEXT NAME=rres SIZE=12> </TD>
</TR>
<TR>
<TD><INPUT TYPE="button" VALUE="Calculate"
onClick=calcvalues(this.form)></TD>
<TD><INPUT TYPE="reset"  VALUE="Reset"
onClick=clearvalues(this.form)></TD>
</TR>
</TABLE>
</FORM>
<A HREF="js.htm"><B>Back</B></A><BR>
</BODY>
</HTML>
```

OTHER.HTM

```
<HTML>
<HEAD><BODY BGCOLOR=WHITE TEXT=BLACK><TITLE>Other</TITLE></HEAD>
<BODY>
<H1>Augs Other Sample Page</H1>
<H2>
<A HREF="clrchrt.htm"><B>Color Chart</B></A><BR>
<A HREF="clrchrt1.htm"><B>Color Chart 1</B></A><BR><BR>
<A HREF="index.html"><B>Home</B></A><BR>
</H2>
</BODY>
</HTML>
```

TEMPTY.HTM

```
<HTML>
<HEAD>
<TITLE>
</TITLE>
</HEAD>
<BODY BGCOLOR=WHITE TEXT=BLACK>
</BODY>
</HTML>
```

TEST.HTM

```
<HTML>
<HEAD>
<BODY BGCOLOR=WHITE TEXT=BLACK>
<TITLE>Augs Test Page</TITLE>
</HEAD>
<BODY>
<H1>Augs Test Page</H1>
<H2>
<A HREF="index.html">Home</A>
</H2>
</BODY>
</HTML>
```

TILECALC

```
<HTML>
<HEAD><TITLE>Tile Calculator (VBScript)</TITLE></HEAD>
<BODY BGCOLOR=BEIGE TEXT=BLACK LINK=RED VLINK=BLACK
LANGUAGE="VBScript">
<SCRIPT LANGUAGE="VBScript">
Sub ClearFields
  dim MyForm1
  set MyForm1 = Document.tileType
  SquareFeet.value = ""
  DisplayText.value = ""
  MyForm1.elements(0).checked = true
  MyForm1.elements(2).checked = true
```

```
End Sub
Sub RunCompute
  dim tilesize
  dim tilespace
  dim sqrefeet
  dim temphold0, temphold1, temphold2
  dim MyForm
  set MyForm = Document.TileType
  if MyForm.elements(0).checked then
    tilesize = 6
  end if
  if MyForm.elements(1).checked then
    tilesize = 2
  end if
  if MyForm.elements(2).checked then
    tilespace = .25
  end if
  if MyForm.elements(3).checked then
    tilesize = 8
  end if
  if MyForm.elements(4).checked then
    tilesize = 4
  end if
  if MyForm.elements(5).checked then
    tilespace = .5
  end if
  if MyForm.elements(6).checked then
    tilesize = 12
  end if
  if MyForm.elements(7).checked then
    tilespace = .75
  end if
  sqrefeet = SquareFeet.value
  temphold0 = sqrefeet * 144
  temphold1 = (tilesize + tilespace) * (tilesize + tilespace)
  temphold2 = int(temphold0 / temphold1) + 1
  DisplayText.value = temphold2
```

```
End Sub
</SCRIPT>
<H1>Tile Calculator (VBScript)</H1>
<HR COLOR=GREEN><BR>
<PRE>
Enter Sq. Ft.    <INPUT TYPE=TEXT NAME="SquareFeet" SIZE=24><BR>
Pieces Required  <INPUT TYPE=TEXT NAME="DisplayText" SIZE=24><BR>
</PRE>
<HR COLOR=GREEN><BR>
<FORM NAME=tileType>
<TABLE BORDER=4 BORDERCOLOR=BISQUE BGCOLOR=BEIGE>
<TR>
<TD BGCOLOR=BISQUE>Floor</TD>
<TD BGCOLOR=BISQUE>Counter</TD>
<TD BGCOLOR=BISQUE>Spacing</TD>
</TR>
<TR>
<TD><INPUT TYPE=RADIO NAME="tile1" CHECKED=TRUE>6X6</TD>
<TD><INPUT TYPE=RADIO NAME="tile1">2X2</TD>
<TD><INPUT TYPE=RADIO NAME="space1" CHECKED=TRUE>&frac14;</TD>
</TR>
<TR>
<TD><INPUT TYPE=RADIO NAME="tile1">8X8</TD>
<TD><INPUT TYPE=RADIO NAME="tile1">4X4</TD>
<TD><INPUT TYPE=RADIO NAME="space1">&frac12;</TD>
</TR>
<TR>
<TD><INPUT TYPE=RADIO NAME="tile1">12X12</TD>
<TD></TD>
<TD><INPUT TYPE=RADIO NAME="space1">&frac34;</TD>
</TR>
<TR>
<TD><INPUT TYPE="BUTTON" VALUE="Calculate"
onclick=RunCompute></TD>
<TD><INPUT TYPE="BUTTON" VALUE="Clear" onclick=ClearFields></TD>
</TR>
</TABLE>
```

```
</FORM>
<P>
<HR COLOR=GREEN><BR></P>
<P><B><A HREF="vbs.htm">Back</A></B></P>
</BODY>
</HTML>
```

TIMEJS.HTM

```
<HTML>
<HEAD><META HTTP-EQUIV="REFRESH"
CONTENT=10><TITLE>Time</TITLE></HEAD>
<SCRIPT LANGUAGE="JScript">
  function getgreeting()
    {
    if (h < 12)
    {
      Document.Write("<HR>Good morning!<BR>")
      return;
    }
     if (h < 17)
    {
      Document.Write("<HR>Good afternoon!<BR>")
      return;
    }
    if (h < 24)
    {
      Document.Write("<HR>Good evening!<BR>")
      return;
    }
    }
  function PrintWelcome()
    {
    AugsDate = new Date()
    h = AugsDate.getHours()
    Document.Write("<H2>JScript Time<BR>")
    getgreeting()
    Document.Write("<HR>Welcome to CheckMaster.<BR>")
```

```
    Document.Write("Just in case you were wondering, it's<BR>")
    Document.Write(AugsDate + "</H2><HR>")
    }
</SCRIPT>
<BODY BGCOLOR="beige" FGCOLOR="black" TOPMARGIN=8>
<SCRIPT LANGUAGE="JScript">
  PrintWelcome()
</SCRIPT>
<A HREF="js.htm"><B>Back</B></A><BR>
</BODY>
</HTML>
```

TIMEVBS.HTM

```
<HTML>
<HEAD><META HTTP-EQUIV="REFRESH"
CONTENT=10><TITLE>Time</TITLE></HEAD>
<BODY BGCOLOR="beige" TOPMARGIN=8>
<SCRIPT LANGUAGE="VBScript">
  ' This line executes when the script tag is parsed.
  Call PrintWelcome
  Sub PrintWelcome
    dim h
    h = Hour(Now)
    Document.Writeln "<H2>VBScript Time<BR>"
    If h < 12 then
      Document.Writeln "<HR>Good morning!<BR>"
    ElseIf h < 17 then
      Document.Writeln "<HR>Good afternoon!<BR>"
    Else
      Document.Writeln "<HR>Good evening!<BR>"
    End If
    Document.Writeln "<HR>Welcome to CheckMaster.<BR>"
    Document.Writeln "Just in case you were wondering, it's<BR>"
    Document.Writeln Time() & " on " & Date() & ".</H2><HR>"
  End Sub
</SCRIPT>
<A HREF="vbs.htm"><B>Back</B></A><BR>
```

```
</BODY>
</HTML>
```

TOWERJS.HTM

```
<HTML>
<HEAD><TITLE>Tower Of Hanoi (JScript)</TITLE></HEAD>
<BODY BGCOLOR = BEIGE TEXT = BLACK LINK = RED VLINK = BLACK LAN-
GUAGE="JScript" OnLoad="resettower()">
<SCRIPT LANGUAGE="JScript">
function resettower ()
{
T0 = "<HTML><BODY BACKGROUND=\"/IMAGE/T0.JPG\"></BODY></HTML>";
T1 = "<HTML><BODY BACKGROUND=\"/IMAGE/T1.JPG\"></BODY></HTML>";
T2 = "<HTML><BODY BACKGROUND=\"/IMAGE/T2.JPG\"></BODY></HTML>";
T3 = "<HTML><BODY BACKGROUND=\"/IMAGE/T3.JPG\"></BODY></HTML>";
T12 = "<HTML><BODY BACKGROUND=\"/IMAGE/T12.JPG\"></BODY></HTML>";
T23 = "<HTML><BODY BACKGROUND=\"/IMAGE/T23.JPG\"></BODY></HTML>";
T123 ="<HTML><BODY
BACKGROUND=\"/IMAGE/T123.JPG\"></BODY></HTML>";
  frames[0].document.write( T123 );
  frames[0].document.close();
  frames[1].document.write( T0 );
  frames[1].document.close();
  frames[2].document.write( T0 );
  frames[2].document.close();
}
function messageboxtimer ()
{
  alert ("Next");
}
function runtower ()
{
T0 = "<HTML><BODY BACKGROUND=\"/IMAGE/T0.JPG\"></BODY></HTML>";
T1 = "<HTML><BODY BACKGROUND=\"/IMAGE/T1.JPG\"></BODY></HTML>";
T2 = "<HTML><BODY BACKGROUND=\"/IMAGE/T2.JPG\"></BODY></HTML>";
T3 = "<HTML><BODY BACKGROUND=\"/IMAGE/T3.JPG\"></BODY></HTML>";
T12 = "<HTML><BODY BACKGROUND=\"/IMAGE/T12.JPG\"></BODY></HTML>";
```

```
T23 = "<HTML><BODY BACKGROUND=\"/IMAGE/T23.JPG\"></BODY></HTML>";
T123 ="<HTML><BODY
BACKGROUND=\"/IMAGE/T123.JPG\"></BODY></HTML>";
  frames[0].document.write( T23 );
  frames[0].document.close();
  frames[1].document.write( T0 );
  frames[1].document.close();
  frames[2].document.write( T1 );
  frames[2].document.close();
  messageboxtimer;
  frames[0].document.write( T3 );
  frames[0].document.close();
  frames[1].document.write( T2 );
  frames[1].document.close();
  frames[2].document.write( T1 );
  frames[2].document.close();
  messageboxtimer;
  frames[0].document.write( T3 );
  frames[0].document.close();
  frames[1].document.write( T12 );
  frames[1].document.close();
  frames[2].document.write( T0 );
  frames[2].document.close();
  messageboxtimer;
  frames[0].document.write( T0 );
  frames[0].document.close();
  frames[1].document.write( T12 );
  frames[1].document.close();
  frames[2].document.write( T3 );
  frames[2].document.close();
  messageboxtimer;
  frames[0].document.write( T1 );
  frames[0].document.close();
  frames[1].document.write( T2 );
  frames[1].document.close();
  frames[2].document.write( T3 );
  frames[2].document.close();
```

```
  messageboxtimer;
  frames[0].document.write( T1 );
  frames[0].document.close();
  frames[1].document.write( T0 );
  frames[1].document.close();
  frames[2].document.write( T23 );
  frames[2].document.close();
  messageboxtimer;
  frames[0].document.write( T0 );
  frames[0].document.close();
  frames[1].document.write( T0 );
  frames[1].document.close();
  frames[2].document.write( T123 );
  frames[2].document.close();
}
</SCRIPT>
<H1>Tower Of Hanoi (JScript)</H1>
<P>
<HR COLOR=BLUE><BR></P>
<IFRAME NAME="t1frame" SRC="tempty.htm" WIDTH=100 HEIGHT=100
SCROLLING=NO FRAMEBORDER=5>
</IFRAME>
<IFRAME NAME="t2frame" SRC="tempty.htm" WIDTH=100 HEIGHT=100
SCROLLING=NO FRAMEBORDER=5>
</IFRAME>
<IFRAME NAME="t3frame" SRC="tempty.htm" WIDTH=100 HEIGHT=100
SCROLLING=NO FRAMEBORDER=5>
</IFRAME>
<P>
<HR COLOR=BLUE><BR></P>
<P></P>
<INPUT TYPE="BUTTON" VALUE="Reset" OnClick="resettower()">
<INPUT TYPE="BUTTON" VALUE="Run" OnClick="runtower()">
<P></P>
<P>
<HR COLOR=BLUE><BR></P>
<P><B><A HREF="js.htm">Back</A></B></P>
<IMG SRC = "images/t0.jpg" HEIGHT = 1 WIDTH = 1>
```

```
<IMG SRC = "images/t1.jpg" HEIGHT = 1 WIDTH = 1>
<IMG SRC = "images/t2.jpg" HEIGHT = 1 WIDTH = 1>
<IMG SRC = "images/t3.jpg" HEIGHT = 1 WIDTH = 1>
<IMG SRC = "images/t12.jpg" HEIGHT = 1 WIDTH = 1>
<IMG SRC = "images/t23.jpg" HEIGHT = 1 WIDTH = 1>
<IMG SRC = "images/t123.jpg" HEIGHT = 1 WIDTH = 1>
</BODY>
</HTML>
```

ZROTTIME.HTM

```
<HTML>
<HEAD>
<TITLE>Rotating Time</TITLE>
</HEAD>
<BODY BGCOLOR=BLACK TEXT=BLACK LINK=RED VLINK=BLACK>
    <OBJECT ID="IeLabel1" WIDTH=192 HEIGHT=181
 CLASSID="CLSID:99B42120-6EC7-11CF-A6C7-00AA00A47DD2">
    <PARAM NAME="_ExtentX" VALUE="3000">
    <PARAM NAME="_ExtentY" VALUE="3000">
    <PARAM NAME="Caption" VALUE="">
    <PARAM NAME="Angle" VALUE="0">
    <PARAM NAME="Alignment" VALUE="0">
    <PARAM NAME="Mode" VALUE="1">
    <PARAM NAME="FillStyle" VALUE="0">
    <PARAM NAME="FillStyle" VALUE="0">
    <PARAM NAME="ForeColor" VALUE="#00FF00">
    <PARAM NAME="BackColor" VALUE="#000000">
    <PARAM NAME="FontName" VALUE="Arial">
    <PARAM NAME="FontSize" VALUE="14">
    <PARAM NAME="FontItalic" VALUE="0">
    <PARAM NAME="FontBold" VALUE="0">
    <PARAM NAME="FontUnderline" VALUE="0">
    <PARAM NAME="FontStrikeout" VALUE="0">
    <PARAM NAME="TopPoints" VALUE="0">
    <PARAM NAME="BotPoints" VALUE="0">
</OBJECT>
    <SCRIPT LANGUAGE="VBScript">
```

```
<!—
Sub IeTimer1_Timer()
stepangle = IeLabel1.Angle + 5
if stepangle >360 then
stepangle = 0
end if
IeLabel1.Caption = Time
IeLabel1.Angle = stepangle
end sub
—>
     </SCRIPT>
     <OBJECT ID="IeTimer1" WIDTH=39 HEIGHT=39
      CLASSID="CLSID:59CCB4A0-727D-11CF-AC36-00AA00A47DD2">
         <PARAM NAME="_ExtentX" VALUE="1005">
         <PARAM NAME="_ExtentY" VALUE="1005">
         <PARAM NAME="Interval" VALUE="100">
     </OBJECT>
<P>
<HR COLOR=GREEN><BR></P>
<P><B><A HREF="vbs.htm">Back</A></B></P>
</BODY>
</HTML>
```

Summary

ActiveX was, on the surface, a renaming of OLE Custom Controls to ActiveX Controls, but the ActiveX initiative covers a much wider range of technology. ActiveX and the Internet go hand in hand. The client side implementation is the Internet Explorer. The server side implementation is the Internet Information Server running on Windows NT. Surrounding that is a whole new world of features designed to move people from the confines of their desktop to the world wide venue of the Internet.

In this book, I have concentrated on the client side, showing you how to build Web pages to take advantage of as much new technology as I could show you. I give you a little more information in the last two chapters about building controls.

Chapter 8

Introducing ActiveX Custom Controls

When you buy a telephone, an amplifier, a set of speakers, a television, or any number of other *components*, you never question whether they will work with the other components you may own. You know that the telephone has an *interface* that will connect it to the local telephone system. You may not even know or care that it's called an RJ11 connector.

An amplifier has inputs for various other components and output jacks to connect the speakers. Those jacks are called RCA jacks. Even the plug on the refrigerator is designed as an interface to the 110-volt circuit in your house. The point is, you never question the interface—you buy components with the full expectation that they will connect with other components in a standard and predictable way.

That, in a nutshell, is the principle behind component software as in ActiveX Controls designed to the Component Object Model (COM) specification.

Now, taking the original analogy a little further, you probably never ask exactly what is inside one of the components you buy. Similarly, you probably don't care what language an ActiveX Control is written in as long as it gets the job done. Ideally, the control will run on a wide variety of hardware under a wide variety of operating systems, and still present the same interface to the outside world.

The ActiveX Controls that I've been discussing throughout this book are designed to run on the client machine (usually a PC running Windows) in conjunction with Internet Explorer. In fact, they will be available to run on Windows, UNIX, Macintosh, and other machines in time. When you reach a Web site that requires your machine to run a control, the server will know which machine is asking for the control and will download the proper control for that system.

These same controls are usually designed to run with various development software as well as on the Internet. This means that rather than build new code every time you want a particular piece of functionality, you can simply look to one of the thousands of vendors who provide controls and you may find exactly the functionality you need. At that point, you need only glue it together with something such as Visual Basic. You might say that controls are like the components you buy for your HiFi system, and scripting languages are like the wires you buy to connect them. Not a great analogy, but it works.

Looking at the Implications

In the early years of the electronic industry, you bought tubes, transformers, coils, capacitors, and resistors to wire together a piece of electronic equipment. Computers with very limited functionality took huge rooms, huge air conditioners, and huge power to run. The transistor was developed and then everything became smaller, but things were still assembled in pieces. That was followed by integrated circuits that led to the present crop of one-chip computers with literally millions of transistors.

A computer with the power of a thousand Univacs or more now sits in a two-inch square socket, though it must be cooled with its own private fan. You can buy a motherboard, disk drive adapter (SCSI or EIDE), modems, and other items, and plug them into a cabinet with the expectation that all will work together.

In a very similar manner, the promise of component software is that huge capabilities can be put together using components just as you now assemble a powerful computer from components. If that promise is fulfilled—and I believe it will be—the ability to develop powerful software with minimal effort will be here.

Examining Scripting Services

I've discussed VBScript and JScript. The fact is that anyone could and well may develop scripting languages to glue the components together. I'm not talking about "object-oriented programming" in the traditional sense; rather, I'm talking about a completely new idea in component software. The components may make use of object-oriented development methods, or any other method, for that matter.

I'm talking about components that expose their capabilities to the world through well-defined interfaces. Scripting software is designed to look at those interfaces by sending and receiving appropriate information to make use of the internal functionality of the component.

Looking at HTML Standards for Active Content

The future of the Internet is the Web. The future of the Web is HTML. To ensure that everyone can connect a coffee pot to the electrical outlet in the wall, the power companies all agree to provide 110 volts AC and 60 cycles per second (your clock wouldn't keep time if they didn't). In a very similar manner, the HTML specifications *must* be carefully standardized. If every browser developer decides to implement slightly different HTML tags that do things that other browsers don't understand, we will have anarchy.

Both Microsoft and Netscape are working to ensure that the standards become just that. Maintaining strong standards is imperative to ensure that the new functionality introduced by components can be used by every Web designer in the world with the full expectation that the browser being used by visitors to that site will not find unpleasant surprises.

Examining "Safe" Code Download and Verification

Just the other day, a virus was reportedly going to trigger and play havoc with computers. McAfee and other virus-check developers made free downloads available. The fact is, viruses are very real and they can be disastrous. The idea of being able to download software in the full certainty that it is safe has value beyond its surface appearance.

The system being implemented by Microsoft works as follows: A developer obtains certifications from a trusted third party. The trusted third party is like a network notary. The system uses public key cryptography to encrypt the developer's status as a trusted supplier. The developer uses software provided as part of Authenticode to hash the application software (code) that he or she intends to make available, and attaches the certificate from VeriSign (in most cases) to the software.

NOTE:
Hashing, as discussed here, simply generates a unique digital signature. If one byte is changed in the original software, a different hash is generated. A hash value is generated when the software is signed. When you download the software, part of the authentication is to generate a hash using the same algorithm and compare it to the hash generated by the software developer. If these two values match, the software has not been tampered with.

When the software begins to download, Internet Explorer looks for a certificate. If it finds one, it decodes it and displays the certificate for the user on the screen. If the user trusts the vendor, the user can agree to allow the software to be copied to the user's machine. This ensures that the user knows who the vendor is and knows that the hash matches the original hash to verify that the software hasn't been tampered with. The result is what has come to be known as *Internet shrink wrap*.

NOTE:
If Internet Explorer fails to find a certificate, it warns you that the software is unsigned and asks whether you still want it installed on your computer.

Unless the software was infected with a virus on the developer's premises, you can be virtually certain that the software is safe.

Security Services

Microsoft and others are making a wide range of services available based on public key cryptography. These services will make it possible for people to conduct business on the Internet in the virtual certainty that they won't be compromised. Let me explain a bit.

You probably played with ciphers when you were young. One that I played with was a simple transposition cipher. Every *A* in a message was converted to the letter *D*, for example. Every other letter was converted to the letter four characters further in the alphabet, and wrapped at the end. Without getting into heavy detail, this system is known as *secret key* cryptography. Each person must know the secret key for it to work. If you live across the street from the person with whom you're exchanging messages, you can each agree—in person—about the day's key. If, on the other hand, you live a continent away, sharing secret keys becomes a real problem.

The modern counterpart of the transposition or substitution cipher is embodied in technology such as DES (Data Encryption Standard) and dozens of other techniques for encrypting messages, with the assurance that decoding them would take years of work. Keys must still be exchanged in some manner, however.

Enter public key encryption or the Public Key Cryptography System (PKCS). This system was invented in 1977 by Ron Rivest, Adi Shamir, and Leonard Adleman, whose last names begin with RSA—thus RSA Data Security. RSA Data Security *is* public key encryption; it holds the patents. Two very large keys, made up of large prime numbers, are generated using some very complex math. One of these keys is called the *private* key; the other is called the *public* key. You keep your private key somewhere as privately as you possibly can. You give the public key to anyone in the world, and here's how it works.

Say that you want to send a message to Jane. You obtain Jane's public key and encrypt your message using that key. After the message is encrypted, the *only* key in the world that will decrypt the message is Jane's private key. You can't even decrypt it using Jane's public key, obviously. It's a little like Jane putting a bank vault on a street corner. You deliver your message to her by putting it in the vault and twirling the dial. Because only Jane knows the combination, only Jane can open it. PKCS is, however, a little cheaper than a vault.

Now Jane receives the message. It was encoded with her public key because she can decrypt it using her private key. But how does she know who sent it? Everyone has access to her public key, so anyone could have sent the message. You need to sign the message before you send it if you want Jane to know for certain that it came from you. You encrypt a hash (an always unique group of numbers generated by a hashing algorithm) of the message using your private key. Jane receives the message and decrypts the hash using your public key. Because only your public key can decrypt a message encrypted with your private key, Jane knows for an absolute certainty that you sent the message, and that it wasn't tampered with enroute. She knows this because the hashes match.

The digital signature is considered nonrepudiatable because no one in the world can forge such a signature.

That is the essence of cryptography. The subject gets very intense as you begin examining it in more detail, but it represents the future of the Internet. Without the security inherent in cryptography, little if any business of any kind could be done on the Internet. With it, the Net becomes safer than your living room for discussing business, signing contracts, buying products, banking, and any other business-related thing you can think of. It is also the heart of the code-signing initiative as represented by Microsoft's Authenticode.

Introduction to Document Objects

The notion of Nashville (the code name for Internet Explorer 4.0) is to reduce your screen to a full-screen browser—uncluttered by desktop icons and multiple applications—that contains your documents as you need them and instantiates the correct software application to read or work on them. In other words, you no longer start applications (Word, Excel, and so on), you select a document and the system knows which application to start. It will incorporate the best of Explorer with the best of Internet Explorer 3.0 to give you a single focus for everything you do. The MS Office binder, Internet Explorer 3.0, and soon Internet Explorer 4.0 are all ActiveX document containers. Storage is in OLE *streams* and *storages* (files and folders) internal to the document container.

When you are working on the desktop, the left panel shows your directory structure or a stream and storage structure. When you're on the Web, a properly designed site shows its structure in the file and folder view of Explorer. Internet Explorer 4.0 will also be highly customizable. You will be able to set virtually everything to look as you want it to look.

In a way, document objects are the future of computing. The notion is that the system will know what application you need to work on a particular document. You will not be required to know that a file with an .XLS extension requires Excel, whereas a document with a .DOC extension requires Word. The system will know, and will run the appropriate application to work on the document that you have selected.

Summary

A sea of change is occurring right now in the world of computing. Your world was your desktop with occasional excursions to the local network. The future is the world with your computer connected anywhere you want to go. Things will smooth out in a few years, but the learning curve is going to continue exponentially for a considerable time. Of one thing, you can be sure: change will come!

Chapter 9

Building Controls with Visual C++

The Internet is young. The world of high-powered, low-cost computers is young. Desktop computers are available today that outstrip supercomputers of a few years ago. Powerful operating systems are young. The problem is that everything about these machines and the technology surrounding them increases on a near exponential curve. The upside is that much of the hardware has been componentized: a new mother board, new disk drive, new com ports, and other items are installed as ready-made components. The downside is that software is not yet at that point. ActiveX Controls, COM, and DCOM have the potential to correct this downside.

Some formidable problems remain to be overcome before we simply plug new functionality into existing applications, but the groundwork has been laid. You are, I believe, looking at the future of software development and the future of computing in general. Your computer will become a window to the entire world. Knowledge will be as close as a few keystrokes or mouse clicks away. The potential for education is staggering. Certainly, the Internet's impact on the future of commerce is profound, but even more significant is the interconnectivity of both private individuals and businesses in ways that will make collaboration far easier than in the past.

The real promise of the Internet is in sharing knowledge with each other and with our children in a far more meaningful way. The promise is new systems of education, research, and entertainment that have never been possible in the history of humankind. So, learn all you can about this technology—it will be more valuable to you than you can possibly imagine.

It would be nice to give you a complete education on building ActiveX Controls (components) but neither space nor time to do so are available with this book. Here, however, is some information to point you in the right direction.

Building Controls

Although Visual C++ Version 4.2 and MFC is the ideal environment for the development of custom controls, Microsoft makes the ActiveX Template Library (ATL) and other tools available to allow the use of existing compilers.

The ActiveX Template Library (ATL)

ATL is a set of template-based C++ classes that allow you to easily create small, fast Component Object Model (COM) objects. Special support for key COM features such as aggregation, dual interfaces, connection points, enumerations, and tear-off interfaces is provided.

Microsoft has been using COM as the basis for binary component reuse for some time. COM solves many of the problems in the component world, including language independence, versioning, licensing, and others. COM now spans machines, contains optimizations for slow-link operation, integrates well with a variety of languages including Java, C++, Basic, Pascal, and COBOL, and is based on DCE standards.

A Template Library

C++ compilers have support for a language feature called *templates*. A template is like a macro in that a template expands to code you have written, with appropriate parameter substitution. Templates go further and allow the creation of new classes based on types that you pass as parameters.

Template libraries differ from traditional C++ class libraries in that they are supplied only as source code. Rather than derive from a class to get the functionality you desire, you instantiate a class from a template. ATL is a small template library designed to help you create small, fast, extensible COM objects.

What's in ATL

ATL is designed for the creation of small, fast COM servers and provides generic custom interfaces and explicit support for dual interfaces. Dual interfaces allow interfaces both through `IDispatch` and through the use of `vtable` entries. Standard COM enumerator interfaces of the form `IEnumXXX` connection points, and tear-off interfaces are also supported. A tear-off interface is an optimization of a regular COM interface in that it doesn't actually exist until it is instantiated by a call to `QueryInterface` on your object for that interface. When the reference count on that interface returns to zero, it is removed from memory.

ATL supplies a custom AppWizard, which can be used with Visual C++ 4.1 and later. The wizard is targeted at creating dual interfaces in particular, although it can be used to create any arbitrary COM interface. ATL code can be used to create single-threaded objects, apartment model objects, and free-threaded model COM servers. ATL can also create aggregated objects.

ATL provides stock implementations of `IUnknown`, `IClassFactory`, and `IDispatch`, as well as an `IEnumXXX` template that, when instantiated for a particular type, implements the enumerator for that type. Likewise, the connection point code implements `IConnectionPointContainer` and `IConnectionPoint`, and supports multicasting.

The Scope of ATL

ATL is not intended to be an all-purpose creation mechanism for OLE or ActiveX servers. The wizard support in this release is limited to the custom AppWizard that generates the shell of an ATL object in Visual C++. ATL is shipped as source code. You don't get runtime support from DLLs or new libraries. This also allows you to select the compiler and linker options that make most sense to you for your application.

Foundations of ATL

ATL uses COM, the fundamental "object model" on which ActiveX and OLE are built. COM defines how objects expose themselves and how this exposition works across processes and across networks. COM also defines the life cycle of an object. Fundamental to COM itself, then, are the following concepts:

Interfaces: The mechanism through which an object exposes its functionality. Each interface is given a unique ID (using the DCE uuid mechanism) called an interface ID (IID). Because these IIDs are unique, supporting interface versioning is extremely easy: a new version of an interface is simply a new interface, with a new IID.

IUnknown interface: The basic interface for a COM object. IUnknown has three methods that every other interface also implements; `QueryInterface`, `AddRef`, and `Release`. `QueryInterface` allows an interface user to ask the object for a pointer to another of its interfaces. `AddRef` and `Release` implement reference counting on the interface.

Reference counting: The technique by which an interface decides to remove itself. COM does not provide automatic garbage collection. That is, it does not attempt to remove an object from memory when it thinks it is no longer required. COM gives the object programmer the task of removing unused objects through the IUnknown methods `AddRef` and `Release`.

`QueryInterface` **method:** Used to interrogate an object for a given interface. Although mechanisms exist by which an object can express the functionality that it provides statically, the fundamental COM mechanism is to use the IUnknown method called `QueryInterface`. Every interface is derived from IUnknown, so every interface has an implementation of `QueryInterface`. `QueryInterface` is called with the IID of the interface to which the caller wants a pointer. If the object supports that interface, it returns a pointer to it; otherwise, it returns the `E_NOINTERFACE` error code.

Marshaling: The mechanism that enables objects to be used across process and network boundaries, allowing for location independence. To use interfaces exposed by an object in one process in another process, COM needs to marshal that interface. This means that COM provides code to pack the parameters of a method call into a format that can be moved across processes, and to unpack those parameters at the other end. Likewise, on the return from the call, COM must pack the outbound parameters and the return value at one end and unpack them at the other.

Aggregation: The way in which one object can make use of another object's interfaces. Many cases occur in which an implementor of one object would like to be able to take advantage of the services offered by another, prebuilt object in such a way that the second object appears as a natural part of the first. This is achieved in COM by containment, usually through aggregation. Aggregation means that the containing (outer) object creates the contained (inner) object as part of its creation process, typically, and the interfaces of the inner object are exposed by the outer.

These, then, are the fundamental concepts behind all COM objects including ActiveX Controls. You should find the ATL available for download at Microsoft's Web site.

Building ActiveX Controls with Visual C++ 4.2

There are purists who would insist that building software using Microsoft's Developer Studio (a.k.a. Microsoft C++ Version 4.*x*) is the lazy way, but doing so will save you literally hours of error-prone data entry in a text editor. Figure 9-1 shows Developer Studio's New dialog box. For ActiveX controls, select Project Workspace.

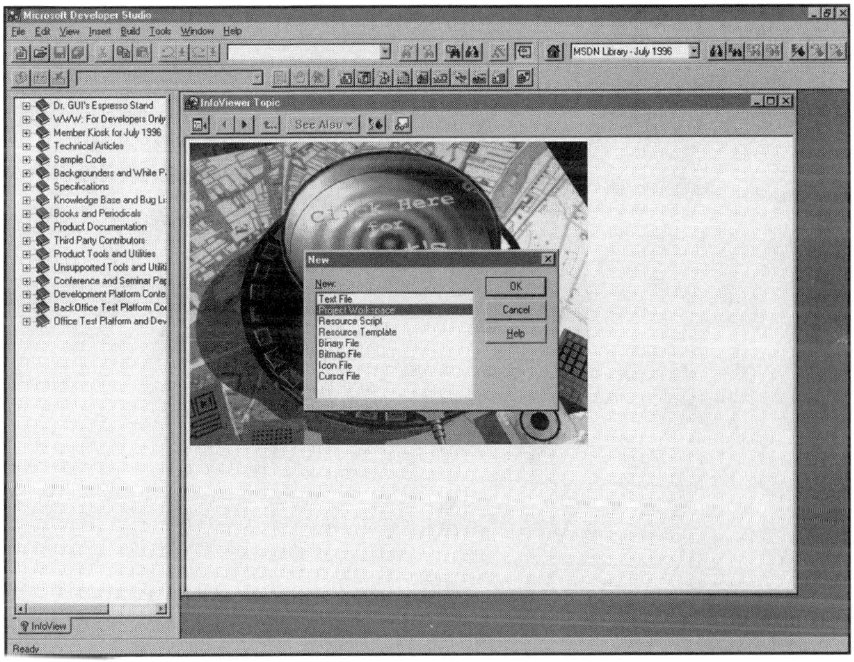

Figure 9-1
The Developer Studio New dialog box

Select OLE ControlWizard, as shown in Figure 9-2. A name, in this case MyControl, needs to be entered. You can also select a location for the project. Click Create... to start building your new control.

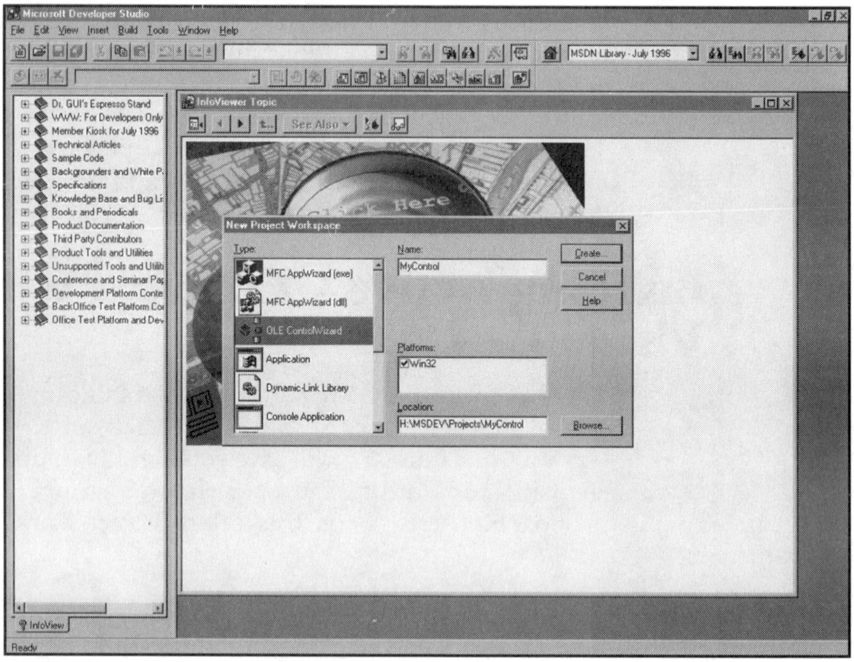

Figure 9-2
The OLE control selection

In step 1 of 2, you are asked to make several selections. As shown in the dialog box shown in Figure 9-3, I've selected a single control (this could be more than one); and I've elected to have a runtime license, comments, and help files.

The OLE ControlWizard, step 2 of 2 is shown in Figure 9-4. At this step, you can edit the name that you selected. You can also activate or deactivate a number of features and decide which subclass, if any, you want your control to use.

The Edit Names button brings up the dialog box shown in Figure 9-5. Here you can edit the names of virtually everything being generated by this wizard.

The Advanced button brings up the Advanced ActiveX Features dialog box, shown in Figure 9-6. Here you decide which ActiveX features you would like your control to use.

Clicking Finish generates a complete application. The classes generated are shown in Figure 9-7. It should be obvious that entering all this code by hand would be a long job and probably full of errors. The tabs at the bottom of the left panel allow you to activate various parts of the project.

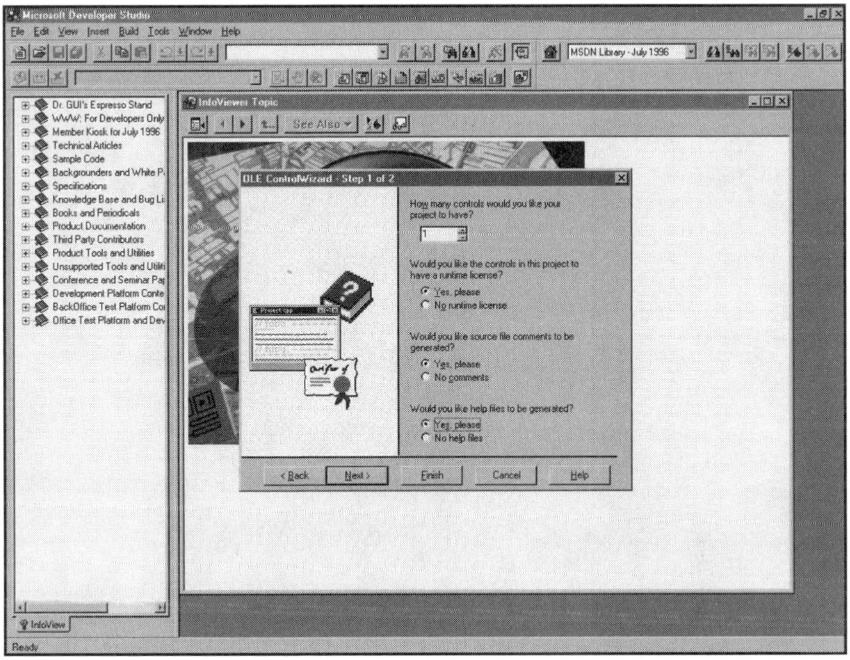

Figure 9-3 The OLE ControlWizard, step 1 of 2

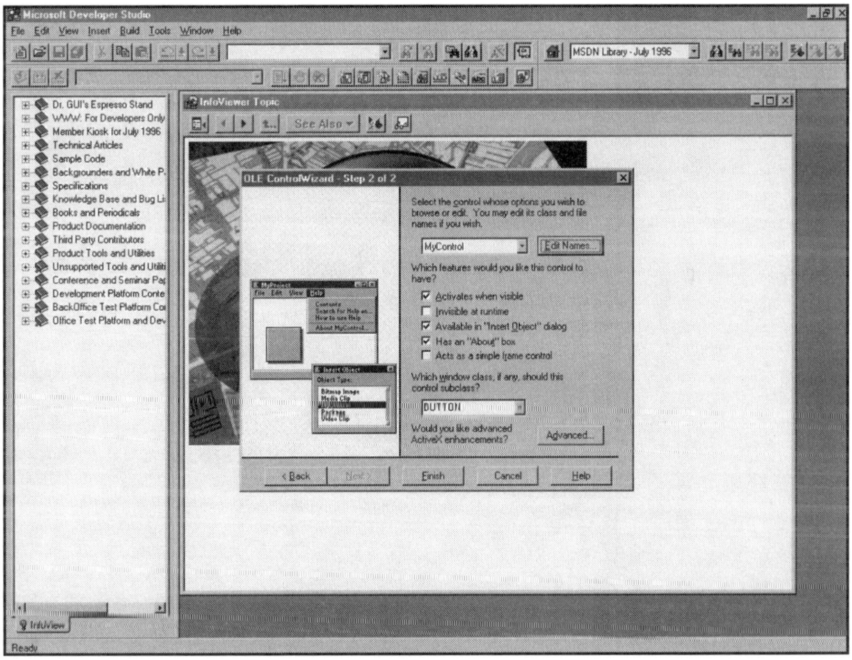

Figure 9-4 The OLE ControlWizard, step 2 of 2

Figure 9-5
The OLE ControlWizard Edit Names dialog box

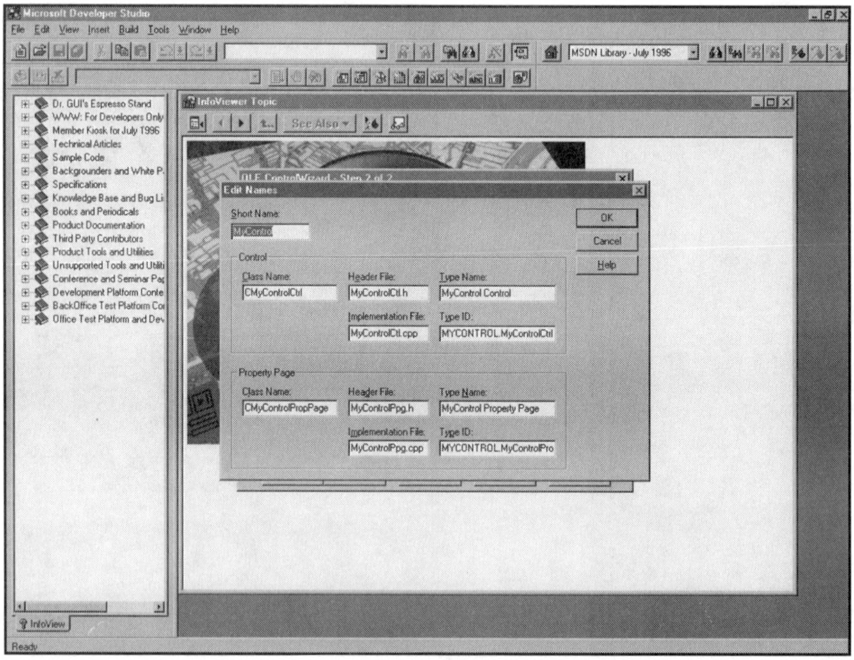

Figure 9-6
The Advanced ActiveX Features dialog box

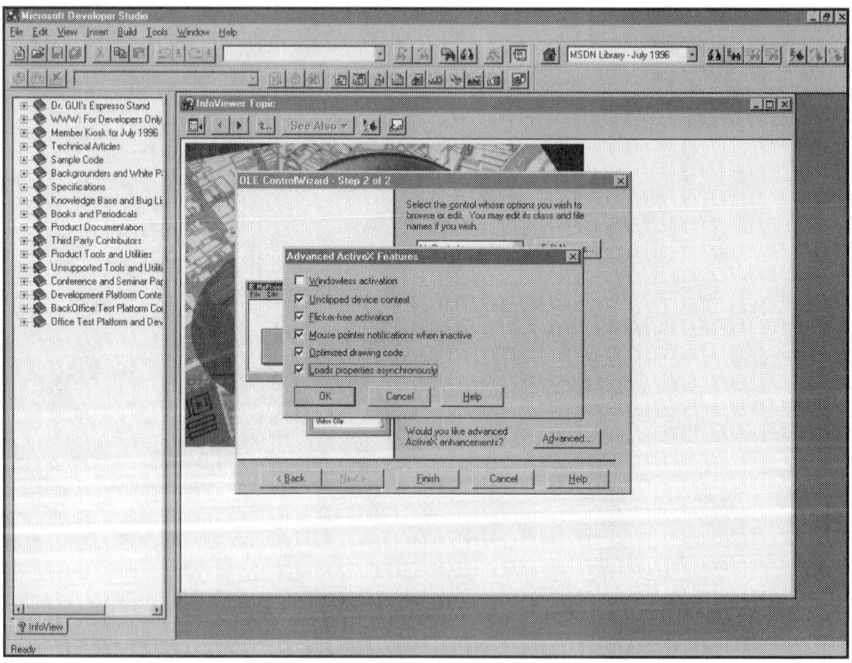

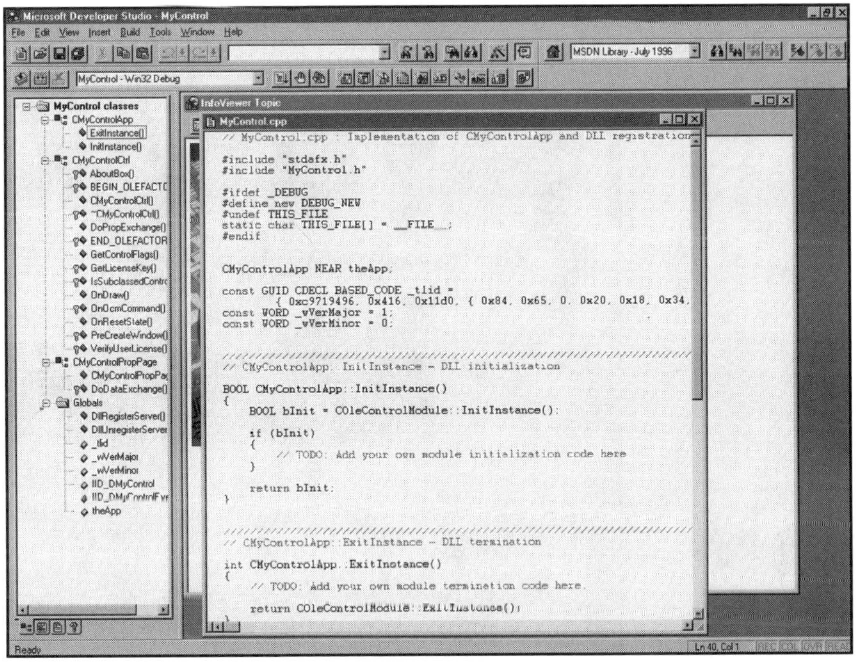

Figure 9-7
The MyControl classes

As shown in Figure 9-8, you need only double-click a resource to edit it in place. In this case, a bitmap resource is displayed with editing tools on the right. All resources can be edited in this fashion.

In a similar fashion, dialog boxes can be edited as shown in Figure 9-9. Again, an editing window and toolbox are available.

What once took days of hand coding can now be done in seconds with the tools available in Microsoft Visual C++. The result is that you can work smarter in developing the functionality you need.

The code generated consists of the following:

- MyControl.cpp
- MyControl.def
- MyControl.lic
- MyControl.odl
- MyControl.rc

Figure 9-8
MyControl resources—
editing a bitmap

Figure 9-9
MyControl resources—
editing a dialog box

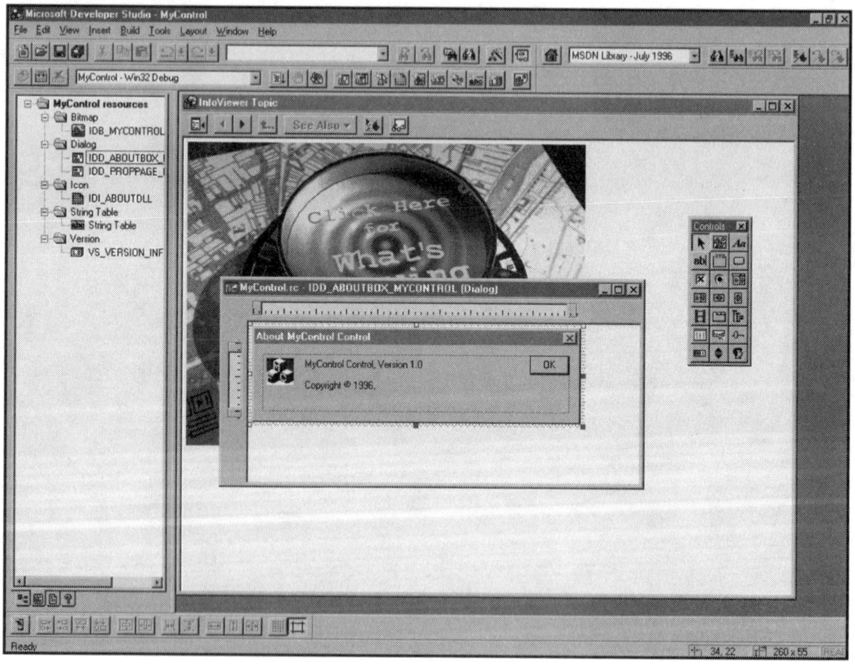

- MyControlCtl.cpp
- MyControlPpg.cpp

and all of the required resource files for the new control. The include files and main code modules are shown here. Notice that you can add your own implementations in many places where the `// TODO` comments are shown.

```
// MyControl.h : main header file for MYCONTROL.DLL

#if !defined( __AFXCTL_H__ )
  #error include 'afxctl.h' before including this file
#endif

#include "resource.h"       // main symbols

/////////////////////////////////////////////////////////////////////
➥////////////
// CMyControlApp : See MyControl.cpp for implementation.

class CMyControlApp : public COleControlModule
{
public:
  BOOL InitInstance();
  int ExitInstance();
};

extern const GUID CDECL _tlid;
extern const WORD _wVerMajor;
extern const WORD _wVerMinor;

// MyControlCtl.h : Declaration of the CMyControlCtrl OLE control
➥class.

/////////////////////////////////////////////////////////////////////
➥////////////
// CMyControlCtrl : See MyControlCtl.cpp for implementation.
```

```
class CMyControlCtrl : public COleControl
{
  DECLARE_DYNCREATE(CMyControlCtrl)

// Constructor
public:
  CMyControlCtrl();

// Overrides
// ClassWizard generated virtual function overrides
//{{AFX_VIRTUAL(CMyControlCtrl)
  public:
  virtual void OnDraw(CDC* pdc, const CRect& rcBounds, const
➥CRect& rcInvalid);
  virtual void DoPropExchange(CPropExchange* pPX);
  virtual void OnResetState();
  virtual DWORD GetControlFlags();
//}}AFX_VIRTUAL

// Implementation
protected:
  ~CMyControlCtrl();

  BEGIN_OLEFACTORY(CMyControlCtrl)        // Class factory and
➥guid
    virtual BOOL VerifyUserLicense();
    virtual BOOL GetLicenseKey(DWORD, BSTR FAR*);
  END_OLEFACTORY(CMyControlCtrl)

DECLARE_OLETYPELIB(CMyControlCtrl)       // GetTypeInfo
DECLARE_PROPPAGEIDS(CMyControlCtrl)      // Property page IDs
DECLARE_OLECTLTYPE(CMyControlCtrl)
// Type name and misc status

// Subclassed control support
  BOOL PreCreateWindow(CREATESTRUCT& cs);
  BOOL IsSubclassedControl();
  LRESULT OnOcmCommand(WPARAM wParam, LPARAM lParam);
```

```
// Message maps
//{{AFX_MSG(CMyControlCtrl)
// NOTE - ClassWizard will add and remove member functions here.
//    DO NOT EDIT what you see in these blocks of generated
➥code !
//}}AFX_MSG
DECLARE_MESSAGE_MAP()

// Dispatch maps
//{{AFX_DISPATCH(CMyControlCtrl)
// NOTE - ClassWizard will add and remove member functions here.
//    DO NOT EDIT what you see in these blocks of generated
➥code !
//}}AFX_DISPATCH
DECLARE_DISPATCH_MAP()

afx_msg void AboutBox();

// Event maps
//{{AFX_EVENT(CMyControlCtrl)
// NOTE - ClassWizard will add and remove member functions here.
//    DO NOT EDIT what you see in these blocks of generated
➥code !
//}}AFX_EVENT
DECLARE_EVENT_MAP()

// Dispatch and event IDs
public:
  enum {
//{{AFX_DISP_ID(CMyControlCtrl)
// NOTE: ClassWizard will add and remove enumeration elements
➥here.
//    DO NOT EDIT what you see in these blocks of generated
➥code !
//}}AFX_DISP_ID
  };
};
```

```
// MyControlPpg.h : Declaration of the CMyControlPropPage
➥property page class.

/////////////////////////////////////////////////////////////////
➥//////////
// CMyControlPropPage : See MyControlPpg.cpp.cpp for
➥implementation.

class CMyControlPropPage : public COlePropertyPage
{
  DECLARE_DYNCREATE(CMyControlPropPage)
  DECLARE_OLECREATE_EX(CMyControlPropPage)

// Constructor
public:
  CMyControlPropPage();

// Dialog Data
//{{AFX_DATA(CMyControlPropPage)
  enum { IDD = IDD_PROPPAGE_MYCONTROL };
// NOTE - ClassWizard will add data members here.
//    DO NOT EDIT what you see in these blocks of generated
➥code !
//}}AFX_DATA

// Implementation
protected:
  virtual void DoDataExchange(CDataExchange* pDX);    // DDX/DDV
➥support

// Message maps
protected:
//{{AFX_MSG(CMyControlPropPage)
// NOTE - ClassWizard will add and remove member functions here.
//    DO NOT EDIT what you see in these blocks of generated
➥code !
//}}AFX_MSG
  DECLARE_MESSAGE_MAP()
```

```
};

// MyControl.cpp : Implementation of CMyControlApp and DLL
➥registration.

#include "stdafx.h"
#include "MyControl.h"

#ifdef _DEBUG
#define new DEBUG_NEW
#undef THIS_FILE
static char THIS_FILE[] =_FILE__;
#endif

CMyControlApp NEAR theApp;

const GUID CDECL BASED_CODE _tlid =
{ 0xc9719496, 0x416, 0x11d0, { 0x84, 0x65, 0, 0x20, 0x18, 0x34,
➥0x9e, 0x95 } };
const WORD _wVerMajor = 1;
const WORD _wVerMinor = 0;

//////////////////////////////////////////////////////////////////
➥//////////
// CMyControlApp::InitInstance - DLL initialization

BOOL CMyControlApp::InitInstance()
{
  BOOL bInit = COleControlModule::InitInstance();
  if (bInit)
  {
  // TODO: Add your own module initialization code here.
  }
  return bInit;
}

//////////////////////////////////////////////////////////////////
➥//////////
```

```
// CMyControlApp::ExitInstance - DLL termination

int CMyControlApp::ExitInstance()
{
  // TODO: Add your own module termination code here.
  return COleControlModule::ExitInstance();
}

////////////////////////////////////////////////////////////////////
➥//////////
// DllRegisterServer - Adds entries to the system registry

STDAPI DllRegisterServer(void)
{
  AFX_MANAGE_STATE(_afxModuleAddrThis);

  if (!AfxOleRegisterTypeLib(AfxGetInstanceHandle(), _tlid))
  return ResultFromScode(SELFREG_E_TYPELIB);

  if (!COleObjectFactoryEx::UpdateRegistryAll(TRUE))
  return ResultFromScode(SELFREG_E_CLASS);

  return NOERROR;
}

////////////////////////////////////////////////////////////////////
➥//////////
// DllUnregisterServer - Removes entries from the system registry

STDAPI DllUnregisterServer(void)
{
  AFX_MANAGE_STATE(_afxModuleAddrThis);

  if (!AfxOleUnregisterTypeLib(_tlid, _wVerMajor, _wVerMinor))
  return ResultFromScode(SELFREG_E_TYPELIB);

  if (!COleObjectFactoryEx::UpdateRegistryAll(FALSE))
  ResultFromScode(SELFREG_E_CLASS);
```

```
  return NOERROR;
}

; MyControl.def : Declares the module parameters.

LIBRARY      "MYCONTROL.OCX"

EXPORTS
  DllCanUnloadNow     @1 PRIVATE
  DllGetClassObject   @2 PRIVATE
  DllRegisterServer   @3 PRIVATE
  DllUnregisterServer @4 PRIVATE

// MyControlCtl.cpp : Implementation of the CMyControlCtrl OLE
➥control class.

#include "stdafx.h"
#include "MyControl.h"
#include "MyControlCtl.h"
#include "MyControlPpg.h"

#ifdef _DEBUG
#define new DEBUG_NEW
#undef THIS_FILE
static char THIS_FILE[] = __FILE__;
#endif

IMPLEMENT_DYNCREATE(CMyControlCtrl, COleControl)

/////////////////////////////////////////////////////////////////////
➥////////////
// Message map

BEGIN_MESSAGE_MAP(CMyControlCtrl, COleControl)
  //{{AFX_MSG_MAP(CMyControlCtrl)
  // NOTE - ClassWizard will add and remove message map entries
  //    DO NOT EDIT what you see in these blocks of generated
➥code !
  //}}AFX_MSG_MAP
```

```
  ON_MESSAGE(OCM_COMMAND, OnOcmCommand)
  ON_OLEVERB(AFX_IDS_VERB_EDIT, OnEdit)
  ON_OLEVERB(AFX_IDS_VERB_PROPERTIES, OnProperties)
END_MESSAGE_MAP()

//////////////////////////////////////////////////////////////////////
➥//////////
// Dispatch map

BEGIN_DISPATCH_MAP(CMyControlCtrl, COleControl)
  //{{AFX_DISPATCH_MAP(CMyControlCtrl)
  // NOTE - ClassWizard will add and remove dispatch map entries
  //    DO NOT EDIT what you see in these blocks of generated
➥code !
  DISP_STOCKPROP_READYSTATE()
  //}}AFX_DISPATCH_MAP
  DISP_FUNCTION_ID(CMyControlCtrl, "AboutBox", DISPID_ABOUTBOX,
➥AboutBox, VT_EMPTY, VTS_NONE)
END_DISPATCH_MAP()

//////////////////////////////////////////////////////////////////////
➥//////////
// Event map

BEGIN_EVENT_MAP(CMyControlCtrl, COleControl)
  //{{AFX_EVENT_MAP(CMyControlCtrl)
  // NOTE - ClassWizard will add and remove event map entries
  //    DO NOT EDIT what you see in these blocks of generated
➥code !
  EVENT_STOCK_READYSTATECHANGE()
  //}}AFX_EVENT_MAP
END_EVENT_MAP()

//////////////////////////////////////////////////////////////////////
➥//////////
// Property pages

// TODO: Add more property pages as needed.  Remember to
➥increase the count!
```

```
BEGIN_PROPPAGEIDS(CMyControlCtrl, 1)
  PROPPAGEID(CMyControlPropPage::guid)
END_PROPPAGEIDS(CMyControlCtrl)

/////////////////////////////////////////////////////////////////////
➥////////////
// Initialize class factory and guid

IMPLEMENT_OLECREATE_EX(CMyControlCtrl,
"MYCONTROL.MyControlCtrl.1",
  0xc9719499, 0x416, 0x11d0, 0x84, 0x65, 0, 0x20, 0x18, 0x34,
➥0x9e, 0x95)

/////////////////////////////////////////////////////////////////////
➥////////////
// Type library ID and version

IMPLEMENT_OLETYPELIB(CMyControlCtrl, _tlid, _wVerMajor,
➥_wVerMinor)

/////////////////////////////////////////////////////////////////////
➥////////////
// Interface IDs

const IID BASED_CODE IID_DMyControl =
  { 0xc9719497, 0x416, 0x11d0, { 0x84, 0x65, 0, 0x20, 0x18,
➥0x34, 0x9e, 0x95 } };
  const IID BASED_CODE IID_DMyControlEvents =
  { 0xc9719498, 0x416, 0x11d0, { 0x84, 0x65, 0, 0x20, 0x18,
➥0x34, 0x9e, 0x95 } };

/////////////////////////////////////////////////////////////////////
➥////////////
// Control type information

static const DWORD BASED_CODE _dwMyControlOleMisc =
  OLEMISC_ACTIVATEWHENVISIBLE |
  OLEMISC_IGNOREACTIVATEWHENVISIBLE |
  OLEMISC_SETCLIENTSITEFIRST |
```

```
  OLEMISC_INSIDEOUT |
  OLEMISC_CANTLINKINSIDE |
  OLEMISC_RECOMPOSEONRESIZE;

IMPLEMENT_OLECTLTYPE(CMyControlCtrl, IDS_MYCONTROL,
_dwMyControlOleMisc)

////////////////////////////////////////////////////////////////
➥//////////
// CMyControlCtrl::CMyControlCtrlFactory::UpdateRegistry -
// Adds or removes system registry entries for CMyControlCtrl

BOOL CMyControlCtrl::CMyControlCtrlFactory::UpdateRegistry(BOOL
➥bRegister)
{
  // TODO: Verify that your control follows apartment-model
➥threading rules.
  // Refer to MFC TechNote 64 for more information.
  // If your control does not conform to the apartment-model
➥rules, then
  // you must modify the code below, changing the 6th parameter
➥from
  // afxRegInsertable | afxRegApartmentThreading to
➥afxRegInsertable.
  if (bRegister)
    return AfxOleRegisterControlClass(
    AfxGetInstanceHandle(),
    m_clsid,
    m_lpszProgID,
    IDS_MYCONTROL,
    IDB_MYCONTROL,
    afxRegInsertable | afxRegApartmentThreading,
    dwMyControlOleMisc,
    tlid,
    wVerMajor,
    wVerMinor);
  else
    return AfxOleUnregisterClass(m_clsid, m_lpszProgID);
}
```

```
/////////////////////////////////////////////////////////////////
➥////////////
// Licensing strings

static const TCHAR BASED_CODE _szLicFileName[] =
_T("MyControl.lic");

static const WCHAR BASED_CODE _szLicString[] =
  L"Copyright (c) 1996 ";

/////////////////////////////////////////////////////////////////
➥////////////
// CMyControlCtrl::CMyControlCtrlFactory::VerifyUserLicense -
// Checks for existence of a user license

BOOL CMyControlCtrl::CMyControlCtrlFactory::VerifyUserLicense()
{
  return AfxVerifyLicFile(AfxGetInstanceHandle(),
_szLicFileName,_szLicString);
}

/////////////////////////////////////////////////////////////////
➥////////////
// CMyControlCtrl::CMyControlCtrlFactory::GetLicenseKey -
// Returns a runtime licensing key

BOOL CMyControlCtrl::CMyControlCtrlFactory::GetLicenseKey(DWORD
➥dwReserved, BSTR FAR* pbstrKey)
{
  if (pbstrKey == NULL)
    return FALSE;
  *pbstrKey = SysAllocString(_szLicString);
  return (*pbstrKey != NULL);
}

/////////////////////////////////////////////////////////////////
➥////////////
// CMyControlCtrl::CMyControlCtrl - Constructor
```

```
CMyControlCtrl::CMyControlCtrl()
{
  InitializeIIDs(&IID_DMyControl, &IID_DMyControlEvents);
  m_lReadyState = READYSTATE_LOADING;
  // TODO: Call InternalSetReadyState when the readystate
➥changes.
  // TODO: Initialize your control's instance data here.
}

///////////////////////////////////////////////////////////////////
➥//////////
// CMyControlCtrl::~CMyControlCtrl - Destructor

CMyControlCtrl::~CMyControlCtrl()
{
  // TODO: Cleanup your control's instance data here.
}

///////////////////////////////////////////////////////////////////
➥//////////
// CMyControlCtrl::OnDraw - Drawing function

void CMyControlCtrl::OnDraw(CDC* pdc, const CRect& rcBounds,
➥const CRect& rcInvalid)
{
  DoSuperclassPaint(pdc, rcBounds);
  if (!IsOptimizedDraw())
  {
    // The container does not support optimized drawing.
    // TODO: if you selected any GDI objects into the device
➥context *pdc,
    // restore the previously-selected objects here.
    // For more information, please see MFC technical note #nnn,
    // "Optimizing an ActiveX Control".
  }
}

///////////////////////////////////////////////////////////////////
➥//////////
```

```
// CMyControlCtrl::DoPropExchange - Persistence support

void CMyControlCtrl::DoPropExchange(CPropExchange* pPX)
{
  ExchangeVersion(pPX, MAKELONG(_wVerMinor, _wVerMajor));
  COleControl::DoPropExchange(pPX);
  // TODO: Call PX_ functions for each persistent custom
➥property.
}

/////////////////////////////////////////////////////////////////////
➥////////////
// CMyControlCtrl::GetControlFlags -
// Flags to customize MFC's implementation of ActiveX controls.
//
// For information on using these flags, please see MFC
➥technical note
// #nnn, "Optimizing an ActiveX Control".
DWORD CMyControlCtrl::GetControlFlags()
{
  DWORD dwFlags = COleControl::GetControlFlags();
  // The control's output is not being clipped.
  // The control guarantees that it will not paint outside its
  // client rectangle.
  dwFlags &= ~clipPaintDC;
  // The control will not be redrawn when making the transition
  // between the active and inactivate state.
  dwFlags |= noFlickerActivate;
  // The control can receive mouse notifications when inactive.
  // TODO: if you write handlers for WM_SETCURSOR and
➥WM_MOUSEMOVE,
  // avoid using the m_hWnd member variable without first
  // checking that its value is non-NULL.
  dwFlags |= pointerInactive;
  // The control can optimize its OnDraw method, by not
➥restoring
  // the original GDI objects in the device context.
  dwFlags |= canOptimizeDraw;
```

```
  return dwFlags;
}

///////////////////////////////////////////////////////////////////
➥///////////
// CMyControlCtrl::OnResetState - Reset control to default state

void CMyControlCtrl::OnResetState()
{
  COleControl::OnResetState();  // Resets defaults found in
➥DoPropExchange
  // TODO: Reset any other control state here.
}

///////////////////////////////////////////////////////////////////
➥///////////
// CMyControlCtrl::AboutBox - Display an "About" box to the user

void CMyControlCtrl::AboutBox()
{
  CDialog dlgAbout(IDD_ABOUTBOX_MYCONTROL);
  dlgAbout.DoModal();
}

///////////////////////////////////////////////////////////////////
➥///////////
// CMyControlCtrl::PreCreateWindow - Modify parameters for
➥CreateWindowEx

BOOL CMyControlCtrl::PreCreateWindow(CREATESTRUCT& cs)
{
  cs.lpszClass = _T("BUTTON");
  return COleControl::PreCreateWindow(cs);
}

///////////////////////////////////////////////////////////////////
➥///////////
// CMyControlCtrl::IsSubclassedControl - This is a subclassed
➥control
```

```
BOOL CMyControlCtrl::IsSubclassedControl()
{
  return TRUE;
}

///////////////////////////////////////////////////////////////////
➥////////////
// CMyControlCtrl::OnOcmCommand - Handle command messages

LRESULT CMyControlCtrl::OnOcmCommand(WPARAM wParam, LPARAM
➥lParam)
{
#ifdef _WIN32
  WORD wNotifyCode = HIWORD(wParam);
#else
  WORD wNotifyCode = HIWORD(lParam);
#endif
  // TODO: Switch on wNotifyCode here.
  return 0;
}

///////////////////////////////////////////////////////////////////
➥////////////
// CMyControlCtrl message handlers

// MyControlPpg.cpp : Implementation of the CMyControlPropPage
➥property page class.

#include "stdafx.h"
#include "MyControl.h"
#include "MyControlPpg.h"

#ifdef _DEBUG
#define new DEBUG_NEW
#undef THIS_FILE
static char THIS_FILE[] = __FILE__;
#endif

IMPLEMENT_DYNCREATE(CMyControlPropPage, COlePropertyPage)
```

```
////////////////////////////////////////////////////////////////////
➥//////////
// Message map

BEGIN_MESSAGE_MAP(CMyControlPropPage, COlePropertyPage)
  //{{AFX_MSG_MAP(CMyControlPropPage)
  // NOTE - ClassWizard will add and remove message map entries
  //    DO NOT EDIT what you see in these blocks of generated
➥code !
  //}}AFX_MSG_MAP
END_MESSAGE_MAP()

////////////////////////////////////////////////////////////////////
➥//////////
// Initialize class factory and guid

IMPLEMENT_OLECREATE_EX(CMyControlPropPage,
➥"MYCONTROL.MyControlPropPage.1",
  0xc971949a, 0x416, 0x11d0, 0x84, 0x65, 0, 0x20, 0x18, 0x34,
➥0x9e, 0x95)


////////////////////////////////////////////////////////////////////
➥//////////
// CMyControlPropPage::CMyControlPropPageFactory::UpdateRegistry -
// Adds or removes system registry entries for CMyControlPropPage

BOOL
CMyControlPropPage::CMyControlPropPageFactory::UpdateRegistry(BOOL
➥bRegister)
{
  if (bRegister)
    return
AfxOleRegisterPropertyPageClass(AfxGetInstanceHandle(),
    m_clsid, IDS_MYCONTROL_PPG);
  else
    return AfxOleUnregisterClass(m_clsid, NULL);
}
```

```
////////////////////////////////////////////////////////////////
➥////////////
// CMyControlPropPage::CMyControlPropPage - Constructor

CMyControlPropPage::CMyControlPropPage() : COlePropertyPage(IDD,
➥IDS_MYCONTROL_PPG_CAPTION)
{
  //{{AFX_DATA_INIT(CMyControlPropPage)
  // NOTE: ClassWizard will add member initialization here
  //    DO NOT EDIT what you see in these blocks of generated
➥code !
  //}}AFX_DATA_INIT
}

////////////////////////////////////////////////////////////////
➥////////////
// CMyControlPropPage::DoDataExchange - Moves data between page
➥and properties

void CMyControlPropPage::DoDataExchange(CDataExchange* pDX)
{
  //{{AFX_DATA_MAP(CMyControlPropPage)
  // NOTE: ClassWizard will add DDP, DDX, and DDV calls here
  //    DO NOT EDIT what you see in these blocks of generated
➥code !
  //}}AFX_DATA_MAP
  DDP_PostProcessing(pDX);
}

////////////////////////////////////////////////////////////////
➥////////////
// CMyControlPropPage message handlers
```

From the Developer Studio Build menu, choose Build MyControl.ocx. The code will compile, generate MyControl.ocx, and register it in the system registry.

Now, start the ActiveX Control Pad and select Insert ActiveX Control from the Edit menu. Scroll down the list of controls until you locate the new MyControl Control. You will see the usual layout control with a button in place and a property page display. When you close the layout control, your new control will be inserted as shown in Figure 9-10. Save the .HTM file as PAGE1.HTM and double-click the saved file to start Internet Explorer.

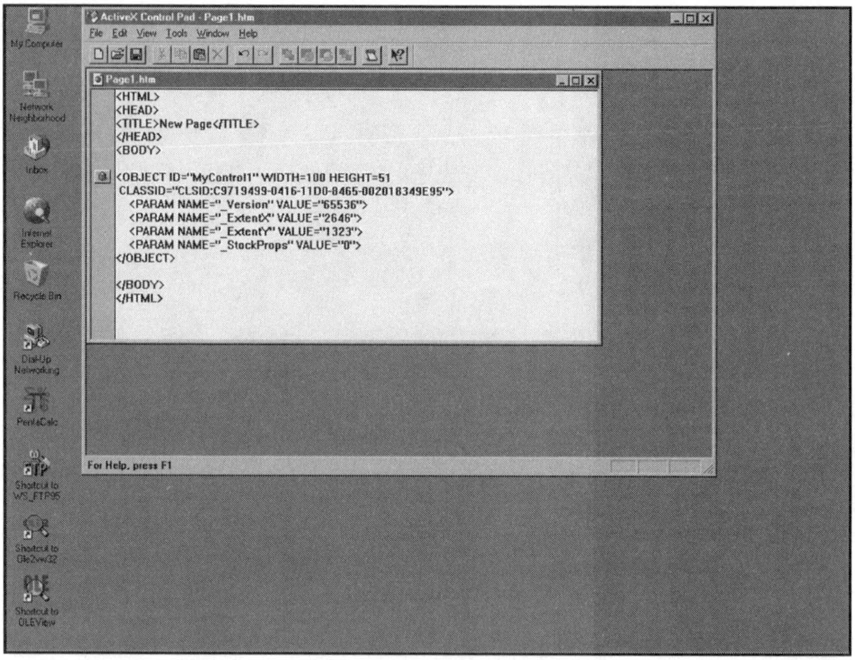

Figure 9-10 Your New Control Inserted in ActiveX Control Pad

Internet Explorer will present the Potential Safety Violation dialog box shown in Figure 9-11. Answer yes and you will see your new button control as shown in Figure 9-12.

Summary

I've tried to cram as much information as possible into a very small space. The subject of developing ActiveX Controls is a very large subject, but I hope that I've given you enough to begin moving forward in this very exciting business.

In this book, I've tried to pull together the essentials of a very disparate and, at times, difficult subject. ActiveX covers such a broad venue that it is probably impossible to enclose it in the covers of a single book. You can literally spend hours browsing through the offerings that Microsoft makes available on its Web site. If it does nothing else, this book may make it easier to follow the links to the information you want.

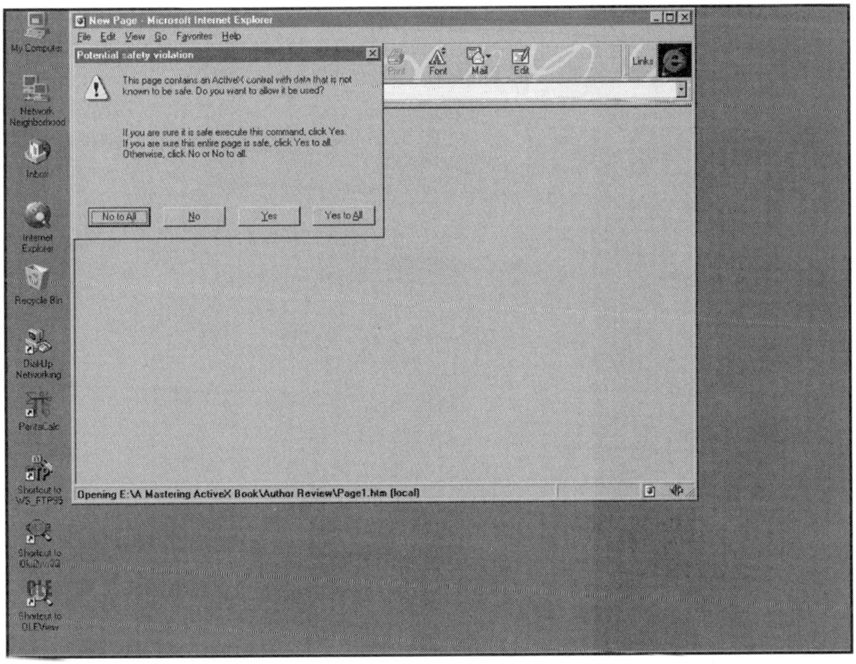

Figure 9-11
The Potential Hazard dialog box

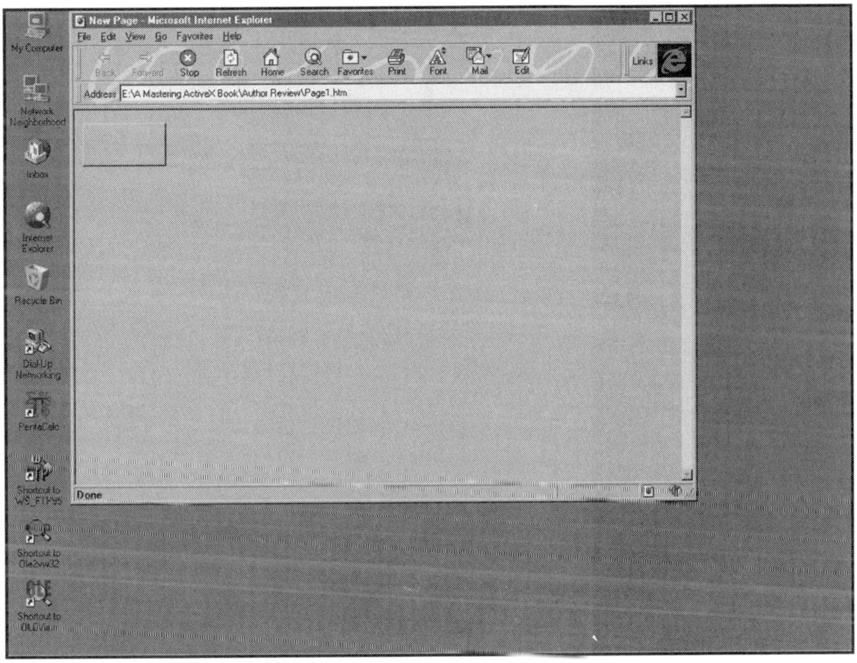

Figure 9-12
Your new control running in Internet Explorer

I hope that I've given you the information you need to create new and exciting Web sites. Between what I've provided and what you can find on the Internet, you should be well on your way to a good understanding of what ActiveX is all about.

Appendix A

Glossary

ActiveX - The rebranding of Microsoft's OLE technology to take advantage of the Internet.

ActiveX Control Pad - A tool developed by Microsoft to simplify using objects and scripting in HTML code.

ActiveX Controls - Formerly OLE Custom Controls, ActiveX Controls normally have an .OCX extension and are components following the COM model.

Applets - These are small executables that are normally associated with Java.

ARPANET - Advanced Research Project Agency network. The original beginnings of the Internet.

Authentication - A method of ensuring that code being downloaded from an Internet site is code coming from a reliable source.

Backbone - The main communications trunks of the Internet.

Bandwidth - Your modem probably has a bandwidth of 28.8 Kilobits per second (Kbps). This represents the amount of data that can be transmitted in a given time.

Browser - Internet Explorer 3.0 and Netscape Navigator are browsers or Web browsers.

Buttons - A clickable device on a form.

Certifications - Certifications are like Internet notarization and are provided by a trusted third party.

CGI - Common Gateway Interface. Used to allow passing information between various operating systems on the Internet.

Chatting - A system that allows two or more people to engage in a live written dialog.

Check boxes - Boxes that can be checked or unchecked on a form to indicate a choice.

Client - The user of a service or application.

Client program - A program that makes use of the services offered by a server.

Client/server - The relationship between clients who use provided services and servers that provide such services.

COM - Component Object Model. COM is Microsoft's initiative to allow the development of software components. Components show an interface to the outside world allowing the use of their functionality.

Cookies - Files downloaded to your computer to indicate conditions appropriate to a particular Web site such as personalization information for `www.msn.com`.

CryptoAPI - Microsoft's cryptography API allowing the development of crypto-enabled applications.

Cryptography - A means of encoding and decoding information.

DCOM - Distributed Component Object Model. An extension of the COM model that allows calls from client to server.

Digital signatures - Cryptographic systems to allow signatures to be applied to transmissions.

DLL - Dynamic Link Library. Libraries of function calls can be statically linked to programs at compile time; DLLs, on the other hand, are dynamically linked at runtime.

DNS - Domain Name Service. Allows names such as `internetchecks.com`, for example, to be translated to 204.134.94.74 (the actual IP address).

Document Objects - ActiveX Documents capable of being instantiated in Document containers.

Domain name - `mycompany.com` and similar names are called domain names.

Download - Moving a file from a server to a requesting client.

E-mail - Electronic mail.

Form - Among other things, a device in HTML for collecting information.

FrontPage - Microsoft's FrontPage Web design software.

FTP - File Transfer Protocol. The system used on the Internet to transfer files from one location to another.

GIF - Graphic Interchange Format. An image format owned by CompuServe.

Gopher - Another Internet service. Gopher is an Internet navigation tool that allows you to browse the Internet. It could be considered a forerunner of the Web.

Host - In Internet usage, the computer used to store Web pages.

HTML - HyperText Markup Language. The language used to build Web pages.

HTTP - Hypertext Transfer Protocol. The protocol used on the Internet to transfer HTML from server to client.

IETF - Internet Engineering Task Force. One of the groups of Internet users who maintain various standards.

IIS - Microsoft's Internet Information Server.

ISAPI - Internet Server API.

Internet Studio - A high-end Web development tool being developed by Microsoft.

Intranet - As differentiated from the Internet, a local network using TCP/IP.

IP - Internet Protocol

IP number - A number of the form nnn.nnn.nnn.nnn. This number, like your telephone number, is the real address of any host on the Internet.

IRC - Internet Relay Chat.

ISDN - Integrated Services Digital Network.

Java - A programming language for the Internet developed by Sun Microsystems.

Java applets - Programs written in Java and compiled to byte code for uses similar to ActiveX Controls.

JScript - Microsoft's implementation of a Java scripting language.

LAN - Local Area Network.

Modem - MOdulator + DEModulator. A modem converts binary information to analog information. The analog information is sent over voice telephone lines to another modem, which converts the signal back to binary.

Mosaic - An early Web browser. Mosaic is the underlying technology in most modern browsers.

NNTP - Network News Transfer Protocol.

PKCS - Public Key Cryptography Standard.

POP - Point of Presence. A local access point to the Internet backbone.

POP - Post Office Protocol. Most mail servers are called POP Servers on your Internet Service Providers sites.

PPP - Point-to-Point Protocol. The protocol that you should be using for connection to your Internet Service Provider.

Radio buttons - Part of a form allowing a one-from-many selection.

SET - Secure Electronic Transaction. One of several specifications for secure money transactions on the Internet.

SLIP - Serial Line Interface Protocol. Another protocol used by Internet Service Providers. A better choice is PPP.

SMTP - Simple Mail Transfer Protocol.

SSL - Secure Sockets Layer. A Netscape system for providing secure transmissions on the Internet. Most modern browsers are designed to use SSL.

TCP/IP - Transfer Control Protocol/Internet Protocol.

URL - Uniform Resource Locator. Your name in a telephone directory is a URL, in a sense. It provides the information that a person needs to find your telephone number and connect.

UUCP - UNIX-to-UNIX copy.

UUNET - One of the major network providers.

Veronica - Very Easy Rodent Oriented Net-wide Index to Computerized Archives.

W3C - World Wide Web Consortium. This is the Web. The World Wide Web Consortium is the standards body for Web-related matters.

WAIS - Wide Area Information Servers.

WAN - Wide Area Network.

Appendix B

HTML 3.2 Plus Reference

In the early days of printing, Linotype operators sat at rustic keyboards and typed lines of text. As they typed, brass slugs dropped from a font (fountain) into a tray. After the line was complete, it was sent to a device that cast the line on a lead slug. Lead shims were placed between lines for proper spacing (thus the term *leading* to describe line spacing) and the entire column was assembled in a case. Printers required a separate font for each type size and type face.

Markup languages were designed to allow editors to convey to the typesetters the manner in which text was to be set. Things have progressed significantly since those days, but we still use markup languages. HTML is based on what is known as Standard Graphics Markup Language, or SGML. You probably will never need this information unless you become involved in developing new HTML tags.

HyperText Markup Language, or HTML, is what the World Wide Web uses to tell browsers how to display the information at a particular Web site. With all of this business being less than six years old, HTML has seen some significant changes—some proprietary, some standard. Basic HTML is quite easy to learn. Putting it all together and using the newer tags can become more difficult. Luckily, a number of HTML editors are available that allow you to do markup in a WYSIWYG fashion. You will still probably find yourself using a text editor to fine-tune your HTML.

First, all tags (see Table B-1) take the general form "<aaa>some text and/or other elements</aaa>," where aaa is the tag, usually the browser will understand it in either upper- or lowercase. You will find tags that do not require the closing "</aaa>" but some editors will automatically insert them anyway.

Table B-1
An HTML 3.2 tag list with descriptions

Tag	Description
<!—...—>	Used to enclose comments or other text, such as scripts, that should not be displayed by the browser.
<!DOCTYPE>	Defines the document type represented by the HTML. Not a required part of a page.
<A>	An anchor point in your document. You can use HREF=attribute to create a hyperlink or NAME=attribute to create a named reference.
<ADDRESS>	Displays enclosed text as a mailing address.
<APPLET>	Defines a Java applet. Scripting in IE 3.0 uses OBJECT.
<AREA>	Defines an area in a graphic as a "hot spot" for client-side image maps.
<B>	Bolds enclosed text, as does <STRONG>.
<BASE>	Names a URL as a document source.
<BASEFONT>	Establishes a base font for a document.
<BGSOUND>	Plays specified background sounds on document load.
<BIG>	Makes a font larger by one HTML size.
<BLOCKQUOTE>	Presents enclosed text to appear as a block quote.
<BODY>	This tag and its end-tag enclose the displayed text in a page.
 	Inserts a line break in a document.

Tag	Description
<CAPTION>	Used in the TABLE element; displays a caption for the table.
<CENTER>	Centers elements including text and images.
<CITE>	Citation. Presents a book, paper, or source material.
<CODE>	Displays enclosed text as a code sample.
<COL>	Sets the properties of a table column.
<COLGROUP>	Sets the properties of one or more columns as a group.
<COMMENT>	The browser does not display enclosed text.
<DD>	Definition data. Formats text for a definition. See DL, DT.
<DFN>	Displays information as a defined term.
<DIR>	Displays text as a directory list.
<DIV>	Document division. Groups related elements in a document.
<DL>	Definition list. Used to display defined terms. See DT, DD.
<DT>	Definition term. Used to display a defined term. See DL, DD.
<EM>	Usually displays text in italics.
<EMBED>	See OBJECT.
<FONT>	Sets the font style, size and color.
<FORM>	Sets up a form for user data entry. See INPUT for a list of form elements.
<FRAME>	Used to set up frames within a page. See FRAMESET.
<FRAMESET>	Sets up the layout for frames within a page. See FRAME.
<Hn>	Used to display headings with a larger size than the body
	text. n can be from 1 to 6.
<HEAD>	Marks the beginning of the HTML document heading.
<HR>	Horizontal rule. Used to separate sections. Not recommended.
<HTML>	The first tag in HTML document.

continues

Table B-1
Continued

Tag	Description
<I>	Displays text in italics.
<IMG>	Inserts an image in a document.
<INPUT>	Sets up a form control such as a checkbox or radio button. See FORM.
<ISINDEX>	Tells the browser that a searchable index exists.
<KBD>	Displays text as fixed-width, boldface type.
<LI>	List item. Adds a character or number depending on use. See UL, OL.
<LINK>	Sets up a link relationship between documents. Used only in HEAD element.
<LISTING>	Displays text in a fixed-width type list format.
<MAP>	Defines hot spots for a client-side image map.
<MARQUEE>	Displays text in a marquee.
<MENU>	Displays text as a list of items in menu format.
<META>	Provides information about an HTML page for use with client pull and by some search engines for indexing.
<NOBR>	Turns off line breaks.
<NOFRAMES>	Provides an alternative for browsers that do not understand frames.
<OBJECT>	Used to insert ActiveX controls in HTML pages.
<OL>	Ordered list. Items have a number or letter reference. See UL, LI.
<OPTION>	A choice in a list box.
<P>	Paragraph break indicating the start of a new paragraph.
<PARAM>	Used to set object properties.
<PLAINTEXT>	Displays text in fixed-width type.
<PRE>	Displays text exactly as typed; that is pre-formatted.
<S>	Displays text as strikethrough.
<SAMP>	Displays text as sample text. See CODE.
<SCRIPT>	Encloses an executable script.
<SELECT>	Sets up a list box or dropdown list.
<SMALL>	Decreases the displayed font size by one HTML size.
<SPAN>	Applies style information to enclosed text.

Tag	Description
<STRIKE>	Displays text as strikethrough. See S.
<STRONG>	Displays text as boldface. See B.
<SUB>	Displays text in subscript.
<SUP>	Displays text in superscript.
<TABLE>	Used to creates a table. TH, TR, and TD are used for further definition.
<TBODY>	Table body.
<TD>	Table data.
<TFOOT>	Table footer.
<TH>	Table header element.
<THEAD>	Defines a table header.
<TEXTAREA>	Used to create a box where users can enter and edit text.
<TITLE>	The document title. Displays in the browser title bar.
<TR>	Table row.
<TT>	Displays text in old teletype format with fixed-width type.
<U>	Underlined.
<UL>	Displays text an an unnumbered list or as a bulleted list.
<VAR>	Displays text in a small fixed-width font.
<WBR>	Inserts a soft linebreak in a block of NOBR text.
<XMP>	Displays text in fixed-width font as example text.

Expanded Definitions and Examples

Each of the tags listed in Table B-1 is expanded here to give you additional information. Each tag is followed with an indication of its HTML level or browser support. That is followed with an illustration of the syntax.

!—...— (HTML 2.0)

```
<!- ... ->
```

This is an unusual tag. The beginning tag is <!–. The ending tag is – >. Any text enclosed within these tags is not displayed by the browser.

This makes an ideal place for comments, obviously, but it can also be used to contain scripts because multiple lines of text can be included between the tags.

> **NOTE:**
> **Most beginning tags are enclosed in a pair of angle brackets, and most ending tags are enclosed in a pair of angle brackets with a slash, as in </>.**

Example

```
<!—This text is not displayed by the browser
and neither is this—>
```

!DOCTYPE (HTML 2.0)

```
<!DOCTYPE>
```

Used to specify the HTML version, !DOCTYPE is the first element in an HTML document and is required for an HTML 3.2-compliant document.

Example

```
<!DOCTYPE HTML PUBLIC "-//W3C//DTD HTML 3.2//EN">
```

A (HTML 2.0)

```
<A
HREF=reference
NAME=name
REL=relationship
REV=revision
TARGET=window
TITLE=title>
```

A stands for anchor and is used to generate hyperlinks. The <A...> and </A> tags can enclose text or graphics. The allowed properties that follow the A are used to further refine the name or link definition. The HREF=reference attribute is used to attach a hyperlink to text or graphics. The NAME=name attribute is used to create an anchor on a page. Anchors cannot be nested.

Attributes

`HREF=reference`

A destination address or a destination file name. The destination address must be in URL format (`http://www.microsoft.com`). A destination file must name a file in the format of the given file system (`temp.htm`).

`NAME=name`

A named reference in an HTML document. The name can be used by its document and external documents in a hyperlink by prefacing it with the pound sign (#).

`REL=relationship`

Defines a relative relationship.

`REV=revision`

Defines the revision number.

`TARGET=windowname`

This capability is used with frames to load documents into named panes. You may, for example, have a table of contents in one pane and want to load a linked document into some other pane. You tell the link where to load the document using the TARGET=window parameter. `windowname` can be one of these values:

Value	Action
`windowname`	**Load the specified document into the named pane. The windowname must begin with an alpha-numeric character to be valid, except for the four target windows listed that follow.**
`_blank`	**Load the link into a new blank window. This window is not named.**
`_parent`	**Load the link into the immediate parent of the document the link is in.**
`_self`	**Load the link into the same window.**
`_top`	**Load the link into the full body of the window.**

```
TITLE=name
```

Defines the title that appears when the hyperlink is selected.

Example

```
<A HREF="http://www.msn.com"> This is a link to Microsoft
Network.</A>

<A HREF="top.htm">This is a link to top.htm.</A>

<A TARGET="body" HREF="newcontent.htm">This will load
newcontent.htm into the frame named body.</A>
```

ADDRESS (HTML 2.0)

```
<ADDRESS>
```

Displays text, usually in italics, as the text might appear in a street address.

Example

```
<ADDRESS>1102 South Pacific Street</ADDRESS>
```

AREA (IE)

```
<AREA
COORDS=coords
SHAPE=shape-type
NOHREF
HREF=url
TARGET=window>
```

Defines the shape of a “hot spot” in a client-side image map.

Attributes

```
COORDS=coords
```

Coordinates that define the hot spot’s shape.

```
HREF=url
```

The destination reached when the hot spot is selected.

`NOHREF`

Clicks in this region cause no action.

`SHAPE=shape-type`

The shape-type can be one of these values:

Value	Action
RECT	**Rectangle. Takes four coordinates: x1, y1, x2, and y2.**
RECTANGLE	**Rectangle. Takes four coordinates: x1, y1, x2, and y2.**
CIRC	**Circle. Takes three coordinates: centerx, centery, and radius.**
CIRCLE	**Circle. Takes three coordinates: centerx, centery, and radius.**
POLY	**Polygon. Takes three or more pairs of coordinates denoting a polygonal region.**
POLYGON	**Polygon. Takes three or more pairs of coordinates denoting a polygonal region.**

`TARGET=windowname`

This capability is used with frames to load documents into named panes. You may, for example, have a table of contents in one pane and want to load a linked document into some other pane. You tell the link where to load the document using the TARGET=window parameter. `windowname` can be one of these values:

Value	Action
`windowname`	**Load the specified document into the named pane. The windowname must begin with an alpha-numeric character to be valid, except for the four target windows listed that follow.**
`_blank`	**Load the link into a new blank window. This window is not named.**
`_parent`	**Load the link into the immediate parent of the document the link is in.**
`_self`	**Load the link into the same window.**
`_top`	**Load the link into the full body of the window.**

B (HTML 2.0)

```
<B>
```

Displays enclosed text in bold.

Example

```
<B>This text is bold.</B>
```

BASE (HTML 2.0)

```
<BASE
HREF=url
TARGET=window>
```

Defines the document's URL.

Attributes

```
HREF=url
```

Defines the document's full URL in case the document is read out of context and the reader wants to refer to the original.

```
TARGET=windowname
```

This capability is used with frames to load documents into named panes You may, for example, have a table of contents in one pane and want to load a linked document into some other pane. You tell the link where to load the document using the TARGET=window parameter. `windowname` can be one of these values:

Value	Action
`windowname`	**Load the specified document into the named pane. The windowname must begin with an alphanumeric character to be valid, except for the four target windows listed that follow.**
`_blank`	**Load the link into a new blank window. This window is not named.**
`_parent`	**Load the link into the immediate parent of the document the link is in.**
`_self`	**Load the link into the same window.**
`_top`	**Load the link into the full body of the window.**

Examples

```
<BASE HREF="http://www.temp.com/hello.htm">

<BASE HREF="http://www.temp.com/hello.htm" TARGET="_self">
```

BASEFONT

```
<BASEFONT
COLOR=color
NAME=name
SIZE=n>
```

Defines the base font values for the document. This value will be used as a default for text not formatted with a style sheet or not using the FONT element.

Attributes

```
COLOR=color
```

Defines the color of the base font.

```
NAME=name
```

Defines the name of the base font.

```
SIZE=n
```

Defines the size of the base font. n can be between 1 and 7 and defaults to 3; 1 is the smallest and 7 the largest.

Examples

```
<BASEFONT SIZE=3> This sets the base font size to 3.

<FONT SIZE=+3> Now the font size is 6.

<FONT SIZE=-2> Now the font size is 1.
```

BGSOUND

```
<BGSOUND
SRC=url
LOOP=n>
```

Adds background sounds to a page. Sounds can either be WAV, AU, or MIDI format.

Attributes

```
SRC=url
```

Defines the location of a sound to be played.

```
LOOP=n
```

Defines how many times a sound will loop when activated. If n=-1, or if LOOP=INFINITE, it will loop indefinitely.

BIG

```
<BIG>
```

Makes text one size larger.

Example

```
<BIG>This text is one size larger<./BIG>
```

BLOCKQUOTE

```
<BLOCKQUOTE>
```

Indents both left and right margins to simulate a block quote.

BODY

```
<BODY
BACKGROUND=url
BGCOLOR=color
BGPROPERTIES=FIXED
LINK=color
TEXT=color
TOPMARGIN=n
VLINK=color>
```

Defines the beginning and end of document body text. You can also set a background image, a background color, a link color, and the top and left margins of the page.

Attributes

BACKGROUND=url

Defines a background picture. The picture is tiled behind the text and graphics on the page. Use care with this; it can get ugly and unreadable.

BGCOLOR=color

Defines the background color for the page. The color can be either a hexadecimal, red-green-blue color value, or a predefined color name. Although IE 3.0 is supposed to recognize only a few color names, it does, in fact, recognize all named colors.

BGPROPERTIES=FIXED

Defines a nonscrolling image or watermark.

LEFTMARGIN=n

Defines the left margin for the entire page and overrides the default margin. If set to zero, the left margin will be exactly on the left edge.

LINK=color

Defines the color of hyperlinks that have not yet been visited.

TEXT=color

Defines the color of text on the page.

TOPMARGIN=n

Defines the margin for the top of the page and overrides the default margin. If set to zero, the top margin will be on the precise top edge.

VLINK=color or colorname

Sets the color of hyperlinks that have already been visited.

BR

<BR
CLEAR=align-type>

Inserts a line break.

Attributes

```
CLEAR=align-type
```

Inserts vertical space so that the next text displayed will be past left- or right-aligned "floating" images.

The align-type can be one of these values:

Value	Action
LEFT	Inserts space so that the next text appears aligned with the left margin directly below a left-aligned floating image.
RIGHT	Inserts space so that the next text appears aligned with the right margin directly below a right-aligned floating image.
ALL	Places the next text past all floating images.

CAPTION

```
<CAPTION
ALIGN=align-type>
```

Defines a table caption.

Attributes

```
ALIGN=align-type
```

Sets the alignment of the caption within the table. The align-type can be LEFT, RIGHT, TOP, or BOTTOM. By default, the caption is centered and at the bottom of the table.

This element is valid only within the TABLE element. The end-tag is required.

Example

```
<TABLE>
<CAPTION ALIGN=BOTTOM>
This caption is centered below the table.
</CAPTION>
```

```
<TR>
        ....
</TR>
</TABLE>
```

CENTER

Centers text and images.

Example

```
<CENTER>Hi there!</CENTER>
```

CITE

```
<CITE>
```

Indicates a citation. Refers to a book, paper, or other published source material.

Example

```
<CITE>Book Title.</CITE>
```

CODE

```
<CODE>
```

Displays text as a computer code sample.

Example

```
<CODE>For x = 1 to 100</CODE>
```

COL

```
<COL
ALIGN=align-type
SPAN=n>
```

Sets the properties of one or more columns in a table. Use this element in conjunction with a COLGROUP element to set the properties of a column within a group of columns.

Attributes

`ALIGN=align-type`

Defines the alignment of text in cells within the column. The align-type can be CENTER, LEFT, or RIGHT.

`SPAN=n`

Sets the number of consecutive columns for which the properties are set.

This element is valid only within a table. The end-tag is not required and not recommended. The properties specified by the COL element always override the properties specified by the preceding COL-GROUP element.

COLGROUP

```
<COLGROUP
ALIGN=align-type
SPAN=n>
```

Sets the properties of one or more columns.

Attributes

`ALIGN=align-type`

Defines the alignment of text in the cells in the column(s). The align-type can be CENTER, LEFT or RIGHT.

`SPAN=n`

Sets the number of consecutive columns that are in the group and for which the properties are set. This element is valid only within a table. The end-tag is not required and not recommended.

COMMENT

The text between the elements is ignored unless it contains HTML code.

Example

```
<COMMENT>This won't show on your display.</COMMENT>
```

DD

```
<DD>
```

The definition part of a definition list. Indicates that the text is a definition and should be displayed in the right column of a definition list.

DFN

```
<DFN>
```

Displays text as a definition.

Example

```
<DFN>HTML stands for hypertext markup language.</DFN>
```

DIR

```
<DIR>
```

Displays a directory list. The block following consists of individual items, each beginning with an LI tag and none containing more than 20 characters.

Example

```
<DIR> <LI>COBOL
<LI>Fortran
<LI>BASIC
<LI>C
<LI>C++
</DIR>
```

DIV

```
<DIV
ALIGN=align-type </DIV>
```

Sets document division. Groups related elements together.

Attributes

```
ALIGN=align-type
```

Sets alignment of block elements within DIV elements. The align-type can be LEFT, CENTER, or RIGHT. LEFT is the default value.

DIV is frequently used in conjunction with .ALX files in the HTML Layout Control.

DL

```
<DL>
```

The block following is a definition list. It is automatically formatted in two columns with terms <DT> on the left and their definitions <DD> on the right.

Example

```
<DL>
<DT>Algebra
<DD>A subject I nearly flunked in high school.
<DT>Calculus
<DD>Huh? What?.
</DL>
```

DT

```
<DT>
```

A term in a definition list. Indicates that the text is a term to be defined, and should therefore be displayed in the left column of a definition list.

EM

Displays text in italics.

Example

```
<EM>This text is in italics.</EM>
```

FONT

```
<FONT
SIZE=n
FACE=name
COLOR=color>
```

Sets the font, size, and color of text.

Attributes

`COLOR=color`

Sets the font color. The color can be either a hexadecimal, red-green-blue color value or a predefined color name.

`FACE="name [,name2[,name3]]"`

Sets the font face name or names. A list of font names should be specified. The fonts will be requested from left to right. If the name, name2, or name3 fonts are not available on the client computer, a default will be used.

`SIZE=n`

Defines font size between 1 and 7 (7 is largest). A plus or minus before the number indicates a size relative to the current BASEFONT setting. The BASEFONT size defaults to 3. A new `<FONT SIZE="n">` will always redefine the font in terms of the BASEFONT setting, not with reference to the last size set.

FORM

```
<FORM
ACTION=url
METHOD=get-post
TARGET=window>
```

Forms are used to collect information..

Attributes

`ACTION=url`

The address to be used to for the action of the form. If none is specified, the base URL of the document is used.

`METHOD=get-post`

Indicates how the form data should be sent to the server.

The get-post can be one of these values:

Value	Action
GET	Appends the arguments to the action URL and open it as if it were an anchor.
POST	Sends the data via an HTTP post transaction.

TARGET=windowname

This capability is used with frames to load documents into named panes. (I cover this in greater detail in later chapters.) You may, for example, have a table of contents in one pane and want to load a linked document into some other pane. You tell the link where to load the document using the TARGET=window parameter. windowname can be one of these values:

Value	Action
windowname	Load the specified document into the named pane. The windowname must begin with an alpha-numeric character to be valid, except for the four target windows listed that follow.
_blank	Load the link into a new blank window. This window is not named.
_parent	Load the link into the immediate parent of the document the link is in.
_self	Load the link into the same window.
_top	Load the link into the full body of the window.

Example

```
<FORM TARGET="viewer" ACTION="http://www.sample.com/bin/search">
    ...
</FORM>
```

FRAME

```
<FRAME
ALIGN=align-type
FRAMEBORDER=1|0
MARGINHEIGHT=height
MARGINWIDTH=width
NAME=name
SCROLLING=yes|no
SRC=address>
```

Defines a single frame in a frameset. There is no matching end-tag because this is not a container. Frames provide capabilities that just aren't available with standard HTML.

Attributes

`ALIGN=align-type`

Sets the alignment of the frame or of the surrounding text.

The align-type can be one of these values:

Value	Action
TOP	Surrounding text is aligned with the top of the frame.
MIDDLE	Surrounding text is aligned with the middle of the frame.
BOTTOM	Surrounding text is aligned with the bottom of the frame.
LEFT	The frame is drawn as a left-flush "floating frame," and text flows around it.
RIGHT	The frame is drawn as a right-flush "floating frame," and text flows around it.

`FRAMEBORDER=0|1`

Renders a 3-D edge border around the frame.

1 (default) inserts a border.

0 displays no border.

`MARGINHEIGHT=height`

Controls the margin height for the frame in pixels.

`MARGINWIDTH=width`

Controls the margin width for the frame in pixels.

`NAME=name`

Provides a target name for the frame. This name is used when directing content to the frame.

`NORESIZE`

Prevents the user from resizing the frame.

`SCROLLING=yes|no`

Creates a scrolling frame if set to yes; otherwise, scroll bars are not applied.

`SRC=address`

Determines which HTML document will be loaded into the frame.

Example

```
<FRAME FRAMEBORDER=0 SCROLLING=NO SRC="sample.htm">
```

FRAMESET

```
<FRAMESET
COLS=col-widths
FRAMEBORDER=1|0
FRAMESPACING=spacing
ROWS=row-heights>
```

This is a container that hosts the FRAME, FRAMESET, and NOFRAMES elements.

Attributes

`COLS=col-widths`

Creates a frame document with columns. You can specify the column dimensions by percentage (%), pixels, or a relative size (*).

`FRAMEBORDER=1|0`

Provides the option to display or not display a 3-D border for a frame.

1 (default) sets a frame border.

0 displays no border.

`FRAMESPACING=spacing`

Creates additional space between frames in pixels.

`ROWS=row-heights`

Creates a frame document with rows. You can specify the row dimensions by percentage (%), pixels, or a relative size (*).

The `FRAMEBORDER=` and `FRAMESPACING=` attributes are inherited from any containing FRAMESET element, which means that you need to set the attribute only on the single, outermost FRAMESET tag to affect all FRAME tags on that page.

Example

```
<FRAMESET SCROLLING=YES COLS="25%, 50%, *">
    <FRAME SRC="contents.htm">
    <FRAME SRC="info.htm">
    <FRAME SCROLLING=NO SRC="graphic.htm">
</FRAMESET>
```

Hn

```
<Hn
ALIGN=align-type>
```

Displays text in one of six heading sizes. Use H1 through H7 to specify different sizes and styles of heading.

Attributes

`n`

H1 through H6. Integer from 1 to 6.

`ALIGN=align-type`

Sets alignment of header text. Align-type can be CENTER, LEFT, or RIGHT. LEFT is default.

The end-tag is required.

Example

```
<H1>Welcome to Internet Explorer!</H1>
```

HEAD

```
<HEAD>
```

Marks the beginning <HEAD> and end </HEAD> of the HTML document heading.

The end-tag is not required but is recommended.

Example

```
<HEAD>
<TITLE>My First HTML Document</TITLE>
</HEAD>
```

HR

```
<HR
ALIGN=align-type
COLOR=color
NOSHADE
SIZE=n
WIDTH=n>
```

Displays a horizontal rule.

Attributes

`ALIGN=align-type`

Draws the rule left-aligned, right-aligned, or centered. The align-type can be LEFT, RIGHT, or CENTER.

`COLOR=color`

Sets the color of the rule. The color can be either a hexadecimal, red-green-blue color value or a predefined color name.

`NOSHADE`

Draws the rule without 3-D shading.

`SIZE=n`

Sets the height of the rule in pixels.

```
WIDTH=n
```

Sets the width of the rule either in pixels or as a percentage of window width. To specify a percentage, the n must end with the percent (%) sign.

Example

```
<HR SIZE=5 WIDTH=80% NOSHADE>
```

HTML (HTML 2.0)

```
<HTML>
```

Denotes the file as an HTML document. All HTML documents begin with <HTML> and end with </HTML>.

This element has no attributes.

Example

```
<HTML>
<BODY>
<P>This is an HTML document.
</BODY>
</HTML>
```

I

```
<I>
```

Displays text in italics.

Example

```
<I>This is displayed in italics.</I>
```

IFRAME

```
<IFRAME
ALIGN=align-type
FRAMEBORDER=1|0
MARGINHEIGHT=height
MARGINWIDTH=width
NAME=name
```

```
SCROLLING=yes|no
SRC=address>...</IFRAME>
```

Defines a floating frame. Requires the end-tag.

Attributes

```
ALIGN=align-type
```

Sets the alignment of the frame or of the surrounding text.

The align-type can be one of these values:

Value	Action
TOP	Surrounding text is aligned with the top of the frame.
MIDDLE	Surrounding text is aligned with the middle of the frame.
BOTTOM	Surrounding text is aligned with the bottom of the frame.
LEFT	The frame is drawn as a left-flush "floating frame," and text flows around it.
RIGHT	The frame is drawn as a right-flush "floating frame," and text flows around it.

```
FRAMEBORDER=0|1
```

Renders a 3-D edge border around the frame.

1 (default) inserts a border.

0 displays no border.

```
MARGINHEIGHT=height
```

Controls the margin height for the frame in pixels.

```
MARGINWIDTH=width
```

Controls the margin width for the frame in pixels.

```
NAME=name
```

Provides a target name for the frame.

`NORESIZE`

Prevents the user from resizing the frame.

`SCROLLING=yes|no`

Creates a scrolling frame if yes; otherwise, scroll bars are not displayed.

`SRC=address`

Determines the HTML source file that will be loaded in the frame.

Example

```
<IFRAME FRAMEBORDER=0 SCROLLING=NO SRC="sample.htm"></IFRAME>
```

IMG

```
<IMG
ALIGN=align-type
ALT=text
BORDER=n
CONTROLS
DYNSRC=url
HEIGHT=n
HSPACE=n
ISMAP
LOOP=n
SRC=address
START=start-event
USEMAP=map-name
VSPACE=n
WIDTH=n>
```

Inserts an image into the display.

Attributes

`ALIGN=align type`

Sets the alignment of the image or of the surrounding text.

The align-type can be one of these values:

Value	Action
TOP	Surrounding text is aligned with the top of the image.
MIDDLE	Surrounding text is aligned with the middle of the image.
BOTTOM	Surrounding text is aligned with the bottom of the image.
LEFT	The picture is drawn as a left-flush "floating image," and text flows around it.
RIGHT	The picture is drawn as a right-flush "floating image," and text flows around it.

`ALT=text`

Defines text that will be displayed in place of the picture if Show Pictures is turned off.

`BORDER=n`

Defines the size of a border to be drawn around the image. If the image is a hyperlink, the border is drawn in the appropriate hyperlink color. If the image is not a hyperlink, the border is invisible.

`CONTROLS`

If a video clip is present, a set of controls is displayed under the clip.

`DYNSRC=url`

Dynamic Source. Defines the address of a video clip or VRML world to be displayed in the window.

`HEIGHT=n`

Along with `WIDTH=`, defines the size at which the picture is drawn. If the picture's actual dimensions differ from those specified, the picture is stretched to match what's specified. Internet Explorer also uses this to draw a placeholder of appropriate size for the picture before it's loaded.

HSPACE=n

Along with VSPACE=, defines margins for the image. Similar to BORDER=, except that the margins are not painted with color when the image is a hyperlink.

ISMAP

Identifies the picture as a server-side image map. Clicking the picture transmits the coordinates of the click back to the server, triggering a jump to another page.

LOOP=n

Defines how many times a video clip will loop when activated. If n=-1, or if LOOP=INFINITE, it will loop indefinitely.

SRC=address

Defines the address of the picture to insert.

START=start-event

Defines when the file specified by the DYNSRC= attribute should start playing.

The start-event can be one of these values:

Value	Action
FILEOPEN	Start playing as soon as the file is done opening. This is the default.
MOUSEOVER	Start playing when the user moves the mouse pointer over the animation.

Both values can be set but must be separated with a comma.

USEMAP=map-name

Identifies the picture as a client-side image map and defines a MAP to use for acting on the user's clicks.

VSPACE=n

Along with HSPACE=, defines margins for the image. Similar to BORDER=, except that the margins are not painted with color when the image is a hyperlink.

```
WIDTH=n
```

Along with `HEIGHT=`, defines the size at which the picture is drawn. If the picture's actual dimensions differ from those specified, the picture is stretched to match what's specified. Internet Explorer also uses this to draw a placeholder of appropriate size for the picture before it's loaded.

INPUT

```
<INPUT
ALIGN=align-type
[CHECKED|]
MAXLENGTH=length
NAME=name
SIZE=size
SRC=address
TYPE=type
VALUE=value>
```

Defines a form control.

Attributes

```
ALIGN=align-type
```

Used when TYPE=IMAGE. Defines how the next line of text will be aligned with the image. The align-type can be TOP, MIDDLE, or BOTTOM.

```
CHECKED
```

Include CHECKED to set a checkbox or radio button to "selected" when the form first loads.

```
MAXLENGTH=length
```

Indicates the maximum number of characters that can be entered into a text control.

```
NAME=name
```

Defines the name of the control.

SIZE=size

Defines the size of the control (in characters). For TEXTAREA-type controls, both height and width can be specified, using this format: "width,height".

SRC=address

Used when TYPE=IMAGE. Defines the address of the image to be used.

TYPE=type

Defines what type of control to use.

VALUE=value

For textual/numerical controls, defines the default value of the control. For Boolean controls, defines the value to be returned when the control is turned on.

ISINDEX

```
<ISINDEX
ACTION=url
PROMPT=prompt-text>
```

Indicates the presence of a searchable index at the Web site.

Attributes

ACTION=url

Defines the program to which the string in the text box should be passed.

PROMPT=prompt-text

Defines a prompt to be used instead of the default prompt.

If the PROMPT= attribute is not used, the element displays the following message followed by a text box: `You can search this index. Type the keyword(s) you want to search for:`. When the user enters text and presses Enter, that text is posted back to the page's URL as a query.

Example

```
<ISINDEX ACTION="http://intranet/search" PROMPT="Type in keywords here.">
```

KBD (HTML 2.0)

```
<KBD>
```

Displays text as it might be typed on a keyboard.

LI

```
<LI
TYPE=order-type
VALUE=n>
```

Defines one item of a list.

Attributes

```
TYPE=order-type
```

Changes the style of an ordered list.

The order-type can be one of these values:

Value	Action
A	Use large letters
a	Use small letters
I	Use large Roman numerals
i	Use small Roman numerals
1	Use numbers

```
VALUE=n
```

Changes the count of ordered lists as they progress.

LINK

```
<LINK
HREF=URL>
```

LINK establishes a hierarchical organization for navigating between documents.

Attributes

```
HREF=URL
```

Defines the related URL.

LISTING

```
<LISTING>
```

Displays text as a computer code listing.

MAP

```
<MAP
NAME=name>
```

Defines a collection of hot spots in a client-side image map.

Attributes

```
NAME=name
```

Gives the MAP a name.

MARQUEE

```
<MARQUEE
ALIGN=align-type
BEHAVIOR=type
BGCOLOR=color
DIRECTION=direction
HEIGHT=n
HSPACE=n
LOOP=n
SCROLLAMOUNT=n
SCROLLDELAY=n
VSPACE=n
WIDTH=n>
```

Creates a scrolling text marquee.

Attributes

`ALIGN=align-type`

Defines how the surrounding text aligns with the marquee.

The align-type can be one of these values:

Value	Action
TOP	Surrounding text aligns with the top of the marquee.
MIDDLE	Surrounding text aligns with the middle of the marquee.
BOTTOM	Surrounding text aligns with the bottom of the marquee.

`BEHAVIOR=type`

Defines how the text behaves.

The type can be one of these values:

Value	Action
SCROLL	Start completely off one side, scroll all the way across and completely off, and then start again. This is the default.
SLIDE	Start completely off one side, scroll in, and stop as soon as the text touches the other margin.
ALTERNATE	Bounce back and forth within the marquee.

`BGCOLOR=color`

Defines a background color for the marquee. The color can be either a hexadecimal number specifying a red, green, and blue color value or a predefined color name.

`DIRECTION=direction`

Defines which direction the text should scroll. The direction can be LEFT or RIGHT. The default is LEFT, which means scrolling to the left from the right.

HEIGHT=n

Defines the height of the marquee in pixels or as a percentage of the screen height. To specify a percentage, the n must be end with a percent (%) sign.

HSPACE=n

Defines left and right margins in pixels for the outside of the marquee.

LOOP=n

Defines how many times a marquee will loop when activated. If n=-1, or if LOOP=INFINITE, it will loop indefinitely.

SCROLLAMOUNT=n

Defines the number of pixels between each successive draw of the marquee text.

SCROLLDELAY=n

Defines the number of milliseconds between each successive draw of the marquee text.

VSPACE=n

Defines top and bottom margins in pixels for the outside of the marquee.

WIDTH=n

Sets the width of the marquee, either in pixels or as a percentage of the screen width. To specify a percentage, the n must end with a percent (%) sign.

Example

```
<MARQUEE DIRECTION=RIGHT BEHAVIOR=SCROLL SCROLLAMOUNT=10
SCROLLDELAY=200>Here's Johnny!</MARQUEE>
```

MENU

<MENU>

Displays a list of items. The block following consists of individual items, each beginning with an LI element.

Example

```
<MENU>
<LI>This is item one.
<LI>This is item two.
</MENU>
```

META

```
<META
HTTP-EQUIV=response
CONTENT=description
NAME=description
URL=url>
```

The meta tag provides information about an HTML document to browsers, search engines, and other applications.

NOBR

```
<NOBR>
```

Turns off line breaking to display text without line breaks.

NOFRAMES

```
<NOFRAMES>
```

This tag is used to create a page that is compatible with browsers that support frames and those that do not. The content between the beginning and ending NOFRAMES tags will be displayed for browsers that do not support frames. Frames-capable browsers will not display the NOFRAMES content.

OBJECT

```
<OBJECT
ALIGN=align-type
BORDER=n
CLASSID=url
CODEBASE=url
CODETYPE=codetype
DATA=url
DECLARE
```

```
HEIGHT=n
HSPACE=n
NAME=url
SHAPES
STANDBY=message
TYPE=type
USEMAP=url
VSPACE=n
WIDTH=n>
```

Inserts an object, such as an image, document, applet, or control, into an HTML document.

OL

```
<OL
START=n
TYPE=order-type >
```

Displays an ordered list. The following block consists of individual items, each beginning with an LI tag. The items are numbered.

Attributes

```
START=n
```

Defines a starting number for the list.

```
TYPE=order-type
```

Changes the style of the list.

The order-type can be one of these values:

Value	Action
A	Use large letters
a	Use small letters
I	Use large Roman numerals
i	Use small Roman numerals
1	Use numbers

OPTION

```
<SELECT
SELECTED
VALUE=value>
```

Denotes one choice in a list box. In a SELECT block, denotes one of the choices that will appear in the list.

Attributes

```
SELECTED
```

Indicates the default item. If not present, item #1 is the default.

```
VALUE=value
```

Indicates the value returned if the item is selected.

P

```
<P
ALIGN=align-type>
```

The paragraph marker.

Attributes

```
ALIGN=align-type
```

The align-type can be CENTER, LEFT, or RIGHT. Default is left.

The end-tag is optional but is inserted by many HTML editors.

Example

```
<P>This is a paragraph.</P>
```

PARAM

```
<PARAM
NAME=name
VALUE=value
VALUETYPE=type
TYPE=type>
```

Sets the property values for an object.

Attributes

`NAME=name`

Defines the property name.

`VALUE=value`

Defines the property value. The value is passed to the object without change except that any character or numeric character entities are replaced with their corresponding character values.

`VALUETYPE=type`

Defines how the value is interpreted.

The type can be one of these values:

Value	Action
DATA	The value is data—the default.
REF	The value is a URL.
OBJECT	The value is a URL of an object in the same document.

`TYPE=type`

Defines the Internet media type.

This element is valid only within an OBJECT element. The end-tag is optional.

PLAINTEXT

`<PLAINTEXT>`

Renders text in fixed-width type without processing tags. Renders text in fixed-width type. Also turns off HTML parsing until the browser encounters the </PLAINTEXT> tag. You might use this pair of tags to display HTML code in a document.

PRE (HTML 2.0)

`<PRE>`

Displays text exactly as entered. “Pre” stands for preformatted.

S

```
<S>
```

Displays text as strikethrough.

Example

```
<S>This text is lined out.</S>
```

SAMP

```
<SAMP>
```

Displays text as code sample.

SCRIPT

```
<SCRIPT
LANGUAGE=scripting language>
```

Defines a script.

Attributes

```
LANGUAGE=scripting language
```

The ActiveX scripting language in which the enclosed script was written. Examples of an ActiveX scripting language are VBScript and JScript.

Example

```
<SCRIPT>
<SCRIPT language="VBScript">
    '... Additional VBScript statements ...
</SCRIPT>
```

SELECT

```
<SELECT
MULTIPLE
NAME=name
SIZE=n>
```

Defines a list box or drop-down list.

Attributes

MULTIPLE

Multiple items can be selected.

NAME=name

Gives the list a name.

SIZE=n

Defines the height of the list control.

SMALL

<SMALL>

Makes text one size smaller.

SPAN

<SPAN
STYLE=value>

Use to apply style information to text within a document. SPAN can be used to do localized formatting to text using STYLE as an attribute.

Example

```
<SPAN STYLE="margin-left: 1.0in"> This paragraph is 1.0 inches
from the left margin.<SPAN>
```

STRIKE

<STRIKE>

Displays srikethrough text.

STRONG

<STRONG>

Displays text in bold.

SUB

```
<SUB>
```

Displays text as subscript.

SUP

```
<SUP>
```

Displays text as superscript.

TABLE

```
<TABLE
ALIGN=align-type
BACKGROUND=url
BGCOLOR=color
BORDER=n
BORDERCOLOR=color
BORDERCOLORDARK=color
BORDERCOLORLIGHT=color
CELLPADDING=n
CELLSPACING=n
COLS=n
FRAME=frame-type
RULES=rules
WIDTH=n>
```

Creates a table. You must create rows and cells using the TR, TD, and TH elements to complete the table.

Attributes

```
ALIGN=align-type
```

Defines table alignment.

The align-type can be one of these values:

Value	Action
LEFT	The table is left-aligned. This is the default alignment.
RIGHT	The table is right-aligned.

`BACKGROUND=url`

Defines a background picture.

`BGCOLOR=color`

Sets a background color.

`BORDER=n`

Size of the table border in pixels. Default is zero.

`BORDERCOLOR=color`

Sets border color and must be used with the `BORDER` attribute.

`BORDERCOLORLIGHT=color`

Sets independent border color control over one of the two colors used to draw a 3-D border.

`BORDERCOLORDARK=color`

Sets independent border color control over one of the two colors used to draw a 3-D border.

`CELLPADDING=n`

Amount of space, in pixels, between the sides of a cell and its contents.

`CELLSPACING=n`

Amount of space, in pixels, between the frame (exterior) of the table and the cells in the table.

```
COLS=n
```

Number of columns in the table.

```
WIDTH=n
```

Sets the width of the table in pixels or as a percentage of the window. To set a percentage, the n must end with a percent (%) sign.

```
FRAME=frame-type
```

Defines which sides of a frame (outer borders) are displayed.

The frame-type can be one of these values:

Value	Action
VOID	Removes all outside table borders.
ABOVE	Displays a border on the top side of the table frame.
BELOW	Displays a border on the bottom side of the table frame.
HSIDES	Displays a border on the top and bottom sides of the table frame.
LHS	Displays a border on the left-hand side of the table frame.
RHS	Displays a border on the right-hand side of the table frame.
VSIDES	Displays a border on the left and right sides of the table frame.
BOX	Displays a border on all sides of the table frame.
BORDER	Displays a border on all sides of the table frame.

```
RULES=rule-type
```

Defines which dividing lines (inner borders) are displayed.

The rule-type can be one of these values:

Value	Action
NONE	Removes all interior table borders.
GROUPS	Displays horizontal borders between all table groups. Groups are specified by the THEAD, TBODY, TFOOT, and COLGROUP elements.
ROWS	Displays horizontal borders between all table rows.
COLS	Displays vertical borders between all table columns.
ALL	Displays a border on all rows and columns.

The end-tag is required.

The optional THEAD, TBODY, TFOOT, COLGROUP, and COL elements can be used to organize a table and apply attributes across columns and groups of columns.

TBODY

```
<TBODY>
```

Defines the table body. This element distinguishes the rows in the table header or footer from those in the main body of the table.

TD

```
<TD
ALIGN=align-type
BACKGROUND=url
BGCOLOR=color
BORDERCOLOR=color
BORDERCOLORLIGHT=color
BORDERCOLORDARK=color
COLSPAN=n
NOWRAP=NOWRAP
ROWSPAN=n
VALIGN=align-type>
```

Creates a cell in a table.

Attributes

`ALIGN=align-type`

Defines the horizontal alignment of text in the cell.

The align-type can be one of these values:

Value	Action
LEFT	The table is left-aligned.
CENTER	Text is centered—the default value.
RIGHT	The table is right-aligned.

`BACKGROUND=url`

Defines a background picture.

`BGCOLOR=color`

Sets background color.

`BORDERCOLOR=color`

Sets border color and must be used with the `BORDER` attribute.

`BORDERCOLORLIGHT=color`

Sets independent border color control over one of the two colors used to draw a 3-D border.

`BORDERCOLORDARK=color`

Sets independent border color control over one of the two colors used to draw a 3-D border.

`VALIGN=align-type`

Defines that the vertical alignment of text in the cell.

The align-type can be one of these values:

Value	Action
TOP	Text is aligned with the top of each cell.
MIDDLE	Text is aligned in the middle of each cell—the default.
BOTTOM	Text is aligned with the bottom of each cell.
BASELINE	Text in adjoining cells in a row is aligned along a common baseline.

TEXTAREA

```
<TEXTAREA
COLS=n
NAME=name
ROWS=n>
```

Creates a multiple-line text entry control in which the user can enter and edit text.

Attributes

`COLS=n`

Sets the width, in characters, of the text area.

`NAME=n`

Sets the name of the text area. This name is used when the element is used within a FORM element.

`ROWS=n`

Sets the height, in characters, of the text area.

The end-tag is required. Any text between the start and end-tags is used as the initial value for the control.

TFOOT

```
<TFOOT>
```

Defines a table footer. Use this element to distinguish the rows in the table footer from those in the header or main body of the table.

TH

```
<TH
ALIGN=align-type
BACKGROUND=url
BGCOLOR=color
BORDERCOLOR=color
BORDERCOLORLIGHT=color
BORDERCOLORDARK=color
COLSPAN=n
NOWRAP=NOWRAP
ROWSPAN=n
VALIGN=align-type>
```

Creates a row or column heading in a table. The element is similar to the TD element but emphasizes the text in the cell to distinguish it from text in TD cells.

Attributes

`ALIGN=align-type`

Defines the alignment of text in the cell.

The align-type can be one of these values:

Value	Action
LEFT	Text is left-aligned.
CENTER	Text is centered—the default value.
RIGHT	Text is right-aligned.

`BACKGROUND=url`

Defines a background picture.

`BGCOLOR=color`

Sets background color.

`BORDERCOLOR=color`

Sets border color and must be used with the `BORDER` attribute.

```
BORDERCOLORLIGHT=color
```

Sets independent border color control over one of the two colors used to draw a 3-D border.

```
BORDERCOLORDARK=color
```

Sets independent border color control over one of the two colors used to draw a 3-D border.

```
COLSPAN=n
```

Number of table columns this cell spans.

```
NOWRAP=NOWRAP
```

Prevents word wrapping with the cell.

```
ROWSPAN=n
```

Number of table rows this cell spans.

```
VALIGN=align-type
```

Defines the vertical alignment of text in the table.

The align-type can be one of these values:

Value	Action
TOP	Text is aligned with the top of each cell.
MIDDLE	Text is aligned in the middle of each cell—the default value.
BOTTOM	Text is aligned with the bottom of each cell.
BASELINE	Text in adjoining cells in a row is aligned along a common baseline.

THEAD

```
<THEAD>
```

Defines the table header.

TITLE

```
<TITLE>
```

Defines a title for the document. Internet Explorer uses this for the window caption.

This element is valid only within the HEAD element. The end-tag is required.

Example

```
<HEAD>
<TITLE>"Welcome To Internet Explorer!"</TITLE>
</HEAD>
```

TR

```
<TR
ALIGN=align-type
BACKGROUND=url
BGCOLOR=color
BORDERCOLOR=color
BORDERCOLORLIGHT=color
BORDERCOLORDARK=color
VALIGN=align-type>
```

Creates a row in a table.

Attributes

```
ALIGN=align-type
```

Defines the alignment of text in the cells in the row.

The align-type can be one of these values:

Value	Action
LEFT	Text is left-aligned.
CENTER	Text is centered—the default value.
RIGHT	Text is right-aligned.

BACKGROUND=url

Defines a background picture.

BGCOLOR=color

Sets background color.

BORDERCOLOR=color

Sets border color and must be used with the BORDER attribute.

BORDERCOLORLIGHT=color

Sets independent border color control over one of the two colors used to draw a 3-D border.

BORDERCOLORDARK=color

Sets independent border color control over one of the two colors used to draw a 3-D border.

VALIGN=align-type

Defines the vertical alignment of text in the cells of the row.

The align-type can be one of these values:

Value	Action
TOP	**Text is aligned with the top of each cell.**
MIDDLE	**Text is aligned in the middle of each cell—the default value.**
BOTTOM	**Text is aligned with the bottom of each cell.** BASELINE **Text in adjoining cells in a row is aligned along a common baseline.**

TT

<TT>

Teletype. Renders text in fixed-width type.

U

<U>

Displays underlined text.

UL

<UL>

Displays an unnumbered or bulleted list. The block that follows the list consists of items beginning with an LI tag.

VAR

<VAR>

Displays text as small fixed-width type.

WBR

Provides soft linebreaks in a block of NOBR text.

XMP

<XMP>

Displays text in fixed-width type.

HTML Color Values

Defining colors within HTML documents is not difficult; finding definitions for available colors *is* difficult. You may well find the material that follows to be one of the most valuable items in this book. The HTML color names are shown with corresponding RGB values in both decimal and hexadecimal notation. You can use the color names or the RGB values to define colors anywhere that a color value is mentioned in HTML.

	Decimal			Hexadecimal		
Color Name	R	G	B	R	G	B
Aliceblue	240	248	255	F0	F8	FF
antiquewhite	250	235	215	FA	EB	D7
aqua	0	255	255	00	FF	FF
aquamarine	127	255	212	7F	FF	D4

Color Name	Decimal R	G	B	Hexadecimal R	G	B
azure	240	255	255	F0	FF	FF
beige	245	245	220	F5	F5	DC
bisque	255	228	196	FF	E4	C4
black	0	0	0	00	00	00
blanchedalmond	255	235	205	FF	EB	CD
blue	0	0	255	00	00	FF
blueviolet	138	43	226	8A	2B	E2
brown	165	42	42	A5	2A	2A
burlywood	222	184	135	DE	B8	87
cadetblue	95	158	160	5F	9E	A0
chartreuse	127	255	0	7F	FF	00
chocolate	210	105	30	D2	69	1E
coral	255	127	80	FF	7F	50
cornflowerblue	100	149	237	64	95	ED
cornsilk	255	248	220	FF	F8	DC
crimson	220	20	60	DC	14	3C
cyan	0	255	255	00	FF	FF
darkblue	0	0	139	00	00	8B
darkcyan	0	139	139	00	8B	8B
darkgoldenrod	184	134	11	B8	86	0B
darkgray	169	169	169	A9	A9	A9
darkgreen	0	100	0	00	64	00
darkkhaki	189	183	107	BD	B7	6B
darkmagenta	139	0	139	8B	00	8B
darkolivegreen	85	107	47	55	6B	2F
darkorange	255	140	0	FF	8C	00
darkorchid	153	50	204	99	32	CC
darkred	139	0	0	8B	00	00
darksalmon	233	150	122	E9	96	7A
darkseagreen	143	188	143	8F	BC	8F
darkslateblue	72	61	139	48	3D	8B
darkslategray	47	79	79	2F	4F	4F

Color Name	Decimal R	Decimal G	Decimal B	Hexadecimal R	Hexadecimal G	Hexadecimal B
darkturquoise	0	206	209	00	CE	D1
darkviolet	148	0	211	94	00	D3
deeppink	255	20	147	FF	14	93
deepskyblue	0	191	255	00	BF	FF
dimgray	105	105	105	69	69	69
dodgerblue	30	144	255	1E	90	FF
firebrick	178	34	34	B2	22	22
floralwhite	255	250	240	FF	FA	F0
forestgreen	34	139	34	22	8B	22
fuchsia	255	0	255	FF	00	FF
gainsboro	220	220	220	DC	DC	DC
ghostwhite	248	248	255	F8	F8	FF
gold	255	215	0	FF	D7	00
goldenrod	218	165	32	DA	A5	20
gray	128	128	128	80	80	80
green	0	128	0	00	80	00
greenyellow	173	255	47	AD	FF	2F
honeydew	240	255	240	F0	FF	F0
hotpink	255	105	180	FF	69	B4
indianred	205	92	92	CD	5C	5C
indigo	75	0	130	4B	00	82
ivory	255	255	240	FF	FF	F0
khaki	240	230	140	F0	E6	8C
lavender	230	230	250	E6	E6	FA
lavenderblush	255	240	245	FF	F0	F5
lawngreen	124	252	0	7C	FC	00
lemonchiffon	255	250	205	FF	FA	CD
lightblue	173	216	230	AD	D8	E6
lightcoral	240	128	128	F0	80	80
lightcyan	224	255	255	E0	FF	FF
lightgoldenrodyellow	250	250	210	FA	FA	D2
lightgreen	144	238	144	90	EE	90

Color Name	Decimal R	Decimal G	Decimal B	Hexadecimal R	Hexadecimal G	Hexadecimal B
lightgrey	211	211	211	D3	D3	D3
lightpink	255	182	193	FF	B6	C1
lightsalmon	255	160	122	FF	A0	7A
lightseagreen	32	178	170	20	B2	AA
lightskyblue	135	206	250	87	CE	FA
lightslategray	119	136	153	77	88	99
lightsteelblue	176	196	222	B0	C4	DE
lightyellow	255	255	224	FF	FF	E0
lime	0	255	0	00	FF	00
limegreen	50	205	50	32	CD	32
linen	250	240	230	FA	F0	E6
magenta	255	0	255	FF	00	FF
maroon	128	0	0	80	00	00
mediumaquamarine	102	205	170	66	CD	AA
mediumblue	0	0	205	00	00	CD
mediumorchid	186	85	211	BA	55	D3
mediumpurple	147	112	219	93	70	DB
mediumseagreen	60	179	113	3C	B3	71
mediumslateblue	123	104	238	7B	68	EE
mediumspringgreen	0	250	154	00	FA	9A
mediumturquoise	72	209	204	48	D1	CC
mediumvioletred	199	21	133	C7	15	85
midnightblue	25	25	112	19	19	70
mintcream	245	255	250	F5	FF	FA
mistyrose	255	228	225	FF	E4	E1
moccasin	255	228	181	FF	E4	B5
navajowhite	255	222	173	FF	DE	AD
navy	0	0	128	00	00	80
oldlace	253	245	230	FD	F5	E6
olive	128	128	0	80	80	00
olivedrab	107	142	35	6B	8E	23
orange	255	165	0	FF	A5	00

Color Name	Decimal R	Decimal G	Decimal B	Hexadecimal R	Hexadecimal G	Hexadecimal B
orangered	255	69	0	FF	45	00
orchid	218	112	214	DA	70	D6
palegoldenrod	238	232	170	EE	E8	AA
palegreen	152	251	152	98	FB	98
paleturquoise	175	238	238	AF	EE	EE
palevioletred	219	112	147	DB	70	93
papayawhip	255	239	213	FF	EF	D5
peachpuff	255	218	185	FF	DA	B9
peru	205	133	63	CD	85	3F
pink	255	192	203	FF	C0	CB
plum	221	160	221	DD	A0	DD
powderblue	176	224	230	B0	E0	E6
purple	128	0	128	80	00	80
red	255	0	0	FF	00	00
rosybrown	188	143	143	BC	8F	8F
royalblue	65	105	225	41	69	E1
saddlebrown	139	69	19	8B	45	13
salmon	250	128	114	FA	80	72
sandybrown	244	164	96	F4	A4	60
seagreen	46	139	87	2E	8B	57
seashell	255	245	238	FF	F5	EE
sienna	160	82	45	A0	52	2D
silver	192	192	192	C0	C0	C0
skyblue	135	206	235	87	CE	EB
slateblue	106	90	205	6A	5A	CD
slategray	112	128	144	70	80	90
snow	255	250	250	FF	FA	FA
springgreen	0	255	127	00	FF	7F
steelblue	70	130	180	46	82	B4
tan	210	180	140	D2	B4	8C
teal	0	128	128	00	80	80
thistle	216	191	216	D8	BF	D8

Color Name	Decimal R	G	B	Hexadecimal R	G	B
tomato	255	99	71	FF	63	47
turquoise	64	224	208	40	E0	D0
violet	238	130	238	EE	82	EE
wheat	245	222	179	F5	DE	B3
white	255	255	255	FF	FF	FF
whitesmoke	245	245	245	F5	F5	F5
yellow	255	255	0	FF	FF	00
yellowgreen	154	205	50	9A	CD	32

An HTML Color Chart Program

The following code is on the CD; you can also enter it. Figure 3-1 shows the display resulting from this code. Although you will not be looking at it in its full, glorious color, it points up a fact or two. Color names are used rather than RGB values, so IE 3.0 supports far more color names than might be apparent. You may want to use this little application to select and control color for your own HTML coding.

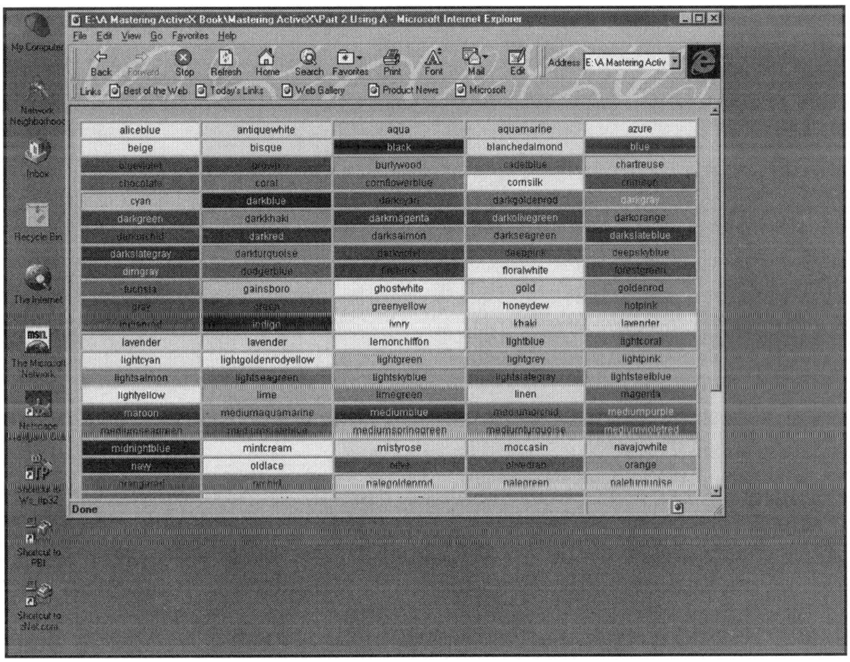

Figure B-1
A color chart for those difficult colors

```
<HTML>
<HEAD>
<TITLE>Color Table using Color Names</TITLE>
<STYLE TYPE="text/css">
<!–
BODY {font-size: 9 pt;
        font-family: "Arial"}
–>
</STYLE>
</HEAD>
<BODY>
<TABLE ALIGN=LEFT BORDER=1 WIDTH=100%>
<TR ALIGN=CENTER><TD BGCOLOR=aliceblue>aliceblue</TD>
<TD BGCOLOR=antiquewhite>antiquewhite</TD>
<TD BGCOLOR=aqua>aqua</TD>
<TD BGCOLOR=aquamarine>aquamarine</TD>
<TD BGCOLOR=azure>azure</TD>
</TR>
<TR ALIGN=CENTER><TD BGCOLOR=beige>beige</TD>
<TD BGCOLOR=bisque>bisque</TD>
<TD BGCOLOR=black><FONT COLOR=white>black</TD>
<TD BGCOLOR=blanchedalmond>blanchedalmond</TD>
<TD BGCOLOR=blue><FONT COLOR=yellow>blue</TD>
</TR>
<TR ALIGN=CENTER><TD BGCOLOR=blueviolet>blueviolet</TD>
<TD BGCOLOR=brown>brown</TD>
<TD BGCOLOR=burlywood>burlywood</TD>
<TD BGCOLOR=cadetblue>cadetblue</TD>
<TD BGCOLOR=chartreuse>chartreuse</TD>
</TR>
<TR ALIGN=CENTER><TD BGCOLOR=chocolate>chocolate</TD>
<TD BGCOLOR=coral>coral</TD>
<TD BGCOLOR=cornflowerblue>cornflowerblue</TD>
<TD BGCOLOR=cornsilk>cornsilk</TD>
<TD BGCOLOR=crimson>crimson</TD>
</TR>
<TR ALIGN=CENTER><TD BGCOLOR=cyan>cyan</TD>
<TD BGCOLOR=darkblue><FONT COLOR=yellow>darkblue</TD>
```

```
<TD BGCOLOR=darkcyan>darkcyan</TD>
<TD BGCOLOR=darkgoldenrod>darkgoldenrod</TD>
<TD BGCOLOR=darkgray><FONT COLOR=yellow>darkgray</TD>
</TR>
<TR ALIGN=CENTER><TD BGCOLOR=darkgreen><FONT COLOR=yellow>
darkgreen</TD>
<TD BGCOLOR=darkkhaki>darkkhaki</TD>
<TD BGCOLOR=darkmagenta><FONT COLOR=white>darkmagenta</TD>
<TD BGCOLOR=darkolivegreen><FONT COLOR=yellow>darkolivegreen</TD>
<TD BGCOLOR=darkorange>darkorange</TD>
</TR>
<TR ALIGN=CENTER><TD BGCOLOR=darkorchid>darkorchid</TD>
<TD BGCOLOR=darkred><FONT COLOR=yellow>darkred</TD>
<TD BGCOLOR=darksalmon>darksalmon</TD>
<TD BGCOLOR=darkseagreen>darkseagreen</TD>
<TD BGCOLOR=darkslateblue><FONT COLOR=yellow>darkslateblue</TD>
</TR>
<TR ALIGN=CENTER><TD BGCOLOR=darkslategray><FONT
COLOR=yellow>darkslategray</TD>
<TD BGCOLOR=darkturquoise>darkturquoise</TD>
<TD BGCOLOR=darkviolet>darkviolet</TD>
<TD BGCOLOR=deeppink>deeppink</TD>
<TD BGCOLOR=deepskyblue>deepskyblue</TD>
</TR>
<TR ALIGN=CENTER><TD BGCOLOR=dimgray><FONT
COLOR=white>dimgray</TD>
<TD BGCOLOR=dodgerblue>dodgerblue</TD>
<TD BGCOLOR=firebrick>firebrick</TD>
<TD BGCOLOR=floralwhite>floralwhite</TD>
<TD BGCOLOR=forestgreen>forestgreen</TD>
</TR>
<TR ALIGN=CENTER><TD BGCOLOR=fuchsia>fuchsia</TD>
<TD BGCOLOR=gainsboro>gainsboro</TD>
<TD BGCOLOR=ghostwhite>ghostwhite</TD>
<TD BGCOLOR=gold>gold</TD>
<TD BGCOLOR=goldenrod>goldenrod</TD>
</TR>
<TR ALIGN=CENTER><TD BGCOLOR=gray>gray</TD>
```

```
<TD BGCOLOR=green>green</TD>
<TD BGCOLOR=greenyellow>greenyellow</TD>
<TD BGCOLOR=honeydew>honeydew</TD>
<TD BGCOLOR=hotpink>hotpink</TD>
</TR>
<TR ALIGN=CENTER><TD BGCOLOR=indianred>indianred</TD>
<TD BGCOLOR=indigo><FONT COLOR=yellow>indigo</TD>
<TD BGCOLOR=ivory>ivory</TD>
<TD BGCOLOR=khaki>khaki</TD>
<TD BGCOLOR=lavender>lavender</TD>
</TR>
<TR ALIGN=CENTER><TD BGCOLOR=lavender>lavender</TD>
<TD BGCOLOR=lavender>lavender</TD>
<TD BGCOLOR=lemonchiffon>lemonchiffon</TD>
<TD BGCOLOR=lightblue>lightblue</TD>
<TD BGCOLOR=lightcoral>lightcoral</TD>
</TR>
<TR ALIGN=CENTER><TD BGCOLOR=lightcyan>lightcyan</TD>
<TD BGCOLOR=lightgoldenrodyellow>lightgoldenrodyellow</TD>
<TD BGCOLOR=lightgreen>lightgreen</TD>
<TD BGCOLOR=lightgrey>lightgrey</TD>
<TD BGCOLOR=lightpink>lightpink</TD>
</TR>
<TR ALIGN=CENTER><TD BGCOLOR=lightsalmon>lightsalmon</TD>
<TD BGCOLOR=lightseagreen>lightseagreen</TD>
<TD BGCOLOR=lightskyblue>lightskyblue</TD>
<TD BGCOLOR=lightslategray>lightslategray</TD>
<TD BGCOLOR=lightsteelblue>lightsteelblue</TD>
</TR>
<TR ALIGN=CENTER><TD BGCOLOR=lightyellow>lightyellow</TD>
<TD BGCOLOR=lime>lime</TD>
<TD BGCOLOR=limegreen>limegreen</TD>
<TD BGCOLOR=linen>linen</TD>
<TD BGCOLOR=magenta>magenta</TD>
</TR>
<TR ALIGN=CENTER><TD BGCOLOR=maroon><FONT
COLOR=yellow>maroon</TD>
<TD BGCOLOR=mediumaquamarine>mediumaquamarine</TD>
```

```
<TD BGCOLOR=mediumblue><FONT COLOR=yellow>mediumblue</TD>
<TD BGCOLOR=mediumorchid>mediumorchid</TD>
<TD BGCOLOR=mediumpurple><FONT COLOR=yellow>mediumpurple</TD>
</TR>
<TR ALIGN=CENTER><TD BGCOLOR=mediumseagreen>mediumseagreen</TD>
<TD BGCOLOR=mediumslateblue>mediumslateblue</TD>
<TD BGCOLOR=mediumspringgreen>mediumspringgreen</TD>
<TD BGCOLOR=mediumturquoise>mediumturquoise</TD>
<TD BGCOLOR=mediumvioletred><FONT
COLOR=yellow>mediumvioletred</TD>
</TR>
<TR ALIGN=CENTER><TD BGCOLOR=midnightblue><FONT COLOR=yellow>
midnightblue</TD>
<TD BGCOLOR=mintcream>mintcream</TD>
<TD BGCOLOR=mistyrose>mistyrose</TD>
<TD BGCOLOR=moccasin>moccasin</TD>
<TD BGCOLOR=navajowhite>navajowhite</TD>
</TR>
<TR ALIGN=CENTER><TD BGCOLOR=navy><FONT COLOR=yellow>navy</TD>
<TD BGCOLOR=oldlace>oldlace</TD>
<TD BGCOLOR=olive>olive</TD>
<TD BGCOLOR=olivedrab>olivedrab</TD>
<TD BGCOLOR=orange>orange</TD>
</TR>
<TR ALIGN=CENTER><TD BGCOLOR=orangered>orangered</TD>
<TD BGCOLOR=orchid>orchid</TD>
<TD BGCOLOR=palegoldenrod>palegoldenrod</TD>
<TD BGCOLOR=palegreen>palegreen</TD>
<TD BGCOLOR=paleturquoise>paleturquoise</TD>
</TR>
<TR ALIGN=CENTER><TD BGCOLOR=palevioletred>palevioletred</TD>
<TD BGCOLOR=papayawhip>papayawhip</TD>
<TD BGCOLOR=peachpuff>peachpuff</TD>
<TD BGCOLOR=peru>peru</TD>
<TD BGCOLOR=pink>pink</TD>
</TR>
<TR ALIGN=CENTER><TD BGCOLOR=plum>plum</TD>
<TD BGCOLOR=powderblue>powderblue</TD>
```

```
<TD BGCOLOR=purple><FONT COLOR=yellow>purple</TD>
<TD BGCOLOR=red>red</TD>
<TD BGCOLOR=rosybrown>rosybrown</TD>
</TR>
<TR ALIGN=CENTER><TD BGCOLOR=royalblue><FONT COLOR=yellow>
royalblue</TD>
<TD BGCOLOR=saddlebrown><FONT COLOR=yellow>saddlebrown</TD>
<TD BGCOLOR=salmon>salmon</TD>
<TD BGCOLOR=sandybrown>sandybrown</TD>
<TD BGCOLOR=seagreen>seagreen</TD>
</TR>
<TR ALIGN=CENTER><TD BGCOLOR=seashell>seashell</TD>
<TD BGCOLOR=sienna>sienna</TD>
<TD BGCOLOR=silver>silver</TD>
<TD BGCOLOR=skyblue>skyblue</TD>
<TD BGCOLOR=slateblue><FONT COLOR=yellow>slateblue</TD>
</TR>
<TR ALIGN=CENTER><TD BGCOLOR=slategray>slategray</TD>
<TD BGCOLOR=snow>snow</TD>
<TD BGCOLOR=springgreen>springgreen</TD>
<TD BGCOLOR=steelblue>steelblue</TD>
<TD BGCOLOR=tan>tan</TD>
</TR>
<TR ALIGN=CENTER><TD BGCOLOR=teal>teal</TD>
<TD BGCOLOR=thistle>thistle</TD>
<TD BGCOLOR=tomato>tomato</TD>
<TD BGCOLOR=turquoise>turquoise</TD>
<TD BGCOLOR=violet>violet</TD>
</TR>
<TR ALIGN=CENTER><TD BGCOLOR=wheat>wheat</TD>
<TD BGCOLOR=white>white</TD>
<TD BGCOLOR=whitesmoke>whitesmoke</TD>
<TD BGCOLOR=yellow>yellow</TD>
<TD BGCOLOR=yellowgreen>yellowgreen</TD>
</TR>
</TABLE>
</BODY>
</HTML>
```

Appendix C

What's on the CD?

The CD that accompanies this book contains numerous tools and utilities to assist the experienced programmer in developing and implementing ActiveX technology. There are Internet servers, ActiveX tools, HTML editors, Windows utilities, and more.

Running the CD

To make the CD more user friendly and take up less of your disk space, no installation is required. This means that the only files transferred to your hard disk are the ones you choose to copy.

CAUTION:
Significant differences between the various Windows operating systems (Windows 3.1, Windows 95, and Windows NT) sometimes render files that work in one Windows environment inoperable in another. Prima has made every effort to insure that this problem is minimized. It is not possible to eliminate it entirely, however. Therefore, you may find that some files or directories appear to be missing from the CD. Those files are, in reality, on the CD, but remain hidden from the operating system. To confirm this, view the CD using a different Windows operating system.

Note: This problem most often occurs while viewing the CD in Windows 3.1.

Windows 3.1

To run the CD:

1. Insert the CD into the CD-ROM drive.
2. From File Manager, select File, Run to open the Run window.
3. In the Command Line text box, enter **D:\PRIMACD.EXE** (where D:\ is the CD-ROM drive).
4. Select OK.

Windows 95

Because there is no install routine, running the CD in Windows 95 is a breeze, especially if you have autorun enabled. Simply insert the CD in the CD-ROM drive, close the tray, and wait for the CD to load.

If you have disabled autorun, place the CD in the drive and follow these steps:

1. From the Start, menu select Run.
2. Enter **D:\PRIMACD.EXE** (where D:\ is the CD-ROM drive).
3. Select OK.

The Prima User Interface

Prima's user interface is designed to make viewing and using the CD contents quick and easy. It contains six category buttons, four options buttons, and a display window. Select a category button to show a list of available titles in the display window. Highlight a title in the window and choose an option button to perform the desired action.

Category Buttons

ActiveX. An assortment of ActiveX tools and add-ons.

Controls. Links to sites with downloadable ActiveX controls.

HTML Tools. A large collection of HTML editors, templates, and add-ons to help you create sophisticated Web pages.

Internet. Web browsers, FTP clients, and other tools for getting the most from the Internet.

Multimedia. A variety of graphics and wave editors.

Servers. An assortment of NT and UNIX Internet servers.

Options Buttons

Install/Run. If the highlighted title contains an install routine, selecting this option begins the installation process. If the title has no install procedure but contains an executable file, the executable is run. If neither an install nor an executable file is present (as in the case of a graphics library), the folder containing the information is shown. In the event that an application contains an exectutable file that will not run from the CD, the entire application is placed in a compressed zip file, which can be accessed by installing WinZip (included on the CD).

> **NOTE:**
> **You can install some of the shareware programs that do not have installation routines by copying the program files from the CD to your hard drive and running the executable (.EXE) file.**

Information. Data about the selection is shown, if available. This information is usually in the form of a Readme or help file.

Explore. This option allows you to view the folder containing the program files.

Exit. When you're finished and ready to move on, select Exit.

The Software

This section gives you a brief description of some of the software that you'll find on the CD. This is just a sampling. As you browse the CD, you will find much more.

Apache Server. The popular http server for UNIX.

Cool Edit. A full-featured wave editor for Windows.

Drag and View Gold. A handy utility that lets you drag, drop, and view word processing, spreadsheet, database, and graphics files without opening the parent application.

Frame-IT!. A feature-packed HTML frame generator, which allows you to generate complex HTML frames using only your mouse.

HotDog. A stand-alone HTML editor that supports extensions from Microsoft and Netscape as well as proposed HTML 3 elements.

HTML Assistant. A simple Web publishing tool for creating HTML Web pages.

Internet Information Server V1.0. The latest in NT Internet server technology from Microsoft.

Kenn Nesbitt's Webedit. The popular HTML editor for novice and pro alike.

Live Markup. It's as close as you can get to a WYSIWYG HTML editor.

Lview Pro. A versatile Windows graphics editor.

Mapedit. A WYSIWYG (What You See Is What You Get) editor for imagemap files.

MS ActiveX SDK. Tools to help you develop Internet ActiveX controls.

MS Internet Explorer 3.0. Microsoft's full featured Web browser with support for HTML, ActiveX, Java, and plug-ins.

Paint Shop Pro. The popular bitmap image editor from JASC, Inc.ats.

PolyView. A multithreaded 32-bit Microsoft Windows 95 and Windows NT application that provides viewing, file conversion, and image manipulation support for most popular graphics image format files.

Vram. Speed up your system performance with this 32-bit virtual RAM file system driver for Windows 95.

VuePrint. This multitalented application lets you view, print, and convert graphics files, as well as play sound and movie files.

Web Weaver. An easy-to-use HTML text editor.

Webber. A fast, flexible HTML editor from Cerebral Systems Development.

Index

D

E

F

G

H

N

T

W

X

Y

Z

Notes

Notes

To Order Books

Please send me the following items:

Quantity	Title	Unit Price	Total
______	______________________	$ ______	$ ______
______	______________________	$ ______	$ ______
______	______________________	$ ______	$ ______
______	______________________	$ ______	$ ______
______	______________________	$ ______	$ ______

Shipping and Handling depend on Subtotal.

Subtotal	Shipping/Handling
$0.00–$14.99	$3.00
$15.00–$29.99	$4.00
$30.00–$49.99	$6.00
$50.00–$99.99	$10.00
$100.00–$199.99	$13.50
$200.00+	Call for Quote

Foreign and all Priority Request orders:
Call Order Entry department
for price quote at 916/632-4400

This chart represents the total retail price of books only (before applicable discounts are taken).

Subtotal $ ______

Deduct 10% when ordering 3-5 books $ ______

7.25% Sales Tax (CA only) $ ______

8.25% Sales Tax (TN only) $ ______

5.0% Sales Tax (MD and IN only) $ ______

Shipping and Handling* $ ______

Total Order $ ______

By Telephone: With MC or Visa, call 800-632-8676, 916-632-4400. Mon-Fri, 8:30-4:30.
WWW {http://www.primapublishing.com}

Orders Placed Via Internet E-mail {sales@primapub.com}

By Mail: Just fill out the information below and send with your remittance to:

Prima Publishing
P.O. Box 1260BK
Rocklin, CA 95677

My name is ______________________

I live at ______________________

City ______________________ State ________ Zip ________

MC/Visa# ______________________ Exp. ________

Check/Money Order enclosed for $ ____________ Payable to Prima Publishing

Daytime Telephone ______________________

Signature ______________________

Other books from Prima Publishing, Computer Products Division

ISBN	Title	Price	Release Date
0-7615-0801-5	ActiveX	$40.00	Available Now
0-7615-0680-2	America Online Complete Handbook and Membership Kit	$24.99	Available Now
0-7615-0915-1	Building Intranets with Internet Information Server and FrontPage	$45.00	Available Now
0-7615-0417-6	CompuServe Complete Handbook and Membership Kit	$24.95	Available Now
0-7615-0849-X	Corporate Intranet Development	$45.00	Fall '96
0-7615-0692-6	Create Your First Web Page in a Weekend	$24.99	Available Now
0-7615-0503-2	Discover What's Online!	$24.95	Available Now
0-7615-0693-4	Internet Information Server	$40.00	Available Now
0-7615-0815-5	Introduction to ABAP/4 Programming for SAP	$45.00	Available Now
0-7615-0678-0	Java Applet Powerpack	$30.00	Available Now
0-7615-0685-3	JavaScript	$35.00	Available Now
0-7615-0901-1	Leveraging Visual Basic with ActiveX Controls	$45.00	Available Now
0-7615-0682-9	LiveWire Pro Master's Handbook	$45.00	Fall '96
0-7615-0755-8	Moving Worlds	$35.00	Available Now
0-7615-0690-X	Netscape Enterprise Server	$40.00	Available Now
0-7615-0691-8	Netscape FastTrack Server	$40.00	Available Now
0-7615-0852-X	Netscape Navigator 3 Complete Handbook	$24.99	Available Now
0-7615-0733-7	Netscape Navigator Gold Master's Handbook	$40.00	Fall '96
0-7615-0751-5	NT Server Administrator's Guide	$50.00	Available Now
0-7615-0759-0	Professional Web Design	$40.00	Available Now
0-7615-0773-6	Programming Internet Controls	$45.00	Available Now
0-7615-0780-9	Programming Web Server Applications	$40.00	Available Now
0-7615-0063-4	Researching on the Internet	$29.95	Available Now
0-7615-0686-1	Researching on the World Wide Web	$24.99	Available Now
0-7615-0695-0	The Essential Photoshop Book	$35.00	Available Now
0-7615-0752-3	The Essential Windows NT Book	$27.99	Available Now
0-7615-0689-6	The Microsoft Exchange Productivity Guide	$24.99	Available Now
0-7615-0769-8	VBScript Master's Handbook	$45.00	Available Now
0-7615-0684-5	VBScript Web Page Interactivity	$40.00	Available Now
0-7615-0903-8	Visual FoxPro 5 Enterprise Development	$45.00	Available Now
0-7615-0814-7	Visual J++	$35.00	Available Now
0-7615-0383-8	Web Advertising and Marketing	$34.95	Available Now
0-7615-0726-4	Webmaster's Handbook	$40.00	Available Now

License Agreement/Notice of Limited Warranty

By opening the sealed disk container in this book, you agree to the following terms and conditions. If, upon reading the following license agreement and notice of limited warranty, you cannot agree to the terms and conditions set forth, return the unused book with unopened disk to the place where you purchased it for a refund.

License:

The enclosed software is copyrighted by the copyright holder(s) indicated on the software disk. You are licensed to copy the software onto a single computer for use by a single concurrent user and to a backup disk. You may not reproduce, make copies, or distribute copies or rent or lease the software in whole or in part, except with written permission of the copyright holder(s). You may transfer the enclosed disk only together with this license, and only if you destroy all other copies of the software and the transferee agrees to the terms of the license. You may not decompile, reverse assemble, or reverse engineer the software.

Notice of Limited Warranty:

The enclosed disk is warranted by Prima Publishing to be free of physical defects in materials and workmanship for a period of sixty (60) days from end user's purchase of the book/disk combination. During the sixty-day term of the limited warranty, Prima will provide a replacement disk upon the return of a defective disk.

Limited Liability:

THE SOLE REMEDY FOR BREACH OF THIS LIMITED WARRANTY SHALL CONSIST ENTIRELY OF REPLACEMENT OF THE DEFECTIVE DISK. IN NO EVENT SHALL PRIMA OR THE AUTHORS BE LIABLE FOR ANY OTHER DAMAGES, INCLUDING LOSS OR CORRUPTION OF DATA, CHANGES IN THE FUNCTIONAL CHARACTERISTICS OF THE HARDWARE OR OPERATING SYSTEM, DELETERIOUS INTERACTION WITH OTHER SOFTWARE, OR ANY OTHER SPECIAL, INCIDENTAL, OR CONSEQUENTIAL DAMAGES THAT MAY ARISE, EVEN IF PRIMA AND/OR THE AUTHORS HAVE PREVIOUSLY BEEN NOTIFIED THAT THE POSSIBILITY OF SUCH DAMAGES EXISTS.

Disclaimer of Warranties:

PRIMA AND THE AUTHORS SPECIFICALLY DISCLAIM ANY AND ALL OTHER WARRANTIES, EITHER EXPRESS OR IMPLIED, INCLUDING WARRANTIES OF MERCHANTABILITY, SUITABILITY TO A PARTICULAR TASK OR PURPOSE, OR FREEDOM FROM ERRORS. SOME STATES DO NOT ALLOW FOR EXCLUSION OF IMPLIED WARRANTIES OR LIMITATION OF INCIDENTAL OR CONSEQUENTIAL DAMAGES, SO THESE LIMITATIONS MAY NOT APPLY TO YOU.

Other:

This Agreement is governed by the laws of the State of California without regard to choice of law principles. The United Convention of Contracts for the International Sale of Goods is specifically disclaimed. This Agreement constitutes the entire agreement between you and Prima Publishing regarding use of the software.